KALLSOY

Trøllanes

Vi

Múli

jógv

DJÚPINI

Mikladalur

HARALDSUND

HVANNA

Skarð

KUNOY

Depil

KÁLLSOYARFJØRÐUR

Hvannasund

SUND

Kirkja

Elduvík

Oyndarfjørður

Kunoy

SVÍNOY

Húsar

Hárald
sund

BORÐOY

Fuglafjørður

Arnafjørður

Heltnin

Syðradalur

Funningsbotnur

Lørvik

KLAKKSVÍK

Norðoyri

NORÐUROYAR

S T U R O Y

Gøtugjógv

Norðragøta

Gøtuvík

Gøtunes

SKALAFJØRÐUR

Selatrað

Sølmundarfjørður

Borðoyarnes

SUNDALAGI

Skála

Mjóvanes

ður

Við Sjógv

Rituvík

TANGAFJØRÐUR

Raktangi

Toftavatn

Nes

Aeðuvík

Kaldbak

Eystnes

Sund

Hvítanes

Havnardalur

Hoyvík

TÓRSHAVN

Nólsoyar Bygd

Argir

NÓLSOY

bastaður

Kirkjubøur

Kirkjubønes

ARFJØRÐUR

Skopun

SANDOY

WITHDRAWN

A Faeroe fjord

THE
ATLANTIC ISLANDS

A Study of the
Faeroe Life and Scene by

KENNETH WILLIAMSON

F.R.S.E., M.B.O.U.

WITH A FOREWORD BY

ERIC LINKLATER

and an additional chapter
on the Faeroes Today by

EINAR KALLSBERG

Pen-and-ink drawings by
the Author,
thirty-five photographs,
and four maps

ROUTLEDGE & KEGAN PAUL
London

Originally published in 1948
by Wm. Collins, Sons & Co. Ltd.
First published in this edition 1970
by Routledge & Kegan Paul Ltd.
Broadway House, 68–74 Carter Lane
London, E.C.4

Printed in Great Britain by
Unwin Brothers Limited,
The Gresham Press, Old Woking, Surrey, England
A member of the Staples Printing Group
© this edition Kenneth Williamson 1970

ISBN 0 7100 6911 1

To
the beloved memory of
NIELS and HANSINE REIN
of Tórshavn

PREFACE

THE IDEA of writing this book first came into my mind on the evening of September 19th, 1941, whilst I was writing long and enthusiastic letters to friends at home describing my first whale-hunt. I little realised then, only a few days after my arrival at Tórshavn, that these letters were to develop into a study of the Faeroe life and scene which would bring me many happy and memorable experiences during the next four years, and would culminate in my taking unto myself a Faeroe wife.

Quite early on, the writing of the book became a personal necessity, proving to be my chief arm against boredom—which, some say, is the most insidious enemy an isolated garrison force has to fight. I hope the logical outcome of having written it can also be justified on the grounds of necessity, for it seems to me that English literature is sadly lacking in authentic accounts of this land and people almost at our very door. At school I was taught nothing about the Faeroes, and I cannot believe that my case was exceptional : the islands were not of any economic or political importance to the British commonwealth, and to the rest of the world they were nothing more prepossessing than a faint smudge on the map of Europe. So it is perhaps small wonder that our system of education considers the Faeroes of no account, and that the little knowledge most English people possess concerning these Atlantic islands is fictitious and not founded on fact.

This state of affairs may excuse the belief held by a good many that the Faeroes have a remote connection with ancient Egypt ; or the vague impression of the more enlightened that these are obscure islands in the high north peopled with polar bears and Eskimos who shiver in the perpetual snows. I have not exaggerated ; we who had to spend two, three or even four years there found abundant evidence of the existence of such myths on our infrequent visits home. And it was often a cause for grousing that our mail not infrequently came to us via the Middle East !

In this book I have attempted to give a faithful portrayal of the Faeroe scene and the life and manners of the diligent, courteous and well-educated people who inhabit it. To do this at all satisfactorily I found it necessary to forgo my berth on the troopship on several occasions and spend my leave in wandering about the islands, studying the bird-life, exploring the countryside,

meeting the people, and watching them at their daily work. If
the reader feels that my enthusiasm has sometimes led me into
tiresome detail concerning certain aspects of the peasant culture
of the Faeroese, then I hope he will grant me his indulgence ;
for ethnology, like natural history, is an exact science, and records
are almost worthless without attention to detail and accuracy in
report. My chief interest is and always has been for bird-life,
but throughout this book I have tried to avoid the rather
specialised approach of the ornithologist, my aim being to relate
the birds firstly to the peasant life of the community, and secondly
to the nature of the countryside. I need hardly add that I found
the Faeroe birds, especially the commoner ones, tremendously
interesting for their own sakes—but that is another story, and one
which I hope to tell some day.

I shall not readily forget those local holidays, and I shall
remember them not so much for their value to my purpose (and
that was immense) as for the truly remarkable friendship and
hospitality I met with at every turn. Everything was done to
make me comfortable : if my boots were dirty, they were cleaned ;
if my socks were wet, they had to be handed over to be dried ;
if I entered a house anywhere at any time I was believed to be in
imminent danger of collapse from starvation ! Although I always
ate as much as I could (for the food was wholesome and deliciously
cooked) I was seldom able to convince my hosts that I had really
eaten enough !

I dwell somewhat on this homely treatment because it brings
out a side of Faeroe nature which (if certain scurrilous articles
that appeared from time to time in the English press are any
criterion) was not fully appreciated in our own country. The
great majority of the Faeroe people were intensely pro-British
even in those dark days when the invasion of Britain from Hitler's
" Fortress Europe " was expected at any time. Very many of
them had family and friends in German-occupied Denmark, but
fear of possible reprisals against their own kith and kin did not
deter them from opening their hearts and homes to the British
troops. Nor, later, did the growing scarcity of foodstuffs and
stringent rationing of tea, coffee, sugar and margarine impair
their generosity. There were, of course, some troops who did
not like the Faeroes, and said unkind things about the land and
the people ; and there were also some Faeroese who never had
any time for the English : but these formed very unimportant
minorities, and throughout the war the relations between the

civilians and the " occupying " forces were excellent indeed. And now I come to my major difficulty—an acknowledgment of my grateful thanks to all those men, women and children who, directly or indirectly, contributed in some measure to the material of which this book about them is composed. First among these are my wife and her family, for their help has been immense. For the rest, it would be invidious to single out particular individuals : most of those from whom I had help and hospitality are mentioned in the text, and to those who are and those who are not I have the privilege and pleasure of saying "Tøkk fyri seinast ! "

During the latter stages, when the book was being prepared for publication, I received from friends nearer home help which it is a pleasure to acknowledge. Among these are my colleague Mr. Reginald Wagstaffe, the Keeper of the Yorkshire Museum, and Messrs. James Fisher, Eric Hosking and Alan Delgado, of Collins. I am also grateful to Major Eric Linklater for so kindly writing a Foreword to the book, and wish to express to Major C. I. Fraser (The Lovat Scouts) and Major R. D. Ball (The Cheshire Regiment) my deep appreciation of their kindness in allowing me the use of their excellent photographs. It is a real pleasure to me to have our association of Faeroe days repeated in this way.

Some of the material in the following chapters has already appeared in articles and papers, and my thanks are due to the editors of *The Field*, *The North-western Naturalist*, *Antiquity*, and *The Ibis*, for permission to reproduce these items in their present form.

Finally, a word about orthography. Throughout the book I have used the Faeroese spelling in place and personal names, and these, together with the names of institutions and special days in the calendar, are given in ordinary type. All other Faeroe words are in italics. It is often difficult to know which of two or more ways is the correct way of spelling certain words— opinions, even among authorities, sometimes differ, and for this reason I have followed whenever possible the dictionary of Jacobsen and Matras. All nouns have been left in the nominative case, but agree with their context in number, and I should point out that this fact explains the occasional disparity in the spelling of names of objects described and figured in the book.

The Yorkshire Museum,   K. W.
          York.
February, 1947.

AUTHOR'S NOTE

THIS BOOK was written during and immediately after the war. It deals with the Faeroe Islands and the Faeroe people as I found them during a prolonged stay in the early 'forties, and although it remains the definitive work on Faeroe social history and natural history I am only too well aware as I re-read it that many things have changed during the past twenty-five years.

The book has been long out of print, and for practical reasons it has not been possible to publish a revised edition. It is hoped that the present re-issue of the text published by Collins of London in 1948 will satisfy the increasing demand which exists both in Britain and the Faeroes, and at the same time provide an authoritative picture of the political, social and economic scene today. For this I am very grateful indeed to Mr. Einar Kallsberg, adviser on Faeroese questions in the Royal Danish Ministry of Foreign Affairs, for the excellent account he has written. Although this appears at the end of the book I strongly recommend the reader to study it first, so that he or she will have the main part of the work in better perspective.

I am grateful to Mr. Mogens Wahl, the Danish High Commissioner at Tórshavn, for his encouragement. The re-issue would not have been possible without financial assistance, and my sincere thanks are due to the Dansk-Faerøsk Kulturfond and the Cultural Foundation of the Faeroese Løgting for providing a grant. A number of new photographs have been included, partly with a view to illustrating modern developments in the Islands, and I thank the Press Department of the Royal Danish Ministry of Foreign Affairs for making these available. The photographs facing page 160 are by the late Leo Hansen. My son Robin kindly provided the photograph facing page 304.

Finally, as I am primarily a bird-man, I could not forego this opportunity of bringing the list of Faeroe birds up to date. Mr. Anders Holm Joensen has kindly helped me over certain points.

Tring, Hertfordshire.   Kenneth Williamson.

CONTENTS

	PAGE
PREFACE	5
FOREWORD BY ERIC LINKLATER	13
Chapter One THE ATLANTIC ISLANDS	17
Chapter Two THE LAND	44
Chapter Three THE SEA	70
Chapter Four WHALE-HUNTING	95
Chapter Five PORTRAIT OF AN ISLAND (1)	120
Chapter Six BIRD-FOWLING	143
Chapter Seven PORTRAIT OF AN ISLAND (2)	168
Chapter Eight HOLIDAY AT FRODBØUR	189
Chapter Nine CORN HARVESTING AND MILLING	206
Chapter Ten CUSTOMS AND FOLK-LORE	230
Chapter Eleven THE FAEROE LAKES	256
Chapter Twelve OTHER ISLANDS	280

Chapter Thirteen

PAGE

THE FAEROES TODAY 305

Appendix " A "

FAEROE MAMMALS 322

Appendix " B "

FAEROE BIRDS 326

REFERENCES 350

GLOSSARY OF FAEROESE WORDS 357

SUBJECT INDEX 368

INDEX TO PLACE NAMES 381

ILLUSTRATIONS

A Faeroe fjord   *frontispiece*

                                                                  facing page
Tórshavn from Kirkjubøreyn   64

Tórshavn:
   (top) The town, (bottom) Suburbia   65

Tórshavn:
   (top) Tinganes, (bottom) Boats in the harbour   80

Kirkjubøur:
   (top) Farmland on the " coastal plain ",
   (bottom) The unfinished St. Magnus' Cathedral
      and St. Olaf's Church   81

Mykines—the *bøur* at haymaking time   112

Sorting and drying " klipfisk "   112

Grindadráp at Tórshavn   113

Boat-building   128

Mykines and its cloud-cap from Sørvágsfjørdur   129

Mykines—looking east from the holm lighthouse   129

Guillemots on a crowded ledge   160

Fowler with *fleygustong*   160

Mykines—the north coast   161

Ringing the young Gannets on Mykineshólmur   176

A *fuglaberg* with its Kittiwake and Guillemot tenements   177

Niðri á bøur farmstead and watermill   208

Nólsoy—a group of *hjallar*   208

Haymaking at Froðbøur:
   (top) Building a *sáta*, (bottom) Carrying *byrdir* 209

Faeroe village and fields   224

The Klakksvík—Arnafjørdur road-tunnel   225

Couple in national dress   256

Church interior   256

Velbastaður   257

Tórshavn—a modern fish-processing plant   257

Klakksvík—the harbour and Kunoy   272

Klakksvík—the town   273

Nólsoy—the village and quay   304

Inter-island communications:
    (top) The old " Smiril ", (bottom) A modern helicopter   305

" S.E.V."—the Faeroe electricity undertaking   320

Fisher girl   321

MAPS

Faeroe Islands (the North, Central and Western
    Islands)   *front endpapers*

Faeroe Islands (the South Islands)   *back endpapers*

Faeroe Islands in relation to adjacent countries   „   „

Mykines—showing division of the outfield and
    the chief sea-bird colonies   *page* 134

FOREWORD

It is a rare experience to find a book that seems to be the perfect and specific response to a private wish for it; but *The Atlantic Islands* has for me this charming and uncommon distinction.

A few years ago I spent some little time in the Faeroes, islands of which, until then, I had known nothing more than that they made a fog-bound archipelago which old fishermen called the Faraways; and before long the heroic vivacity of their people, and the menacing abruptness of their scenery, had so stirred my imagination that I urgently wanted to take away some enduring and adequate record of them. I wanted a generous biography of the islands : a description of the people, and their towering coastline, and the multitudes of sea-fowl that fish their stormy channels ; a sample or two of the stories that are told in the red-walled grass-roofed houses at night ; an account of their painstaking agriculture and their riotous hunting of caain' whales ; of their weaving and their proverbs and the small flowers of their precarious spring ; a book well written, out of wide knowledge and deep affection, about the whole life and circumstance of the islands. That is what I looked for, but could not find.

Then, when the war was over, my friend James Fisher came to Orkney and said casually that he had with him the manuscript of a book about the Faeroes, written by an able naturalist who had served in our small garrison there. Would I care to read it ? And before I had read forty pages, I realised with the liveliest satisfaction that this was precisely what I had wanted.

Mr. Williamson is a practical and sagacious man. He knew, when he went to the Faeroes, that garrison life is apt to be boring, and he was aware that boredom has little defence against the counter-attack of an active mind. He set himself, therefore, to study the unknown country to which he had so roughly come ; and study begat knowledge, knowledge enthusiasm, and enthusiasm a book so various and richly full of life—life on the wing, life at strangely furnished tables, life colouring the steep fields and turbulent sea—that boredom's poor ghost must have fled whimpering down the mountainside at the mere sight of his battle-dress and bulging note-book. So much for the resolution

of Mr. Williamson's private affairs. More important is the public
expression of his activities ; and his book I believe to be a
masterpiece of its kind, that will live for long in the affectionate
knowledge of bird-lovers, and island-lovers, and lovers of men's
hardihood against the heavy odds of nature. Mr. Williamson is
an admirable writer, and a naturalist whose broad interests are
everywhere sustained by acute perception and the most in-
dustrious curiosity. He is a naturalist of that catholic sort which
includes humanity in its field, and was singularly happy on the
island of Mykines, where he could not study the kittiwakes that
flew like a snowstorm before its sombre cliffs—or the auks and
the puffins and the crimson-footed guillemots—without also
considering their vital relationship to the inhabitants.

He begins well, with a description of Tórshavn showing to the
sea like pieces of a rainbow through swirling mist that draped
the dark wet rock behind ; and quickly, to prove he has more
solid fare than views to sell, he is sitting down to wind-dried
mutton and pancakes, sweet soup and a stewed puffin or two.
A writer should always have a good appetite, and Mr. Williamson
has a nobly accommodating stomach for the many dishes—some
primitively robust, some rich with Danish addition—of the
Faeroe table. He has the good sense, moreover, to perceive that
anthropology is incomplete without some recipes, and presently,
between a description of fishing-grounds and a note on the
fishermen's superstitions, there come a gracious tribute to the
Faeroe housewife and appetising instruction how to make *fiska
gratin* and *knettir*. But he does not dally too long at the table,
and a few paragraphs later he has discovered, in a little week-end
suburb on the landward side of Tórshavn, the strangest birds
that ever invaded a suburban garden : wheatears and Faeroe
snipe, oyster-catchers and golden plover, and whimbrels crying
at the valley's edge.

I should be much at fault, however, if I suggested that the
book is merely a hotch-potch of interesting impressions. It is,
on the contrary, an orderly and learned presentation of almost
everything that comprises life in the islands : land-tenure and
the farmers' heroic industry, boat-building and folk-lore, milling
and peat-cutting, dancing and bird-snaring and whale-hunting.
But Mr. Williamson always writes with his eyes open ; there is
always the impression of things seen ; and whenever he looks
round he is likely to notice a fulmar sailing on stiff wings, a
saxifrage in the wet grass, or rocks that gird the dark hills like

iron bands round a cask—and because of the visibility in his writing, there is often the suggestion of a whole landscape behind whatever he may be describing in the foreground. The effect is singularly happy, and I can hardly remember a book that contained so much information as this, and was so easy to read.

On one occasion, when visibility almost fails because the night has fallen, a shadow-play is presented with an astonishing power to evoke the twilit scene of rushing wings. The storm-petrel and Leach's petrel both nest in Mykines and a nearby holm, and Mr. Williamson describes a night when he, and a friend with a fowling-net, spent some hours of feverish excitement in a ghostly multitude of the little birds, swirling and crying about them, dancing like great butterflies in the summer darkness, calling to their mates in high, clear voices. It must have been a wild, enchanting experience, and the frenzy of the birds, coming aland for a few weeks only after long months on the deep Atlantic, is very like the vivid, delicate, and almost desperate growth of a northern spring, when all the flowers and sweetness of the year are crammed into a single month. This haunted night among the petrels must be compared, as a piece of writing, with Mr. Williamson's description of a *grind*, or communal whale-hunt ; for both are done with a fine regard for pictorial effect, and a scientist's scrupulous obligation to be accurate. The *grind* is a superb spectacle, and I am sadly tempted to redescribe the turbulence in the harbour as the boats drive in their captured herd, and the sea turns red with blood, and men and boys go out waist-deep into the fearful flux to meet the boats and hasten the slaughter. It is a cruel and revolting scene, yet thrilling to read of or to watch, and justifiable to the most shrinking conscience. Mr. Williamson recreates the exhilaration of the hunt, and calmly explains its importance in the economy of the islands.

But what, you may ask, is the importance of the Faeroes, that small and stormy archipelago, that justifies the expenditure of so much labour, love, and talent on description of them? It is worth recalling, to begin with, that during the war the Faeroe men brought to us most of the fish that we ate ; the Iceland trawlers objected to being sunk by U-boats, but the Faeroe men accepted the risk of bombs and torpedoes, and maintained a traffic of great value to us at heavy loss to themselves. That quality, moreover, of being undeterred by hardship and danger is typical of life in the islands : without it, the people would not survive. Their agriculture is a miracle of hard, imaginative, and continuous toil. Their seafaring is adept and bold as the voyaging of their Viking ancestors : in small wooden boats, bought from Britain sixty years ago, they regularly fish the far-off grounds south-west of Greenland, and the navigation of their own island firths, that boil with the Atlantic tide, requires the liveliest strength and skill. They furnish their tables with sea-birds caught on dizzy ledges of the precipitous cliffs—taller by far than any in these islands—that overhang the loud Atlantic. And in such circumstances, of hardship and hard weather, their houses and their social life are not, as you might suppose, somewhat roughly ordered, and indifferent to dirt, and surly ; but lively and clean and gay. Their housekeeping is characterised by a passion for cleanliness and a warm regard for conviviality. They like bright colours, and are tireless dancers. They are imaginative cooks, and highly literate. They are immensely patriotic, but no xenophobes. They have retained a primitive virtue, and added to it the graces of a native culture ; they appear to have escaped the vulgarity and inertia of civilisation.

Their material assets are meagre, except for the vast, uncountable host of guillemots and kittiwakes and puffins that cover the cliffs in summer ; and the fish that swim in the surrounding sea. The land they can till is only a frill or a flounce of green below the knees of their cloud-capped mountains, and a warm sunny day is a day to remember. They cannot grow corn or wine, and their mineral wealth is small. But there are thirty thousand people in the archipelago, and every school is packed with hearty, fair-haired children. Native hardihood and energy have conquered a hostile environment, and given to it geniality and grace. Surely such a triumph of vitality and the spirit deserves its historian ?

I remember, when I was in the islands, saying to an officer of the Lovat Scouts that it would be an excellent thing for Scotland if every man in the regiment married and brought home with him a Faeroe wife ; but the opportunity was unfortunately neglected. Mr. Williamson's book, however, will explain what may appear to be an immoderate admiration ; and though I am reluctant to cast the smallest shadow over the delight of his pages, I do suggest that they can be read, not only for pleasure and information, but for the example they offer of a people who, by their indomitable spirit, have made a fair haven on the windy edge of nothing.

ERIC LINKLATER

Chapter One

THE ATLANTIC ISLANDS

1. Introducing the Faeroe Islands and the people who inhabit them (*page* 17).
2. Arrival at Tórshavn, and a description of Faeroe houses and Faeroe food (*page* 24).
3. The capital's amenities, and its " suburbia " (*page* 31).
4. A winter journey in a typical fiord (*page* 35).
5. Winter and Summer in the hills—mainly a brief sketch of the bird-life, with some notes on the national emblem of the Faeroese (*page* 38).

I

THE FAEROE ISLANDS lie in the North Atlantic, between Shetland and Iceland. There are, excluding small holms and stacks, over twenty islands covering an area of 540.55 square miles, and of these seventeen are inhabited. They fall readily into four main groups :—

The North Islands (*Norðuroyar*)—from east to west

Fugloy	Two villages.
Svínoy	One village.
Viðoy	Two villages.
Borðoy	Five hamlets and one important town, Klakksvík (population over 2,000).
Kunoy	Two villages.
Kallsoy	Four villages.

The Central Islands—from east to west

Eysturoy	Some 25 villages and hamlets, of which Fuglafjørður (population over 1,000) is the most important.
Nólsoy	One village.
Streymoy	Some 20 settlements, including the capital, Tórshavn, and a second port, Vestmanna (population about 1,000).

Hestur   One village.
Koltur   Four farms.

The Western Islands—from east to west
Vágar   Three large and three small villages.
Tindhólmur   Uninhabited.
Gáshólmur   Uninhabited.
Mykines   One village.
Mykinsehólmur   Lighthouse only.

The Southern Islands—from north to south
Trøllhøvdi   Uninhabited.
Sandoy   Seven villages.
Skúvoy   One village.
Stóra Dímun   One large farm.
Lítla Dímun   Uninhabited.
Suðuroy   Some 14 settlements and two impor-
                      tant towns, Vágur and Tvøroyri,
                      each with more than 1,000 in-
                      habitants.

The islands, the sounds between them, and the fiords indenting the coasts run generally in a NNW.—SSE. direction. The land may be regarded as the highest part of a submarine ridge connecting Scotland with Iceland, the remnant of a deeply-eroded plateau which was thrown up by volcanic action in the Tertiary Age, during a series of eruptions which have given a very distinctive appearance to the islands' contours. Successive sheets of flowing lava were laid over each other at long intervals of time, and in the interim shallow beds of tuff, usually of a reddish colour and derived from volcanic ashes, were deposited between them. In the Miocene Era the gradual breaking-down of the plateau began, due to subsidence and erosion, and the remnants are to be found to-day from County Antrim northwards through the Hebrides and north-west Scotland to the Faeroe Islands, Iceland and Greenland. The chief rock is basalt—a hard and fine-grained anamesite basalt in the two oldest islands, Mykines and Suðuroy, and a coarser and more recent porphyritic basalt over the rest of the archipelago. Where the two strata meet on Mykines, Vágar and Suðuroy there are narrow beds of a poor-quality coal, pointing to the existence of a rich flora in the islands during a lull in the volcanic activity at the end of the Tertiary epoch.

Since they came into being as such, the islands have lost much of their size, by erosion during the Ice Age (when they were covered by an ice-sheet separate from that of northern Europe) and subsequently by frost and storms. Most of the country lies at an elevation of between 1,000 and 2,500 feet, and is totally unsuited to cultivation. The hills rise very steeply, and the exposed edges of the lava-flows, called *hamrar*, form rocky walls alternating with grassy, rock-strewn shelves, where the soft tuff and a good deal of the basalt have been ground down to form a thin covering of soil. On the western side of the islands the hills often fall precipitously to the sea from a height of over a thousand feet, forming immense cliffs in which great quantities of sea-fowl, of considerable economic importance to the people, have their nests. Characteristically alpine conditions prevail on the mountainous North Islands, and on the northern peaks of the central group, whilst Sandoy and Suđuroy are more fertile and enjoy a less rigorous climate. The moorlands have a considerable depth of peat, invaluable as fuel, and provide rough grazing for the flocks of sheep. There are no large streams, as is to be expected in such small and mountainous islands, and the bodies of inland water are few and unimportant.

The climate is mild, since Faeroe waters are visited by a branch of the Gulf Stream, but very wet and often stormy : the rainfall reaches sixty inches or so annually, most of it falling between October and January. Precipitation is heaviest in the north, there being nearly twice as many foggy days as in Suđuroy, and although a normal summer produces a fair amount of fine, sunny weather, entirely cloudless days almost never occur, and heat-waves such as we experience in England are a phenomenon unknown. Every winter brings heavy snowfalls, and the " white weather " may last up to three weeks or more during the early part of the year, but intense frost is rare and conditions are not nearly so arctic as popular imagination appears to credit.

The 30,000 inhabitants (more than four times as many as a century ago) are of Viking stock and form a distinct Scandinavian race, with a culture originally brought from Norway when the islands were settled in the tenth century, and since developed almost entirely without the interference of extraneous elements until quite recent years. To-day, features of our western civilisation are increasingly affecting life in the islands, especially in the capital and other towns which, since the rise of the fishing industry, have achieved some importance as ports. These are Klakksvík

(Borðoy), Tvøroyri and Vágur (Suðuroy), each with about two thousand inhabitants ; and Fuglafjørður (Eysturoy) and Vest-manna (Streymoy), which have rather more than a thousand. Such changes are only natural, especially in such a place as Tórshavn, where the population rose from 554 in 1801 to 1,656 at the beginning of the present century, and is more than three times that figure to-day.

The early history of the islands is little documented and as a result obscure. The first settlers appear to have been of Celtic origin. This occupation, dating back to the eighth century, secured for the Faeroes an honourable mention in the Irish monk Dicuil's description of the world, " De mensura orbis terrae." He wrote in 825, saying that the islands had been inhabited by Irish hermits for about a century, but that these men had been constrained to leave on account of the ravages of sea-rovers. Only at one place, Kirkjubøur in south Streymoy, is there conclusive archaeological evidence of Celtic occupation, and there is a Celtic place-name, Brandansvík (the creek of Saint Braddan, or Brandon) there to this day. Doubtless the settlement extended to other parts, and the name Vestmanna (stream of the west-men) suggests original occupation by Irish or Hebridean Celts.

A further clue, surely, is to be found in the name of the archi-pelago, Professor Brøgger having pertinently suggested that *Føroyar* is ultimately derived from the Gaelic " fear an," meaning " the far islands." This seems to me to be a much more likely derivation than the one usually given—that the name comes from the Danish " faar," meaning a sheep. The first Vikings are not likely to have spoken Danish, but the Old Norse from which the present Faeroe name for a sheep, *seyður*, is descended. Professor P.A. Munch, in his " Chronicle of Man and the Sudreys," states that the sheep of Iceland and the Faeroes were of Scottish origin, and quotes Dicuil as saying that they were introduced by the Scoto-Irish culdees.

Grím Kamban was the first Viking to make his home in the Faeroes, and he was soon followed by other Norse colonists who sailed to the west to escape the rule of Harald Haarfager, who had succeeded in unifying Norway. The earliest document describing life among the islands is a part of the famous Flattey Book of Icelandic sagas. There is an excellent English translation of this and therefore little need to say much about the story here. Briefly,

it describes the life-long feud between Sigmun‹
Skúvoy, friend of the Norwegian king and a de¹
and the independent, heathen and cunning Tróndu
this saga we learn many interesting facts—of the
ting or parliament (ancestor of the present Løgtin
in the tenth century, of the presence of Hebrid
islands at that time, of occasional journeying to Norway with wool
and the visits of foreign merchants, of strong opposition to the
introduction of Christianity, and so on. The tale is told with a
forthright, unvarnished simplicity which characterises the Norse
sagas, and there are many dramatic scenes. Not the least of these
describes the death of Sigmund, who was foully murdered at
Sandvík in Suđuroy when lying exhausted on the shore after
swimming from Skúvoy to escape Tróndur, whose men had
successfully breached the defences of the homestead in a surprise
attack. The translation by Muriel Press makes stimulating
reading, and can be recommended to any one who has an interest
in this land.

The saga closes with the words, " And it is not told that any
other great things happened in the Faeroes in the days of Sigmund
and his descendants." Thus heralded, the Dark Age of the Faeroes
begins. They were incorporated with Norway about the year
1035 and continued so under the union of that country with
Denmark, remaining united to Denmark when Norway was ceded
to Sweden in 1814. Even in the very early days it seems as though
some fairly regular contact must have been maintained with the
outside world, for in decrying the evils which the merchants of
the German ports brought to Norway in 1168, the king (reported
by Snorre Sturlason) said :

" We wish to thank all Englishmen who have come here
with wheat and honey, flour and homespun. We thank those
who have brought flax, wax and kettles. We mention with
friendship those who come from Orkney and Shetland, from
the Faeroes or Iceland, and all who have brought to this
country the things we cannot do without."

It would be most interesting to know what was the staple of the
Faeroe trade in those distant days, but perhaps we may be
allowed the guess that wool and woollen goods comprised the
chief export.

There is a brief description of conditions in the islands in an

.d law made by Hertug Haakon, the son of King Magnus of orway, and duke of the Faeroes and Shetlands, in 1289. Cultivation of the land does not appear to have been long established—at any rate, its importance seems to have been almost negligible in comparison with the sheep-rearing. The Faeroes appears to have been a lawless country : each man put as many animals as he wanted into the outfield, without regard for its capacity and the rights of his neighbours, and we have a sorry glimpse of the more powerful landowners crowding the poorer settlers out, and even openly stealing their sheep. Three hundred years later much the same state of affairs persisted, and Frederick II of Denmark found it necessary to rebuke the bigger farmers in 1559 for trying to squeeze their poorer neighbours out of existence.

For most of the mediæval and early modern period the islands appear to have enjoyed but little contact with the outside world— indeed, it may be doubted that they experienced enjoyment in their contacts at all ! Most of the visitors seem to have been blood-thirsty and acquisitive pirate bands. To deal with such visitations the people maintained a system of " watch and ward " at the villages, and indeed it is only in comparatively recent times that this home guard has been discontinued. There is a mass of evidence for the existence of this organisation in the place-names alone. At Eiði, for instance, Vaktarahúsbrekka, " watch-house hill," is on the west side of the great eminence called Kollur which dominates the village ; and on the hill-top south-west of Klakksvík the ruins of the watch-houses may still be seen. The watch-keeper's house as Tórshavn is still known by the name Vaktarastova, and the street leading out of the town to the point where observation was kept has a similar name. The people, being few and unarmed, took to prepared hiding-places among the hills when strange ships came towards the shore, and there is a legend that one village was moved bodily to another site, so that it would be less noticeable from the fiord, following unpleasant experience of pirate raids.

It was in order to defend commercial interests against such raiders that Tórshavn's two forts were erected. In 1578 King Frederick II gave Magnus Heinason the exclusive right to trade with the Faeroe Islands, and because of the ever-present danger from English, Dutch, French and other privateers, Heinason set up a fortification at Skansin, overlooking the entrance to Tórshavn. Later, about 1630, King Christian IV built a fort on Tinganes, but the two strongholds gradually fell into disrepair. In 1677 the fort of Skansin was razed by French ships, and half a century later the one on Tinganes was demolished. Skansin was rebuilt in 1780 and manned by a sergeant and twenty-four riflemen under the direction of a commandant, who was also the governor of the islands. This, the only army the Faeroes has had, gave place in later years to a police force, which used the fort as a prison until the British naval authorities made it their headquarters from 1940-45. This was the second occasion on which Skansin had surrendered to the Royal Navy, for an English brig, *Clio*, captured the castle in 1808.

The turning-point in Faeroe fortunes was the abolition of the Danish crown monopoly on trade in 1856. Before that date the Faeroes had been virtually a closed land, remote from the rest of Europe and having but little intercourse with other countries. But if the economic situation kept the people poor, it also gave them great opportunities for developing their culture undisturbed, and forced upon them the necessity for perfecting a peasant life of such economy that they could be self-supporting in every way. This isolation also permitted them to keep their language very much alive, and it can be said that much of the nationalist fervour which sways Faeroese political thought to-day had its origin in that long period when the islanders were forced to live unto themselves.

Politically the Faeroes form a county division or *amt* of Denmark, and although they have their own parliament, called Løgting, its powers are very limited, and generally speaking its duty is to propose rather than effect legislation. This is done by the Danish Rigsdag, to which the Løgting sends two members, one to sit in the upper house and one in the Fólkating. There is a good deal of political unrest in the islands to-day, a large body of the people, who belong to the Fólkaflokkur party, desiring home rule—or, at the least, a more democratic form of government.

Such new influences as have arrived in the islands from time to time have come mainly from Denmark : nevertheless, they have been of political, commercial and religious rather than of materially ethnological significance, and the Faeroese national characteristics have been strengthened rather than weakened by their intrusion. Although Danish has long been the official language, and was formerly the only one allowed in the law-court, churches and schools, the Faeroese tongue is gradually replacing it in daily life.

During the present century association with Denmark has been very pronounced, but there are many people living to-day who can recall the times when there were not more than two boats a year between Tórshavn and Copenhagen. Many children have received their higher education in Denmark, and many Faeroese have emigrated to take up trades and professions there. Indeed, during the recent war some 3,000 Faeroese—a tenth of the whole race—were cut off from their homeland by the German invasion of the Danish state in 1940. Throughout that period, of course, the Faeroe Islands were under British protection, but it is doubtful if the native culture has been much affected by this new association (except that a large number of people have added a third language to their vocabulary), although it is probable that the increased communication and business intercourse with Britain will have its results in years to come.

Such changes as have been brought about by the union with Denmark and the growing attention to the fishing industry have been largely confined to the ports, but have also led to improvements in housing and household comforts and utensils, the addition of the petrol engine to the rowing-boats, the introduction of the motor lorry and private car to the narrow roads, the importation of knives from Sheffield, scythes from Norway, spades from Sweden, canned fish from Iceland—and so on—in the smaller villages. But in these remoter settlements, especially the more isolated ones on the small and lonely islands, the daily life (as we shall see) remains conservative in character and self-sufficient in a high degree.

2

When I first saw Tórshavn on the day we sailed down the fairway into its little bay, I thought it one of the most picturesque places I had seen. Round about the town the hills were a watery green, rock-scarred and boulder-strewn, and seared with trickling rills. They rose in dreary, inhospitable slopes that looked devoid of interest or charm, rearing steeply to jagged crests of broken rock and scree beyond which one could imagine a great stony plateau ranging away for mile upon mile. The monotony of the surroundings cast into bold relief the attractiveness of this tiny, compact

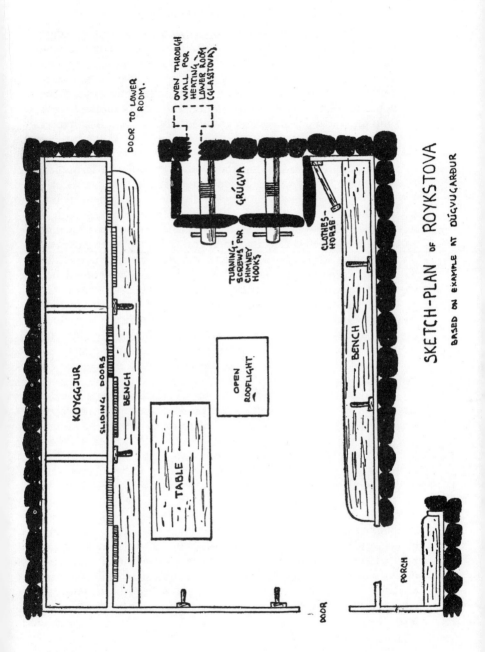

SKETCH-PLAN OF ROYKSTOVA

BASED ON EXAMPLE AT DÚÇVUGARÐUR

town spreading over the lowest slopes towards the water's edge.

Only occasionally, however, could the ragged edges of the hinterland be seen, combing the passing clouds. For there was a mistiness everywhere—a swirling, patchy, sunlit-gossamer September mist. Time after time as the troopship lay outside the harbour, waiting for the berth to clear, the many-coloured town was almost blotted out, or appeared dimly to view, like pieces of a shattered rainbow thrown into confusion behind the lurking cloud.

The buildings crowded together with disdain for pattern, plan or uniformity of any kind. There were all shapes and sizes and kinds of buildings clinging to the knolls and the shreds of fields, their roofs and walls shining with the wetness, glowing with a gay medley of colours. Tórshavn has been described as a town of wood, concrete and corrugated iron, and so for the most part it is. This much is apparent before one sets foot on shore, but the definition conveys an impression of cold, ugly, comfortless dwellings that is entirely foreign to the truth. It even goes so far as to suggest a place where, at long last, the army nissen-huts which awaited us might have found a sympathetic environment, and even some pretensions to architectural merit! But the Tórshavn whose smiling face I looked upon that day, despite all I had heard about it, held out no hope that such a miracle would ever come to pass !

This island capital presents a totally different aspect to a small English town or village. Here bricks and mortar and slated roofs are practically unknown, and the fashions of building houses in rows, semi-detached pairs and " garden estates " have failed to impress the Faeroe mind. The homes stand singly, and the shape and size and colour of each gives it an individuality that most English town houses do not have. It is to the credit of the Faeroeman that he has achieved such picturesqueness, and such efficiency, with the poor materials at his disposal. The narrow, often hilly streets ; the simple, unadorned frontages ; the long grass growing profusely on the roofs ; the liberal use of bright paints that shine through the damp mists, or of darker hues that draw back like shadows in contrast—all of these so enliven every change of scene that one cannot but marvel at the inspiration which so obviously dwells in the shelter of those hopeless-looking hills.

The older houses are small, some little more than mere cabins, and almost invariably their wooden walls are covered with pitch as proofing against the weather. Their roofs consist of sods on which the living grass flourishes no less than in the fields, and buttercups, sorrel, and other field-flowers grow when the roof is new. I might add that the hens delight to wander there in search of food. Many of the larger and more recent houses also have the characteristic sod roofs, but their walls are almost always brightly painted white, yellow, red, cream or brown. Nowadays cement for the walls and corrugated iron sheeting for the roofs are replacing the older and far more pleasing style.

Indoors, the houses are scrupulously clean and tidy, with tastefully decorated and well-furnished rooms. At first the English visitor misses the lazy comfort of his home—for there is no roaring coal-fire with a contented cat snoozing in the hearth, no deep arm-chair by the fireside, nor mantel-shelf to rest his weary feet upon ! Large ornate stoves, burning peat or imported coal, heat the rooms, and the arm-chair gives place to a divan which often serves as a bed for the chance visitor. Next to the kitchen is the *spisustova* or dining-room : formerly, on the farms and in many of the town houses, these were combined in the *roykstova*, " smoke-room," so-called because the smoke from the *grúgva* or open hearth, in seeking its exit through a hole in the roof, filled the room with a thin, turf-scented fog. A plan of a typical *roykstova*, one of the few remaining examples, is given on page 25. A communicating double-door joins the dining-room and the sitting-room, *dagligstova*, where the guests are entertained and the family sit at ease on Sunday afternoons. In earlier days this was the *glasstova*, the only room in the house to boast a window. The bedrooms nowadays are in the *loft* (or, as we would say, upstairs), another change from the older life, when there was usually only a half-loft over the *glasstova*, as there is in Celtic cottages to-day. The sleeping accommodation then was in half-neuk beds called *koyggjur* in tiny curtained cubicles against one wall of the *roysktova*. It was a warm place to sleep, and even if the space was somewhat limited, it was at least adequate for the people's needs. The half-loft was seldom used for sleeping in : it was more important to the economy of a people who had to make all their own clothes and furnishings to reserve this space for the loom and spinning-wheel and their accessories (see page 28).

Almost every house, except the older and poorer ones, has its small flight of steps leading to the kitchen door, and a little cubicle at the top where muddy shoes, wooden sabots or rubber

sea-boots are removed before their owner steps inside. The steps
are necessary because the dwelling-portion is raised eight or ten
feet above ground level by the stone walls of the basement or
kjallari. This is the storehouse of all the fishing, farming, whaling
and bird-fowling gear without which the Faeroeman would find
it well-nigh impossible to live. It is in a corner of the *kjallari*
that the cow is kept throughout the winter months—and if this
fact occasions any raising of the eyebrows, let it be remembered
that until quite recently, in many parts of Celtic Britain, the

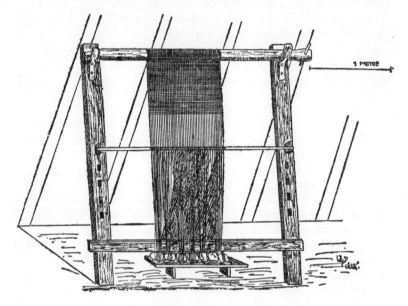

VEVUR (LOOM) - example in TÓRSHAVN MUSEUM

cattle byre was actually the lower portion of the dwelling, and
at best was separated from the family only by a wooden screen.
Keeping the cow below the house has great advantages—one
need only descend the ladder from the kitchen in order to milk
her or give her hay, and no matter how furious the elements one
will return from the duty warm and dry. One will be sure to
spend a sleepless night, however, should nature choose the dark
hours in which to bring her a calf! In another corner roost the
hens, and the cock sounds the coming of the new day as vigorously
as any alarm-clock, summer and winter alike. And it is in the

kjallari that the week's washing is done, or the day's catch of fish
and birds is sorted and cleaned, whilst here too the farmer turns
butcher in the autumn months.

The Faeroese depend to a large extent on dried and salted
food, and we find another use for the *kjallari* in the preparation
of such food for winter consumption. The drying of fish and meat
takes place in the open air, and a row of split cod, saithe or
whale-meat suspended from a rod beneath a loft window, or
ranged along the wall of the *hjallur*, is a common sight. The
hjallur is a small outhouse usually made of upright wooden laths
spaced a little apart, so that the wind can blow through the hut
and cure the mutton and legs of lamb hanging within. It is
sometimes a lean-to shed against the house itself, but is more often
separate : in it more of the farming and other tackle sometimes
finds storage, and often enough some hay, peat and potatoes are
kept.

Here, perhaps, we may lightly touch upon the subject of
Faeroe food and Faeroe meals. After a few months suspension in
the *hjallur* the mutton, now called *ræst kjøt*, is a great delicacy
(though not perhaps, for delicate English stomachs !). It is served
boiled, with potatoes, usually at supper on special occasions, as
when guests have been invited to the board. A few months more,
and the remaining mutton has turned to *skerpikjøt*, and I have
often heard it said that if there was enough of this commodity
Faeroemen would eat nothing else. It has a strong flavour and a
stronger smell, is the dark red colour of congealed blood, and is
like toffee to chew. Its taste is an acquired one which most
Britons at once decide they can very well do without ; but,
having persevered, I am inclined to agree with Faeroe folk that
nothing more tasty or sustaining is to be found in the islands.
It is put on the table just as it comes from the *hjallur*, and as the
piece goes round the table you take it in your hands and carve
long slivers of meat from it, with your own pocket-knife if you like.
(It is a singular fact that Faeroese pocket-knives are always kept
sharp—for carving *skerpikjøt*, I believe !) Sometimes the housewife
will braise it on the top of the stove for a few minutes, but my own
opinion is that it tastes much better when raw. And the fatter
it is, the nearer it approaches to perfection.

When the master of the house slaughters the sheep in autumn
he does all the work, from the actual killing to hanging up the
meat, himself. Butchers have a lean time in the Faeroes !

Nothing of the sheep's anatomy is wasted : the outside will make a splendid rug, and the inside a quite remarkable number of meals. The head is taken to the blacksmith's forge and singed, and appears on the dinner—or supper—table as *seyðarhøvd*. The " parson's nose," as we shall see later, is a special Christmas dish. The tallow finds its way into *knettir* and other dishes ; the stomach is used to contain *blóðpylsa* or *blóðmørur*, a kind of " black pudding ; " and the blood is collected and preserved for this and *blóðpannukøka*, which is a fried pancake of blood and flour and tallow mixed. The intestines are useful in making a species of sausage, *kjøtpylsa*, formed from minced meat and fish ; and the thin layer of meat covering the ribs is rolled up on the " swiss roll " principle with onion and condiments to taste, sewn with a needle and thread and boiled for a couple of hours. The result, *rullupylsa*, is one of the nicest meats ever to grace a sandwich.

Breakfast, *morgunmatur*, is a light affair, usually of sandwiches and coffee, though eggs and *skerpikjøt* are likely to appear. The sandwich is a great stand-by in this land, and takes such an immense variety of forms that a book could be devoted to it alone. It is a property of a Faeroe sandwich that you are permitted to see what you are expected to eat, for the meat or fish or fruit salad (or whatever it is) sits on a single slice of buttered bread. The coffee is strong and dark, with thick cream if you wish, and is far better than the nondescript liquid that passes for the same beverage in England. On the other hand, I prefer the English idea of tea—in the Faeroes tea has a tendency to be weak.

Lunch is *døgurði*. It may consist of fish, fried or boiled or served as *knettir* or in some other way—fish dishes I have reserved for description in a later chapter. If it is braised meat or boiled birds we shall be surprised to see rhubarb or even strawberry jam on the table to use as a sweet sauce with the boiled potatoes. Potatoes, incidentally, are never mashed, and rarely baked. It may be a whale-meat day, with pancakes and tea to follow ; or, if it is winter, salt herring, salted birds, *blóðpylsa* or *blóðpannukøka* may appear. The soup-course comes at the end of the meal— except at dinner in the evening, when it plays its usual *rôle*. A fish-soup goes well in its appropriate context, *ræst súpan* accompanies *ræst kjøt*, and bird-soup is the usual dessert with guillemot or puffin. There are, of course, many sweeter soups, such as a delightful one made from a mixture of fresh and sour milk, *kyrnumjólksuppa*, sweetened with raisins or prunes, and served with cream. That does not cover the range of Faeroe lunch-time foods by any means, but will serve to give the reader a general idea.

Afternoon tea with cakes is English enough, except that on party days no housewife would consider *millummáli* a success unless she were able to put a dozen different varieties of cakes and biscuits on the table, and give her guests chocolate (with whipped cream), followed by coffee, to drink. Supper, *nátturði* is sometimes not unlike breakfast, and is dominated by the sandwich—usually preceded, however, by a lightly cooked dish of meat or fish. It is at breakfast and supper that such delicacies as *skerpikjøt* and *rullupylsa* hold pride of place, and in summer *rómastampur*—curds and whey—often figures at the evening meal.

I have tried only to give a general outline—any attempt at a fuller treatment would be doomed to failure because Faeroe meals are so varied and the dishes so diverse. The standard of cooking is very high in most families, and one is right in suspecting that it owes much to Danish influence. Much of the food is strange to English eyes, and stranger still to English palates—but we are terribly afraid of dishes we do not understand, and miss much as a result of our timidity. The English visitor to the islands, however, need have no fears as to the provision that will be made for the inner man : the Faeroese are perfect hosts, and will never offer him their peculiar foods unless he first expresses a desire to sample them himself.

3

Tórshavn, as might be expected, is the big shopping-centre of the Faeroes. Cargo steamers from British ports bring flour, coal, cement and general merchandise to the quay, and, more frequently, there are visits by Danish ships with butter, bacon, eggs, other foodstuffs and beer. The last is for private consumers only—the Faeroes is a "dry" country and there are no public-houses. The town has three hotels, and although other smaller establishments take in visitors during the summer months, there is really little accommodation for tourists. Other amenities include three dance-halls and two very tiny cinemas, whilst one of the first, the Sjónleikarhúsið, is also used as a theatre.

The main streets are named in honour of famous sons of the islands, such as Niels Finsen, discoverer of the curative properties of ultra-violet rays, who was born in Tórshavn in 1860, and whose monument was made from a stone on which he had carved his initials when a boy ; Dr. Jacobsen, the greatest authority philology has had on the Norn language of the Shetlanders, and one of the pioneers of written Faeroese ; V. U. Hammershaimb, who also did a tremendous amount of work on the Faeroese grammar ; and J. C. Svabo, who wrote a description of the islands in 1781-82. In Tróndargøta we find the malicious Tróndur of saga fame commemorated, whilst Tórsgøta takes us still deeper into the past, remembering the heathen god Thor after whom the town was named.

The great majority of the inhabitants are Lutheran by religion, thus following the established church of Denmark, and a dean or próstur has charge of the ten parishes into which the islands are divided. The late próstur, Jákup Dahl, who died in 1944, will take his place in history alongside such worthies as Hammershaimb and Jacobsen, for it was due to his unceasing efforts that the Faeroe language was established in the schools and churches, and that Faeroe people were enabled to enjoy a marriage service in their own tongue. There is a Roman Catholic church with a small congregation at the Convent, and the Baptists and Salvation Army have considerable followings. There are two troops of Boy Scouts and one of Girl Guides in the capital, and sports organisations for soccer and handball exist all over the islands. There are choral and orchestral societies which give occasional recitals, and an amateur dramatic society produces plays now and then at the theatre. The Merkið is a very successful social and political organisation which holds dances and parties in the winter, and also meets for lectures and discussions : it has its counterparts in most of the villages, these units coming together at some central venue several times a year to hear addresses and sing national songs. There is a strong nationalist flavour about these gatherings, and they are certainly important as pillars of Faeroe culture.

In Tórshavn there is a chess club with many adherents, and the standard of play is extraordinarily good considering the small population. Perhaps the most popular indoor pastime in the winter months, however, is contract bridge. The only museums are at Tórshavn and Kirkjubøur, and both have good collections of Faeroese " bygones," whilst the former building also houses the county library. The county hospital is situated at Tórshavn, in charge of an expert surgeon, and there are " cottage hospitals " at Klakksvík and Tvøroyri. In Hoydalur, two miles to the east in a grassy bowl-shaped valley, is the tuberculosis sanatorium, and there is a convalescent home just outside the town, adjacent to the plantation.

There are a number of schools. The Franciscan sisters keep an infants' school at the Convent, and also teach languages, art and domestic science to older students. The Føroya Fólka-háskúli gives courses of from three to six months, in general subjects, for young people from the outer villages. The " Kommune " School and Realskúlin are state-endowed, and of elementary and high school standard respectively. The Læraraskúli trains young men and women to be school teachers ; the Handilsskúli caters for those who want careers in business, and there are also technical and evening schools. The Studentarskeið enables High School students to proceed to universities in Denmark, whilst the Navigation School trains young sailing-men for their mate's, skipper's and engineer's tickets. Small though their country is, the Faeroese are not behind neighbouring peoples in enjoying facilities for a sound education and owe much to Denmark for help in this respect.

Just outside the town, on the road to Hoydalur, is a plantation of larch, white spruce and silver fir, with a few blighted maples and other deciduous trees thrown in for good measure. This plantation is the best of four in the islands, was begun at the end of the last century, and is now the local park and beauty spot. On fine summer days many people walk its pleasant, shady paths, or sit lazing on the rocky outcrops among the little trees, sometimes (but, alas, too rarely !) basking in the sunshine. Near the top of the hillside there is a wide marshy hollow with a pool in one corner, and at one end of the pool a grand show of yellow iris gives fragrant charm and colour to the scene, whilst the marsh forget-me-not blooms profusely when the water-flag has gone. From the high points surrounding the pool there is a splendid panorama of the painted town reaching to the sea, and of the ships in the fairway and the fine shape of Nólsoy beyond. At the foot of the tree-clad slope the stream runs musically over its rocky bed, eventually to run down to the harbour side by side with Niels Finsens-gøta, the town's main thoroughfare.

Beyond the plantation is the sports ground—football field, handball pitch, tennis courts and swimming pool—all in the middle of the moor, and standing on the very edge of Tórshavn's " suburbia." This modern extension of the town fills the vale of the Hoydalur stream, where it runs below Ternuryggur, and extends also to the lower slopes of Húsareyn on the north side of the town. Here many of the townsfolk have bought or rented from the Council parcels of land in the outfield, and have tilled small areas for the cultivation of potatoes, rhubarb, carrots and other root-crops. The plot is at first rented, and as soon as one-fifth of it is under cultivation the lessee may buy the land on condition that he fences it to prevent encroachment by stock.

In these little enclosures, called *urtagarðar*, many people have built summer-houses to which they retire at the week-ends for a change and respite from the town routine. Most of the summer-houses are in the recent tradition of Faeroese building, gay and colourful, neat in outline and execution. Others are more ambitious bungaloid growths of unenlivened cement, but neat and comfortable enough inside. A few are well-planned permanent dwellings, and some at the other extreme are merely untidy, uncouth shanties and coops which tend to detract from the wholesomeness of the general scheme. Probably they are inhabited only by the gardening tools—certainly they seem too restricted in space and poor in material to have been intended for any higher purpose.

In these gardens of Tórshavn's " suburbia " you find the desert and the sown side by side ; you find nature's pools changed to ornamental waters, and rockeries ready-made to receive the gardener's alpine plants. You find a curious bird-life for the suburb of a town. Wheatears perch with cheerful song on rocks and posts, and Faeroe snipe trouble the sky above. I trespassed in one garden to put rings on a brood of oyster-catcher chicks, and among heather in the untilled part of another found my first young golden-plover—one moment a bundle of gold-spangled feathers half-hidden at my feet, and the next a writhing mass of quite astonishing energy doing its utmost to squirm out of my hand. A few yards away a gardener had set his seed and, full of abounding hope, had planted the empty packet on a stick in the ground—presumably in order that the picture would remind him later of what ought to be blooming there.

On the moorland rim of the valley's edge the whimbrels breed, bringing tuneful wood-wind music to the workers below. The snipe persistently slant down the sky, and the dun-coloured meadow-pipits rise and fall in the cheerful ecstasy of their song-flight. Everywhere you can hear the water rushing over the rocks and stones of the river bed to the waterfall below which its slower

journey across the flat land of the little Hoydalur plain begins.
The coming of man to make his own good use of this rock-littered
peaty soil has certainly failed to extinguish the beauty with which
the lives of birds enrich wild and lonely places. Indeed, it has
perhaps given to the birds added protection and new feeding-
grounds, for the golden-plover, wheatear, Faeroe snipe and
oyster-catcher are every whit as common as on the barren heath
about.

The summer-houses are for the most part small, and models of
economy in furnishings and space. A table and a few chairs, a
small stove for cooking, a small kitchen sink, and double tier bunks
flush with the inner wall or fitting cosily into a corner of the room
are the chief items. The bunks are a modern adaptation of the
space-saving sleeping accommodation which was an invariable
feature of the big kitchen or *roykstova* of old Faeroe homesteads.
Tórshavn's " suburbia " is indeed an interesting place, reflecting
an important and progressive side of modern Faeroe life, which
seems to be dominated now no less than in the past by the will to
make the best possible use of unpromising surroundings. You
find here the holiday-spirit that properly belongs to all town-
dwellers ; and beyond that you find also something of that force
which has made the Faeroe nation a thriving race in a land of
alien conditions—a force which embraces a love of making poor
soil productive, and of harnessing wild nature to their own
purpose.

4

My early wanderings in the Faeroes were confined to journeys,
on duty bent, " up the fiord,"—as the protecting power, excusably
cowed by the unpronounceable mien of its proper name, called
Skálafjørður. This long arm of the sea, reaching to the heart of
Eysturoy, makes a splendid anchorage and natural haven in
rough weather, but quite apart from its inestimable value to the
Royal Navy in those difficult days of war, it provided an excellent
introduction to the Faeroe scene. Indeed, perhaps no other part
of the archipelago can give the newcomer a more forceful first
impression of this strange and interesting land. The topography
is typical. The settlements are not so characteristic of the older
life, perhaps, as those on Nólsoy and Mykines, but they teach their
lesson.

Sometimes, on these journeys, the snow lay in dingy whiteness on the bodies of the pyramidal hills which are ranged around the fiord, the grey sky pressing on their tops. With the pallid hue of the hills stamped on their wings the big glaucous-gulls, winter visitors from arctic coasts, moved silently about the boats. It was a quiet world, in winter, and even the turning of the screw and the swish of water divided by the bows seemed a part of the great silence. There were times when the bold outlines of the hills were more beautiful, with a blue sky beyond them, and yellow clouds sailing there only a tone deeper than the sun's gleam on the snow-slopes. The country had a kindlier aspect then—but one could not escape the feeling that the kindliness was only superficial, for other impressions were always subdued by the startling desolation of the scene.

Beyond the head of the fiord the highest mountains in the Faeroes vie with each other to stand first before the sky. I will not deny their rugged, majestic beauty, especially under the Midas-touch of the winter sun. But they are a little frightening too—not in their immensity (for they are not great mountains), nor in the steepness of their slopes, but in their obvious hostility to human life. One feels that in the beginning (long æons ago) this country may have glowed with radiant health : but now, when spring scrapes the snow off their sides, the hills are revealed as old skeletons to which the brown flesh clings in frayed ribbons, tatters and shreds. The panorama is a reflection of the weather, of the storms that in the course of centuries have worn the mountains down to jagged cores of rock to which life clings precariously, holding to the poor, thin covering of soil that remains. You can find places, on the tops of these hills, where the grass-bound soil has been torn up by the force of the wind, or literally rolled back like a carpet by a winter storm.

The rocks go round the hills in irregular walls, as iron bands run round the staves of casks. I have often thought that if you were to heap soil and sods on the steps of the famous pyramid at Sakkara, you would have an exact replica of a Faeroe hill. There are innumerable places where these walls, called *hamrar*, have collapsed, and the rocks and scree dribble down the grassy slopes. There are picturesque cataracts bounding over the walls, and here and there long black chimneys deep in eternal shadow. The tiny watercourses, so busily employed in winter in carrying off the heavy rain and melting snow, are legion. The sea licks the feet of the hills as though fawning on the power that feeds it.

The land, the sea and the elements are in perpetual league against all human kind.

And yet the Viking chiefs fleeing from the fear of thralldom, saw in this a promised land ! There can be no better commentary on the quality of Viking mettle than that they should have chosen to settle on such forbidding soil, and no finer compliment to their endeavour than that, ten centuries after, their lineal descendants can still force that soil to pay. There is no air of poverty about these brightly coloured homes that cling, with the tenacity of limpets, to the strips of habitable shoreline where a great hill has dropped its guard, throwing out a sloping shelf instead of a nearly precipitous brow to meet the sea. In such places, a little less steep and brighter green than the rest, the Vikings seized their chance and drove home against nature one of the mighty warrior-punches with which their sagas resound. But is any saga more heroic than this—of how Scandinavia beyond the sea, the Faeroes, Iceland, and Greenland too, were forced into subjection by this most vigorous, virile and cultured of Nordic folk ?

There is evidence of Norse cunning in the sites chosen for the settlements, most of them sufficiently removed from the furies of the open sea, sheltering in the comparative calm of the fiords and bays, and squatting on the best that these towering hills can afford. All along the eastern shore of Skálafjørður the settlements string out, from Nes, through Toftir, round the bight of Kongshavn to Saltangará, Glyvrar, Sølmundarfjørður, and so to Skipanes, so that it is sometimes difficult to tell where one place-name ends and another begins. Most of the houses step down jauntily to the water's edge, and behind and about them is the chequer-board of fields where fertility has been created on the lower slopes. So vivid is the green that the fields gleam with it, making the rough grass of the upland beyond a drab and dirty brown in comparison. The houses make a mosaic of colour which contrasts oddly with the grey monotone of the alien rocks —as though flaunting in nature's face that irresponsible cheerfulness and unflagging optimism which the Vikings must have possessed in good measure, and which is reflected in the hopeful outlook of the Faeroe race to-day.

5

Tórshavn's neighbouring hills, Húsareyn and Kirkjubøreyn, are hardly worth climbing in winter unless you are in search of exercise rather than a pleasing countryside. Both are small plateaux rather than hills, and their upper reaches present a wide expanse of broken rocks covering the ground in the wildest confusion, at once depressing to the spirit and tiring to the eyes. The best hour I spent on Húsareyn was on a bright October morning when hoar-frost glittered in green and blue and violet points on the rocks about my feet, and the small areas of crisp grass crunched as I walked across them, leaving grey-green footprints stamped on the ground behind. Almost the only life was the quick, athletic loping of an alpine hare, and the lilting call of an occasional snow-bunting overhead. The hills and high moors in winter are wet, wind-swept and almost utterly deserted ; the change from the summer scene is so immense and so incredible that one feels the hills must hibernate !

Apart from the shepherds who must see to their sheep ; the postman who goes between Norðradalur and Syðradalur and the capital with mail, and must surely have one of the most exacting rounds in the history of postal services ; and the few men who go out with guns to shoot the mountain hares, the hills are little visited at this time of the year. The hares, originally brought from Norway, are common, and good numbers can be shot during the first few days of the season, before they become shy. They are most plentiful in the high hills in the north of Streymoy, but are subject to large-scale weather movements. Thus, the onset of cold and snow in the north sends practically the whole population scurrying to the south, where the weather is usually less severe ; and during a spell of cold east wind the hares show a tendency to move across to the lee side of the island. Heavy snow drives them down to lower ground, and if it falls early in north Streymoy, before the shooting opens in mid-November, it is a not uncommon sight to see hares in the fields and even the streets of the villages.

Winter may make much difference to the wild life, but it does not lessen the magnificence of the scenic panoramas to be had from the higher hills. A little beyond Húsareyn, above the western coast, is Tungulifjall, which affords the climber splendid views of Koltur, Hestur and Trøllhøvdi on the Atlantic fringe, as well as the Sandoy and Vágar coasts. From the southern side of the summit you can gaze down into the magnificent round-valley, a great natural amphitheatre, in which the new houses of the Syðraðalur homesteads, white-walled and red-roofed, stand in the dark shadow of encircling cliffs. Crossing to the north side, you can look over a terrifying precipice to the tiny roofs of the Norðradalur farms, as though seeing them from an aeroplane. Beyond the narrow valley in which they lie Núgvan rises steeply aloft to a broken craggy top, whilst the sheer cliffs of the equally rocky Stiðjafjall close off the head of the dale. From the top of any of these mountains on a clear day you can gaze into the south beyond Nólsoy and Sandoy and the Dímunar to the mountains of Suðuroy forty miles away.

It is in April that the hills begin to change, and by early May they are very wide awake. They are far different and far pleasanter company then, and the wanderer who knew them at their winter worst realises very forcibly to what an immense degree bird-life can bring about a change of scene. The moors and their intersecting valleys are thronged with birds, and their numbers and variety are more impressive than it has ever been my lot to see on similar ground at home. Their colour, form and music—to say nothing of their abundance—is so vital a character of the country scene in the summer time that it is impossible to deprive them of a place in this book.

First home is the golden-plover : he comes quietly, un-obtrusively, and goes straight to the hills. Those Faeroe snipe which migrated in autumn return close on his heels. Shortly afterwards the vanguard of the oyster-catcher host arrives, and the villagers are visibly cheered when they see and hear these greatly beloved creatures back among them once more. For the oyster-catcher, *tjaldur* as he is called, is right at the top of the avine hierarchy, and much more than a mere bird. He is as strong a symbol of Faeroe nationhood as the Faeroe flag. His name has been given to boats and businesses, and his effigy is painted on " Presents from Tórshavn " and appears as a common motif in decorative needlework. Perhaps Faeroe history will record that the soldiers of the protecting power, out of respect for a people they grew to like very much, adopted the *tjaldur* as their shoulder-badge, and pictured him on the cover of their magazine, *Fanfaroe !*

The oyster-catcher was raised to eminence by Páll Pállsson of Nólsoy, better known as Nólsoyar Páll, a late eighteenth century poet and patriot, and a very clever man. He could speak several European languages, and built and sailed the first Faeroe sailing-ship, in which he was eventually lost at sea. Taking a mediæval bird-ballad, " Fuglakvædi," as a model, he composed a satirical ballad in which he championed Faeroese culture and the cause of freedom, representing himself as a *tjaldur* attacking the governor, police chief, and other officials of the Danish administration, who he depicted as raven, hooded-crow, greater blackback and other predatory birds. Thus he shielded the people, the puffins of the cliffs, from alleged tyrannies and oppressions. This observation on the courage of the *tjaldur* must be an ancient one, for the root *tjald* signifies " a tent," the bird providing cover for the smaller species by its fearlessness in attacking any large bird which enters its domain.

So it is small wonder that the Faeroese have a special " welcome home " song for this colourful creature. Traditionally he comes back from the south at Grækarismessa, March 12th ; but always a few blithe spirits arrive earlier than that, whilst the main body does not come until the third or last week of the month. If the first to arrive flies in from the north, the people say it will be a bad summer that year ; if, however, *tjaldur* flies in from the south (as he ought), the portents are good. They say that if you hear the first bird before you see it, people will talk about you a lot during the year. (A good deal of scandal must have circulated about me, for I invariably heard my first oyster-catchers passing in the darkness as they finished their day-long flight across the sea !) If the first bird you see is facing you, you will have bad luck, but if it is retreating and you get a tail-view all will be well. If you see the bird in profile, Rasmus Rasmussen says, then you must make sure of your good luck by saying, " Eg síggi teg í lið, alt gangi mær við ! " meaning literally, " I see you in the lee, all goes with me ! "

There is little else to say about this interesting and amusing bird, except that in summer it is the life and soul of Faeroe hill and dale, and is more plentiful in the neighbourhood of the settle-ments than are lapwings about English farms. The oyster-catchers' spring piping is a song of hope for the new season, and it is good to sit on the heath beside some little tarn and watch the scores of birds, got up like pierrots with their long red noses and orange legs, as they meet for communal piping ceremonies. Gradually, as April advances, they go off in pairs to scrape a hollow in the gravelly patches or the grey-green *Grimmia hypnoides* moss, to receive their eggs. At the end of the month you cannot walk across any Faeroe moorland, or climb the slopes of any hill, without having half a dozen of these handsome (but now rather tiresome) creatures buzzing about your ears.

By this time another bird, the whimbrel, is busy imprinting his charming personality on the scene. He comes a full month later than the oyster-catchers, together with the dainty wheatears and white-wagtails. At the end of May, when the green cushions of the moss-campion are sprouting their frail pink flowers and the shy butterwort gleams in the grass, the wild, sweet song of the whimbrels floods the dales. Their song is the final triumphant fanfare proclaiming the season's conquest of the grim desolation which held the land in thralldom during the winter months. With slow wing-beats, the males fly in wide circles, their fluted, mournful notes increasing gradually in tempo until, with wings held in a shallow downwards glide, a long bubbling trill breaks forth. To listen to half-a-dozen birds performing above the same hillside on a warm and sunny evening is an experience of ineffable beauty, and I know of no richer reward for the patience of watching birds. There is no voice that expresses so eloquently the spirit of wildness, remoteness and strange charm with which the summer endows these northern solitudes.

There is not room enough to continue with a full account of all the denizens of these bird-thronged moors—of the wheatear with his stony voice and jaunty movements, the hooded-crow on evil bent, the obscure brown meadow-pipit, and even the starling and the wren. For these two are almost as much birds of the *hamrar* and the coastal cliffs as they are of the settlements ; and incidentally, like the eider-duck and rock-pipit, they are special insular forms which differ slightly in certain characters from representatives of the same species in other parts of Europe. Nor can we afford more than a fleeting reference to the sometimes extensive colonies of lesser black-backed gulls and arctic-skuas which give certain parts of the outfield a character of their own. In a wide and shallow valley just south of Kirkjubøreyn, only a few miles from the capital, the knolls and wet depressions among the innumerable wandering streams are studded white with thousands of nesting gulls, and the great colony overflows on to the shelves of the hill itself. The biggest of the skua colonies is probably that on the wet moss surrounding Fjallavatn, the

picturesque lake in the north of Vágar island, but there are other
fine groups in the hills above Saksun and Skúvoy.

So the season comes, stays for a brief time in a blaze of wild
music and scattered colours, and then slowly but surely fades
away. The stone-grey chicks of the oyster-catchers and the
buffy-brown young of the whimbrels are guarded through countless dangers by bold and watchful parents, until finally they learn
the power of their wings. The bird-ringer may well marvel at
the sturdiness of the young whimbrels' grey-blue legs and feet,
which are disproportionately long and large, but if he uses his
rings to good advantage he will soon learn from " recoveries "
that nature has an excellent reason for equipping them in this
way. They take between five and six weeks to fledge, and during
that period they perform a migration from the hill nesting-
grounds to the valleys below which may take them upwards of
a mile and a half from the nest. The parents divide the brood
between them if there are three or four, and after a week or so
the two groups appear to separate—perhaps intentionally, as
an insurance against loss at the hands of predators—only to
re-unite when the valley is reached. Why they desert the hills in
such numbers I do not know : perhaps food is more plentiful
on the lower ground, or perhaps the growing young need the
longer vegetation to give them cover from their enemies.

A shy-flowered saxifrage, *Saxifraga stellaris*, like a miniature
London-pride and one of the most distinctive of Faeroe plants,
grows with them on the wetter patches where they feed ; the
dense mosses run the gamut of all colours from yellow-green to
polished bronze ; the caddis-flies skim about the little pools, and
sometimes (if you are quick) you can catch tiny leverets as they
crouch forlorn among the rocks. Silver-spangled russet snipe
chicks remain at your feet when their guardian adults wing
suddenly away, and golden-plovers run at a little distance with
the most pathetic note in the bird-world whilst their downy
young (perhaps the most beautiful young of all) evade the eye
by harmonising wonderfully with the grass. The sheep lose their
coats, and look even sorrier spectacles than before ; the migrant
silver-Y moths, and later the dazzling red-admiral butterflies,
finish their quite astonishing journey of hundreds of miles across
the sea. . . .

In late August there is a great and sorry change. You can
walk for miles, and not a single oyster-catcher will come to meet
you, nor will more than an odd late whimbrel or golden-plover

cross your path. The season is done. The oyster-catchers, with those of their young that have survived the quest of crows and gulls and skuas for living food, have all gone to feed in the stubble-fields or gather in noisy bands near the newly-arrived turnstones on the shore. There is a delightful saying that when the whimbrel sees the first *sáta*, the large tramp-cock that heralds the close of the haymaking, he feels a " tickling in his head ! " In other words, the whimbrels begin to be affected by the restlesssness which precedes the autumn migration, and towards the end of this month their departure begins. High above, their seven-whistling whinnies floating down the sky, they move off in small parties along their high-road into the south. The wheatears, white-wagtails and meadow-pipits again pass through the villages and haunt the trees of the plantation on the edge of the town : but this time all movement is outwards, and by the middle of September the moorlands are alseep once more in that deathly hush which will cover them for more than half the year.

References to Chapter One

Brøgger, A. W. (1939) ; Killerich, A. (1928) ; Munch, P. A. (1860) ; Niclassen, P. (1938-39) ; Press, M. (1934) ; Walker, F. .and Davidson, C. F. (1935-36) ; Williamson, K. (1946-47 and 1947a).

HUNDAGONGUR
(Dog)

Faeroese knitting pattern.

Chapter Two

THE LAND

1. The situation of the infield or *bøur* and notes on its plants and their uses (*page* 44).
2. The tenure of land and the various types of holding (*page* 48).
3. The measurement and valuation of the land and manorial rights (*page* 52).
4. The characteristic appearance of Faeroe fields, their drainage, and the chief methods of cultivation (*page* 54).
5. Manure, and how this and other burdens are carried, with a note on Faeroese roads (*page* 57).
6. An account of the peat-cutting, the first harvest of the year (*page* 60).
7. A review of the farmer's lore concerning birds (*page* 65).

I

THE SUMMER LIFE of a Faeroe village is dominated by activities in the *bøur*, the cultivated area in the neighbourhood of the houses. The fishing, bird-fowling and whale-hunting, though of vital importance to the economy of the islanders, are incidental to the labour on the land, except in the few ports which have begun to flourish in modern times through taking up the fishery on a commercial scale.

So much of the islands is mountainous that the geographical features which lend themselves to the development of settlements are few and never extensive. Less than four per cent of the total land-area of more than five hundred square miles is under cultivation, and this small part doubtless represents a very high proportion of the ground that it is possible to till successfully under the existing system of tenure, and by such primitive means as Faeroe husbandry employs. The *bøur* that is being tilled to-day has been invested with the toil and care of generations of Faeroemen, and now as in the past the gain is little when one considers the immense amount of labour involved.

This *bøur* or infield usually lies at the head or *botnur* of a fiord or bay, or on the more gradual slopes along its shores ; or it may lie, as at Gásadalur, Funningur and other villages, where a valley debouches on the coast. Sometimes the shelving slope of a great hill will provide a soil-covered ledge or ledges between the *hamrar* of sufficient compass for a settlement, as at Hamar (the upper part of Froðbøur) and Velbastaður. To the south of Velbastaður this widening of the hillside has formed a narrow coastal plain, a feature unique in the islands, where the fertile infield of the farm Kirkjubøur is situated (see facing page 81). The lower regions of such small islands as Koltur, Skúvoy and Stóra Dímun are very fertile ; whilst at several places in Suðuroy a curious geographical formation called *eiði*, caused by the east-side fiords cutting back through the chain of hills almost to the western coast, has created suitable conditions for the development of a fine *bøur*. This is especially the case with Hvalbøur and Vágur and the existence of a similar type of lowland is reflected in the names of two of the chief villages in the north of the islands, Eiði and Viðareiði.

The *bøur* consists primarily of grass fields which produce fodder for the 3,000 head of cattle, and give winter grazing to a small number of the 80,000 sheep. Formerly a considerable amount of barley was grown, and the manner in which it was harvested and made into meal is dealt with fully in a later chapter. During the last hundred years this crop has been largely replaced by potatoes, and to a less extent by carrots and other root-crops. It is with the cultivation of the soil for grass and potatoes that the present section is concerned.

When preparing the infield for meadow-grass in olden times it was customary to grow barley in the first year, and leave the field fallow in the second, allowing the grasses and weeds to invade the plot from the surrounding land. The weeds, of which hemp-nettle, chickweed and shepherd's-purse seem to be the most vigorous and omnipresent, usurped the plot in this fallow season, but by the end of the third summer the annual grasses had taken hold and ousted most of the perennial weeds. The poor grass-crop would then be cut, and in subsequent seasons—up to ten years in most places—there would be good yields of hay. Occasionally a field would be sown with barn-sweepings when it was put down to corn, but usually little or no attempt was made to establish the grass in this manner. Foreign seed, as a general rule, is still sown only on the larger farms : there is little advantage in using it, for, as Feilberg has pointed out, the native grasses of the Faeroes yield an excellent hay of a high nutritious value.

The Faeroese field has been likened to the Norwegian " sæter " and Swiss " alpen," and certainly it has a wealth of flowering-plants and emerald grass. The flowers are not dissimilar to those of many English meadows, and in different districts different species dominate the scene. At Sandur and Nólsoyarbygd on a warm summer's day the homely scent of white-clover pervades the still air ; on Mykines in August the uncut fields are burnished with the rust of sorrel-heads ; at Argir in July the purple crane's-bill is the most striking bloom, whilst some of the Tórshavn meadows at the same time are gold-spangled with innumerable buttercups. One misses the red-clover, which is an introduced plant at Kirkjubøur, Stóra Dímun and a few other farms, but there are other gay blooms to make good the deficiency—the abundant, small-flowered northern eyebright, the frail pink ragged-robin, and the beautiful *Adam og Eva*, as the red and white forms of the spotted-orchis are called.

The old fields develop a soft carpet of mosses which eventually choke the grass—a sign that the soil should be turned, and rejuvenated with potatoes or barley again. Among the mosses grows a greyish-brown lichen called *jarðarsipa* which was used in Suðuroy in former times to make an infusion for the treatment of sores and wounds. This same lichen, curiously, was once used in England to cure rabid dogs, as well as the unfortunate people who were bitten by them—hence its scientific name, *Peltigera canina !* As in country districts the world over many plants were similarly used and misused in the cult of healing, and others had their importance in the manufacture of dyes for wool and cloth. Indeed, in olden days, the fields and *hagi* or moorland beyond anticipated in a sense the social services of the doctor's dispensary, the industrial chemist's lab, and even the greengrocer's and confectioner's shops.

Landt, in his section on the plants, gives many notes of the domestic uses to which they were put, and although some of this lore was obviously founded on superstitious beliefs, much of it was exceedingly practical, and provided yet another illustration of the Faeroeman's ability to put to good purpose Nature's bounteous store of raw materials. Hansina Rein has told me of the many applications of wild plants which were still quite common three and four decades ago. A green dye was obtained from the devil's-bit scabious and the leaves of white-clover, a black dye from meadow-sweet and crane's-bill, and a red one from the root of crosswort. *Steinamosi*, the moss known to botanists as *Parmelia saxatilis*, gave a brown dye : it was scraped off the rocks and boiled in water, the infusion being sieved off and the wool or cloth steeped in it.

The leaves of common sorrel were boiled and served as the vegetable with the meat, or gave additional flavour to the bird-soup. Its leaves, like the stem of *heimahvonn* and the berries of some hill-plants, were relished by the children. *Heimahvonn* is the home-grown form of wild angelica, which attains a vigorous and well developed form in the nitrogenous soil of the bird-inhabited cliffs. In the vicinity of the older houses one will often find tiny walled enclosures, usually no more than five or six feet square, to which the angelica was transplanted. The chopped stem, served with sugar and cream, was a most refreshing dish on summer days.

The leaves of bogbean (which, incidentally, is a very local plant, and seldom blooms in the Faeroes) and dwarf-honeysuckle were shredded and smoked in times of tobacco scarcity—the former as recently as the first great war. Cotton-sedge and common rush both provided wicks for candles and *kola* lamps. The pith was removed from the core of the rush-stems and rubbed between the hands until a thick strand eight or nine inches long had formed, and then tallow was melted and the strand placed in the middle. Tormentil rhizomes provided an excellent tanning agent. They were thoroughly cleaned by rubbing them against a stone, and then pulverised ; hot water was then poured over the powder and the sheep-skin was steeped in the solution. When yellow (either light or dark, depending upon the length of time it was immersed) the skin was removed and dried, then stretched against a chair-back. It was then ready for making into *rotuskó-gvar*, light skin slippers which even to-day are in very common use among men and women both in and out of doors.

From *hundaland*, under which name go several species of agaric, an antiseptic was produced. My informant remembered a farmer of Kallsoy who enjoyed a local reputation as a leech, employing toadstools in this way less than forty years ago. It is doubtful, however, if *hundaland* was a more efficacious medicine than silverweed, which must have been a panacea for almost all conceivable ills. Landt says it would " heal inward wounds and bruises, stop spitting of blood, hæmorrhage at the nose, remove the toothache, check dysentery," and perform other wonders of a range and variety such as no maker of a modern patent medicine would ever dare to claim !

2

Before we deal with the variety of methods by which the shallow but invaluable soil is cultivated, it is as well to gain some understanding of the structure of the Faeroe village community, and of the farmers' difficulties and problems, by looking into the question of tenure and valuation of the land. It is a question of supreme interest to the historian and student of folk-culture, but its importance is not merely academic : it will need to be examined very closely in the near future by those who are more immediately affected, for unless sweeping changes are brought about it is difficult to see how life on this grudging soil can be made to give an adequate return for the time and labour involved.

All the land in the Faeroe Islands, whether the cultivated *bøur* or infield, the untilled grazing of the outfield, the foreshore, the bird-fowling cliffs or the offshore holms and stacks, is owned by the Danish crown, by private individuals, or by the village communities. Certain areas in the neighbourhood of Tórshavn belong to the town council, but this fact is exceptional and due to the rapid growth and importance of the capital, and need not concern us here. It is probably true to say that there is hardly an acre in the archipelago that is not used in one way or another by the people for their profit.

A farmer who leases Crown land is known as *kongsbóndi* ; usually the lease-fee is small and the property fairly extensive, and the largest farms, such as Kirkjubøur and Stóra Dímun, belong to this category. Such holdings and the rights appertaining to them pass intact on the death of the lessee to his eldest son ; or, if there is no male heir, his eldest daughter, although the government (on behalf of the Crown) reserves the right to consider such cases on their merits and dispose of the holding to another tenant if it thinks fit to do so. The private owner is called *óðalsbóndi*, and under present law his land is inherited in equal parts by all his children, though up to about a century ago it was divided in the ratio of two to one in favour of male heirs. The

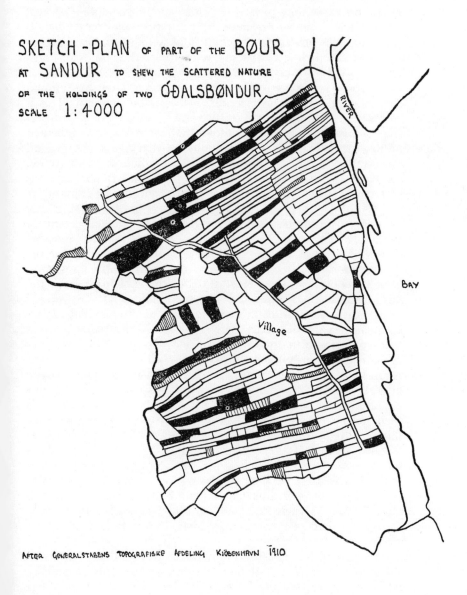

SKETCH-PLAN OF PART OF THE BØUR
AT SANDUR TO SHEW THE SCATTERED NATURE
OF THE HOLDINGS OF TWO ÓÐALSBØNDUR
SCALE 1:4000

RIVER

BAY

Village

AFTER GENERALSTABENS TOPOGRAFISKE AFDELING, KJÖBENHAVN 1910

D

" allodial " ownership, originating in Norway, was formerly the system of land-tenure in the Shetlands, and, far back in mediæval times, obtained in the Orkneys and north Scotland, too. There it was gradually superseded by the feudal system under which rich and powerful men were able to buy or appropriate lands and turn the " udalers " into their tenants.

"Kongs " land has the great advantage that the ground generally undergoes no division, and can be maintained as a comparatively large unit. On the other hand, " óđals " ownership, whilst it had the advantage that all the children benefit in the succession, has the manifest drawback that the ground inevitably becomes split up into small and often widely-scattered strips, and is therefore very laborious to work. It also happens that many of the female inheritors marry outside the community and go to live on other islands : in such cases the holding may be sold outright, but the owner will often appoint a trustee (usually a near relative) in the village to look after her interests there. She will claim her due share of wool and mutton from the flocks and the trustee will take as his fee the entire grass-crop from her holding in the bøur, and her share of birds from the fowling-cliffs.

As an illustration of the remarkable way in which " óđals " land can become dispersed there is the case which came before a land commission in 1908 of a farmer at Sandur whose holdings in bøur and newly-tilled trađir comprised nearly a hundred separate parcels of ground ! Another villager owned between fifty-one and sixty, and a third between forty-one and fifty, whilst a quarter of the land-owners had between ten and twenty parcels each (see page 49). A number of these were owned in partnership, by two, three and even four men. In many respects " óđals " tenure is reminiscent of the " rundale " open-field system common in Ireland years ago, of which Dr. E. Estyn Evans has written : " There are cases on record where twenty-nine partnership-peasants shared four hundred and twenty-two plots of ground, where one man held thirty-two different patches, or again where twenty-six people had shares in a field of half an acre."

At a few places, notably Vestmanna and Frođbøur, a practice called útskift has been adopted in recent years, the land being redistributed among the farmers so that each has his holdings concentrated in one area. One of the results of útskift at Vestmanna, I have been told, is that the inhabitants have been able to double their head of cattle, whilst there are other obvious advantages in the amount of time saved in tilling the soil, and in the fact that the larger areas involved render the use of the plough economical. In the absence of new legislation regulating the succession, however, the advantage gained can be only a temporary one, and several generations hence the holdings will require reshuffling once again.

Not all the villages in the Faeroes have their *bøur*, for several have grown up on land that has been taken into cultivation during the last hundred years or so. Such places are Slættanes at the northern tip of Vágar, whose tilled soil was formerly a part of the outfield of Sandavágur in the south of the island ; Hvítanes, where settlers on a spit of land reaching out into Tangafjørđur have bought parcels of ground from the Hoyvík outfield ; and Argir, which may now be regarded as a suburb of Tórshavn, and whose fine fields were once a part of the rich Kirkjubøur estate. Such new land is technically known as *trøđ* (in the plural, *trađir*), and as the people have either rented or purchased the ground only, they have no rights in the outfield for turf-cutting, bird-fowling or grazing sheep. For this reason these are, generally speaking, poor communities. The people of Hvítanes regularly get wool from Sund and Hoyvík at the beginning of the winter, so that they can make clothing. They do not buy the wool, but keep for themselves one in every three of the items they make, the other two being the property of the owner of the wool. Such an arrangement of working for a third part as payment was more customary in the old days than now, and extended sometimes to such occupations as haymaking and the slaughter of the sheep if one farmer had to call in another's help. Some of these *trađir* villages, such as Víkar on the north-west coast of Vágar and Bøur to the south of Kirkjubøur, had only a short career before the settlers decided that the independent life was too precarious, and abandoned their fields in favour of the greater security of employment in the towns or on the larger farms.

An annual meeting of the landowners is held in all the villages in the spring. It is called *grannastevna*, and there policy with regard to the administration of the outfield is discussed. Decisions taken at such meetings are by vote, and the biggest landowners always have the biggest say because the votes belong to the ground, not to the man, there being one for every unit called *gyllin*. Adjacent villages often combine to form a *komuna* or council for the administration of the school, the building and upkeep of roads, provision

for the poor and so on. Each *komuna* pays a small tax to the
Government, from which in turn it receives financial help for
public works. In former times when roads and schools were
built, a man gave one or two days' labour on the project in lieu
of paying a tax.

3

The value of the land was fixed in accordance with the old
Nordic measurement at some time in the remote past. The basic
unit is the *mørk*, which contains 16 *gyllin*, 1 *gyllin* containing 20
skinn. The unit varies from place to place both in its intrinsic
value and in the extent of land it represents : thus, in Mykines
the commonwealth has the value 40 m., at Froðbøur 24 m.
(although the area concerned is actually larger), and at Hvalbøur
97 m., the highest figure for any settlement among the islands.
These and similar totals bear absolutely no value for practical
comparison, the area and resources of the land being different in
each case, and in some cases covering manorial rights (such as
bird-fowling) which are not present in others. At each of the
old settlements a man has wealth in the resources of the outfield or
hagi corresponding to the amount of *bøur* he holds. This holding
in the *hagi*—a term which covers all land in the country not
actually under cultivation—corresponds to the " scathold " of
the old Scottish " runrig " system, which appears to have had
the same Norse origins.

In view of the absence of any clear historical records one can
only surmise as to the origin of the " kongs " system. It is
possible that it goes back as far as the tenth century, and the
Faeroe saga gives a hint as to how it might have arisen. The chief
characters in this fine story are Sigmund, the son of Bresti, whose
estate was on Skúvoy and the Dímunar, and Tróndur, the " villain
of the piece," who lived at Norðragøta on Eysturoy. The child
Sigmund was banished to Norway by Tróndur, who, with his
henchmen, had surprised and slain Bresti and his brother Beini
during one of their periodic visits to Stóra Dímun. When
Sigmund attained manhood he was befriended by the king of
Norway, who equipped him with an expedition, and enabled
him to return to the Faeroes and take his hereditary possessions.
Sigmund swore fealty to the king, and later embraced the
Christian religion, and it is recorded that he collected an annual

tribute for his overlord from some of the settlers. It was only by guile and force of arms that he was able to make Tróndur and his numerous followers pay this tribute or accept the Christian faith, and it is certain that when they finally succeeded in disposing of Sigmund they reverted to their heathen and independent ways, and, one imagines, maintained the original allodial owner-ship which the earliest settlers had brought from Norway. Sig-mund and his friends, on the other hand, seem to have been the first " kongs " men, and it is probably significant that Skúvoy and Stóra Dímun consist of " kongs " farms to-day, whilst Lítla Dímun also belonged to the Crown until it was sold to the Hvalbøur community late in the last century.

It is certain that most of the present " kongs " land belonged, prior to the Reformation, to the Church. Its earliest holdings may have been received from the Crown; some was no doubt given later by ardent catholics, and it is equally certain that some was confiscated in reprisal for spiritual delinquency, for here as elsewhere the Church was powerful enough to deal harshly with offenders against the faith. There is always an abundance of " kongs " holdings in the neighbourhood of religious centres and the residences of the priests—as at Nes and Miđvágur, for instance —and conversely " óđals " holdings predominate at places which appear to have been far removed from Church influence. Kollafjørđur, judging by remains discovered there, was once the site of a religious institution, and for very many years it has been the seat of the priest for the Norđstreymoy district : it comprises 51½ m. " kongs " holdings, and a freak ½ m. " óđals " land whose existence history has tantalisingly failed to explain.

The great farm at Kirkjubøur provides the best example : this was once the seat of a bishop, and throughout the early history of the Faeroes was the religious and cultural centre. Prior to the Reformation, when the Crown took all the Church's wealth, the Kirkjubøur estate extended northwards to Hórisgøta, between Kvívík on the one side of Streymoy and Kollafjørđur on the other, and included the islands of Koltur and Trøllhøvdi. Such settlements in this area as Kaldbak and Velbastađur, which are certainly pre-Reformation, came under the Church's domination, and have no " óđals " holdings. After the fall of the Church some of the Kirkjubøur estate was dispersed by the Crown and resulted in the formation of new settlements, such as Sund, which has a small bøur but a rich and extensive outfield, and is valued at 12 m. ; Skælingur, where there are now two 7½ m. farms, and probably also Norðradalur, where two brothers own 5 m. 10 g. each. A further 8 m. in the Tórshavn district were leased as a separate farm, and the 2 m. Sandagerði was established as the living of the priest for the South Streymoy district.

By private agreement with the families concerned, or by other arrangement made with the consent of the crown, " kongs " holdings have been split occasionally between two or more sons of the original tenant. Koltur island, on which there was probably originally one farm, to-day comprises four equal holdings amounting to 17 m. Skælingur and Norðradalur provide other examples ; whilst at Hoyvík there is a farmer with 5 m. and a government experimental farm with a like amount. In the same way, Húsagarður, the original 8 m. " kongs " farm in the Tórshavn area, is now equally divided between a private farmer and the town council. On the other hand, " kongs " land has sometimes been sold to *óðalsbøndir*, as in the case of Lítla Dímun, the farm Steigagarður at Sandavágur, once the living of the Speaker of the Løgting, and several farms in other places which were formerly part of the living of the priests.

In former times the lease-fee of Crown land was substantial and was paid in produce—so much wool, butter, meat, etc. to the *mørk*. In the middle of the last century the fee was converted into the equivalent amount of cash, but as the sum has never been adjusted to conform to the depreciation in the value of the *króna* since that time the lease-fee of all " kongs " holdings to-day is a nominal one only. The government taxes both categories of land at a standard rate per *mørk*, and also the newer *traðir* holdings, these, however, being assessed at a considerably higher rate than the old *bøur*.

4

At haymaking time in August and September the fields are more beautifully variegated than before, with the small plots at the various stages of harvesting, and the ground ribbed with the curious drainage channels—exposed now that the grass has been felled by the scythe, and cast into relief by their own shadows as they ripple down the hillside to the valley floor. The top photograph facing page 112 of the Mykines *bøur* in mid-August shows this picturesqueness to advantage, but unfortunately a photograph cannot depict those subtle, charming shades of difference in soft colouring which make such a beautiful patchwork of the scene. The absence of walls and fences enhances the loveliness of the village setting at this time, for although there are so very many fields, a few widely-separated stones are the only boundary marks between one man's property and another's. In spite of the rocky nature of the countryside and constant weathering of the basalt by heavy rains and frost the Faeroese keep their fields remarkably clean, sometimes gathering all loose stones together in a corner (see top photograph facing page 208) or removing them to the shore.

The ditches are the most important feature of the fields. They have an ancient history, and have determined not only the curious topography, but also the high fertility of the shallow soil. The

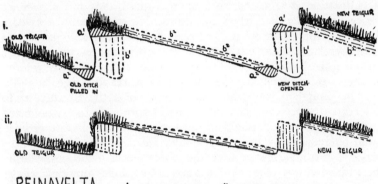

REINAVELTA   i. on wet ground   ii. on dry ground

heavy rainfall and impervious peaty subsoil lying on a rocky bed make an efficient system of surface drainage essential, for the little rills which are normally mere trickles descending the slopes swell into angry spate after an hour of heavy rain, and ground that has no channels to lead off the load of water very quickly becomes a bog. The ditches are usually parallel and run with the slope, if the slope is even, seldom more than ten feet apart and often less ; but where the surface is undulating the ingenuity of the Faeroeman has often been taxed in planning the most efficient course, and the fields often appear to have been built in broken terraces or steps.

These ditches have determined the special manner of cultivation, *reinavelta*, which is peculiar to the islands. This field has the name *teigur*, and diagrammatic sections of it on wet and dryer ground are shown on page 55, whilst a photograph of the latter is facing page 112. During the winter some of the perpendicular bank of the ditch crumbles away, eroded by rain and frost, leaving a slight overhang at the top where the grass-roots bind the soil. In preparing *teigar* for corn the overhang is cut away and put into the ditch below and a sod is lifted from the topmost part of the grassy incline (a1), turned over, and trampled down at the foot of the slope (a2). Manure is then spread over the grassy surface remaining (b1) and slices of earth from below the position of the removed sod are taken with the spade and spread over the manured area (b2). It will be seen that when this process is complete the field has " moved " about a foot, and a new ditch has been opened up adjacent to the old one. Corn is grown, then hay is raised for several seasons, and then the process of cultivation is repeated, so that in a number of stages over a period of twenty or thirty years the field is completely renewed. This ingenious method is becoming rare, but is still practised in many of the outer settlements. A modified form of *reinavelta*, as shown in the figure, takes place on drier fields—usually where there is a steep, even slope giving good natural drainage.

The plough is still practically unknown in the Faeroes, and indeed, with the fields so small and widespread, its use would be uneconomical. The chief tool of cultivation now as formerly is small-bladed, general-purpose spade, *haki*, shown on page 61. To-day, in tilling new ground, the whole plot is turned over with this implement, a deep " V "-shaped furrow being first dug along one side of the field. With three cuts of the *haki* a trapezoid block of soil is lifted, turned grassy side down, and laid against the far side of the furrow. The next and successive *bøkkar* fit closely and firmly against each other along the row, opening up another " V " for the following row as digging proceeds. Usually a man does the digging whilst other members of the family follow on, breaking up the surface with light spades such as are used for cutting peat, and an example of which is shown on page 61.

If potatoes are to be grown, the ground is then dug into alternate ridges and furrows. The seed is put into the furrows and covered with soil from the ridges on either side, so that the finished plot is either fairly flat, or slightly ridged above the potato rows. In a few places, as at Kvívík, this method is modified by first denuding the whole area of the top sods and stacking these in a bank on one or more sides of the plot. Whilst the plants are growing these banks serve to keep off the cold rough winds, in the same way as the earth banks and stone walls I have seen on the weather side of potato-patches on Mykines. When the potatoes have been gathered in the autumn the sods are replaced, the grass downwards to form green manure, and the land is left fallow for the new grass to grow.

Another way of preparing the ground for potatoes is *flagvelta* or *tvørvelta*, " sod-cultivation." The land is tilled in strips, the sods being lifted and turned down again on the same spot when the manure and seed-potato have been laid on the exposed surface. This method is much used on Vágar, and another common type of cultivation also originated there, and has spread to other islands in recent years. It has the advantage of being less laborious, as only half of the plot need be dug, and it is good for a following grass-crop as the ridge can be turned straight away into its original position when the crop has been removed. Potatoes can only be taken from such a field for one year, however, and if successive crops are required true *velta* or *flagvelta* must be employed. The patch is marked out for alternate furrows and ridges ; fish-heads, or other manure, are strewn along the ridges, and the seeds are set on top. This is sometimes a woman's task, whilst the man follows behind, digging a slice of earth the full width of the furrow and turning it grass down over the seed and manure to make a ridge above them. It is a curious coincidence that this method is called *letivelta*, " lazy cultivation " because only half the field is dug—and for the very same reason that the identical Irish field is called a " lazy-bed ! "

5

Cultivation takes place as a rule in April or May, although Landt records that in places where much seaweed was washed ashore in the autumn the ground would be dug at that time so as to make the best use of this invaluable manure. Animal dung is the fertiliser most commonly used to-day, often mixed with seaweed, and of course phosphates and other artificial preparations are in growing demand. The offal of a whale-hunt is considered excellent, especially for grass, but very little use is made of it at the present time.

With the decreasing production of barley, seaweed is declining in importance, for it is of but little value to the potato grower, dung and fish offal giving better yields. At Nólsoyarbygd, Sandur and other villages, however, one may still see small stone enclosures, about ten feet square, along the foreshore—middens called *tarakøstar* in which the wrack is stored until it is time to spread it on the fields. At Søltuvík, a lonely shore four miles north-west of Sandur, seaweed is cast ashore in such abundance as to have made it worthwhile constructing a road across the moorland to the deserted creek, so that cartloads of wrack can be brought to the village. In less favoured settlements men would formerly go out in their boats to suitable places along the coast and cut the ribbon-weed from the sea bed with a scythe or reaping-hook attached to a long pole. This practice was described by Landt a hundred and fifty years ago, and was still to be seen in Tórshavn in quite recent years.

Although there are now roads of some sort at most of the Faeroe settlements, and wheeled traffic has increased in recent years, much of the manure and the produce of field and sea is still borne on the backs of men in the characteristic wooden *leypur*. This is a box, tapering slightly towards the base, and consisting of four posts joined either by spars set an inch apart, or by solid boards. The upper ends of the posts nearest to the body are joined by a short rope, padded with a cloth band in the middle, which presses against the forehead of the bearer. The solid one, *tøðleypur*, is the smaller : it is used for carrying manure, and also by older men for potatoes. Younger and stronger men use the *byrðarleypur* for these, as it will lift a greater quantity—about a hundredweight. This kind is also used for turf, whale-meat and seaweed.

Two special types of *leypur* must be mentioned : one is now obsolete, and the other but little used. The first, *prestaleypur*, held the parson's vestments and books on his journeys between the villages : it had a lid to keep out the rain, and a compartment under the lid for his ruff-like collar, *prestakragi*, so that this carefully laundered item would not be creased by his books and the other contents of the box. The other, *grótleypur*, was used during building operations : it is not a box, but is more like a chair without legs and was for carrying big roughly-hewn stones from the quarry to the site of the house. Niels Rein told me that when the lighthouse was in course of erection at the south end of Nólsoy one of the labourers, called Gutta Jógvan, carried barrels of cement on his *grótleypur* from the landing-place to the site— a distance of five or six hundred yards, and all uphill ! The weight of the cement alone was 180 kilos, so that, with the extra

weight of the barrel and
the *leypur* itself, this Faeroese Samson must have
carried over 400 lb. on
each trip !

The wheeled cart is a
very recent introduction,
as all the roads are new,
but pony transport has
been employed from early
times by those able to
afford draught-animals.
The horses are small and
similar to the Iceland
breed, sturdy and hard-
working, usually of a roan

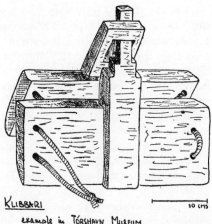

KLIBBARI

10 cms

example in TÓRSHAVN MUSEUM

colour and a pleasant disposition. Their load is put into
two large *rossaleypar*, which are of similar form to the *byrðarleypur*,
and are slung one on each flank in the manner of side
panniers. Landt describes the equipment, which is called *týggj*,
in some detail. Firstly, a sheepskin covering is put over the
horse's back, the woollen side against its skin, and a mat, made of
hay-bands fastened together with a coarse woollen thread, is put
on top of this as an added protection. Then a wooden *klibbari*
(see above) or crook saddle is fixed in position, and the *leypar*
are suspended from its boards : the saddle is held fast by two
ropes, wrapped round with wool to prevent chafing, the first
passing round the horse's breast, and the other beneath its tail.

The roads in the neighbourhood of Sandur, where the
countryside is tolerably flat, have greatly eased the transport
problem for the local farmers. In this village there are numerous
small box-carts, drawn by a single pony, and with boards about
eighteen inches high. They are two-wheeled and about five feet
square, and their carrying capacity can be increased if desired
by fitting a wooden framework inside the boards, raising them to
about two feet in height. The carts are made to tip backwards,
so that unloading is simple. A longer, narrower and somewhat
deeper four-wheeled wagon, of a type introduced from Denmark
in recent years, is owned by a few of the " kongs " farmers, and
this has a centre shaft for two ponies harnessed abreast. The bodies
of the carts, I was told, are made locally, but the wheels have to be
imported from Norway as there are no wheelwrights in the Faeroes.

Faeroe roads are mostly of very inferior construction, but it must be borne in mind that linking up the scattered settlements of this mountainous country is a tremendous and costly task. Again, although the roads are all comparatively recent, the fact that they would soon have to bear a good deal more mechanical than horse-drawn transport was not envisaged when they were laid down. Suðuroy has two good highways, the southern one connecting the Vágur district with Lopra and Sunnbøur—and thus opening up one of the most beautiful areas in the Faeroes to the tourist—and the other joining Froðbøur and Fámjin, through Tvøroyri and Øraðvik, farther to the north. Probably much the longest road runs from Nes and Toftir along the eastern arm of Skálafjørður to Skipanes, with a branch over the hills to the settlements at the head of Gøtuvík, and on through a hill-pass to Fuglafjørður. Vágar is the most fortunate island, for during the war British military works necessitated the construction of an excellent highway from Sørvágur in the west to Miðvágur and Sandavágur in the south, where the new road meets the older one to Fútaklettur, a landing-place opposite Kvívík on the Streymoy shore.

On Streymoy itself a mountain highway is in course of construction between the two chief ports, Tórshavn and Vestmanna, but the work has proceeded very slowly owing to the lack of sufficient funds. The section between Kvívík and Vestmanna was opened in 1944, but much the most costly and difficult portion has yet to be begun. Besides proving a boon to the towns at its termini, and the large villages between, this road will bring some of the finest and most typical scenery in the islands within easy reach of the traveller, even if his stay at Tórshavn is of a few hours duration only.

6

Turf—or " peat," as the Englishman prefers to call it—is the staple fuel of the Faeroe folk. In the largest settlements such as Tórshavn, Klakksvík and Vestmanna, some English coal is imported in normal times, but in these places the recent war witnessed a great revival in the use of peat, and a much greater quantity than usual was cut in the surrounding countryside by those who own turbaries as a part of their manorial rights, or hire them from the town council.

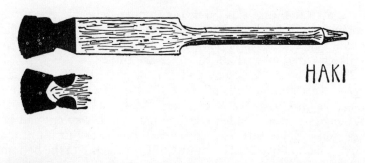

HAKI

PINNAGREV

TORVSKERI

10 ·20 30
CMS.

In the outlying settlements the turf harvest remains an interesting and important feature of the material folk-culture, and to me it had a special appeal because I found in it many affinities with the same occupation in the Celtic provinces of Britain, and in particular with memories of the turf-cutting in the Isle of Man. In the Faeroes the harvest begins later and is more protracted than in Man and other parts of western Britain, for the winter is invariably wet and the springtime generally so, so that the moors do not " dry out " sufficiently to permit cutting until the beginning of June. A fickle summer will prolong the period necessary for the spreading and drying of the peat, and a wretched one such as the islands experienced in 1942 may well ruin a large part of the harvest.

The method of cutting is much the same as in Britain. Two types of spade are used, the comparatively broad *haki* for lifting the top sods to expose the surface of the peat, and a special lighter one for excavating the turves themselves (see above). The grassy sods must always be replaced and stamped down when the peat has been taken so that the grass will continue to grow and provide pasture for the sheep, and failure to observe this rule will result in the offender receiving a summons from the *sýslumaður*, who can be placated only by the payment of a fine. In former days there were similar penalties in the Isle of Man for those who left the face of the turbary exposed, though delinquents were few because the work was carried out under the eagle eye of the Captain of the Parish, who was responsible for seeing that the families cut in their rightful places, did not quarrel with their neighbours, and obeyed all the necessary rules.

The cutting-spade is long and narrow and has an iron blade or *grev*. In common with many of the British varieties it has a small *pinnagrev* (the Manx call it a " feather ") projecting at right-angles to the rounded edge, so that a two-way cut can be made and a single turf released by each downward thrust of the blade. The iron blade is bound by turned " wings " to the bottom of the wooden *fótur*, which has a flat surface flush with the blade so that the peat will slide easily along it. A nail driven through this *fótur* some 15-18 inches from the cutting-edge marks the limit to which the tool should be pushed into the peat, and so decides the length of the turf. The *fótur* has its counterpart in the Celtic spades, but in these it is usually much shorter and greater in width : the Faeroe *torv* has to be long and thin or it will not dry well in this damp climate. The handle is in one piece with the *fótur* and, unlike many British examples, is without a cross-piece at the top. The form of the spade has many local variations in Man and other Celtic areas, but in the Faeroes it is remarkably uniform. It is called *torvskeri* among the islands, a name which has an obvious etymological relationship with the Shetland " tuskar."

The harvest is a family affair. The man will strip the ground with the *haki* and cut and lift the turves on to the bank above the bed, whence his wife and children will carry them to sloping ground, preferably facing south, and lay them down a few inches apart so that each may have the full benefit of exposure to the wind and sun. After a day or two they will be turned so that the undersides can dry, and later several will be stood together on their ends, leaning against each other in pyramid form, so that the wind can pass between them and continue the drying. In Ireland these little stacks of five, six or more turves are called " foots " or " castles," and they are of a variety of shapes. Later still, when drying is almost complete, small dome-shaped mounds of thirty or forty turves will be made, pending removal to the store.

If you were obliged (or found it convenient) in former days to cut peat on land which was not your own, you would pay for the privilege with a day's labour in the owner's fields. Three " man-cuts " are reckoned to be sufficient for a year's supply of fuel for a normal household : this is the amount a man can cut in three full days, and it will generally make about sixty loads if carried in the *leypur*. In late summer the turves are gathered up and built into a *lutur* or *krógv*, the latter very similar in appearance to the Hebridean " cleat," or they are stored in a special *torvhús* or *gróthús* standing on the moor. The *krógv* is usually rectangular in plan, some 12-15 feet long by 4 feet wide, and it is enclosed on the long sides (and sometimes at the rear as well) by a loosely-constructed wall of moorland stones. The top of the stack is ridged so that the rain will drain off, and it is sometimes covered with sacking held in place by ropes or wire-netting, or may even have a rough *flagtak* or straw thatch. The *lutur* is a stack without the protection of the stone walls. There are different local traditions in the form of the stack : in some places it is square rather than rectangular, and walled on all sides ; and on the heather-grown moors about Toftavatn, where the people of the Skála-fjørður settlements cut their peat, stone walls are dispensed with (perhaps because the area is more sheltered than most) and the turves are surrounded by wooden palings made of barrel-staves obtained from the fish-drying establishments of Toftir and Saltangará.

Towards the end of July in 1942 I was staying at Eiði, and at that time the turf-spreading was in full swing on the upland moors to the south and east of the village. Early in the day the families, carrying their satchels of food and the inevitable kettle, trekked out along one or other of the two roads leading to the turbaries, and passed the whole day working on the moorland in the shadow of the great hills.

Along one of these roads I climbed to Suðiravatn, a quiet lake in the lap of the hills. The road rose from the church in a succession of hairpin bends to gain height on the steep coastal slope above the Sundalagi. Most of the returning people, heavily laden with their *leypur*, preferred to use the little hillside paths which served as short cuts eliminating the deep turns, and when tempted to save time in the same way I had to stand aside many times whilst some sure-footed villager tramped by in his sheepskin shoes, his head bowed by the burden on his back. The road came to an end at the northern side of the lake, at a shaky wooden landing-stage on which were piled sacks of turves awaiting transportation to the picturesque village a couple of miles below.

All round the shore of Suðiravatn shafts of smoke rising in the still air betrayed the presence of turf fires over which the diligent workers brewed tea to wash down their midday meal. My fragrant memories of the lake are of the bathing kittiwakes going in a never-ending procession to and from the water, of two ravens high aloft nonchalantly evading an angry whimbrel, of an agile brood of merganser ducklings (the only creatures I have yet seen actually walking on water), and of these straight grey-blue plumes seeking the zenith against the splendid background of the Faeroes' highest hills—Slættaratindur, Svartbakstindur and Bláamanstjall.

Later I stayed for a week on Mykines. The splendid folk who form this island community are fortunate in having their turbaries within a mile of the village at the head of a well-made road. The *krógv* is infrequent : usually the peat is given better storage, and the lower zone of the outfield is dotted with small stone *gróthús* built specifically for this purpose. They have loosely-constructed walls so that the wind can seep through and so continue the drying ; in a few the upper portions of the gable walls are wooden planks set an inch or so apart for the same reason. Similarly many of the doors are lath-like in structure, and they are almost invariably fitted with the large and efficient wooden locks which I have described on page 300. Almost all the huts are roofed with sods, weighted down in some cases by large stones, but one, standing by the roadside, is ingeniously roofed with an old upturned rowing boat—an architectural innovation which Dr. E. Estyn Evans tells me he has also found on the west coast of Ireland.

Many people bring peat two or three times a week throughout the year from these moorland stores, sometimes travelling five or six miles over rough country, burdened for half the distance with a two days' supply in the *leypur* on their backs. In former days it was nothing for men to rise an hour before first light and go out to the turbary for a *leypur* of fuel, arriving as dawn flooded the sky, so that they would have daylight in which to pick their way homewards along the uneven path. Then they would get breakfast and be ready by six o'clock to start the day's work. My father-in-law assures me that even in the capital half a century ago the time to begin work, for the merchants as well as the farmers and fishermen, was six o'clock in the summer months and eight in the winter time. Small wonder the people were often in bed by nine o'clock on a summer evening !

Where there is a good road to the turbaries, it is possible to employ a pony and cart (or the local motor-lorry, if one exists) for transporting the turf, for many families keep a large stock at

Tórshavn from
Kirkjubøreyn

Tórshavn   (*Top*) The town   (*Bottom*) Suburbia

home. A wooden stretcher-like affair, as in the Highlands and Orkney, is often used for manhandling the turves to the site of the *krógv* or *gróthús*, or to the roadside if the owner intends to take his fuel to the village. In other places boats must be brought into play, as on Vágar, where much of the peat for Miðvágur and Sandavágur is ferried across Sørvágsvatn from the western shore of the lake. On Nólsoy the turbaries are at the south end of the island, and the fuel is packed in bags and sent down to the landing-place at Borðan by means of an ingenious overhead ropeway, whence the boats carry it to the village four miles distant. On Hestur the bags are lowered to the village from the hill rising almost precipitously behind by a similar device. At Suðiravatn a lot of the peat cut on the south side of the lake is ferried to the road-head at the other end, and as I sat by the water on that late July afternoon many small craft, loaded high with sacks, took their cargoes to swell the growing pile on the little wooden jetty where the Eiði road begins.

7

It is only to be expected that in these islands, where birds (as we shall soon see) are so abundant and of such importance to the people, there should be a good deal of interesting lore concerning them. In concluding this chapter on the land we may, as a diversion, consider how these small creatures affect the farmer's outlook and daily life ; for some of the trite and pithy sayings in general usage show an unusually keen observation of the habits of birds, and reveal a sense of humour in its application to human foibles and failings.

That magnificent scoundrel the raven is well to the fore of the farmer's black-list, for, as in other farming lands, he is considered an inveterate enemy of new-born lambs and sickly sheep. When visiting Koltur I was shown a small semi-circular butt constructed against a big rock on top of the western cliff, from which periodic attempts are made to shoot these birds. It is a dry-stone wall about five feet high, camouflaged with a row of grassy sods along the top, and has a small entrance low down on the seaward side so that the hunter can crawl into position. This he does at night, leaving some meat on the grass several yards away as a lure to draw the ravens to their doom when they go forth to forage in the early morning.

E

" Seldom do young doves hatch from ravens' eggs ! " is an old proverb, and its implication is that you cannot expect bad parents to rear good children. " He is stealing like a raven ! " is another indictment. For all his shortcomings, however, the raven is not altogether evil : there is a saying (which I have heard of the same species in the Isle of Man, and of the rook in England) that the cunning fellow never does any hurt to the farm on which he builds his nest, taking care to perpetrate his mischief on other land. Perhaps not unconnected with this belief is the solemn warning, " Never kill a good raven—you may get a bad one in his place ! "

Incidentally, the word *ravnabøli* is used of an untidy house where things are left lying about in utter confusion, and it recalls the mess of feathers, bones and castings at the raven's eyrie. An even worse epithet, one would imagine, is *skarvabøli*, denoting a home like a shag's. Having had experience of the nests of both species I can attest that the latter is infinitely the worse, and I should think that its chief claim to unpleasantness is not so much the general untidiness as the possession of a characteristic and overpowering smell !

The hooded-crow, *kráka*, also looms large in the folk-lore and the farmer's hymn of hate. From early times until late in the nineteenth century all able-bodied men had to render annually one or more beaks of such birds as the eagle, raven, hooded-crow and greater black-backed gull as a proof of their zeal in ridding the community of these age-old enemies of sickly sheep and lambs. Debes said this *nevtollur* or " bill-tax " was of very ancient date, an agreement of old times by which every man who entered into part-ownership of a boat was under a moral obligation to pay. However, the duty came to be lightly held and was not sufficiently enforced by the district officers, until public opinion awakened and insisted that something must be done to check the birds' increase. In May of 1741, by royal resolution, all men aged between fifteen and fifty were made subject to the tax, with the exception of the townsfolk of Tórshavn, who held no ground. Each year thereafter the bills were brought to Tórshavn, counted before the judge—who imposed a fine on any district sending an insufficient supply—and burnt on a flat rock near the Skansin Fort. Although it is more than seventy years since the last tax was burnt there, the immediate vicinity of the rock is still known as Krákustein.

The hoodie suffered numerically to a greater extent than any other victim of the *nevtollur*, but shooting him cannot always have been easy, for he is a wary bird. Among the islands they say *krákumáni* ! when they mean "a very short time"—"a crow's time," because he never stays for more than a few seconds in one place. On Kallsoy and Kunoy (and doubtless other islands) the people will tell you that the hoodies come among the houses only on a Sunday, because they know that no man will raise a gun against them on the Sabbath day ! Although the bill-tax was abolished many years ago, raven and hoodie still have a price on their heads.

Their artfulness will not surprise those who are acquainted with the superstition that the crow can see into the future. Jákup Guttormsson á Ryggi, who lived in the late sixteenth century, was sowing his seed one spring when a *kráka* told him he would never taste the corn. Nor did he, for he died before the autumn. Mikkjal á Ryggi, who has recorded this story, tells me that Snorre Sturlason, the famous sagaman and historian, told a very similar one concerning a Norwegian king over seven hundred years ago. So the belief that the crow is a seer must be an ancient one.

The communal judicial assemblies which English folk-lore ascribes to the rook are here the perquisite of the hooded-crow. A century and a half ago Landt described how the birds gathered in conclave, nodding their heads wisely as they cawed their solemn decisions. " It is not uncommon," he wrote, " when they have gone away, to find one or two dead on the spot," sentenced and executed by the court ! Such an assembly is called *krákuting*, and the expression is often used jokingly—or deprecatingly—of assemblies of people, especially of politicians. Not once but many times have I heard the august Løgting ridiculed by this expressive word !

Some of the smaller birds are consulted instead of the weather-glass, or have association with certain seasons or seasonal work. The white-wagtail, named *erla kongsdóttir*—" Princess Erla "— comes at the beginning of May to see if the farmers have emptied their middens and spread the manure on the fields. It is considered a disgrace if any farmer has not completed this part of the season's labour before Princess Erla arrives to seek the juicy worms that have lain all winter under the muck. In the olden days, when the islands were cut off from the outside world throughout the winter time, the arrival of the white-wagtail was taken as a sign that the longed-for trading vessels were on their way. When the rock and meadow-pipits are numerous about the houses in the early morning they promise a good day for catching sea-birds on the cliffs. Sverri Patursson gives the name *vátiskolli* " wet-head," to the wren, because the farmers anticipate a good " growing rain " for their crops if he sings in the early morn. His more usual (and more poetic) name is *músabróðir*, " brother to the mouse," and *mortítlingur*, an allusion to the dark reddish-brown of his feathers, is another.

The arctic-tern traditionally arrives at Halvarðsøka, May 15th, and it is not unusual for a spell of bad weather, with stormy winds and snow, to succeed a fine spring-like period at this time and delay the terns' land-coming for several days. Such a setback is called *ternusnertur*. By the type of cry he utters the red-throated diver foretells a wet or a fine day ; the " drumming " noise made by the snipe portends rain (or snow before the summer if it is heard on Mariumessa, March 25th) whilst his " chipper, chipper " call-note is said to bring fine weather. If gulls fly low over the fields, it will be wet ; and if a flock of starlings rises suddenly from the grass, it is said that a shower of rain is imminent.

When a man who is thoroughly disliked as a nuisance and a bore intrudes upon a harmonious gathering the effect is like " smyril í stariflokki "—a merlin dashing into a flock of starlings ! I learned from Niels á Botni that in former times the starling was blamed for the diffusion of a red " rust " which periodically attacked the barley crops, and also for *svartaspilla*, a blackish blight which despoiled the potatoes. As a result there was a certain amount of fowling of this species on Nólsoy and probably other islands, the young being drawn from their nesting-holes in the cliffs when fully-fledged and sold to epicures among the business and governing class in Tórshavn. One wonders if the recent English belief that immigrant continental starlings brought to this country the dreaded foot-and-mouth disease is to be interpreted as an analogous myth—although, even if it is, it is hardly likely to lead to an increased consumption of starling-pie ! Because it was regarded as an enemy of the crops at seed and harvest time the rock-dove was also subjected to a certain amount of fowling on Nólsoy, where it is a tolerably common bird, its young meeting the same fate as those of its partner-in-crime. To-day the starling is not only protected but encouraged, and almost every house has one or more nesting-boxes on its walls. The people did not eat these birds themselves as they had no taste for *klófuglar*, or birds with other than webbed feet, but fortunately for their purses the Danish element in the town regarded the fat young birds as a delicacy.

References to Chapter Two

BAERENTSEN, C. (1911) ; DANJALSSON, M. (1940a) ; DEBES, L. (1673) ; EVANS, E. E. (1944) ; FEILBERG, C. (1908) ; FEILDEN, H. W. (1872) ; LANDT, J. (1810) ; MEGAW, B. R. S. (1939) ; NICLASSEN, P. (1938-39) ; OSTENFELD, C. H. (1908) ; PRESS, M. (1934) ; WARMING, E. (1908) ; WILLIAMSON, K. (1942 and 1946b).

TURF-STORES ON MYKINES.

Chapter Three

THE SEA

1. Faeroe boats and all about them (*page* 70).
2. Fishing in olden times for saithe and cod, with a digression on the words " Væl afturkomin ! " (*page* 74).
3. The preparation of food, delectable and otherwise, from fish (*page* 80).
4. Some sailors' superstitions, and explanations of how to box the compass and tell the time (*page* 83).
5. The modern fishing industry, its history and its help to Britain during the war (*page* 87).
6. The whaling industry in Faeroe waters (*page* 90).

I

WHEN YOU SEE the small boats of the Faeroes plying to and fro in the sounds and fiords it is difficult to believe that so important and practical an object can have survived a thousand years of everyday use, and have undergone so little change. For the Faeroe boat of to-day is almost unaltered in form and the principles of its construction from the galleys in which the Vikings hoisted sail and steered towards the sunset when the proud chieftains, rather than acknowledge one stronger than themselves as king, left their homeland and sought new realms in which to develop their culture undisturbed.

Those ships came ashore here and in Iceland, in Orkney and Shetland, the Outer and Inner Hebrides, Ireland and the Isle of Man. They were once the only ocean-going traffic between the Minch and Davis Strait, and in them the discoverers of a new continent planted a colony in Greenland and explored from Labrador to Nova Scotia and perhaps beyond. And these ships, with the shield-bosses shining on the bulwarks, were merely large editions of the modern Faeroe rowing-boats, with the rudder fixed to the starboard gunwale instead of to the stern. One might justly claim that the historic achievements of the Norsemen as explorers and colonists are in themselves sufficient proof of their incomparability as builders of ships ; but if an even stronger vindication is needed, then it is surely to be found in the survival of this type of craft through centuries of trial and hazard in these tricky and often treacherous waters.

EYSKAR
TÓRSHAVN MUSEUM 2123.

Faeroese boats are beautiful craft. Their picturesqueness is derived from their wide beam and the pleasing curve or "sheer" that sweeps upwards from amidships to the high, pointed stem and stern. Beside them the small rowing-boats of English shores would seem coarse and clumsy tubs ; and although these natives of the northern seas, for all their pedigree, look delicate and frail, they are in fact very sea-worthy and well fitted for the heavy work required of them in the strong tides and changeable weather among the islands. The high, slender bow lifts buoyantly above the rollers ; the stern, too, contributes to sea-worthiness, dividing the attack of a following sea without shipping water as a boat with a transom stern would do.

The deep keel gives the boat a firm grip of the water, so that it is readily manoeuvrable and quickly answers the helm. The keel-planks form a " V "-shaped channel at the bottom of the boat, making bailing easy, for there is a specially-shaped wooden scoop called *eyskar* (see above) which fits this channel neatly, so that the water is soon ladled overboard. The oar does not have a wide blade as in the English varieties, but is almost the same width over its whole length, its narrowness reducing wind resistance to a minimum. There are no crutch-pins, but instead flat pegs called *tollar* which fit into slots in the gunwale. On two sides of the oar below the rounded grip is a shaped wooden piece, *árarskeyti*, one part of which bears against the edge of the *tollur*, whilst the other slides on a wooden cushion, *borðskeyti*, on the gunwale. A thong, passing through a hole in the

OAR DETAIL

a. Tollar ; b. Borðskeyti ; c. Árarskeyti

gunwale and around the *árarskeyti*, prevents the oar from sliding out of position. In former times these thongs were strips of the dried skin of the caaing-whale.

The rudder swings on the sternpost and is deep and narrow, widening gradually below the waterline (see below). This type of rudder, which has been universal in the western world for many centuries, is the only major departure from Viking tradition, for the ship of the old Norsemen was steered by a modified oar trailing aft on the starboard quarter. The present type of rudder, however, appears to have been but lately introduced into the islands, and indeed its use may not have become general until motor-power was installed. At the end of the eighteenth century, according to Landt, the boats were steered by means of the oars,

RUDDER DETAIL

or were furnished with an implement called *stýri*, " like a short oar." This certainly seems to have been a lineal descendant of the Viking steering-oar. The tiller may consist of short ropes attached to each end of a wooden bar which passes through the head of the rudder, or may be a short rod attached to one side only of this bar.

The hull is clincher-built (*klinkubygdur* or *súðbygdur*) and there is little freeboard, only two strakes rising clear of the water-line amidships. There are six strakes and each has a special name, and, ranging from the gunwale to the garboard strake next to the keel, they are : *rímin, remmuborð, slagborð, lívflýggj, flábord* and *kjalarborð*. Only the keel, stem and stern are made of oak, white wood being used for the remainder of the boat. The two fore and two aftermost ribs were sometimes cut from tree-roots, *klóta*, washed ashore as driftwood, because they often had the required curvature : they were supposed to come down from Siberia on the ocean currents. The remaining ribs are in two sections, and curiously enough, in all the boats I have seen, these are jointed along the same plank. Tallowed hemp or wool, *síggj*, was put between the planks where they overlapped in order to make the hull watertight. Wooden pegs were considered superior to nails for binding the planks to the ribs, but in many present-day craft iron nails are used.

Six types of craft exist, and they are :—

Tristur or *tríbekkur* ; for two or three men (two pairs of oars).

Fýramannafar ; for four men (three pairs of oars, the first and third pairs each handled by one man).

Seksmannafar ; for six men (each taking an oar).

Áttamannafar ; for eight men (each taking an oar).

Tiggjumannafar ; for ten men (each taking an oar).

Seksáringur ; for twelve men (each taking an oar).

Sometimes the larger boats for ten or twelve oars had two masts, but in the North Islands the usual practice, following ancient tradition, was to have only one. This mast is stepped well forrard, passing through the first thwart, four or five feet from the bows. The sail is a dipping lug, like the square-cut sail we see in reconstructions of Viking craft, and it is set by halyards which are tied to small holes in the *tollar*. In former times, Landt says, there were no ropes, and the sail was held in position by the two men nearest the mast.

The usual length of a *seksmannafar* is about twenty feet, and of a *seksáringur* a little less than thirty feet. The first-named, and the *áttamannafar*, are the general-purpose craft and in former times every *bóndi* maintained at least one. The *seksáringur* was used by the Suðuroy people for the journey to Tórshavn when they came with goods to the agent of the royal monopoly business : it is a fine sea-going boat, and not infrequently travelled between the Faeroes and Shetland. Niels Rein told me that the Klakksvík people kept such a boat at Sølmundarfjørður, near the head of Skálafjørður, in former days as an emergency measure : for sometimes, especially if the wind was in the south-east, the weather off Mjóvanes was too heavy for the boats to make Tórshavn by sailing round the coast. So if a doctor were required at Klakksvík, for instance, two small boats would put into Gøtuvík and the men would disembark and go overland to their *seksáringur* at Sølmundarfjørður. Sailing down the fiord they would try to make Tórshavn in the lee of Nólsoy ; or, if that were not possible, would cross Tangafjørður and land at Sund, walking thence across the hills to the town. It was a long and arduous journey and reflects on the precariousness of life in Faeroe settlements years ago.

Some of the villages had full-time shipwrights in former days, and one who lived on Nólsoy is said to have made close on five hundred boats before nature brought to an end a busy career. There were then two boat-builders on that island, and work enough for them both, for Tórshavn was without a shipwright at that period. One's boats, it is said, were better for rowing, the other's being superior under sail. If you wanted a boat you bought the necessary nails and timber, and invited the ship-builder to come along and build it for you. It was your obligation to feed him and give him shelter during the time he was busy on your commission, and it was also understood that you or your servants would give him what unskilled help he required. Pay-ment was on a sliding scale : in addition to his lodging, he received four sheep for a *fýramannafar*, six for a *seksmannafar*, and so on up to a dozen for a *seksáringur*.

When they sail in the fiords, swiftly, buoyantly and with consummate grace, their brightly coloured lug-sails billowing out before a fair breeze, Faeroe boats are indeed beautiful to see. As you watch, you might be forgiven the fanciful thought that time has taken you away down the centuries to the days when the hardy settlers flocked to Tórshavn to attend the *ting*. Unfortunately, such a charming scene is all too rare nowadays, for most of the boats have their little petrol engines and are independent of the wind. Thus, more and more, the Faeroe fleet is relying upon the skill of the mechanic rather than the old wisdom of the sailor. One wonders—especially after hearing the views of some of the older Faeroemen on this new-fangled evil for indulging ignorance and laziness—what the ancient Viking chiefs would think if they could but return to this land to-day !

2

In the autumn months, half a century and more ago, great catches of *seiður* or coal-fish were made in the harbour at Tórshavn by means of nets. Any man in the town who wished to do so could take part in this communal fishing, and practically the whole male population was engaged. The fishermen formed themselves into five companies, with about forty men in each, and these were known to every one by special nicknames given in a spirit of fun. There was the " Big Men's " company, for example, and another which in modern colloquial English might be called the " Old Crocks' Brigade."

The decision to spend the day taking saithe in the nets was

characteristically spontaneous, as decisions affecting the lives of small fishing and farming communities so often are. All villages have their traditional meeting-places, and in Tórshavn to-day knots of temporarily unoccupied men come together at the heads of the east and west harbours to discuss the local news and political developments, as men have done for many years. Doubtless it was at such meetings that the earliest risers would consider the prospects for the day, and agree that saithe-netting was likely to prove the most profitable occupation. They would send the children running among the houses to call out the men, and by six or seven o'clock the first team would be ready to make a start. The nets would be shot outside the harbour and brought ashore by the small boats, and whilst the catch was being sorted and divided, No. 2 company would prepare to follow on. Each man was allowed one *leypur* of fish, except that by customary right the foreman of each company got a double share.

In a good autumn catches would be very heavy and the first company might land many more fish than would fill their own *leypar*, in which case the residue would be set on one side as a nucleus for No. 2 company. If No. 2 was equally fortunate, its surplus would be passed on to No. 3, and so on. Sometimes the first haul was so good that there was more than sufficient to satisfy both Nos. 1 and 2, in which event the latter party would not go out with the nets at all, No. 3 following on in its place. These men might conceivably land enough for themselves and No. 4 as well, so that No. 5 would be the next to shoot the nets, hoping to supply its own needs and also relieve the first team of the necessity of going out a second time.

None of the catch was sold. A little of it would be eaten fresh, usually prepared as *knettir*, and the rest would be split and salted or hung against the wall of the *hjallur* to dry in the wind and become *ræstur seiðar*. Saithe was said to be very fine food when dried, " good for both man and beast," and if there had been an abundance of it in the autumn a quantity of the dried fish would always be used to supplement the winter fodder ration for the cow. Saithe liver was (and still is) considered a delicacy when fresh, but no Faeroeman will eat it if it is more than about thirty hours old. In former times a favourite way of preparing the liver was to bake it in the middle of a loaf of *drýlur* in the ash of the turf fire, as described at the end of Chapter Nine.

In its hey-day the great farm at Kirkjubøur employed about

twenty servants, all of whom lived at the farmhouse, receiving their food and shelter free, and a good wage as well. The men slept in the half-neuk beds in the *roykstova*, the women in small rooms in the loft. Not infrequently on the farms a man and woman servant would marry and continue to live at the big house. Sometimes an old and trusted servant would receive a sheep as an extra present, and so he was able to add to his savings by selling the lambs. A *bóndi* would not usually sell any of his lambs in the autumn, but would often give away one or two to poor neighbours.

At Kirkjubøur the *bóndi* kept two eight-oar boats for the spring and autumn fishing, and all the farms maintained either one or two craft, according to the number of *húskallar* they employed. The insurance agent would have found little business in the Faeroes in those days, for if a man, owning a share in a boat, died leaving a son too young to take his place, the other part-owners invariably allowed the widow and children their share of the fish—perhaps over a period of many years until the boy was old enough to take up his father's responsibilities. Cod, halibut, haddock and saithe were the fish most sought after, and the best seasons were the early spring and autumn. My friend Óla Jákup Jensen, who has fished in Faeroe fiords since he was a mere boy, says of the former :—

Á Grækarismessu var fiskurin bestur
Men á Mariumessu var han mestur,

implying that the best fish were to be caught about the time of Saint Gregory's Mass, March 12th, but that fish were taken most plentifully about Mariumessa, the 25th of the month. This period falls partly in *torri* and partly in *gø*, the first two months of the year according to the old calendar : *torri* extends from January 25th (Pálsmessa) to February 24th (Leypársmessa), whilst *gø* closes at Mariumessa, when the third month, *einmánaður* begins.

January was a bad fishing month, but the *torrafiski* during February was very productive. It was succeeded by the *várfiski* or " spring fishing " which went on throughout March and April. May was a bad month, and so was devoted to work on the land, especially the sowing of barley and the peat-cutting. When that was at an end it was time to take part in the *summarfiski* of June and July, which was varied in certain districts

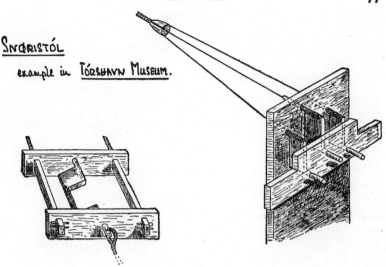

SNØRISTÓL

example in TÓRSHAVN MUSEUM.

(where there was a sandy bottom) with the *sildafiski* or " herring fishing." August was another bad month for the boats, but this was no great loss, for with the stacking of turf and haymaking it was unquestionably the busiest month of the summer on land, and all hands were needed for work at the farm. The autumn fishing, *heystfiski*, succeeded the harvest, extending from September to Christmas time.

Although fishing by long line is now practised in several districts, it is of rather recent introduction, and the hand-line remains the most popular technique

In the little bays at some of the villages, as at Nólsoyarbygd and Argir near the capital, one will see wooden boxes of loosely joined boards, about five feet long and two or three feet wide, floating on the water. They contain the store of cockles and other shell-fish which are used as bait. The villagers set long-lines with numerous cods' heads along them at intervals to catch these shell-fish, which they transfer to the boxes, where the continuous flow of sea-water keeps them alive and fresh until they are required. The flesh of *rita*, the kittiwake gull, is rated very high as bait, and fishermen will often shoot one or two for this purpose on their way out to the banks.

In former days the lines were twisted on a simple arrangement of curiously shaped pieces of bone or wood called *teymaspjaldur ;* thicker ropes, for use at sea and on the bird-fowling cliffs, were made on a wooden machine called *snøristól*, the two parts of which I have drawn on page 77 from an example in the museum at Tórshavn. The lines are carried loosely-wound on a forked wooden holder called *súla* (see page 79) and are paid out over a T-shaped rest on top of the gunwale. A metal bow, whose apex is attached to the heavy lead sinker at the end of the line, carries a hook at either tip. The fishermen carried their day's food, together with the compass, spare hooks and other small impedimenta in a rectangular box called *útróðrarskrín*.

Landt has much to say concerning the *mið* or customary fishing-grounds. At certain places—sometimes on an area of the sea-bed no larger than the floor of a fair-sized room—those who were " in the know " could always rely upon making a good catch, and the location of some of the *mið* in former times was a jealously guarded secret. Indeed, there are good stories of men whose fishing seems to have been for information rather than the legitimate reward, and whose expeditions were spent largely in sailing from point to point in surreptitious attempts to get the necessary bearings on their more fortunate neighbours ! Some of the larger *mið* have been productive of fish for many years, but the smaller ones appear to be curiously unstable, and many of them have been fished out altogether. For a while the bank yields good, big fish in quantity, and then, quite suddenly, it becomes barren, as though the remainder of the stock has migrated elsewhere. For many years the *mið* is one only in name and memory, and then, with an equally surprising and inexplicable suddenness, it becomes a profitable ground once more.

Some of the larger grounds are a considerable distance out to sea ; the well-known Faeroe Bank lying to the west of the archipelago is one, and the Suðuroy Bank to the ESE. of that island is another. In order to exploit these grounds the small boats would often be away for three or four days in good weather : and at other times, by accident and not design, they would be away even longer. Always there was the serious risk of sudden gales or squalls catching the fishermen off their guard and driving them out to sea, in spite of all they could do with the oars. There are stories of men who were a week away from home, and given up for lost, before they managed to regain their native village, and stories also of boats which did not return at all. One can perhaps imagine the depth of feeling with which the words

" Væl afturkomin ! " were uttered on the arrival of those whose
return had been delayed by stress of weather.

" Væl afturkomin ! " means something much more than
" Welcome home ! " It is one of the many social formulae which
soon convince the visitor to this country that he has the honour
of being among a courteous people. Although to-day it appears
at times•to be a very casual greeting (you will hear it spoken, for
instance, to those who have just returned from their summer
holiday, or from a short business trip to another island) it remains
as in olden days, much more a prayer of thanksgiving for safe
deliverance than a salutation. Perhaps the war, with its greatly

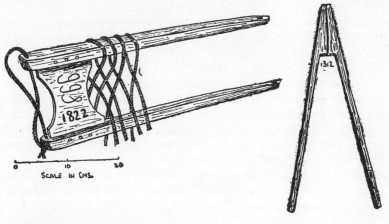

SÚLUR
    examples in TÓRSHAVN MUSEUM.

increased risks for the sailor, served to reinvest the expression
with something of its pristine sanctity. One had this feeling
whenever one was standing on the quayside when a smack
returned from the hazardous round voyage which had taken it
first to Iceland, then south to Aberdeen.

I think I came nearest to a full understanding of its true
significance, however, one late summer evening when I was with
the crowd that welcomed " Mjóvanes." She, with another
fishing-smack, " Bjørgvin," had been to Copenhagen to bring
back to their native land the vanguard of the exiles who had
spent the war-years in enemy-occupied Denmark. It was dusk
as she passed the harbour light, rocking gently on the swell.

There was no waving, no cheering, as she crept towards the quay ; indeed, the slightest noise within the crowd called forth an impatient hiss for silence. For, very faintly at first, the breeze bore to our straining ears the singing of those in the boat. As " Mjó-vanes " swayed gracefully nearer to the land so the voices grew stronger, and the formless shadows of her deck took the shapes of men standing together bareheaded as they sang Martin Luther's famous hymn . . .

> " For God he is so safe a fortress
> He will keep us well
> He is our help in all our sorrow
> Our guard in all our danger . . ."

It is the hymn the Danes and Faeroese have for their great and solemn occasions, as we keep " O God our help in ages past," and whilst the choir of twenty men sang on, clearly and beautifully, to the end, many times that number listened in rapt silence on the shore. For four or five of the most dramatic minutes that ever flew past these islands, there was no sound other than the lapping of the water, the soft pulse of the motor, and this song of praise and thankfulness for deliverance at last to family and friends and the land of their birth. Only when the hymn had ended did the hearts and throats of those who had waited long years to say " Væl afturkomin ! " find a natural and spontaneous release in happy cheers.

3

The cod taken on the Faeroe Bank, sixty miles or so west of Suðuroy, is reputed to be the best in the world. Nearer to the islands, it is said that the best cod is found in Nólsoyarfjørður, and I can certainly testify to its excellence. There is still plenty of cod at this station, but all round the islands the fishing has been spoilt for the Faeroemen by too much trawling in recent years.

Cod liver is a favourite supper-time dish when flavoured with pepper and salt to taste, and it is really enjoyable food. I would certainly far sooner have it in the Faeroe way than drink its extract out of a tablespoon ! It is served in a picturesque manner, the cods' heads being boiled and placed in the centre of the table with their livers protruding from their mouths. Cods' heads are

Tórshavn (*Top*) Tinganes (*Bottom*) Boats in the harbour

Kirkjubøur   (*Top*) Farmland on the " coastal plain "
(*Bottom*) The unfinished St. Magnus' Cathedral and St. Olaf's Church

also relished in another way : they are kept in a box or tin in the *hjallur* (or even buried in the earth !) until they get very " high." They are then resurrected, thoroughly washed and scraped, and the gills removed. After being boiled for a quarter of an hour they are brought to the table and eaten with *spik*, the blubber of the caaing-whale. Done in this manner *grunningshøvd* is very, very nice—so they say ! I have at one time or another tried most of the foods peculiar to the Faeroes, and in nearly all cases have thoroughly enjoyed them, but I could never muster up enough courage to face cods' heads that were three weeks old. The name *grunnings* is archaic Faeroese for the cod, which is called *torskur* to-day.

The Faeroe housewife can teach her English counterpart a good many points when it comes to preparing fish for the table —although not all the dishes, I dare say, would be acceptable in an English home ! I think the tastiest dish of all is *fiska gratin* (it is one which the Faeroese have learned from the Danes) and as some English housewives might feel disposed to try this and other fishy dishes in the dim and distant future when rationing is no more, I will attempt to compete with Mrs. Beeton for a few paragraphs. *Fiska gratin* is made as follows. First make a stiff sauce of flour, lard and milk over a low light, allow to cool, and then add one yolk of egg for each person. Boil the fish (cod for preference, but haddock will do) for a quarter of an hour, then bone it well and remove the skin. Next take the whites of the eggs and whisk them until the fluid is very stiff, so viscous that it will not pour. Mix the fish with the sauce, add the white of egg, and bake the mixture in the oven for an hour or so. It should be served hot, with melted butter : no potatoes or other vegetables are required.

A very good and peculiarly Faeroese dish is *knettir*. For this you require three parts of fresh cod, haddock or saithe (but preferably cod), and one part of sheep's tallow. You put the fish through the mincing-machine three times, then knead it with a little water into lumps about the size of a cricket ball, adding the finely-chopped suet and a little salt and pepper and chopped onion during the process. The fish-balls are then put into a pan of cold water, which is brought to the boil and left thus for a quarter of an hour.

Equally tasty and easy to prepare is a Danish dish, *frikkadellir*, which is very popular among the islands. For this you need three or four fresh cod of medium size, which you mince three times

F

with a little onion. You mix the result with three parts of white
flour and one part of cornflour, and add a little salt. Knead it
with milk into small oval cakes, fry these in margarine until they
are brown, and the lunch is ready for serving. Both these dishes
are delicious, and the residue left from lunch is always cut into
slices and made into sandwiches for the supper table.

Ræstur fiskur is a different proposition—like old cods' heads, it
has always succeeded in terrifying me ! The fish hangs outside
against the *hjallur* or the house-wall for a month or more, and when
required is taken down, skinned and cleaned, and boiled. Some
hardy individuals do not trouble to boil it, but merely remove
the skin and chew the fish just as it is, with obvious relish. It is
a great stand-by when fresh food is difficult to obtain, but Faeroe
people do not eat *ræstur fiskur* because they must : it is considered
almost as great a delicacy as *skerpikjøt*, and has pride of place even
to-day in many homes among the Christmas fare. *Ræstur fiskur*
develops best in fine dry weather, and is liable to spoil if the weather
is wet. It is very surprising how little of this wind-dried meat and
fish becomes maggoty, considering the abundance of blue-bottle
flies of the genus *Calliphora* in the summer months.

The finest fish caught on the *mið* is undoubtedly the halibut,
both for its size and delicious flesh. There was always great joy
in the family circle when a growing lad, out fishing with his
father or older brothers, caught his first *kalvafiskur*, for this
achievement was regarded as a notable step forward on the road
to manhood, and as such was a matter demanding proper celebration. So there was a fine feast of halibut on the return home, and
no doubt all the menfolk (except the idol of the hour !) indulged
themselves in a little brandy ! Niels Rein told me that he was
aged ten or eleven when he and the halibut first brought good
cheer to his home, but his only clear memory of the affair was
his mother's insistence that he should make a gift of part of the
fish to the old lady who had taught him his letters—a courtesy
in accordance with custom. The curious implements figured on
page 83, and called *kleppar*, are employed by the fishermen to
gaff halibut and lift it over the gunwale.

Herrings can be taken all the year round, but are caught mostly
in the late summer. They do not appear to come in the usual
immense shoals, but as they are caught only in the fiords and
sounds and no drifters work the Faeroes area this may not be
altogether true. The nets are shot close inshore at night and
drawn early the next morning ; and in the late summer, soon

after nine o'clock, one sees the boats from Nólsoy, Skálafjørður (where good catches are made in the bight at Kongshavn) and the Sundálagi arriving at the main quay brimful of the gleaming fish, and the townspeople crowding round to make their purchases. Many herrings are eaten fresh at this time, and of course many are salted for the winter. Salt herring, with a few slices of onion and vinegar to flavour it, is one of the favourite dishes at the supper table—a very good appetiser at the beginning of the meal. It is also eaten with boiled potatoes as a midday meal in the winter.

KLEPPAR.

examples in TÓRSHAVN MUSEUM.

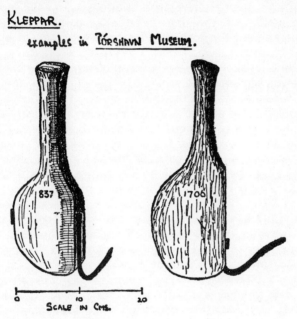

837

1706

SCALE IN CMS.

4

As in other sea-faring nations, a good deal of superstition is rife among Faeroe fishermen. Like other sailors, they have a particular aversion to weighing anchor on a Friday, and many skippers will flatly refuse to do so even to-day. Nor will Faeroese boats, even following a poor week on the banks, break the Sabbath in order to increase their catches.

They say you will have a poor day if you clean out the boat

whilst you are fishing—the dirtier the boat, the better the fish
like it ! If you put some seaweed into the boat on Jóansøka
morning, June 24th, you will ensure a successful season. Landt
records the belief that a heron's foot carried under the sleeve of
the jersey or *skipstroyggja* would bring good fishing—probably a
case of sympathetic magic, since the heron is a doughty fisherman
himself ! The migrant phalaropes were welcomed in the late
spring because they were regarded as the precursors of the herring,
and were called *sildhønir*, " herring-hens," for this reason. Niels
á Botni says that he interprets an old passage in the bird-ballad
" Fuglakvæði " as implying that the appearance of the scarce
king-eider among the flocks of eider-ducks was a sign of prosperous
fishing.

As among sailors the world over, there are certain animals and
objects which must on no account be referrred to by their proper
names whilst at sea. These things are given their own peculiar
titles, called " haf-names " by the folklorist, who ascribes to the
superstition a Nordic origin. In Faeroe boats the cat is never
ketta, but *stuttnøs* or " short nose." Instead of *knivur* you must say
hvast, " the sharp one." A cow, *kúgv* to the farmer, is *langhøla* to the
fisherman ; and conversely a ewe is known by her short tail as
stutthøla. The parson is mentioned in a mildly libellous fashion
as *lundi*, the puffin. Smoke is *vesa*, and the seal is *munnbeiski*,
" strong taste in the mouth," apparently a reference to its meat.
The shearwater, *skrápur*, is *tannhali* at sea, from the manner in
which he rides the waves, with his body canted slightly forward
so that his tail is higher than his head.

When you take a boiled egg to your tea you must always crush
the shell in your egg-cup afterwards, or it is feared a ship will
be lost at sea. (Another interesting table trait, although it has
nothing to do with fishing, is an old saying heard from Niels á
Botni—if you have something on your plate, and you take another
piece when the food is passed round, you must have a hungry
friend somewhere !) Once a year in former times, customarily
during the Christmas week, the owner of a boat gave his crew a
party, called *bátsgildi*. The master provided a midday meal,
usually of *ræst súpan* and *ræst kjøt*, for the men, and they passed
the afternoon in card-playing. The women and children joined
the company later, for tea, and the evening was spent in singing
and dancing, with coffee before the party broke up.

Boxing a compass among the islands seems at first just about

as complicated a business as telling the time, and I think a few
words should be devoted to each of these accomplishments. I
give below a list of the points of the Faeroe compass in relation to
our own. The Faeroese system must be a very ancient one : the
four points represent the direction of the four most prevalent
winds, and there can be no question but that the same notation
was used by the Vikings a thousand years ago. Consider the
application of the terms *landnyrðingur*, which implies a wind
coming from the north with the land, and *landsynningur*, a wind
coming from the south out of the land, to the Norwegian coast,
which runs roughly NE-SW. To-day, at the Navigation School
at Tórshavn, students are taught the orthodox compass : but
almost every child, before he or she is old enough to go to school,
knows the Vikings' compass by heart, and there are still Faeroe
skippers who start to box their compass with the north-east point.

In days past the Faeroeman's compass was not only a naviga-
tional instrument, but also a ready-made means of expressing
the time ; whilst then, as now, the names of the chief points
were used without further qualification to indicate the prevailing
wind—as they are, of course, among our own sailors to-day. In
the table below I have set out the compass points side by side
with their Faeroese equivalents (the cardinal points in capitals)
and the corresponding times of the day. It should be noted that
only the working day is really concerned—from 6 a.m. to 6 p.m.,
" fra eystri til vesturs," with a three-hours' extension for the light
summer evenings—for, naturally enough, there was little need to
label the hours during which nature slept.

Compass Point	Faeroese Name		Corresponding Time	
NORTH	Norðan	Midnight		
NNE	Landnyrðingur-norðan	1.30 a.m.		
NE	LANDNYRDINGUR	3. a.m.	Økt fyri degi*	
ENE	Landnyrðingur-eystan	4.30 a.m.	Hálvga-eystur	
EAST	Eystan	6 a.m.	EYSTUR	
ESE	Landsynningur-eystan	7.30 a.m.	Hálvga-landsuður	
SE	LANDSYNNINGUR	9 a.m.	LANDSUDUR	
SSE	Landsynningur-sunnan	10.30 a.m.	Hálvga-suður (or Hálvga-middagur	
SOUTH	Sunnan	Noon	SUDUR (or MID-DAGUR)	
SSW	Útsynningur-sunnan	1.30 p.m.	Hálvga-nón	

*" Økt fyri degi," i.e. 3 hours before day.

Compass Point	Faeroese Name	Corresponding Time	
SW	ÚTSYNNINGUR	3 p.m.	NÓN
WSW	Útsynningur-vestan	4.30 p.m.	Hálvga-vestur
WEST	Vestan	6 p.m.	VESTUR
WNW	Útnyrðingur-vestan	7.30 p.m.	Hálvga-útnorður
NW	ÚTNYRÐINGUR	9 p.m.	ÚTNORDUR
NNW	Útnyrðingur-norðan	10.30 p.m.	
NORTH	Norðan	Midnight	

Finally—before we pass on to time, a word about tides. The two main flows are *eystfall* and *vestfall* : the former sets SE in most of the fiords and sounds (but runs NNE in Nólsoyarfjørður), and the latter sets NW (but southwards in Nólsoyarfjørður). A most peculiar and apparently inexplicable phenomenon is that there is practically no rise and fall of water with the tides on the south side of the central islands, between Kirkjubønes and Mjóvanes. The level remains constant in the Sundalagi between Eysturoy and Streymoy as far to the north as the narrows at Norðskála, beyond which there is a noticeable rise and fall. So noticeable is it in fact that I have been told that when sailing south towards the narrows at low tide, when the eight or nine knot current is pouring through the bottle-neck towards you, you can actually see that the sound beyond the narrows is at a higher level, and that your boat will have to go " uphill " to get there !

In the good old days, before pocket watches became a mixed blessing, time was assessed by observation of the sun—or, one assumes, by guesswork on those days when the sun failed to report for duty ! The day was divided into eight parts, called *øktar*, and the *økt* was divided into two halves, so that time was reckoned by intervals corresponding to one and a half hours of our reckoning.

The modern clock is followed to-day, but it is read in a different fashion to that obtaining in our own country. One o'clock is *klokkan eitt*, and so on round the clock to *tolv* : but half-past one is *hálvgun tvey*, or " half an hour to two," and so on round the face to *hálvgun eitt*, which is 12.30. A quarter-past one is called one quarter of an hour to two, *eitt kvartur til tvey*, and a quarter to two by our reckoning is " three-quarters to two " by the Faeroese.

So far, so good, but when the fingers get round to twenty-five minutes past one, you have to think about it as " five minutes to half an hour to two o'clock." As a result of the same painfully

meticulous approach, it is *tiggju minuttir yvir hálvgun tvey* (" ten
minutes over the half-hour to two ") when your watch shows
twenty minutes to two o'clock. From all of which it will be clear
that when somebody asks you " Hvussu nógv er klokkan ? " much
the wisest plan is to show him your watch and let him work it
out for himself !

5

The abolition óf the Danish crown monopoly on trade in
1856 opened up an opportunity for the Faeroese to develop their
home fishery as an export trade, and they were not slow to grasp
its potentialities. Hitherto the fishing had been confined to home
waters, the fiords and the nearer banks, and had provided only
for the immediate needs of the community ; after 1856, by adopt-
ing the technique of preparing sun-dried cod or *klipfiskur*, the
Faeroese were able to enter the world market and to extend their
activities to the seas off Iceland and later Greenland, with the
consequence that the fishing soon achieved paramount importance
among Faeroe industries.

Between 1870 and 1880, when the fleets of Hull and Grimsby
and other British ports were converted to steam, many of the
obsolete sailing vessels were bought at low prices by the Faeroese.
It is a reflection on British ship-building prowess that many of
these vessels are sailing to-day, and a happy thought that during
the years 1940-45 they played a part in helping Britain to win her
war. As the smacks sail in and out of harbour it is not difficult
to guess their country of origin, for among them few were re-
christened. To those of us who watched their comings and goings
(for many of them had our friends on board) it was always a
little strange, though satisfying, to see *John Brown*, *Energy*,
Westward Ho! and *Morning Star* southward bound under a foreign
flag to feed a land the Germans were trying to starve.

During the first decade of the present century there were about
a hundred smacks, but the fishing was still largely confined to
home waters. Towards the end of the decade several boats
ventured farther afield to the seas around Iceland : the year 1911
proved an exceptionally good one for these pioneers, and
encouraged by their success many vessels followed suit in
subsequent years. By 1920 fishing in Faeroe waters for commercial
gain had almost entirely ceased.

One or two boats went even farther, to Greenland, in 1925,

and from 1930 until the outbreak of the war most of the fleet worked in that region ; and indeed, the Faeroe boats were largely responsible for opening up the productive fishing on the west Greenland banks. The south of Iceland remained the venue in early spring, the boats bringing home their catches in May, and then sailing out again to reach west Greenland or sometimes Bear Island and Spitsbergen in June. The journey out was about 1,800 miles, a fortnight's sailing in good weather for the little boats.

Cod and halibut provided the catch, and most of the boats employed hand-lines, although latterly many went over to long-line, working ten or twelve thousand hooks a day. The first trawlers came about 1906-07, but they were not successful, and trawling did not assume important dimensions until the decade before the war. By that time there were ten trawlers owned and sailed by Faeroemen and about 120 smacks and schooners fitted with diesel motors, and they were constantly at sea from the beginning of March to the end of October each year.

The industry gave employment to one-sixth of the population of 26,000 in the years before the war, and fish—mainly salt-fish and dried salt-fish—assumed well over ninety per cent of the total exports. But the industry was not able to flourish as it might have done owing to the restrictions imposed on trading by the Danish government. The Faeroese were not permitted to export to Germany, and of the 22,000 tons quota for iced fish which Denmark had from Britain only 450 tons was given to the Faeroese, although this figure was later increased to about 900. Thus, the only market open to the Faeroemen was for salt-fish, and most of this was prepared as *klipfiskur* and exported largely to Spain. The salt-fish went to Italy, and after the outbreak of the civil war in Spain, Italy, Portugal and Greece were the chief buyers of Faeroe fish.

The fish is split and salted immediately it has been taken from the hook, and when the boats reach their ports the catch is thoroughly washed and spread out to dry in the sun. This is done on the shore rocks where these are sufficiently low and flat, or on artificial drying-grounds paved with numerous flat stones as shown in the photograph facing page 112. It is a long and laborious process, for the fish cannot be left out without spoiling in rainy weather, and may have to be gathered in, and subsequently put out again several times in the course of a day. The shore work is done by women and children, and in its heyday in the early thirties this occupation absorbed a considerable amount of labour. More recently, the installation of artificial drying plant brought greatly increased efficiency in the preparation of this commodity.

Soon after the war broke out, the Faeroe fishery underwent a complete change. The production of *klipfiskur* ceased, and the boats concentrated on ferrying iced fish from Icelandic waters to the market at Aberdeen. Despite the greatly increased risks of this always dangerous trade the Faeroese boats did not stop sailing ; and even in 1940, when the Iceland boats, deterred by the rising toll of vessels the enemy was taking, refused to sail until air escort could be provided, the Faeroemen carried on. At the worst period of the war, in the spring of 1941, they were responsible for no less than seventy-five per cent of the fish landed at British ports ; and later, when the Icelanders put to sea again, the proportion of Faeroe landings was about forty per cent of the whole. Throughout the war the small boats, a Bren gun their only armament, sailed constantly with food for Britain with only an occasional day's rest at their home port, and it was only to be expected that they would not sail unscathed. As the little ships sailed out of sight past Glivursnes, relatives and friends on the quay wondered if they would ever see their menfolk again— and hoped and prayed that they might. One by one ships were reported lost : some, like the trawler *Narðaberg*, were bombed between the Faeroes and Scotland ; some struck floating mines, others were torpedoed, and some had the unpleasant experience of being raked with the machine-gun bullets of German aircraft. A few, like the trawler *Nýggjaberg*, merely vanished on the high seas and were never heard of again. Altogether, as a result of enemy action or tempestuous weather, four trawlers and thirty-two smacks were lost during the war, nearly a third of the active Faeroe fleet of 1939. And the Faeroe nation sacrificed more men per population as a direct result of the war than any of the combatant powers.

What of the future ? Their refusal to be cowed by mines, bombs and torpedoes has meant that Faeromen have emerged from the war in a strong position to establish their fishing industry on a sound footing. The markets varied, as markets always do, and so did fortunes ; but during those hectic years the great majority of those engaged in the industry enjoyed a financial success which they will probably never achieve again. To-day the Faeroe shipowners are spending their profits in rebuilding

and re-equipping their fleet, and many of the existing vessels are
going over to seine and trawl net fishing. Whole villages are
subscribing together to purchase trawlers. The Faeroese have
worked hard and unremittingly, and in the face of considerable
dangers, to achieve this longed-for reorganisation and extension
of their fishing industry : but success or failure, and indeed the
well-being of the whole community, depends largely on the
availability of markets for the catch. Throughout five of the most
difficult years of our history the Faeroe Islanders gave Britain a
helping hand ; it is our turn now, and so long as Britain remains
grateful and will keep her markets open for the Faeroese, this
small nation of good neighbours should have nothing to fear.

6

I shall always remember our return from Hvalvík one late
summer evening, shortly before I left the Faeroe Islands. We had
walked the eight miles through the quiet valley from Saksun in
the failing light, had been well fortified with strong coffee in the
village as the result of a chance meeting with friends, and, after
much fiddling about with a stubborn engine, had started on what
I expected would be a dull and uninteresting journey home. But
there is some indescribable quality of charm about travelling in
an open boat at nightfall in the shelter of the land : in deep
shadow the cliffs seem incredibly more sheer, and in dark
silhouette the distant mountains are more towering than they
appear to be by day. The little volatile wave-crests, glistening
with phosphorescence, strew beauty along the waterway.

The night wind was cold, as always in the Faeroes, and came
off the land : and when we crossed the entrances of the long
inlets Kollafjørður and Kaldbaksfjørður the pressure of the wind
which streamed down from the heights of Skælingsfjall and
Stiðjafjall was like a miniature gale, making the sea boisterous.
We were obliged to head well up the fiords, close-hauling the
land, and then race across in the teeth of the wind and the
flying spray, to avoid being driven out to sea. The rocking-horse
motion of the brave little boat, the unruly caress of the spume and
its salty kiss, the dull thudding of the waves under the lifting bows,
the twinkling lights of the hamlets, and above all the sense of
aloneness in the great engulfing gloom . . . all these were made
for memory and pleasurable recall. It cannot be without some

aesthetic joy in their surroundings and a deep fondness for the unruly nature of their homeland that the fishermen return to the villages following a long day out at sea.

But I digress. Before we were fairly on our way, and in the last of the failing light, we drew in to the wooden quay at við Áir, the whaling-station whose ugly sheet-iron buildings occupy a low point midway between Hósvík and Hvalvík on the Streymoy shore. Previously, whenever I had passed that way, the ramshackle, unpainted sheds had looked deserted and derelict : but then, of course, no whaling had been attempted during the war. Now the whaling had begun again, and in the dusk the place was populous, a shadowy scene of brisk activity. We tied up our boat by the heads of two fifty-foot finners and climbed ashore.

A third whale was on the flensing-plane, looking an indescribable mess. We stood on the edge of a sloping open space of wooden boards, at the head of which was installed a steam winch for winding the whales on to the slipway. The plane, quite literally, was running with blood. Men with long-handled flensing-knives, and others whose duties were not so clearly apparent, picked their ways gingerly from place to place : had any one slipped, I think he would have slid slowly but quite inevitably down to the sea. The place was a confused and gory shambles : I have never seen anything quite so bloody, nor have I ever had my sense of curiosity completely routed by such a disagreeable smell. A lively interest in the station's affairs proved quite untenable, and we very soon returned, through a shed stacked high with dark red lumps of whale-meat, to our boat.

There is perhaps no country in the world in which the whale fishery has achieved such remarkable proportions as in the Faeroe Islands, or has such general interest. One can divide the Faeroe whale-fishery into two quite distinct categories, for on the one hand there is hunting—organised by big business—of the great leviathans of the deep, and on the other there is the slaughter of the lesser whales by the co-operate endeavours of the people. The first is of commercial importance only : the second is a phase of folk-culture of such importance in the economic structure of the island life that it deserves, and must have, a chapter to itself.

When the great whales—the blue, the humpback and the sperm —grew scarcer year by year on the grounds off the Norwegian coast towards the close of the last century, the whalers pushed farther out into the Atlantic in search of their prey. In 1883 the fishery was established in the waters south of Iceland, and by 1894 it had found the Faeroes area so profitable that stations began to be established in the islands. For the first few years the boats had good hunting, many blue whales and some humpbacks being captured, and by 1905 a dozen boats were catching some thirty or forty great whales each year.

The northwards migration of the blue whale at this period brought it very close to the islands, and although the greatest passage took place some twenty or thirty miles seawards of Mykineshólmur, many fine monsters were caught much closer to the land. Peder Michelsen, a famous whaler of the period, sometimes followed them from a hundred miles south of the Faeroes, and marvelled at their trick of " heading so straight for the opening between Koltur and Vágar that no helmsman could do it better." Many of these seventy and eighty foot mammals, —the biggest ever known on earth—which yielded up to a hundred barrels of oil if in good condition, were killed within a few miles of the Vágar shore in the hey-day of Faeroe whaling.

However, the stock of blue and humpback whales soon decreased, and latterly one or two only have reached the flensing-planes each year. Sei-whales were common up to the first great war, and no less than 503 were slaughtered in 1909. Because this is a plankton-eating whale, however, its movements are very uncertain and unreliable, the abundance of its food being dependent on the sea currents and sudden changes in the weather. It is, moreover, the least valuable of the larger whales from the whaler's point of view, and the industry in the Faeroes came to be more and more dependent upon a somewhat larger species, the finback, for its revenue.

The finwhale begins to be common in the neighbourhood of the fishing-banks to the south of Suðuroy in April, and towards the end of that month the whaling season usually begins. The numbers rise steadily to a peak in June, then fall away gradually towards the autumn so that the fishery ceases to be productive in September. The finwhale's occurrence in numbers is regular : probably, since it devours herrings as well as krill, it is less susceptible to sudden changes in the temperature and direction of the ocean currents. In the 1920's three-figure catches were obtained every year, but immediately prior to the war the numbers showed a falling-off. When the fast little boats with the harpoon-guns mounted in their bows were able to go about their lawful occasions once more in the summer of 1945, it was the finwhale they met with on the grounds, and the numbers were said to be high.

It is not often that the boats pay attention to the smaller whales, but sometimes they will bring in a few bottlenoses, which normally attain only twenty to thirty feet in length. But the *døglingur* (as this mammal is called among the islands) is by rights one of the species which comes within our second category, being hunted by the people for food and oil. According to Meikel Ibsen's accounts on behalf of His Majesty for the Faeroes, a Suðuroy man caught a bottlenose whale alive as long ago as 1584. Men from northern Suðuroy, particularly the village of Hvalbøur, have continued to catch them ever since. Most are taken in September, a few sometimes appearing in August and October, and the greatest catch on record is of seven together at Hvalbøur on September 16th, 1880. Although it is almost annual in its occurrence at this settlement it is only very rarely that the bottlenose brings excitement and joy to other parts of the archipelago, and it would appear that some few must pass through the sound between the Dímunar and Suðuroy every year on migration southwards from the arctic, where they summer near the edge of the ice.

Killing these whales appears to be a simple matter : they are slow, good-natured creatures and easy to embay. Once near the shore the hunters drive their strong iron hooks, to which long ropes are attached, into the thick layer of blubber covering the beast's head. The whale, apparently, does not object to this rough usage—indeed, the Hvalbøur people say, it appears to enjoy the slight tickling sensation thus caused ! The trouble does not start until the ropes are thrown ashore, and the tug-of-war to get the *døglingur* on to the beach begins. A male bottlenose may measure up to thirty-six feet, so is no weakling : but with the whole man-power of the village pulling on the ropes, its struggles are invariably short-lived.

Sometimes schools of dolphins appear in the fiords and sounds, and attempts are made to run them ashore. These *springari*, however, are fast swimmers, restless and very active and always a great trouble to drive, so that good catches are very rarely effected. The most notable kills ever made were of schools of 308 at Vágur, in Suðuroy, on September 24th 1904, and of 143 at Hvalbøur on August 4th of the following year.

These lesser fry have lost something of their economic value since the rise of the commercial interests, for there is no market to-day for the small quantities of oil they produce. Similarly, the caaing-whale, whose long and interesting obituary notice is the subject of the next chapter, is of no importance from this aspect, but all three species provide the Faeroe folk with meat, sport and social celebration. The meat of the larger whales is also in good demand for the table, and in the summer of 1945, when imported beef and mutton were very difficult to obtain, the flesh of the finback whales was often on sale in Tórshavn and other places.

Providing it is fresh, it makes a very enjoyable dinner, tasting rather like an inferior veal ; and although, being English, I have a marked suspicion of foreign foods, I must say I can find nothing in the slightest degree objectionable about whale-meat if it is well cooked. Whale-meat should always be steeped in a mixture of half vinegar, half water, for two or three hours before it is prepared for eating, as this treatment removes the oily or " fishy " taste which some people find objectionable. It is always better, too, for being pressed overnight on a deep plate, under a bread board supporting a heavy stone or similar weight. The meat should be cut into thick slices, as with steak, flavoured with salt and pepper, and fried, and should be served with gravy and fried onions.

References to Chapter Three

DEGERBØL, M. (1940) ; LANDT, J. (1810) ; NICLASSEN, P. (1937) ; WEIHE, A. (1928).

Chapter Four

WHALE-HUNTING

1. The importance of the caaing-whale or *grind* in Faeroe culture (*page* 95).
2. An eye-witness account of a whale-hunt (*page* 96).
3. The manner of raising the alarm or *grindaboð* (*page* 101).
4. How the driving and slaughter of the schools are organised (*page* 103).
5. The distribution of the meat at the present day and half a century ago, and the division of the islands into "whale districts" for administrative purposes (*page* 106).
6. Some historical, culinary and other miscellaneous observations (*page* 112).
7. A review of this form of whaling in Shetland, Orkney and north-west Scotland years ago (*page* 116).

I

THE BLACKFISH or caaing-whale has a wide distribution in the North Atlantic from Labrador and Greenland eastwards to Norway and the island groups to the north of Britain. It is a small whale, adult males measuring from twenty to twenty-five feet in length, and it is gregarious, roaming the seas in schools of a few dozen up to a thousand or more strong. A full description of its zoological characteristics, if one is required, can be found in Millais's and similar works : the present chapter is concerned only with a review of its place in the social and economic life of the Faeroe people.

Schools of these whales, known in the Faeroes as *grind*, occur regularly and in some years frequently in the summer in the sounds and fiords, and they are also to be found, though less commonly, in the winter time. No single opportunity of hunting them is missed by the Faeroese, for the *grind* has a long and venerable history as a source of food. Its importance to the well-being of the community has been recognised for upwards of a hundred years by statutes ratifying age-old usage and traditions. At its best the hunt, which consists of the driving (*grind-*

arakstur) and slaughter (*grindadráp*) of the schools, is a supremely well-organised affair in which most able-bodied men, whatever their vocation, co-operate. It relies for its success on the disciplined obedience of the participants to the orders and instructions of a chosen master of the game, and although disobedience is punishable by the law, the shame of it is feared more greatly than any fine. It is only natural that such a remarkable phenomenon as this should have made many ineradicable marks on the material culture of the Faeroese.

To the casual observer from abroad the *grindadráp* must seem to be one of the cruellest forms of hunting in existence. The Faeroese, who are by natural temper a kindly, hospitable and well-educated people, admit this much themselves. But the *grindadráp* is the only method by which these whales can be killed successfully, and the conditions of life among the islands are such that the *grind*, like the sea-fowl, remains a vital source of the country's meat supply. For the land is shockingly desolate over the greater part of its 540 square miles, and will never produce fresh meat in sufficient abundance to satisfy the needs of its 30,000 inhabitants. It is a land accursed, moreover, with a stormy and unproductive winter, so that the provision of a good stock of dried and salted meat must always be the primary consideration of the summer toil.

Knowing the conditions, it is easy, and only right, to condone the *grindadráp*. And to any one who is interested in ethnology, its picturesqueness as a form of hunting, its moral value as a skilful and exciting sport and excuse for social celebration, and its importance as an event upon which something of the economic structure of the Faeroe Islands rests, have great appeal. Should this very remarkable practice ever vanish from the Faeroe scene, then this small nation will have lost an integral part of its nationhood, and one of the most significant factors in the curious identity of its life.

2

The afternoon of September 19th, 1941, three days after my arrival in the islands, was a phenomenon in Faeroe weather—a clear, warm, sunny day as good as any Indian summer day you would get at home. I was walking in the countryside near Hoyvík, between the froth-rimmed coast and the boulder-strewn

hills. Around me, on the hard-won greenth of land which generations of Faeroemen had found it profitable to till, men and women
were busy spreading grass to catch the drying sunheat, or were
tying bundles of it to upright wooden posts to grow fit for
garnering.

The scene was one of slow, peaceful, pastoral activity—until
a solitary figure appeared in silhouette on the skyline, and the
magic cry " Grindaboð ! " swept like a sudden breeze across the
fields. Its effect was electric. Instantly the farming ceased, and
the men and women shielded their eyes against the sun's glare
and looked out to sea. Then they hurriedly gathered up their
implements and, whilst one of their number ran to the top of the
next rise to pass on the call to other workers down below, they
separated to their respective homes.

The green land was deserted, the farming forgotten. That
cry, which burns its way wildfire through the town and the
spacious countryside, driving along the fiords and the valleys
and up over the stony hills, had set the life-blood of south
Streymoy tingling with the promise of another harvest, borne
to the people unexpectedly by the sea.

As I made my way quickly towards Tórshavn I watched the
distant cluster of small boats working together as a team out in
the fiord, and the white-streaked wakes of other craft speeding
out from the harbour to join them. The faint pulse of the motors
was carried to me on the breeze, and alongside the slower moving
boats wet oar-blades glistened in the sunlight. Hoyvík was not
far behind me when I heard the engine of the boat in its landing-
place throb eagerly into life. Soon afterwards I had to step off
the road to let a pony-cart pass by, with four erstwhile farmers
urging their small beast onwards to the town. A Faeroeman I
met a little later beamed upon me in his excitement and said,
" There is whale in the fiord—plenty whale ; it will give us a
little pleasure if we can kill him ! " I was to recall that remark
later—as a classic understatement of the truth !

In the town scores of people were going down to the quay.
The children, released from school, ran pell-mell, dodging in and
out among their hurrying elders. Soldiers, grateful to a kind
chance for this new diversion and eager to lend their Faeroe
friends a helping hand, moved along at a more military pace
than usual. Men in blue and brown jerseys, sea-boots and skin
shoes, peaked cloth caps and the striped red hat worn in the
islands passed along the crowded thoroughfare on cycles or afoot,

G

carrying long spears on their shoulders, and wearing their sharp knives in leather scabbards at their waists.

The quayside was crowded. Adjacent offices and houses, the roofs of sheds and boat-houses, and even the backs of stationary lorries whose drivers had gone off to the hunt had been occupied by the early comers who wanted grandstand views. When the *grind* came into the harbour with the shepherding craft behind, and the people saw the sleek black bodies curving rhythmically under and out of the waves in a scurrying of white foam, they raised a full-throated, happy cheer. It was like some thrilling phase of a first-class sporting event at home in the good old days, only one felt that the cheering had seldom reached such a peak of spontaneous joy.

Now there were men standing in the boats, and they had drawn the wooden sheaths from the keen-edged whale-weapons. Those on the edge of the quay stood ready with lances poised, and when the school was still some fifty yards from the harbour-head, some men, fully clothed and armed like Viking warriors wading ashore on some strange coast, leapt off the quay into three feet of water to get to close grips with the *grind*.

The stupid whales came on, raising cockatoos' crests of foam on the little waves. They swam unfalteringly, with the surge and grace of strength in the regular turning of their smooth gleaming bodies, thrusting forwards as though the safety of the seven seas lay before them. It was then, when the leaders were almost in the shallows at the harbour-head, that the captain chose his victim and the slaughter of the whales, the *grindadráp*, began.

The whales were in dire trouble. In water too shallow for swimming they rocked and rolled without control. Their great tail-flukes reared many feet into the air as some of them caught their heads among the rocks. The water roared and seethed, and was churned to an apple-green ribbed and veined and crested with white foam.

The long whale-weapons did terrible work, and soon the water and the foam were gashed with crimson veins. Running rivulets and sordid pools of blood welled up from hidden bodies and trailed and spread over the surface of the sea. The backs of swimming whales broke the surface and their blood leapt in a steaming, crimson spout more than a foot into the air ; blood oozed and flowed in the wake of whales as they ploughed madly through the waves. They squealed in their agony beneath the

reddening water, their cries—like plaintive, pathetic whimpers—
only just audible to those watching from the quay.

More men waded out from the harbour-head, lunging and
thrusting with their lances as the stricken whales sheered by.
Men and beasts seemed inextricably confused in the bloody,
quaking turmoil of the sea. The spear-thrusts sank deep, viciously
biting into blubber and flesh. Within a few minutes of the start
of the kill the harbour was a scene of gory madness and carnage,
and the strong smell of blood was in the air.

The whaling-men on the quayside worked with as much skill
and energy as those in the boats, or wading waist-deep in the
water. Most of them had taken up stations at the slipways where
the small craft are run down to the sea, and each time a weakened
whale came near to the slip they hacked at its head with the
sharp iron hook, *sóknarongul*, often jumping into the water by
the side of the threshing beast to make fast the hook in the big
square head. When the hook was fixed the rope was paid out
quickly to eagerly awaiting hands in the crowd, and to the accompaniment of a great deal of shouting and rhythmic heaving on
the line the whale was brought on to the quay.

As soon as the whale was out of the water the hauling ceased
for a few moments whilst one of its captors took the gleaming
knife from the sheath at his belt, cut a gaping wound in the
blubber and flesh behind the whale's head, and severed the spinal
cord. The convulsive shudder of the beast as the knife sank to
the hilt was the last real movement it made, and the hauling of
the carcase then began anew. I saw one reckless man actually
leave his boat to sit astride a dying whale and administer this
coup-de-grâce.

All along the quay the hauling went on accompanied by the
lusty shouts of the men, and often of the women and children
too, whilst at many points the regular " Heave ! Heave ! " of
British soldiers and sailors was the operative cry which punctuated
the death-ride of the whales to the growing morgue on the roadway. Sometimes a rope snapped, and the shouts died in a gale of
laughter as the ardent pullers tumbled backwards upon one
another, or rolled over the quiescent bodies of beasts that had
been already laid in position. There was plenty of fun for watcher
and worker alike, and excitement ran like a fever in everyone's
veins. Often, whilst the whale was being drawn, somebody
would cut the belly open, and after a short exploration with the
knife extract the kidneys and liver from behind the steaming

viscera. These delicacies are highly prized, and by ancient tradition are the property of any one who cares to take them.

So this gruesome business continued, the crowd surging in sections to the help of some man who had hooked a dying whale, and joining with might and main in the tug-of-war to bring it on to the quay. The roadway ran with streams of blood, and the streams grew and merged together until the quayside was carpeted with a slippery crimson, and the blood oozed around the soles of one's boots.

An hour after the beginning of the *grindadráp* there were whales still swimming strongly in the red sea around the boats, but half-an-hour later the killing was virtually at an end. Nearly a hundred and fifty whales, cut and bleeding and all of them steaming and dead, lay side by side in well-ordered rows along the quay, so closely packed together that in some places you had to walk on their bodies to pass along the road. Only one craft had been sunk, a surprisingly small loss ; it had been smashed to pieces by the tail-flukes of a desperate bull, and luckily its occupants had got off with nothing more serious than a good ducking and a few moments of apprehension whilst they swam to other boats. In the *mêlée* of a *grindadráp* duckings, bruises and cuts from mishandled knives and whale-weapons are of singularly little importance in face of the mounting quantity of meat.

The day was a holiday for all Tórshavn, but especially for the boys and girls. The children helped to pull on the ropes, and two small girls had managed to get their hands red to the wrists with blood, so that they seemed to be wearing scarlet gloves. Some of the children stole pick-a-back rides on the whales that were being dragged, stood by phlegmatically and watched the slaughter of their steeds, and pounced on the heart, liver or kidneys when these were removed. At the head of the harbour boys not yet in their teens swam in great glee in the red water when the killing was at an end, seeking and hooking whales that in dying had sunk to the harbour bed, and bringing the ropes to those on shore. They had tremendous fun, and their enthusiasm gave a great deal of amusement and called for no small admiration from the English folk.

The water in the harbour seemed to reflect the roseate glory of a vivid sunset sky as the crowd thinned away, and people went home to change their wet and blood-bespattered clothes, carrying their weapons and their spoils. Some routine work, such as dragging up the carcases that had sunk, drawing up the craft to the boat-houses, and swilling down the quay to clear it of the blood continued until well on into the evening.

The excitement was not all at an end. In the deepening dusk the people flocked down to the sea front once more, many this time resplendent in their national dress, and full of carnival spirits. In an ever-widening ring they danced at the harbour-head, the dead whales lying round about them in the gloom, and they sang verse after verse of monotonous and seemingly tuneless ballads, until their voices were hoarse. For hours the dancing and singing continued : those who grew tired (and despite the labours of the afternoon they did not tire easily) fell out, but always there were others to take their places.

This was their celebration of a harvest home, and as I watched I fell to wondering if the man who had spoken to me outside the town that afternoon was having his little pleasure here in the midst of the joyous throng.

3

Most of the schools which meet their Nemesis on Faeroe shores are found by the small boats when they are fishing outside the fiords. As soon as one is seen, the boat making the discovery hoists a flag, which may be any piece of cloth or clothing that comes readily to hand, such as a shirt or jacket, or the blue woollen jersey worn by almost all Faeroe fishermen. The important thing is that it must be large enough to catch the eye of all other fishermen in the vicinity, so that these can at once haul in their lines and go to join the finding-boat, which will be closely shadowing the whales. If the flag itself is not immediately seen from the land then the movements of the boats will soon attract attention and the *grindaboð* will rise and quickly spread.

The fluttering of this nondescript item of clothing, usually tied to an upraised oar, is the birth of the most powerful cry in the Faeroe tongue—a cry which throbs with as much excitement as that of " Fire ! " in a crowded city. The message flies with incredible swiftness through the whole district, workers in the fields yelling it at their neighbours and staying only long enough to know that it has been understood. " Grindaboð ! " is a call to those who have places in the boats to forsake their farming, their school-teaching, their office stools or their benches in the Løgting, and take to the sea. To those who will play their part on land, it is a summons to tour the rough tracks on pony-cart, cycle or afoot, until it is known where the kill is likely to be made. Nowadays the main channel for communicating the *grindaboð* is the telephone system, and, needless to say, the message has priority over all other calls. The directory carries a long and carefully-worded instruction to subscribers as to the correct procedure in regard to this call, with the assurance of reimbursement of any charges which may be incurred. Before the installation of the telephone circuit in 1906 the message was distributed by runners, and by lighting beacons of damp hay, or laying out sheets, at certain well-known places on the coast or in the hills.

Such a beacon is—or was—a *grindaglaða*. I say " was " because its day is now past, although men are still appointed to act in the capacity of *grindaboð* in their particular districts should the telephone system fail ! Near Argir, on the south side of Tórshavn, are three sites where fires were lighted in former times to transmit the warning to Nólsoy across the fiord ; one was for use only if the hunt was proceeding in the fiord itself, a second if the hunt was taking place in Tangafjørður, whilst the third denoted that the school was being driven on the western side of Streymoy. In the latter event Tórshavn would first have to get its warning by runner from Velbastaður, since the intervening heights rendered the use of a *grindaglaða* impracticable. Velbastaður, too, would warn Kirkjubøur and the islands of Koltur and Hestur by beacon, and also Miðvágur and Sandavágur on Vágar island. By laying white sheets at the top of a certain hill, the people of the last settlement would pass the news to Kvívík and Leynar on the Streymoy shore of Vestmannasund. In no case was a beacon allowed to burn down until a similar signal was seen at the receiving end, acknowledging the message.

At each settlement the runner was relieved on the discharge of his mission, another carrying the news post-haste to the next village. This runner, called *grindaboð*, had a very close kinship with the *tingakrossur*, who carried a sign from one village to another in olden times to summon the menfolk to a court or *ting*, or to call them to arms so that pirates and other invaders could be repulsed. The Faeroese *tingakrossur* (who survives only in the name of a local newspaper !) was the lineal descendant of the *tingboð* of Viking Norway, and analogous with the bearer of the " Fiery Cross," a well-known symbol in former times in Shetland, Orkney, the Hebrides, parts of Scotland and the Isle of Man. In Norse times there can have been few more important public offices than this, and the laws contained minute instructions regarding the proper mode of delivery : if there was no one in the house, for instance, the symbol must be laid in the master's great chair by the fireside—no other place would do. The penalties for failing to pass the token on, or for concealing or mutilating it, were considerable. So powerful a symbol was the " Fiery Cross " that in the British Isles it outlived the period of Norse supremacy by hundreds of years : it was sent round a Manx parish to summon a public meeting as late as 1843, and Edmonston tells us that it was carried in the middle of the last century in Shetland to give warning of the presence of caaing-whales in the firths.

4

The driving is at once the most skilful, troublesome and exciting part of the hunt—at any rate for the participants, for the observer on shore is too distant to understand much of what is happening. The men of the finding boat, in consultation with the captain of the hunt when he arrives, choose the *grindapláss* to which the whales will be taken for slaughter, and it is then the responsibility of the captain to get them there. He has many problems to consider, such as the set of the tide, the strength and direction of the wind, the amount of daylight remaining, and so on. The *grind* cannot be driven against the tide, and it prefers to swim against the wind. It is reluctant to move after nightfall, and in any event a nocturnal hunt would be a tiresome and even dangerous proposition. If there is insufficient daylight, an adverse tide, or an insufficient number of boats to begin the drive, then the captain's first concern is to find a suitable inlet in which to " lay by " the school until conditions are favourable. This in itself is no easy task, but once it is accomplished the whales are quiet and docile, swimming slowly round and round within the cordon of boats, and making no attempt to break away unless frightened by some clumsiness on the part of the men. They behave, indeed, very much as though they were a flock of sheep.

So too when the driving begins in earnest. The secret then is to guide the whales rather than force them in the required direction. The boats form a crescent behind the school, and gently urge it forwards by throwing the *kast*, or the loose stones which the children and women hastily threw into the craft before its departure from shore. The *kast* is a white stone tied at the end of a long line, so that it can be retrieved after each throw : the whales shun the splash and the whiteness and the stream of air bubbles as the stone sinks, and move away from the disturbance. It is therefore easy to keep them herded, or steer them in any given direction by varying the frequency of the casts on one side or the other. The drive may last for a few hours, or it may last, on and off, for several days. Owing to some mismanagement or unforeseen factor of tide or weather the school may be lost, perhaps later to be recaptured—and perhaps subsequently to be lost once again. It is by no means a foregone conclusion that the drive will culminate in the grindadráp, and many a battle of wits has been won by the whales.

HVALVÁKN AND SLÍÐRI

Tórshavn Museum, scale ca. 1/10

The kast is part of the statutory equipment of the whaling boats, which are usually the eight or ten-oared craft—although, of course, boats of all types may take part in the hunt. They must also carry lances or whale-weapons (hvalvákn), which are also fitted with a line, one end of which is tied to a thwart, so that the chances of loss are minimised ; and iron hooks (sóknaronglar) to which a grindalína is attached, on the following scale :—

Number of Oars	Whale-weapons	Hooks and Lines
10	4	3
8	3	2
6	2	1
4	2	1

Harpoons are often taken, but their use is absolutely forbidden unless and until the captain and the district officer decide that it is impossible to put the grind ashore. It is then a case of " every boat for itself," and the harpoon is the only weapon that will capture a whale successfully at sea. The Løgting imposes a small money tax on every whale so caught.

The best whale-bays are those with a gently-shelving muddy or sandy bottom, on which the luckless beasts can be stranded. If the whales are going in well the men in the boats will often speed them over the last few hundred yards by shouting and making as loud a noise as they can. The choice of a propitious moment to initiate the kill is another of the ticklish decisions the *grindaformaður* must make, for immediately the first-wounded whale runs amok in pain and fright the whole school takes alarm and stampedes. It is therefore essential that the whales shall be moving steadily towards the shore, and that proper care be exercised in piercing the initial victim. If it is wounded in the

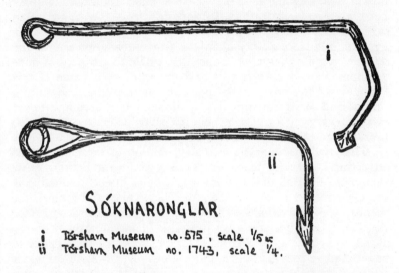

SÓKNARONGLAR

i Tórshavn Museum no. 575, scale ⅕ us
ii Tórshavn Museum no. 1743, scale ¼.

hind part of the body the animal will bound forward, and the rest of the *grind* with it, to their general destruction. If the spearman is clumsy and lances the animal in the side or in front of the dorsal fin, it will probably veer sideways, taking the school with it through the ring of boats, so that they regain the open sea. I saw this happen at Tórshavn on New Year's Day of 1943, the whales sounding when less than fifty yards from the shore and reappearing in a surprisingly short time well outside the harbour mouth. When alarmed, they can travel with incredible speed. Fortunately they were recovered on this occasion, but often will be irretrievably lost in such cases, or will have to be overtaken, calmed down, and driven once again—this time, perhaps, too late in the day or too near the change of tide for the whalers to kill before the *flok* has been " laid by " overnight.

Of the slaughter little more need be said. The spectacle is novel and exciting on the first occasion : thereafter it impresses one as a sordid and sanguinary job of work—the light in which, I believe, most of the experienced *grindamenn* regard it. The main business at the beginning is one of blood-letting, for, together with the mud and sand stirred up during the first mad rush,this serves to blind and still further confuse the whales. In the turmoil of the kill it sometimes happens that one beast or another escapes through the cordon of boats unwounded, and reaches clear water ; but it is a singular fact that such animals return with awful persistency to their death in the dark crimson waves. Faeroemen say that they " return to the blood " as though this exerted some hypnotic influence. Very likely the true explanation is that the instinct of self-preservation impels the whale to escape, but once the immediate danger is past and the extraneous cause of this " first law " removed, the powerful herd-instinct reassumes control and sends the animal to its doom. Whales almost never escape singly from a *grindadráp*, but if a party, no matter how small, breaks clear of the boats it will not return.

The *grindadráp* marks the real beginning of the celebration, attracting a considerable crowd among whom the holiday spirit runs high. Not all of them are would-be sightseers : whaling is too deep rooted in the heritage of Faeroe men and women for them to remain content as onlookers, and there is little need for the law which declares that it is the bounden duty of every citizen to help drag the victims so far on shore that their heads lie above high water mark. In the evening of the hunt the town celebrates its good fortune in no mean fashion. Besides the dancing at the head of the quay, the two dance-halls are crowded with perspiring but happy people. The *dansuringur*, which is more fully described in Chapter Seven, continues until five or six o'clock in the morning, a matter of twelve hours or more. And not once during that period does this marathon effort stop !

5

The laws governing the distribution of *grind* have undergone many changes during the last hundred years, consequent upon the increasing density of population in certain areas. It is unnecessary to discuss these changes in detail, but in order to show how a *grind* is administered I propose to take two actual examples—a recent one from the capital, and another of fifty years ago from one of the outlying villages.

To-day, as from time immemorial, the first consideration after the whales have been counted and measured by the sworn *metingarmenn*, whose duty is to assess the total value of the catch, is the payment of certain traditional entitlements. The largest whale is *finningarfiskur*, a reward to the boat which first sighted the *grind*, and by ancient custom the head of this whale is the sole property of the member of the crew who was the first to raise the alarm. I have been told that in the smaller settlements those who won the *finningarfiskur* unselfishly shared it among their neighbours—a trait typical of the fine fellowship which is still to be found among the older Faeroe folk. In the rare event of a *grind* being first sighted by a man on shore, and the warning passed to a boat, the biggest whale was shared equally between the finder and the crew.

Next, a quantity of meat is set aside as *matarhvalur*. This is given to all the houses at the settlement where the kill is made, so that the whaling men will have a hot meal of fresh meat to go home to at the end of their arduous day. The amount to be set aside for this purpose rests with the discretion of the *sýslumaður*, the chief district officer who supervises the distribution, and it is largely dependent on two factors—the size of the *grind*, and the number of visitors present in the town or village at the time. At Vestmanna, for instance, where a kill usually occupies two or three days owing to the peculiar nature of the bay, the spectacle and the promise of festivity attract many outsiders, so that the proportion of *matarhvalur* is higher than at other settlements.

A sufficient quantity is then put aside as *skaðahvalur* for sale to compensate the owners of damaged boats and whaling gear. Such damage is assessed by two valuers, a boat-builder and a blacksmith, who are each paid 2 *skinn* of meat for their services. Payment in kind is also paid for *vaktarhald*—" watch and ward " over the meat to prevent pilferage, and the search for whales which on dying sunk to the harbour bed. This quest is given up after forty-eight hours, and if any one discovers a whale after that time it is his personal property. The *vaktarhald* is assessed at the rate of $\frac{1}{4}$ s. per man by day, and $\frac{1}{2}$ s. per man by night.

The *metingarmenn* also receive payment in kind. For their work they have a long rod, calibrated in divisions representing *skinn*

—the ancient Norse measurement of land and produce—and they lay this rod along the whale's body from the eye to the anus, and take the reading. One man enters the details on the record from which the *sýslumaður* will work out the distribution, whilst the other cuts the serial number of the whale on its head, and marks the value in Roman figures on one of its flippers. The *sýslumaður* is paid 2 *s.* for his work, and the *grindaformenn* or captains (besides being recompensed under the *vaktarhald*) get a commission of ½ *s.* each. Usually four captains are appointed in every district, and they serve for five years : they reside in widely separated parts of the district so that, no matter where the whales appear, there is always one captain almost immediately available. In south Streymoy, for instance, the present captains reside at Rituvík, Nólsoy, Tórshavn and Hestur respectively. As a sign of their authority they are required by law to fly the Faeroe or Danish flag from the stern of their boat. Technically the *sýslumaður* takes over control of a *grind* as soon as he arrives, but in actual practice he usually controls the shore-work only : his authority is superseded by that of the *amtmaður*, the Danish " governor " who, however, wisely refrains from interfering !

The sum total of these initial payments is deducted from the grand total, and the remainder is declared *partahvalur*, for equal distribution among the inhabitants of the district in accordance with the names entered on the *grind* register at the district office. It is the duty of the *sýslumaður* to take a census every four years in order to check the accuracy of this register, and to forward copies to interested neighbouring districts. Once a year he must also check his register of boats, and ensure that they and their equipment are in good condition. Any deficiencies must be remedied at once by the owners, on pain of fine.

At the present time the law states that if the *heimapartur* works out at ½ *s.* or more per individual, a free and straightforward distribution is to be made. The people come down to the quay with their *leypar*, buckets, and other receptacles, are told the number of their whale and their entitlement, cut the allotted portion from the body under the watchful eye of the *vaktarhald* and take it away. This continues all night long, since the law requires that the *heimapartar* must be removed within twenty-four hours of the announcement that it is ready for issue. Any remaining uncollected at the expiration of that time is sold for the benefit of the Løgting's *Økonomisk Fond*. If the part works out at less than ½ *s.*, a free distribution of fifty per cent of the *partahvalur* is made to the whaling men only, and the rest is sold for the benefit of this fund, which finances the improvement of roads and landing-places and other public works.

The total value of the sixty-six whales killed at Tórshavn on July 21st, 1944, was 324½ s., worth 9,735 *krónur*, or about £434 10s. Out of this were taken :—

Finningarfiskur	21	*skinn*
Matarhvalur	100	„
Skaðahvalur (30 s. damages, plus 2 s. valuers' fees)	32	„
Vaktarhald (44 men and 6 boats for 1 day)	12½	„
Metingarmenn	2	„
Sýslumaður	2	„
Grindaformenn	2	„
Total	171½	„

Thus 153 s. remained for *partahvalur*, giving a " part " of well under ½ s. As there is always some doubt in a big place like Tórshavn as to who are entitled to the name of *grindamenn* and who are not, the *sýslumaður* based the free distribution of the first 76½ s. on the number of registered boats in the south Streymoy district, which includes Tórshavn and several nearby villages, and the islands Koltur, Hestur and Nólsoy. Actually only 71½ s. were available for the 231 boats, for a gift of 4 s. was made to a boat from outside the district which happened to be present at the hunt. The law of 1909 states that any boat from an outside district, arriving before the *grind* is killed, is entitled to 25 *heimapartar*, this being based on an ancient rule that an eight-oar boat represents 25 head of the population—the oarsmen and their dependents. Similarly, a " foreigner " present at any hunt may claim not one but three *heimapartar* as his lawful share.

The Tórshavn town council purchased the Løgting's portion, and also bought the 30 s. *skaðahvalur*, so that it became the owner of 106½ s. This quantity was divided among the town and the nearby islands and villages, again on the basis of the number of boats, the town council recovering the cost from the village councils concerned, but distributing the meat free within its own administrative area.

In former times there were other substantial items, besides those already enumerated, to be taken from the grand total before the general distribution could be made. At a *grind* at Miðvágur on September 28th, 1894, a total of 186 whales, valued at 1,360 *s.*, was slain. First of all, a tithe of ten per cent was deducted ; then *finningarfiskur* and the other traditional entitlements were met, whilst in addition one per cent was taken for the Poor People's Fund, and a similar amount for the benefit of the schools. There remained 980 *s.* From this, twenty-five per cent *jarðarhvalur* or " ground-whale " was deducted to satisfy the claims of the landowners at the *grindaplàss*. The remainder was *partahvalur*.

The tithe was divided between the Church desmesne at Midvágur, the Danish government, the state endowment funds for the Faeroe church, and the living of the *prestur*. The amount taken for the landowners was split in two parts, there being one for each type of holding. The land at Miðvágur is worth 48 *m.* and of this 8 *m.* are farmed by men who hold their land in fee from the crown, and the remainder by freeholders. The latter received meat in proportion to the size of their holdings, but as the *kongsbøndur* did not customarily benefit unless the *grind* was a big one, their share in this instance was returned to the common pool.

The tithe was abolished towards the end of the century, together with the tithes on fish, barley and other produce. At this period, faced with the problem of a growing population, the Løgting was considering a means whereby the *partahvalar* might be increased, and decided that this could best be done by buying out the landowners' claim to *jarðarhvalar* at every *grindaplàss*. So the farmers were compensated on a scale based on their receipts during the previous fifty years ; and in order to recover the very considerable amount of money paid out to these men, the Løgting appropriated the ten per cent formerly demanded as tithe. The debt was liquidated after about twenty-five years, and thereafter the ten per cent also was merged with the *partahvalar*.

The endpaper maps of the Faeroes, examined in conjunction with the key given on page 111, illustrates the division into *grindadistrikt*. The places named in small capitals are the primary *grindaplàss*, and the schools must be killed there if at all possible. If these cannot be used, then the whaling men may have recourse to the second-class bays whose names are shown in normal type. None of the other settlements is suitable.

With the exceptions of Sandoy and Suðuroy, which are too far from the other islands for any active co-operation to be worth while, the districts are not self-contained, and neighbouring areas among the north, central and western islands are linked together in the administrative scheme, as the key shows. The scheme was evolved with the intention of ensuring as fair and regular a share of the meat as possible for every man, woman and child in the archipelago : it is an example of " communism " on the grand scale. These are the divisions as cited in the law of June 14th, 1909 ; they had already existed for many years, and indeed, with certain modifications, still hold good at the present day. The considerable increase in the population within recent years at such places as Klakksvík and Tórshavn, however, has made certain adjustments essential for the benefit of all.

" WHALE-DISTRICTS " AS LAID DOWN BY LAW OF 1909

District	Whaling-bays	Areas receiving :—	
		Full " part "	Half " part "
1. North Islands	HVANNASUND Veðvík	All North Islands (Fugloy east to Kallsoy)	East side Eysturoy (Gjógv south to Lamba)
2. Klakksvík	KLAKKSVIK	All North Islands, east Eysturoy	West side Eysturoy (Rituvík north to Eiði), Nólsoy, east side Streymoy
3. Eysturoy	NORDRAGOTA Funningsbotnur	All North Islands, all Eysturoy	Nólsoy, east side Streymoy
4. Norð í Sund	NORD I SUND	All Eysturoy, all Streymoy, Nólsoy, Koltur, and Hestur	Villages of North Islands west of Múli, all Vágar and Mykines
5. South Streymoy	TORSHAVN	West side Eysturoy, Nólsoy, all Streymoy, Koltur and Hestur	Villages of North Islands west of Múli, all Vágar and Mykines

District	Whaling-bays	Areas receiving :—	
		Full " part "	Half " part "
6. North Streymoy	VESTMANNA Saksun Leynar	Nólsoy, all Streymoy, Koltur, Hestur, all Vágar and Mykines	West side Eysturoy
7. Vágar	MIDVAGUR Tindhólmur	West side Streymoy, Koltur, Hestur, all Vágar and Mykines	West side Eysturoy Nólsoy, easy side Streymoy
8. Sandoy	SANDUR Húsavík Skálavík	All Sandoy, Skúvoy and Stóra Dímun	None
9. Suðuroy	HVALBOUR VAGUR FAMJIN Trongisvágur	All Suðuroy	None

6

The first record of these whales being put to good use in the Faeroes is dated 1584, when four luckless blackfish were stranded on Lítla Dímun (of all unlikely places !) following stormy weather about Saint John's day. It is interesting to note that the words " In defe Voort comen veel Walvifsen " (" In this part come many whales ") are written between the islands of Borðoy and Kunoy on the maps produced by Lucas Waghenaer in 1592 and Joris Carolus in 1634, pointing to the antiquity of the bay at Klakksvík as a noted whaling place. Earlier, in 1539, two men carving up a whale were figured on the map of Olaus Magnus, in addition to two barrels which may suggest that whale-oil was an exported commodity as early as the sixteenth century.

The whaling is doubtless of much greater antiquity than 1584, the first year of the written records which thereafter were kept inconsistently on behalf of the Danish treasury, since the Crown derived a certain income in tithe. H. C. Müller, for many years sýslumaður on Streymoy, published abstracts from these records,

Mykines—the *bøur* at haymaking time

Sorting and drying " klipfisk "

Grindadráp
at Tórshavn

and from these it is apparent that the late summer is the most profitable period, whilst there is a secondary " migration " in the early winter months—actually more pronounced in some years than in others. October and November catches showed a substantial increase between the years 1931-38, and it is possible that this is to be correlated—like the greater abundance of the blue and sperm-whales in the autumn—with the higher temperature of the Gulf Stream noted in recent years. Midwinter catches are rare but very welcome in view of the scarcity of fresh meat at that time, and also because the whales are then in a much fatter condition than in the summer months.

The best *grindapláss* in the Faeroes, judging from these records, is Norð í Sund, and its reputation must be ancient if the name, Hvalvík, of the contiguous settlement is any criterion. Hvalbøur may have got its name from the bottlenose rather than the caaing-whale ; nevertheless, it is the best of the four good stations in Suðuroy. Miðvágur is an excellent bay, but Sørvágur, the largest settlement on Vágar, must kill its schools on the northern shore of Tindhólmur, far away from the village. Klakksvík had the record kills in 1944, and Vestmanna is now one of the most important places, although until 1843, when the local parson conceived the idea of rigging up a huge net to keep the whales confined to a corner of the deep bay, the *grindadráp* was almost always a dismal failure because of the absence of a suitable shore. Between 1843 and 1878 over 6,000 whales, valued at £20,100, were slaughtered in the bight, with the aid of a net which cost £100 to make—a tremendous improvement on the 2,169 recorded for the previous 260 years !

Practically all the *grindahvalur*, except the head and flippers, is used for food. The meat is boiled and eaten with boiled potatoes and mustard when taken fresh : it is very tender, a rich chocolate brown in colour, and has a peculiar but by no means unpalatable flavour. It is customarily followed by a second course of pancakes. The fried liver is excellent, the heart, kidneys and tongue less so. The greater part is either salted for the winter or is dried in the wind, being cut into strips and hung outside the loft window or *hjallur* on special racks. After several weeks of this treatment I defy any but a Faeroeman to find and appreciate its much-boosted but singularly elusive qualities. The blubber, *spik*, is always served with the meat, and Faeroe medical opinion rates it very high among nutritious, body-warming foods. Formerly the heads were rendered down for the oil, a large amount of which

H

was exported to Denmark, but the establishment of whaling stations interested in bigger game destroyed the market value of this commodity, whilst in the Faeroe household electricity and paraffin have taken its place. To-day most of the heads, with other offal, are committed to the deep.

Following the distribution of the meat the viscera and offal must be removed to sea within seventy-two hours : little use is made of it on the land, although those who have taken the trouble to save it for their fields declare that there is no finer manure, especially for grassland. The stomach-skins are tanned and inflated for use as buoys with the long-lines, and in former days thongs of the dried skin were used in the boats to tie the oars to the wooden *tollar* which take the places of rowlocks. Several people are expert at working the whalebone into brooches, paper-knives, penholders and other small ornaments, and this work is generally of a very good quality. The whale itself is a characteristic motif in other artistic work, such as the fashioning of brooches, pendants and rings, and the decoration of scabbards worn with the national dress. These tiny effigies are of beaten silver, inlaid in ebony, and are very neat. In two places among the islands I have seen garden walls built entirely of the skulls of caaing-whales.

There is a wide vocabulary connected with the whaling, but— apart from a rich fund of stories—surprisingly little folk-lore. Most of the special words connected with the occupation have been mentioned, but a few interesting ones remain. A *grindaboð* which embraces more than one district is a *grindabreiðsla*, and the weapons of the chase shown on pages 104-5 are collectively *grindareiðskapur*. Boats putting out from the shore would some-times experience hard rowing in order to reach the drive in time to be of assistance, a sentence which the Faeroese language disposes of in the single word, *grindaróður*. Jacobsen and Matras give *grindamjørki* in their dictionary for a murky fog, such as is not infrequent in the late summer, and which descends suddenly and hides the school from its pursuers. It is interesting to note that the crane-fly is called *grindalokkur* because its appearance in summer is said to herald the coming of the whales.

It is said that there will always be a change for the worse in the weather on the day following a *grindadráp*, and this is not so much folk-lore as observed fact. Such a change will often bring strong winds and heavy seas, and it is on record that boats returning to their own villages after the distribution of the catch sometimes met disaster—probably because they were overloaded, and the water-line above the margin of safety, which is a hand's spread below the gunwale at the middle of the boat. So real was this danger in former times, when the boats were without engines to speed them on their way to shelter, that families always welcomed their menfolk home with " Væl afturkomin ! "—not so much a greeting as a thanksgiving for their safe return.

The best of the many good *grind* stories comes from Hvalbøur, and it is not much more than ten years old. One day the men were away helping to drive a *grind* (a very paltry one, it is said !) into the fiord at Trongisvágur, and the village was left to the old men, the women and the children. Suddenly the quietness of the scene was shattered by the magic cry of " Grindaboð ! " and, almost to a woman, Hvalbøur took to the remaining boats ! In great style these Amazons drove a huge school into the bay, and the kill began. When the menfolk came home at night, with their meagre *heimapartar* in the boats, they found a thousand whales lying dead on Hvalbøur shore ! This, I agree, sounds a fantastic yarn ; but I happen to know the man who, together with the local parson, filled the *rôle* of *grindaformaður* that day. He is an old and respected citizen of Vágur, and I have heard the truth of the story attested by others besides himself.

The sporting parson, apparently, is no rarity in the Faeroes but it is considered most unlucky for the boat containing him to get between the *grind* and the shore. It is also very unlucky to have a woman bearing an unborn child present at the slaughter—a taboo which, one imagines, was originally designed for the woman's sake rather than any advantage which might accrue to the hunt ! If the *grindamenn* were experiencing difficulty in bringing the school to the shore, it was thought a good thing to open the church doors—why, I do not know ! A picturesque and poetic phrase applied to any one who is in a great hurry is that he or she " tók sjógv á bák "—" took sea on the back "—and is derived from the way in which the *grind* rushes away from the hunters when alarmed.

Perhaps the best conclusion for this section is the final paragraph of Müller's paper, since it concerns an old and pleasing custom which seems now to have quite died out. After the distribution of the meat, " No boat leaves the place without striking up a song of praise to the Lord as a thanksgiving for the gift. It is a solemn sight to behold the boats as they, often in the quiet midnight hour of the clear nights, glide over the glassy level of the sea . . . and hear the notes of praise sounding over the calm ocean."

7

Schools of caaing-whales were also hunted until the early years of the present century in the Orkney and Shetland Islands. The name, in fact, comes from Shetland, and is derived from the herding of the whales to the place of slaughter. Tudor says it is " the same as ' kaing,' which is applied in Shetland to driving the sheep into the ' cra' for roving or marking." Edmonston gives the native word as ' caaed.' There has been great confusion over the correct form, and it is perhaps best taken for granted that in its English rendering the spelling is optional.

Probably the earliest record of a whale-hunt in Orkney is that dated 1691, when 114 were driven ashore near Kairston on Mainland. The largest kill ever known in Shetland was of 1,540 whales, at Quendale Bay on September 22nd, 1845, but the story that they were all despatched within two hours must be a wild exaggeration. Whale " draves " are said to have been frequent in Shetland between 1860 and 1880, and to have taken place for the most part in Weisdale Voe, Dales Voe in Delting, and the bays on the east side of Yell : they had become very infrequent when Millais recorded these facts in 1906. The winter kill of a hundred whales in Weisdale Voe on February 7th, 1903, may well have been one of the last organised whale-hunts in these islands. That the excitement of the hunt dies hard, however, is borne out by the words of Mr. F. C. Kelly in a letter to me in 1942. A small school made its appearance in Stromness Harbour " about ten years ago," but the alarm was late in being given and the whales got away into Scapa Flow, " having only to outwit a few small boys who put out in dinghies."

The value of such catches appears to have fluctuated very considerably, else it has been incorrectly reported in some cases. Edmonston says the value of a whale was " about two pounds," Millais between £1 and £1 10 0. Yet the catch of sixty at Sourin, Rousay, in 1861, is said to have been worth £260, and a kill of 195 at Flotta in August 1839 is reputed to have fetched £500 12 6. Other figures given by Tudor are £300 for a school of 154 killed on March 4th, 1882, in Weisdale Voe, and £88 only for 108 slain in Catfirth Voe, Gletness, on August 11th and 12th, 1879.

One of the few records I have seen of a kill of caaing-whales in the Outer Hebrides comes from the island of Lewis where, in 1859, a school of 128 was driven up Little Loch Roag as far as Kinloch Roag, and there slaughtered. The corpses were sold to a firm in Leith for the blubber, and after the barrels had been shipped the offal was used as manure. This note is given by MacGregor. Millais also mentions that occasional kills were made in Loch Seaforth in the island of Harris, and that a small number of whales were driven ashore at Thurso Bay in Caithness on June 19th, 1899.

This form of whaling does not appear to have been taken nearly so seriously in Orkney, Shetland and the Hebrides as in the islands to the north, nor had it anything like the same strong sociological significance. The best accounts I have seen are those of Eliza Edmonston (1856) for Shetland and Daniel Gorrie (given by John Gunn, 1909) for Orkney and substantially these accounts agree. In outline the technique was similar to that employed in the Faeroes to-day; and we have the same picture of great excitement among the people, the rush to the small boats on the part of all able-bodied men, the careful driving of the school towards a selected beach, the stampeding of the whales by making a great noise in the boats, and the ultimate carnage on the shore. Gunn says that the muster of men and boats was " under the leadership of some recognised master of the game " similar to the Faeroese *grindaformaður*. He and others stress the fact that all who participated stood to benefit equally in the sharing of the spoils, and indeed the distribution appears to have been much less complicated than in the Faeroe Islands, although at the same time less favourable to those who actually did the work. According to Tudor, a tithe was claimed by the Church, although other authorities do not say if this was so. The laird on whose foreshore the whales were stranded had claim to one-third of the catch, but in latter days this manorial right was waived. During the eighteenth century, however, again according to Tudor, another third was appropriated by James, the sixteenth Earl of Morton, and his successors.

The caaing-whale seems to have been without any marked food value in Orkney, Shetland and the Hebrides, doubtless because these are much better agricultural lands than the Faeroes, and there was seldom the same serious shortage of meat. Millais, however, says that the whale-meat was dried and pickled, and that the intestines were made into buoys. Tudor writes that

whilst the Faeroese look upon the flesh as a luxury, " their Shetland cousins cannot face it, though during a famine in North-
maven in 1740 they are said to have been compelled by necessity
to overcome their repugnance." Curiously, he adds that the fins
—a part of the anatomy which the Faeroese never eat—were
generally eaten by the poorer crofters about the middle of the
eighteenth century, the taste being described as " like ox-cheek."

Nor does the caaing-whale—or what remained of it after it
had been rendered down for its chief asset, the blubber—appear
to have been used on the land, though MacGregor reports that
this occurred in the outer Hebrides. " The carcases and bones
are in too many instances suffered to lie on the beach as a
nuisance, or are again committed to the sea " wrote Eliza
Edmonston, " Whereas if the Shetlanders were as active and
energetic in the agricultural line, as they are in the sea-faring,
quantities of most valuable manure might be obtained from what
is thus heedlessly wasted."

It is well worth while quoting Edmonston again in illustration
of the inefficacious manner in which many of the Orkney and
Shetland hunts were conducted. " The people are not sufficiently
amenable to discipline or law, so that for lack of due concert and
regulation, the whales are quite as often frightened off, as driven
on shore." She describes how the inhabitants of a neighbourhood
spontaneously answer the call to arms, leaving whatever task
they have on hand, and rushing pell-mell to the shore, where
" there is a scramble for the boats " and " private rights seem for
a time to be merged in ' first come, first served.' "

The Shetlanders and Orcadians do not appear to have had any
special equipment for this form of whaling, and in the various
accounts we read of the oddest assortment of lethal weapons being
used in the chase—old rusty harpoons, " formidable three-
pronged ' graips ' and long-hafted hayforks," the ' toysker ' or
turf-cutting spade, and even guns ! Again, we hear of all manner
of weapons being used by those on shore following the stranding
of the luckless whales.

No review of whale-hunting in Orkney and Shetland would
be complete without the delightful yarn told by Millais. " When
the whales chose to enter the voes on the Sabbath Day even the
Sabbath was not respected. In Shetland they tell a story which
is probably true enough. The minister of Dunrossness was in
the middle of his sermon one Sunday afternoon when he noticed
that several members of the congregation were feeling for their

hats. When some of them stole out of the church he understood, and closed the service hurriedly with these words ' I have only one final word to say, my brethren, and that is : Let us all have a fair start—just a fair start.' Then he opened his pulpit door and ran out as fast as his legs would carry him ! "

References to Chapter Four

BONNEVIE, E. and MITENS, E. (1932) ; BUCKLEY, T. E. and HARVIE-BROWN, J. A. (1891) ; DEGERBØL, M. (1940) ; EDMONSTON, E. (1856) ; GORRIE, D. (1909) ; GUNN, J. (1932) ; JACOBSEN, M. A. and MATRAS, C. (1927-28) ; MCGREGOR, A. A. (1933) ; MEGAW, B. R. S. (1941) ; MILLAIS, J. G. (1906) ; MÜLLER, H. C. (n. d.) ; NØRLAND, N. E. (1944) ; TUDOR, J. R. (1883) ; WILLIAMSON, K. (1945 c).

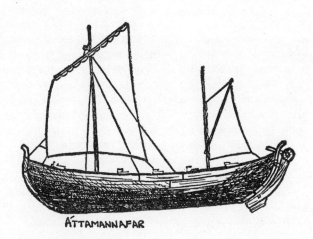

ÁTTAMANNAFAR

Chapter Five

PORTRAIT OF AN ISLAND (1)

1. Describing how we set out for Mykines, and admire the scenery on the way (*page* 120).
2. How we close the island, and marvel at the astonishing abundance of seafowl (*page* 124).
3. How we walk over the *lundaland* to Mykineshólmur, observing the innumerable puffins and other items of interest (*page* 127).
4. How we descend the cliff to the gannets in order to put rings on their young (*page* 131).
5. And hear legends and stories of Mykines in which they figure (*page* 135).
6. How we visit the Kittiwake tenements with our bird-rings, the use and importance of which are here more fully explained (*page* 138).

I

THE POST-BOAT, a diminutive and retired fishing-smack, was waiting at the quay. Somewhere inside it a diesel engine was being stirred into drowsy wakefulness, for the hour of departure was at hand. The scene was dominated by the exciting personality of the skipper, a jovial little man whose tongue, like his body, would not stay still. He bustled about the deck, pretending to superintend the stowage of the curiously assorted cargo in the tiny hold, or made frequent excursions to the quayside to examine bags and packages lying among the cods' heads, ropes and multifarious signs of Sørvágur's fish-procuring life. Piece by piece the cargo came overside—foodstuffs and farming tools, bags of flour and salt, buckets and pans and a miscellany of other household chattels for the inhabitants of Europe's most Atlantic isle.

He had time to spare, however, to talk to his passengers, for we were there a very long time. What he said nobody ever fully understood, for he was always in so great a hurry to burst into a cackle of mirth that the end of almost every sentence became a problem for the imagination. He addressed the old lady who had already made up her mind to have an uncomfortable crossing, the little girl going away on holiday, and myself standing on the threshold of an adventure. Then he returned to his preparations with such zeal and enthusiasm that I felt we might be embarking on a voyage into the unknown, instead of a purely routine run that he had made every Wednesday and Saturday, weather permitting, for donkeys' years.

At length all the packages and the people were aboard, but still we did not cast off. I grew tired of the noise of the terns on the stony hillside above the harbour, bickering as they flickered in the sunlight above their nesting-ground. And the sight of barrels and smell of cods' heads grew ever more objectionable as time rolled by. At last the reason for our delay became apparent— we were waiting for the most important passenger of all ! A single mailbag, sealed with a bright brassy padlock, was brought down from the road and reverently handed aboard. The skipper took it into his personal charge, and there was no mistaking his air of importance as he did so. The man and the mailbag disappeared into the wheelhouse, and the engine burst into renewed vigour as though to welcome them. We were now in a position to look the people of Mykines squarely in the face, and within a few minutes the popping of the exhaust punctuated our journey along the fiord.

At first there was little to see except the green hills closing in the waterway on either hand, and the small bands of kittiwakes against this background, wending their way listlessly towards the gap behind the town, on their bathing trip to the lake. You could, if you wished, look at the wheelhouse, and see the wide grin of the skipper lurking behind the dusty pane ; but very soon the scenery changed, and with a mental effort I dismissed him from mind as we approached the mouth of the fiord, and gave my full attention to the splendid panorama gradually unfolding in the south.

The western promontory of Vágar has an exquisite outline. It is really a double headland, one raised about the other, and each finely traced in a free-flowing curl, gently rising, turning and steeply falling. Opposite the headland are the Drangarnar, two offshore stacks of fairyland form, gleaming with countless kittiwakes, and bathing their feet in the surf of the racing tide. In the larger of the stacks the sea has worn a picturesque archway through which, when the stream permits, a small boat may sail. They introduce a view that has been painted and photographed and reproduced in books and on postcards to a greater extent than any other scene among the islands, and on a close approach one ceases, in a flow of admiration, to wonder why.

Beyond stands all that remains of Tindhólmur, by repute a once inhabited island, but now so battered by the sea's cold furies that it is not worth while living on any more. The only record of occupation I can find tells of one Rasmus of Sørvágur, who was banished to Tindhólmur because he was always making trouble in the town. He appears to have lived well enough. The island produced some sixty lambs a year, more than enough sea-birds for feathers and food, an adequacy of turf for fuel, good fishing in the summer and sufficient hay to feed a few cattle. Andrias Weihe, who recounts his story, says his only misfortune was to have a two years' old child carried by a sea-eagle to the topmost pinnacle of the isle. Legend improves upon this by crediting the babe's mother with the feat of scaling the pinnacle, which no one had ever climbed before—but her courage was in vain, for when she reached the eyrie the child was dead.

Tindhólmur is the quaintest and certainly the most strikingly beautiful islet in the Faeroes. Its shape proclaims the monstrous destructiveness of ocean storms. You would think that some huge giant, some mighty *trøll* of Faeroe legend, had cleaved Tindhólmur in two and stamped one half away beneath the greedy waves. For the south side is a terrific precipice rising from a mass of rock debris to a summit ridge of lofty pinnacles and minarets more than seven hundred feet in height. In the sunlight it glows with rainbow colours, the red of tufa, grey and grey-brown of basalt, and the green, blue-green and yellow of scattered vegetation. On the near side this half-mountain sweeps steeply downwards to low flat shelves of pasture land reaching to the rocky shore, and because such pasture is scarce in the Faeroes many sheep are brought here from Sørvágur and left to crop the precious grass. Tindhólmur is now privately owned and in a sheltered hollow by the shore is its owner's summer house, and a dwelling used by the shepherd and bird-fowlers when business brings them to the isle.

Outside Tindhólmur lies Gáshólmur, its opposite in islands, and an anti-climax—a clear contrast of small, straight cliffs supporting a flat green top. This also is a grazing ground for sheep. In juxtaposition to its fantastic neighbour it is simple and uncomplicated as a child, and this simplicity is the final touch of nature's genius in a splendid and unforgettable scene. Beyond, there is only the hulk of misty Mykines, another half-hour's sailing over the long rollers of the Atlantic swell. In the south you can see the greyness of Sandoy and Skúvoy, the dot of Lítla Dímun, and finally the mass of Suðuroy sprawling vaguely across the horizon nearly forty miles away.

I turned my eyes to the north-western part of Vágar when the beauty of the islets had passed astern. There too the land is immense, the mountains sliding in long slopes to the white surf at the edge of the sea. The cliffs are neither so high nor so sheer as those on the south side of the fiord, now emerging as immense precipitous walls from behind Tindhólmur, but that steep rise of the blue-green hills gives to the land-mass a grandeur no less superb. The single tiny settlement, Gásadalur, sits above a small cliff, a tight cluster of coloured houses at the mouth of a deep valley, its position in the ring of hills impressing forcefully upon you the solitude and remoteness of Faeroe villages. The shining fields gloss the feet of Árnafjall, Vágar's highest hill, and nearly a mile away from the houses a brown zig-zag line marks the way down the cliff to the landing place. Not far away a stream pours out of the valley in a white cascade, and, by a strange optical illusion caused by the distant view, all movement seems to have been arrested, so that it hangs over the dark cliff like a long, narrow scarf of lace.

Two of the extinct breeding-birds of the Faeroes are com-memorated by these names, the sea-eagle and the grey-lag goose. Centuries ago Árnafjall was doubtless the home of the noble erne, and Tindhólmur is known to have been its last regular haunt among the islands. There is a great crag, also named Árnafjall, dominating the south-east coast of Mykines, so the eagle must have been a frequent visitor—and may even have had an eyrie—there. It is difficult to imagine better settings for sea-eagles than these. The ørn was never common, and it was lost to the Faeroes through the curious and only too efficacious " bill-tax," *nevtollur*, described in Chapter Two. The high price set on the eagle's head in those days may be appreciated from the fact that the man who gave up its beak was exempt from any further payment during the rest of his life. By 1869, the last year in which the *nevtollur* was brought to Tórshavn and publicly burned, the ørn had been extinct well over a century and a half.

As to Gáshólmur and Gásadalur, there are two suggestions as to the derivation of the names, and you can have your choice.

Perhaps the root-word is *gás*, a reference to the grey-lag goose
which nested on Vágar until persecution ended its days early in
the last century. At that time the élite of Tórshavn thought it
great sport to go out in a small boat on Sørvágsvatn when the
geese were in moult, and unable to fly, and shoot as many of the
wretched birds as possible at point-blank range ! The other and
more romantic explanation is that the names recall the sad story
of Gaesa, who, according to tradition, was the rich owner of the
great Kirkjubøur estate late in the eleventh century. She built
a fine stone church, dedicated to the Virgin Mary, and entertained
with great hospitality the bishops and other preachers who came
to the islands soon after 1100. In history it is usually the woman
who does the plotting and scheming, and the man whose head
falls as a result, but at Kirkjubøur the sordid story was reversed.
It is said that one Matthias, a priest, distressed that the Church
must rely upon a woman's whim for its wealth and power,
conspired against her and brought her into disgrace. Her lands
were confiscated, and she fled to the protection of a nephew in
Vágar, from whom she received the farm now known after her as
Gásadalur.

2

When our boat had pitched and tossed its way through the
racing tide between the islands we gained the shelter of Mykines'
southern coast, and sailed more peacefully in the shadow of the
mighty cliffs. The land rises in alternating terraces of naked
basalt bands and steep grassy shelves reaching up to the overhanging pall of cold, grey mists shrouding the island's summit.
Great daubs of green ground spill out of the land, slopping over
the cliff-face to the sea, and here and there immense grassy
buttresses, stippled with the white fronts of innumerable puffins
sunning themselves outside the earthy portals of their homes,
bolster the fortress wall. Everywhere against this wall, and covering the dappled expanse of the waves and the mottled sky, are
countless thousands of birds : without the actual experience,
one would find it hard to believe that any place on earth could
be so lavishly stocked. We seemed to sail through a world
seething with the eager, throbbing life of a tremendous hive,
thrumming with a million wing-beats and gay everywhere with
movement and bright colour.

For a time the birds around us were almost exclusively puffins and fulmars. The puffins hurried to one side, paddling furiously or taking headlong dives to get out of our way ; but the fulmars seemed inquisitively interested in the boat and time after time swept low across the bows, or sidled up on the wind to look at us out of their cold, expressionless eyes. Gull-like in the distance with their white bodies and greyish wings, they are curiously changed when close at hand ; their bodies are short and fat, their yellow bills a different shape because they are among the few birds to possess a nose—a short horny tube along the top of the beak—and their wings straight-cut and rigid as they swing round on the wind, not sharply angled like those of a gull.

As we drew farther to the west it became obvious that two species were largely responsible for the character of the scene, and that although others were present they were noticeable only by the sudden contrast they made with the two hordes, the puffins and kittiwakes, which shared between them the onshore and off-shore realms. The puffins flew past in busy crowds, trailing little streaks of bright colour where their legs and splayed feet supplemented inadequate tails. All around the boat the water was darkly mottled with the birds, and the air vibrated to the thrum of their fast-winnowing wings. Not a second passed by without a spattering of orange-vermilion paddles as birds leapt out of our path, to rise clear or change their minds and vanish as suddenly as they had appeared in a headlong plunge under the waves.

The disturbance of land, sea and air was chaotic. The puffins were the nature and the spirit of the scene everywhere except in the immediate vicinity of the cliffs, where the kittiwakes floated as thickly against the dark backdrop as snowflakes against a midwinter sky, stealing the picture from them. Their voices rose in a perpetual threnody of sound, and although the sheer walls were plastered white with sitting birds, it seemed that thousands more swirled madly on restless wings. By contrast of colour, voice or form other species intruded on the scene. Their lithe fork-tailed bodies and shrill screams announced the arctic terns. The crimson legs and dazzling white blur of the black guillemots' wing-patches attracted attention to this most lovable of all sea-birds. Occasionally the slender brown silhouettes of arctic skuas caught the eye as they planed past above, looking for some laden kittiwake to rob. Herring and lesser blackback gulls flew past, looking lonely indeed among the crowds of auks and kittiwakes. Once I caught sight of a single gannet some way out at sea : otherwise the only evidence that a gannetry existed close at hand was provided by the gleaming white caps of Flatidrangur and Píkarsdrangur, twin stacks at the south-western corner of the holm, on which were sitting innumerable birds.

At length we turned into the landing-place, a large rock-lined cleft open to the south-west, and obviously the kind of place where disembarkation is always a little uncertain unless the wind and tide and sea are just right. One could well imagine the inaccessibility of this small cove under certain complications of these elements, so all-important in the lives of small maritime communities ; and it was significant that the boathouses were perched at the end of a promontory a good fifty or sixty feet above the sea, out of harm's way of the winter storms. I had been told during the journey that it is usual for Mykines to be isolated for long periods in the winter months, and that sometimes the Christmas mail does not reach the inhabitants until March ! It was not at all difficult to visualise this place with the white surf seething at the rocky walls, nor did one need much experience of small islands to guess what terrors a heavy ground swell would have within this narrow *gjógv*.

To-day conditions were peaceful enough, and without difficulty we jumped ashore and made our way across the sloping rocks to the foot of the steep pathway which is in reality the beginning of the village street. Very soon I saw the village and its spacious green *bøur* for the first time, for during the approach by boat one sees only the jumble of *hjallar* and boathouses on the point. The village lies low in the valley, pleasing and picturesque like all Faeroe *bygdir*, because each house is different in size, shape, and hue from its neighbours. Some are brightly coloured, or painted white, and in contrast there are the older houses with their sod roofs and pitch-black walls. Clustering about them all are dingy outhouses of stone, or stone and wood combined, and the meat-drying *hjallar* of upright wooden planks set an inch or so apart, so that flickering shafts of daylight seem to ripple through the hut as you stroll by. Below the houses runs the little stream, crossed by a concrete bridge, and standing on a knoll above the northern half of the settlement is the white church of simple, traditional design, and near to it another white building with a red roof that is self-evidently the school. Below this cultural seat I found the house of Abraham Abrahamsen, with whom I was to stay.

Here on the ocean fringe is a place that is at once one of the most wholesome and characteristic of Faeroe settlements, quite unspoilt by the influence of modern civilisation which has permeated the fishing towns on other islands. And it is, moreover, more worthy than any place I have visited to be called a birdman's paradise. Not only are the birds here in prodigal abundance, living amid the loveliest surroundings you will find in this strange and beautiful group of islands ; but they are also, as perhaps nowhere else in the world, so closely bound up with the daily life of the people and the economic structure of their community that it is quite impossible to study them without considering their relationship to mankind. Mykines, as a result of centuries of winter hardships and isolation, has learned to live alone. The chief concern of the fruitful summer must always be the provision of sufficient food to tide the people over the harsh and unproductive winter months. The bird-fowling, by which the chief of the island's natural resources is conserved, keeps this village alive, and at the same time helps to maintain in this pleasant place those customs and traditions which have made Faeroe folk-culture unique in the civilised world.

3

The walk from the village over the *lundaland* to the holm is one of the finest afternoon strolls you will find, and you need only an ordinary man's interest in bird-life to enable you to appreciate it to the full. The meaning of *lundaland* is " Puffin's land," and the western part of Mykines is crowded with this and other equally interesting birds.

When you pass through the break in the stone wall that separates the *bøur* and Dalið you become conscious immediately of trespassing on ground which is wholly and completely theirs. Down below, against dark cliffs which are mostly hidden from view, the restless chorus of the kittiwakes, " kitti-werk, kitti-werk," fills the air. Dalið is a long grassy slope littered with rocks, great and small, and in and around and beneath them the thousands of puffins have made their homes, in many places so ruining the pathway that you must skip and leap along to clear the gaping mouths of the burrows or small piles of displaced rocks. Semi-human snores and moans come from among the boulders and under the soil, and all the time a loud and ceaseless whirring of wings goes on above your head as the birds scurry busily to and from the sea. Puffins are everywhere, not by the score, nor by the hundred, but in multitudes. Red-legged, white-smocked, they sit in groups on the grass and the sun-warmed rocks, or waddle with a caricature of a sailor's gait from a position which does not suit them agreeably to a new position which does.

It is good to sit and watch the multitudes of birds going urgently about their daily tasks. Small crowds of them rise from the rocky ground before you, going off to the shining sea with a great rush of air from their vibrating wings. Sometimes, of course, it is your approach which causes this flurried movement, but even if you sit quietly in some inconspicuous place you will see similar communal behaviour among the scattered groups. One second the birds are standing together outside their burrows, doing nothing in particular, and the next—as though each bird had been visited by the same idea in the very same moment—the flock is scudding through the air to the puffin-dappled water below. When you gaze out to sea black spots dance in your vision, as in an attack of giddiness, but resolve themselves as your eyes focus into the distant mites of this vast horde of birds who spend the one half of their lives here on the ocean fringe.

As I have said, they are not the only birds, although the others are likely to pass unnoticed amid this overwhelming abundance of puffins. The Faeroe starlings, a sturdier breed than our own, are also frequenters of the *lundaland*, and on every day of my stay a flock of pied oyster-catchers sought the larvae of the crane-flies, *grindalokkar*, at the roots of the grass. Sometimes the blue-black ravens sit on Klettur or feel the air above with pinions spread like fingers against the sky, and nearly always one or two of their poor relations, the hooded-crows, pass to and fro with hoarse barks. Lithe terns beat up and down the puffinries quartering the ground systematically as they scavenge for small fish dropped by the hasty inhabitants outside their burrows. The puffins are shy of the terns, especially when the latter hover low to take their gleanings, and dive in precipitate and amusing fashion into the security of their holes. Their fears are groundless, however, for the terns are quite content with their scavenging and never oppress the fish-bearing puffins in any way. I have not seen this habit recorded for arctic-terns, and fancy that the birds thus engaged were non-breeders ; most of them swallowed their

Boat-building

(*Top*) Mykines and its cloud-cap from Sørvágsfjørdur

(*Bottom*) Mykines—looking east from the holm lighthouse

finds straight away, although one was seen to bear off a sand-eel towards the colony on the holm.

The Daliđ rocks and Rógvukollur are a sanctuary for the tiny Faeroe wrens, delightful bouncing balls of dark brown feathers with a handsomely chequered wing-edge and incredibly loud voices for such insignificant mites. They are more abundant on Mykines and the holm than I have found them elsewhere in the Faeroes, despite the damage wrought by the village cats, which get many of the young. On one morning of my stay I counted a family party of ten very confiding birds on the rocks just above the kittiwake colony of the holm. On another I was privileged to observe a pretty courtship display in which a male who sang every morning in the village, just outside my window, moved about the road trying hard to attract the attention of his mate, who was diligently examining crannies in a stone wall. He stood still as he sang, his tail uptilted, and his wings spread and upraised to form a deep " V " ; when each stanza was completed, he relaxed, so that the wings were only half-open and the " V " was much shallower. Several times he flew close to his mate, as though he would attract her attention ; but, to her shame, it should be recorded that she never once showed the slightest interest in his performance.

The path climbs through long grass lit by yellow buttercups and hawkbits, and in places gay with the wild angelica, rusty sorrel, yellow-rattle, forget-me-not and red campion—the last a rare plant in Faeroe—to the narrow knife-edge of the Rógvukollur ridge. Almost immediately beneath this ribbon of bare soil the north cliff sweeps down to the sea three hundred feet below—it is no path to walk for pleasure on a wet and windy day ! At the end of the ridge overlooking the village stands a proud memorial raised by the men of Mykines to those of their comrades and kinsfolk whose lives were lost at sea : the long list of names inscribed on the sides of the plinth makes tragic reading, for in some cases the passing of all the menfolk of a single family is commemorated. The monument, etched against the sky and visible almost everywhere you go in the village area and the fields around, is an eloquent reminder of the dangers and hardships to which those who live on such isles as this are ever exposed.

The opposite end of the ridge, from where you have your first view of the whitened gannet ledges of the holm, is associated with joy, not sorrow, for from this high point the Mykines children roll their Easter eggs down the long Lambi slope, having

I

first coloured them brown in an infusion of *steinamosi*—which, as its name implies, is a moss growing plentifully among the rocks. Here too, the women came on Pálsmessa many years ago to welcome the gannets to the breeding-cliff in a little ceremony which must have been one of the most picturesque that Nordic history has known. The feast-day of St. Paul falls on January 25th, which day traditionally marks the return of the gannets to the land. The maidens put on their handsome national costumes and went out to the Lambi summit to wave their white aprons in imitation of the gannets' wings. This must surely have been a survival of an early fertility ritual by which the women sought to attract a great assembly of birds, and so ensure a successful harvest for their menfolk later in the year. There is no clear memory of the festival on Mykines to-day, and it must have become obsolete well over half a century ago.

For a short space the path zigzags down the north cliff, and then turns the corner of Rógvukollur to wind down the Lambi slope to the suspension-bridge straddling Hólmgjógv below. Lambi is a very different place from Dalið, though the puffins are there in the same uncountable hordes. Gone are the grey rocks and scattered boulders and the bright flowers embroidering the grass, and in their place is a dark green carpet with large patches of a glaucous colour in those areas where the puffin-burrows are most abundant. The dark green is a vigorous growth of chickweed that has smothered almost every other plant out of existence, and in the glaucous places the chickweed has itself been ousted by the rich *lundasina*, a variety of the common festuca grass which flourishes only on the bird-manured soil of the fowling-cliffs. The Faeroese consider this blue-green growth superior to any grass in the islands, and the Lambi *feitilendi*, " fat land," is the pasture of the finest rams you will find in the whole country.

It is a long walk down Lambi, and on a hot day the air reeks with the stench of stale fish from the burrows, to whose entrances bluebottle and greenbottle flies are attracted by the score. Against the cliff-face carrying the Rógvukollur ridge the kitti-wakes swirl and the fulmars wheel about their nesting-sites ; and now and then, as you watch, a great net at the end of a long pole moves in a wide arc from the clifftop, propelled by some unseen hand at the Óyggjarmúlan catching-place, and one atom of this realm of birds goes to his doom, destined to help fill the dinner pot. The suspension-bridge at the bottom of the slop will surprise you : with the holm lighthouse and the radio-telephone service

it seems to be the island's only concession to the scientific genius
of man. When erected early in this century it was probably
painted black, but since then it has been completely and perpetually white-washed by the winged traffic plying constantly
overhead.

4

Mykineshólmur is an almost rectangular islet about six
hundred yards long by two hundred wide, with its surface tilted
towards the south, so that this shore is quite low compared with
the northern one, a precipitous cliff where live puffins, fulmars,
kittiwakes and the only gannets in the Faeroe Islands. The
pasture is again of splendid quality, richest towards the lighthouse
enclosure, where a large colony of arctic-terns hide their eggs and
youngsters in the long grass. They are continually having
trouble from the heavy-footed bullocks which graze here, and
which unwittingly stamp many of the chicks to death. One
afternoon I saw a bullock pick up a nearly fledged youngster
with a mouthful of grass, and on going to where the bird was
dropped found it alive, but with one wing crushed at the carpal
joint.

The terns do not seem to be nearly so enraged against the
bullocks as against human intruders, and a journey through the
heart of the colony can be an unpleasant affair. With angry
cries numbers of the white birds swirl and sway above your head,
and here and there one pair bolder than the rest stoops swiftly
and subjects you to persistent physical attack. My nerves are
good enough to sustain this treatment for some time, but on
occasion it can be painful, and a discreet retreat is the better
part of valour. When able to control this aggressive flight, in
calm weather and against a stationary foe, the bird always strikes
with the beak—hard enough to administer a painful prick and
draw blood on one's forehead. If you care to stand still, you will
see that the flight conforms to a beautiful pattern, the birds
dipping suddenly from a height of ten or a dozen feet, striking,
and sweeping upwards almost without slackening speed, to
regain position by means of a short but clever backwards flight
and a deft sideslip and turn.

The lovely black guillemot or tystie is another of the holm's
inhabitants, and several pairs are scattered along the south shore

rocks. They are pleasantly confiding and allow a close approach for admiration of their neat white wing-patches and scarlet legs. From several vantage points at the other side of the islet, if you have a head for heights, you can get splendid views of the gannets' ledges, and eavesdrop their guttural love-making, greeting and parental solicitude. These are big snow-white birds, so white that they make the plumage of gulls look dowdy, and they have long wings over five feet in span, jet black at the sharply pointed tips. Close at hand you can see their buff-coloured heads and strong, heavy beaks. Their manner of hunting is as remarkable as the Faeroeman's method of hunting them, an incident in the life of Mykines which is earmarked for the next chapter of this book. The birds go out from the great cliff to glide in wide lazy circles some sixty feet or more above the sea, and when a fine coal-fish takes their fancy they descend in a hurtling power-dive, swift bolts of gleaming white against the blue. As they crash into the water without slackening their speed one whit, a column of splash and spray soars ten feet into the air and hides their going. Watching them, you involuntarily shudder when the moment of impact comes, wondering how any living creature can do that and yet live. Perfect streamline, the astonishing strength of the skull, and perhaps the curious collection of air-sacs underneath the spongy skin (which, although their purpose is as yet incompletely understood, must act in a measure as shock-absorbers) do the trick.

My best afternoon during the first of my holidays on Mykines was that which brought me to close grips with the gannets—or, more truthfully, their young. Sofus Sivertsen and I were lowered to one of the upper ledges by our friend Jákup Nielsen, so that we could put some British Trust for Ornithology bird-migration rings to good use. The young were fat puff-balls of greyish-brown down, with evil tempers and an admirable, if unpleasant, fighting spirit. They were inclined to view our visit with the gravest suspicion, shuffling awkwardly along the ledges (but taking great care not to fall off!) and lunging viciously at our hands with their long, hook-tipped beaks—weapons which were not to be treated with disdain. "Keep your face out of reach!" Sofus warned me, and I obeyed, having no wish to go through the remainder of my life looking at the world, like a Cyclops, out of one good eye! I remembered, not without apprehension, that during the April hunt Jógvan Abrahamsen—my host's son—had been stabbed through the hand by an adult bird, and had been unable to do any manual work for a month afterwards. However, as I sought the youngsters' legs beneath their downy skirts, and clipped the rings in place, I suffered nothing more alarming than long scratches and minor cuts. My companion, who had had dealings with gannets often before (and who stands no nonsense from them !), worked expertly and fast, keeping his elbow pressed against the young bird's neck to minimise the force of its blows. In about twenty minutes we had ringed all the young we were able to reach—seventeen in all—and, helped by Jákup's sturdy heaving above, we climbed aloft, leaving the strange and bewildered kindergarten behind. Abraham Abrahamsen, who always showed the kindliest interest in the peculiar activities of his guest, promised that the fowlers would leave those particular ledges alone when the autumn hunt took place.

Bird-ringing, especially when there is some energetic climbing to do, is a fine sport—a splendid mental and physical exercise, and a useful piece of scientific work. There is a great exhilaration in climbing sound rock under good conditions—in being able to lean outwards and look down, feeling a comfortable sense of security as the rope draws taut behind you, and see an entirely new vista unfolding before your eyes. You gaze out to the rocks and the deep shadows of rocks and the waving tentacles and heaving beds of weed under the sea, down past a perpendicular world of gannets and fulmars, kittiwakes and puffins, who grow smaller and smaller as your eyes reach towards that moving translucent wall beyond which lie the fields they reap for a livelihood.

Each year during the war, subsequent to 1942, my Mykines friends took rings with them on their day-time visit to Flatidrangur at the beginning of the autumn hunt, and by the end of 1945 some two hundred young gannets had been marked. At the time of writing only two have been heard of again. One of these was ringed by Sofus on August 25th 1944, and was caught in a fishing-net off Agadir, Morocco, ten weeks later. When ringed it was a bird in down (otherwise it would not have been spared) so very likely it did not start its journey until towards the end of September, so that its rate of travel south may well have been about 300-350 miles a week. The other, ringed in August, 1945, was reported a few weeks later from the west coast of France. The recoveries suggest that the autumn movements of the Mykines birds are in line with those of gannets from British colonies.

The immensity of the puffinries and the economic value of

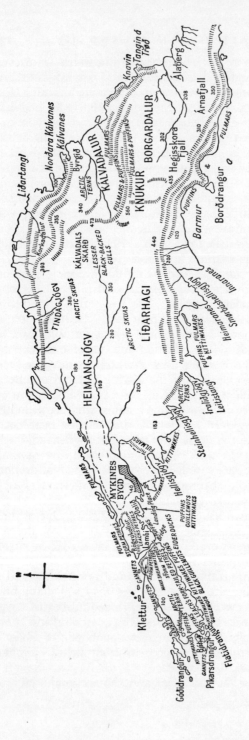

MYKINES

To show division of the outfield
and the chief Sea-Bird Colonies
described in Chapters Five-Seven

Adapted from the 1:20,000 map
of the Geodetiske Institut, Copenhagen

SCALE

0   1000   2000 METRES

Liðartangl

Norðara Kálvanes

Kálvanes

ARCTIC
TERNS

Byrgið

Qrðafjøll

FULMARS

Knøvin

Tanginá
Trøð

Alaberg

Árnafjall

208

310

350

FULMARS

Hegisskora
Fjall

302

KNÚKUR

BORGARDALUR

435

FULMARS & PUFFINS

FULMARS & PUFFINS

PUFFINS

550

Borðdrangur

Barmur

120

440

KÁLVADALUR

340

355

393

Qrðafjøll

180

TINDAGJÓGV

ARCTIC SKUAS

380

KÁLVADALS
SKARÐ

473

LESSER
BLACK-BACKED
GULLS

350

ARCTIC SKUAS

280

HEIMANGJÓGV

169

200

153

FULMARS

MYKINES
BYGD

200

200

LIÐARHAGI

Innaranes

Heimaranesgjógv

Suðuracelsisgjógv

PUFFINS, FULMARS
& KITTIWAKES

FULMARS, FULMARS
& KITTIWAKES

Íraliðagjógv

Leiðisong

Steinhelisið

ARCTIC
TERNS

KITTIWAKES

Hellisið

PUFFINS
GUILLEMOTS
KITTIWAKES

FULMARS

RED PETRELS
Róvnuhøllur
STORM PETRELS
Lambi
MANX SHEARWATERS

landing place

Bridge

PUFFINS

GANNETS

Klettur

100

RED PETRELS
GANNETS
Stóru Petrels

BLACK GUILLEMOTS EIDER DUCKS

ARCTIC
TERNS

PUFFINS

MANX SHEARWATERS
LEACH'S
PETRELS
KITTIWAKES

GANNETS

FORK-TAILED PETRELS

KITTIWAKES

PUFFINS
STORM PETRELS

KITTIWAKES

BLACK GUILLEMOTS

KITTIWAKES

GANNETS

Góðdrangur

Píkarsdrangur

Flatidrangur

the gannetry are not by any means the only striking features in the natural history annals of this isle. As Mykines unfolds her wonders we shall see more, such as the great ternery of Kálvadalur and the curious night life of the petrels on the holm ; but in closing this section I feel I must mention one of her past glories— the amazing black-browed albatross who won the name of *súlukongur*, " king of the gannets." The albatross is a bird which hardly needs an introduction to any one, although very few people whose travels have not extended beyond the northern hemisphere have ever seen one, alive or dead. The several species of albatross roam over the seas south of the Equator, and although the black-browed is the one which most frequently strays to the north Atlantic, it has been taken only once in Britain, and is indeed an exceedingly scarce vagrant to any of the maritime countries of Europe. Yet this *súlukongur* came with the gannets to Mykine-shólmur every year for thirty-four years, between 1860 and 1894 and stayed with them throughout each season ! Towards the end of its career it lived among the gannets on the extreme western point, Bóliđ, and there—for no good reason—it was shot on May 11th, 1894. It is a great pity that its sensational existence should have had such an unkind and ignominious end. The skin, incidentally, is preserved in the Natural History Museum at Copenhagen ; and it is interesting to note that when examined after death this aristocrat proved to be not a king, as had been long supposed, but a queen !

5

Nobody knows how this island came by its name. *Nes* denotes a headland, and the prefix *myki* is said to mean the muck with which the diligent farmer endows his fields. As always, legend rushes to the rescue with an explanation that is ingenuous rather than ingenious, and is dreadfully unkind to this most beautiful of the Atlantic isles.

In olden days there was a Sørvágur man who was often out fishing west of the land. He was a fine fisherman, but timid, and always took a big piece of muck with him because he was afraid of whales—for, you must know, there is nothing like a lump of manure for making a whale keep a respectful distance ! One day, when the mist was very thick, our hero was alarmed to see a great shape looming out of the water very near to the boat. At once he grew panicky and had unpleasant visions of becoming another Jonah ; so he threw the lump of muck in the direction of the ominous shape and applied himself vigorously to the oars. Just then the fog lifted, and he saw not a whale, but an island that no one had noticed there before. So, because of the way in which the timorous fisherman anointed it, the new island got the name of Mykines.

A much better legend is the epic of Tórur and Óli. Tórur was a giant who lived at Gásadalur, and who, coveting possession of the lovely island in the west, decided to slay the head man, Óli, and wrest the tiny kingdom from him. One day he ran down the dale and with a flying leap cleared the intervening sea, landing at the foot of Borgardalur, where the imprint of his feet can still be seen. He strode eastwards to the village, but Óli saw him coming and beat a hasty retreat towards the long western headland. With Tórur hard on his heels, Óli came to the end of the high ridge, Rógvukollur, and, hoping to trap the giant, he caused a deep chasm to open up behind him. That is how Hólmgjógv and Mykineshólmur were made. However, a giant who had leapt across nearly five miles of open sea only a few minutes before was too nimble to be caught napping by such a poor subterfuge, and he took the chasm in his stride and pounced on the magician.

So the two began to fight, and remained locked in combat many days, so that gradually they wore a knee-deep hollow in the ground. The spot where the battle-royal took place is called í Trakki, and no grass will grow there to this day. Eventually Óli got the giant down and gouged out one of his eyes, so that Tórur was in great fear and trembling for his life. He begged for mercy, and promised to make the islanders three fine gifts each year if Óli would spare him. They were, firstly, a large whale ; secondly, a great piece of driftwood, and thirdly, a big bird that would never be found anywhere else in the Faeroes than Mykineshólmur. There was a condition—that the Mykines folk should not laugh at or deride any of these things, on pain of losing them. Óli accepted the promises, and gave Tórur his life. Thereafter the two lived together on Mykines and became fast friends, and they lie buried close together beneath the Rógvukollur ridge.

It turned out as Tórur had said. Each year, at haymaking time, a big *døglingur* was stranded in Hvalagjógv, bringing meat, and oil for the lamps ; and each autumn a great piece of driftwood

floated into Viðarhellisgjógv, providing material from which boats could be made. From that time, too, the gannets have come annually to make their nests on the holm, and the Mykines folk have found them exceedingly good to eat. But as time went on the people were not so mindful as formerly about the condition that Tórur had imposed, and one year they laughed at the whale because it had only one eye—and that was the last whale to come ashore. They laughed also at the driftwood one year because it was so gnarled and twisted as to be almost useless—
—and thenceforth they searched Viðarhellisgjógv in vain. Since that time the Mykines men have been very careful not to give offence to the gannets, and they do not like outsiders to poke fun at these fine birds either, for fear that they too should come no more.

Whilst on the pleasant subject of fairy-tales we might as well take this opportunity of recounting a charming story of the early days of the gannet-hunt, although it is a chapter out of place. One year two rivals for the hand of a fair Mykines maiden went out with the party, and on the following morning they were the last to leave the holm. In those days there was no bridge, and the men crossed Hólmgjógv by rope. The first of the rivals crossed the chasm, and as soon as he set foot on the main island he loosened the rope and cast the end into the gulf, leaving his enemy fuming on the holm.

But the deceitful one had reckoned (as villains so often do) without the resourcefulness of a woman in love. When only one of her suitors returned, the lady went in search of the other, and from the summit of the Lambi slope observed his plight. There and then she decided to whom she would give her hand in marriage. But that was not all ! Immediately she went back to the village, procured a strong rope, a fishing line, and a goose which was, fortunately, the proud possessor of a pair of unpinioned wings. With these she returned to Lambi, and proceeded to put her ingenious plan into effect. Making the line fast to the goose's leg, and tying the other end securely to the rope, she threw the bird into the air on the very brink of Hólmgjógv. Bravely the bird struggled across, the line running out behind—the whole future, one might say, hanging on a slender thread—and made a perfect landing at the feet of the admiring swain. The lucky man pulled the line, and so the rope, across the gulf, and was able to make his way in safety to his lover's outstretched arms.

6

The prating of the stream to its narrow stony bed and the clamour of the sharp-tongued kittiwakes make a constant musical background to the Mykines life and scene. The village has character from this endless argument of the crowds of white birds nesting so close at hand, for, even though they are for the most part out of sight, they are never beyond hearing. You wake in the morning to this babel of tongues ; you walk and work and eat with it as a perpetual accompaniment, and when you go to bed it is still singing in your ears. Throughout the half-darkness that passes in the Faeroe summer for dead of night it is the stuff of the village silence. For silence exists in the familiar sounds you do not consciously hear rather than in no sound at all, and if you take the silence of Mykines apart it resolves itself into these components, the garrulity of the little stream and the high-pitched voices of the innumerable gulls. They create a kind, comforting, friendly silence, for after the first few hours you cease to think of it as noise. Perhaps the Mykines men, despite their playful remark that " Rita will stop crying before women stop talking ! " are not really aware of it at all—until they realise with sorrow in September that the sound has stopped, the kittiwakes have left, and the long and stormy winter is at hand.

East of the village, looming up above the lower ground which forms the southside bøur, there rises a precipitous wall of packed basalt columns, white-flecked with one of the largest single colonies of kittiwakes I have seen. Before the dark cliff the birds float as thickly as thistledown above an English heath : like their tongues, their bodies are never still. Behind the headland on the western side of the landing-place is another large and noisy colony, and down under the height of Rógvukollur is a third. Here also, along two wide parallel ledges, is one of the few guillemot colonies on Mykines, consisting of some three hundred birds. Thence there is a gap until you come to the middle of the holm, where hundreds more ritur breed on the low south and south-west cliffs.

It was at this colony that my ringing was done, for it is accessible from the land and parts of it can be worked with com-parative ease, the big basalt blocks of the lower part of the cliff providing good hand and foot holds and sound rock which it

was a pleasure to climb. Sofus Sivertsen made the rope fast round
the base of a boulder on the clifftop (judging by its smooth, shiny
surface it had held many a good rope before) and we lowered
ourselves hand over hand to the foot of the cliff, and clambered
across the rocks to the first of the breeding-places.

At intervals Sofus stopped to flay the air for the adult birds, for
he had brought his bird-fowling net along. They poured off
the cliff above us and cried harshly in anger and alarm, eddying
about our heads. Although his skill met with some initial success
at the various places we tried, the Kittiwakes soon tempered
their anger with temerity and were content to do their complaining
from a longer range. Sofus did well to take a dozen birds on the
wing, and to " bag " in addition three adult guillemots as they
leapt off their tiny ledges.

When business with the net was slack we climbed to the lower
nests and at the end of the morning had ringed over fifty young.
All the nests had young, but it was interesting to see the wide
difference in their ages ; some were only two or three days old,
small bundles of grey-brown down with the kittiwake's look of
innocence already in their eyes ; most were half-grown, a mixture
of soiled down and new feathers, and a small number were already
on the wing. This disparity in age is to be explained by the fact
that kittiwake eggs are a food-crop early in the season and (as
the polished sides of the clifftop boulder testified) men come from
the village to gather eggs from the more accessible nests. The
birds lay again, and may lose their clutches again, so that in the
more unfortunate families the domestic cycle may be much
retarded.

To look at, kittiwakes are the daintiest of the commoner
gulls, but it is a great pity that their domestic habits do not match
their appearance. Small, trim and immaculate, they are a joy
to watch on the wing, and when looking down from their nests on
the cliff-face, with heads inclined to one side, they have a demure
expression that is quite remarkable in a gull. But they have
astonishingly filthy habits, and if you want to find abject squalor
in the bird-world the kittiwake colony is the place to look for it.
It is anomalous that such a pretty creature is not more fastidious
in its home-life—just as it is that the kingfisher, sparkling gem of
English waterways, lives in a nesting-tunnel like an open drain.
Because their persons are so pleasing one is disappointed that
their habits are not equally above reproach.

When new the kittiwake's nest is a wonder of skill and tidiness :

a compact cushion of grass and seaweed, it is placed—almost glued—against the cliff-face on any slight projection big enough to support its base. For economy of living-space reduced to a fine art there is nothing in nature to compare with a crowded kittiwake tenement. Now, however, at the end of the season, the nests were chalked and filthy with fishy offal and the birds' own droppings, and they reeked offensively in the summer sun. Not only were the nests themselves badly fouled, but the cliff was everywhere splodged with white patches, or held small gutters and channels in which fish-castings and droppings blended together in a noisome, fly-delighting mess. There were times when climbing was difficult because the rocks were slippery with this semi-liquid ooze, or was impossible because the only available handhold had been anointed by innumerable birds in the most disgusting fashion !

The whole time we remained at the colony we were exposed to a ceaseless rain of droppings from the excited mob wheeling above. In a large ternery one also becomes a target for this unpleasantness, and so marked is it in big colonies that there are naturalists who seriously believe that it is a form of " missile warfare " on the part of the birds. It was ten times more pronounced in this kittiwake colony than I have found it at any ternery, and I do not believe that it is an intentional attack, or anything other than a purely reflex action caused by the mental stress of anxiety and fear. With so many birds about one is bound to be hit frequently or alarmed by the " near misses " which spatter the rocks around. As we went about our dirty but important job that morning something of the mystery of the tremendous " bathing parades " which I had watched at Eiði and Saksun, and which are described in Chapter Eleven, was explained, for if this is the way he chooses to live, the kittiwake needs to bathe well, as often as he can !

In spite of the deplorable conditions we did our job assiduously and it has since brought its reward. For one of the juvenile birds caught in the net that morning turned up a little over three months later in Newfoundland, whilst another was reported in 1945 in Norway. Bird-ringing is a twice happy pastime : it provides excellent sport on the cliffs and in the countryside, putting in your way many novel experiences and intimate bird-life glimpses that you would not otherwise enjoy ; and it gives delight also in its results. Some of my most energetic, enjoyable and useful birding has been done with aluminium rings, and on a few occasions the investment has paid good dividends. A few recoveries, as we term the unfortunate birds which happen to die in the right place at the right time, are in a class of their own because they add something of importance to ornithological knowledge and at the same time look well—and even sensational —on a map. Swallows from South Africa and terns from the Gold Coast are cases in point : so also, of course, are trans-atlantic kittiwakes.

There had been others before the Mykines bird, eight or nine in all. Newfoundland is the nodal point in the lives of these young adventurers—for all the American recoveries are of immature birds—and it was at Cape St. John that our own was found in early November, 1942. Two birds summered in Newfoundland waters when a year old : one belonged to the Farne Islands off the Northumberland coast, and the other to the Bull Rock, Co. Cork. Another Farne Islands bird has been reported in its second winter from the coast of Labrador. Still another came aboard a factory-ship which was attending a fishing-fleet in the Davis Strait a hundred miles west of Disko Island, in midsummer of its second year : very likely it had moved northwards with the arctic summer, following its food-supply, from a winter base in the Newfoundland area. One ringed on the Farnes in June 1936 and recovered on the south coast of Greenland in October of the same year may well have been on its way to the vicinity of the Grand Banks. Of three others which have reached Newfoundland, the record journey of a bird from the Murman coast of Russia suggests an important point which our own case supports—that the urge to cross the Atlantic is shared by kittiwakes born along the whole of the western and north-western seaboard of Europe, and is not confined to those from the British area alone.

Ringing has gained us much valuable information : neverthe-less, recoveries are still too few to provide us with true pictures of the movements of this and other species. That a great many kittiwakes cross the Atlantic as young birds to winter in the very profitable area of the Newfoundland Banks is certain ; but that some do not is equally certain as there are recoveries of first and second winter birds from the North Sea area to prove it. Birds of a similar age from Scottish colonies have been picked up at Sandoy and Miðvágur on the western side of the Faeroes, but it is difficult to decide to which category these properly belong. They might have been on their way to the American side via the Faeroes, Iceland and south Greenland, where other recoveries have occurred.

That a large number of transatlantic wanderers spend their immaturity on the American side is more than likely, though they probably disperse northwards and eastwards in summer in pursuit of their food supply, returning to the Newfoundland area in winter time. How long the majority stay we do not know : a Fair Isle bird occurred in Notre Dame Bay in its third autumn, and a Farnes bird was still in this area in its third winter, when it should have been in breeding-condition and seriously thinking of home. Most of the birds probably return to the vicinity of their native colonies after the second winter abroad ; it is unusual, even rare, to see a year-old " tarrock " near a breeding-colony, but on the outlying stacks and skerries of the North Antrim coast my friends Dr. M. N. and the late D. H. Rankin have seen second-year birds in large non-breeding flocks, and this is equally true of at any rate a part of the immense number which passes the summer on the picturesque Góðidrangur and its neighbouring *flesjar* at the western end of Mykineshólmur. Some day the mystery of the movement of kittwakes may be unravelled, but it will not be solved without the continuous ringing of large numbers of young and adult birds.

References to Chapter Five

HAMMERSHAIMB, V. U. (1891) ; HARVIE-BROWN, J. A. and POPHAM, H. L. (1894) ; LEACH, E. P. (1937-44) ; RASMUSSEN, R. (1928) ; WEIHE, A. (1928).

Chapter Six

BIRD-FOWLING

1. Introducing another important folk-industry, the bird-fowling (*page* 143).
2. The relative importance of certain birds, and the manner in which they are prepared as food (*page* 145).
3. Catching puffins with the special fowling-net, and by another method (*page* 149).
4. Some notes on the fowlers' lore (*page* 153).
5. Catching guillemots on the cliffs and at sea (*page* 156).
6. The value of the fulmar, its place on the cliffs, and the tragic consequences of eating its young (*page* 158).
7. Some species of minor importance, the Manx shearwater hunts on Trøllhøvdi and Koltur, and some folk-lore concerning them (*page* 161).
8. The classic performance—the annual hunt for gannets on Mykineshólmur (*page* 164).

I

THE SEA-BIRDS, resorting in their millions to the tremendous coastal cliffs, form one of the most important natural resources of the Faeroes. From time immemorial the people have taken their toll of the guillemots and puffins which live among the ledges and screes, winning fresh meat for their summer food, and large stocks to prepare and set aside for winter use. It is with this great phase of Faeroese summer life, still of vital importance except in the largest towns, that this chapter is concerned.

Most of the fowling-cliffs, the *fuglabjørg* (" bird-mountains "), are on the northern and western coasts of the islands, for it is on the oceanic sides that the cliffs are greatest, often rising sheer from the sea to heights ranging from a few hundred to nearly two thousand feet. The peculiar structure of these cliffs, in which the rocky bands or *hamrar* of the exposed edges of the lava-flows alternate with steep grass-grown slopes and buttresses, is particularly suited to the breeding requirements of these north Atlantic hosts. Often, at the foot of the towering cliffs, heaped-up masses of fallen rocks or talus, known in the Faeroes as *urð*, give shelter to innumerable birds.

The kittiwakes and guillemots whiten the lower ledges of the bare cliff-face, and myriads of puffins, and often Manx shearwaters too, haunt the softer grassy areas where they can burrow freely in the soil. High on the successive *hamrar*, where there are thousands of nooks and crannies with just sufficient vegetation for their liking, the fulmars now breed by the hundred thousand, although little more than a century has elapsed since this species succeeded in establishing itself among the islands. Among the talus, too, are colonies of puffins, and often many fulmars, and in the early days of the season the non-breeding guillemots haunt these gigantic heaps of stones and rubble whilst the nesting birds are busy high on the cliffs.

This great tide of bird-life sweeps in to the cliffs in March and April, and from then onwards until breeding is at an end the islanders gather in this rich harvest by many varied means. Each species, by virtue of its habits or its place on the cliffs, has demanded its own particular treatment and technique, and in different districts different local conditions have created special fowling traditions. No opportunity is missed of exploiting to the full this tremendous population of sea-fowl, and in some districts, where the fulmar has increased enormously during the present century, fowling now goes on throughout the winter as well as during the summer months.

The fowling has its social as well as its economic side—a psychological as well as a culinary value. Indeed, it has been said that its most picturesque form, the annual gannet-hunt on Mykines, is now maintained by the people only for tradition's sake and for its value as a sporting event ; and although this is at present far from the truth, it is perhaps conceivable that the spirit which impels men to this hazardous undertaking almost every year of their adult lives may help to preserve the hunt long after the economic need for it is dead. On the other hand, it might be argued that Faeroemen are busy people, and cannot afford to dissipate their time and energies in unprofitable pursuits, even when the demands of custom are strong. The cessation of parts of the hunt, the April slaughter and the autumn visit to Píkarsdrangur, bear witness to this. Mykines is so isolated in the winter, however, and meat often in such short supply, that the question of whether or not the hunt will survive seems remote. In 1943, for instance, following one of the poorest summers and worst winters for many years, there was so little food on Mykines in the spring that a revival of the April capture of adult birds was essential to the well-being of the community.

Economic needs apart, it cannot be denied that this and other forms of fowling possess that recreational and mentally stimulating quality which belongs to all kinds of hunting and adventurous occupation. Despite the acute discomfort and danger of days and nights on open ledges or in cramped dug-outs in the cliffs, and the loss of life which attends this calling nearly every year, the bird-fowling is universally regarded as the most pleasurable of the summer tasks. In common with the driving and slaughter of the schools of caaing-whales, its importance to Faeroese culture has been in no way diminished by the varied influences of modern civilisation. Both remain economic necessities which have, by virtue of long centuries of usage, become hallmarks of the national life of the people, deeply affecting their folk-lore and customs, and providing outlets for the sporting instinct which is inherent in Faeroese character. And, happily, there is every reason to believe that they will long remain as vividly alive as they are at the present day.

2

The puffin is unquestionably the most valuable item of food among Faeroe seafowl, and in a good year the total catch for all the islands must be in the region of four or five hundred thousand birds. An average summer's harvest on Mykines is reckoned to be about 30,000, but in a good year the toll may well be twice and even three times as much. The average on Nólsoy is about 20,000, on Kunoy 13,000, and on Koltur about 8,000. Large numbers are " fleyged " in Suðuroy and the north islands, and I have been told that Viðareiði on Viðoy claims the record for any one season with no less than 120,000 birds ! A satisfactory day's work on Mykines will yield between 200 and 300 per man, but many more are taken on days when conditions are extremely good. For example, Hr. Abrahamsen's best performance at his *rók* on Tangi amounted to more than 900 birds, on a day of such ideal weather that nearly 10,000 puffins were " fleyged " along the south coast of the isle !

K

During my stay with the Abrahamsens I was given *lundi* for lunch on several occasions, and found it delicious meat—rich and tender, and very tasty. Two birds are considered a sufficient meal, with a good helping of boiled potatoes—which means, in this hospitable land, that at least twice that number are set before you ! I always ate my own brace " Danish fashion," as Hr. Abrahamsen termed it (meaning, I suppose, " in the genteel manner "), without the skin and neck, and in fact consisting only of the breast and the very small amount of meat on the legs. He preferred to eat his in the approved Faeroe fashion, which acknowledges the incontrovertible fact that fingers were made before forks, and demands that the bird shall be cooked in the skin, and appear at the table with all the curious appurtenances of its physiognomy retained. Everything is devoured with gusto, save the larger bones.

With boiled potatoes, thick brown gravy, and rhubarb jam applied liberally as a sweet sauce, a *lundi* lunch is certainly one to write home about. The guillemot and razorbill are often eaten in the same manner, sometimes stuffed with a " pudding " containing currants and raisins. Although there is more meat on a guillemot, it is generally conceded to be of inferior quality to both *álka* and *lundi*.

Most of the puffin catch is salted for the winter. My hosts told me they regularly put down 200 or so for their household of five, and in former times when there were twelve in the family (and before the days when the fulmar was " fleyged ") a thousand birds were required for the winter stock. The guillemot catches too are usually salted down, and although the auks lose much of their flavour when treated in this way, most Faeroe people prefer the meat to the tasteless flesh of the fulmar—whose only recommendation, indeed, appears to be that it is fresh.

Salomonsen puts the annual slaughter of guillemots at some 60,000 birds, but it is certainly very much higher than that. Indeed, any attempt to assess the total casualties in this species, the fulmar and the puffin must be largely a matter of guesswork, since no records are kept. A tremendous number of guillemots' eggs, sometimes up to 80,000 in a week, are gathered on the western cliff of Skúvoy, and also on the fowling-cliffs of Hestur and Stóra Dímun. Most of these are preserved in a " water-glass " mixture of salt water and peat ash, and eggs and potatoes form a staple winter meal on these islands. Many eggs are exported in the season, and in early summer make a colourful show in the shop windows of Tórshavn. I have tried them hard-boiled, and must admit that their chief appeal is to the eye.

The young fulmars are said to have been very good eating when fresh, but again the majority were put in salt for winter use. Fisher and Waterston record that the annual slaughter of young in all the Faeroes amounted latterly to over a hundred thousand birds. Nowadays an average catch of adult birds on Mykines is about 200 per fowler in the winter and spring, which means that between three and four thousand must be taken on that island. Niels Petersen gives the corresponding figure for Nólsoy as 1,000 birds, and several thousand fall annually to the fowlers on Sandoy and Suðuroy.

The number of young gannets killed varies each year, sometimes considerably, as can be seen from the table below ; for the later the date of the hunt (and it cannot take place during inclement weather), the fewer are the birds remaining at the cliff. The best total in recent years was 937 in late August, 1944, and the poorest 395 on September 25th, 1940 ; the average is fairly high, and works out at 818 over the nine years 1936-44. When the adults are taken in spring they are eaten fresh, but the majority of the young birds are salted down. There is much meat on a single bird, and when Jákup Nielsen treated me to a *grásúla* lunch one year I thoroughly enjoyed it, finding the meat very tender, and quite devoid of the objectionable " fishy " flavour I had expected. The Mykines folk say that a gannet is worth as much as a goose, and it can in fact be said that the species does replace the domestic goose on that island.

Young Gannets Killed on Mykineshólmur in Recent Years

Year	Flatidrangur	(Date)	Holm Cliff	(Date)	Total	Remarks
1936	(included)		420	(10.9)	420	
1937	„		640		640	
1938	„		893	(End Aug.)	893	
1939	„		839	„	839	
1940	„		395	(25.9)	395	
1941	„		840		840	210 adults
1942	125	(21.8)	785	(25.8)	910	were taken in
1943	90	(20.8)	560	(10.9)	650	spring 1943 on
1944	165	(18.8)	772	(30.8)	937	Flatidrangur.

The names given to the gannet are varied and interesting. The fully adult bird is usually *súla*, but I have also heard *havsúla* and *hvítsúla*. The immature bird, from its first to third summers when the plumage is a mixture of white and brown, is called *oydisúla* ; the juvenile bird is *grásúla*, and the chick in down is *ompil*.

Of the shag, Landt rather surprisingly says : " The young especially, when taken from the nest, are among the best of the Faeroe seafowl for the table. When properly prepared and roasted, they taste nearly as well as roast hare." I have not tasted either this bird or the fulmar, and somehow think I would have to be tricked into making the experiment, being told the nature of the dish only when the meal was over ! Landt also speaks highly of the flesh of Cormorant, now almost extinct in the Faeroes, and young black guillemot, which was " much sought after " in his day, but is now strictly protected.

Young shearwaters, according to Sverri Patursson, are for the most part salted, being eaten with potatoes and plenty of flavouring in the way of pepper, vinegar and mustard. Formerly the Faeroe barley-bread, *drýlur*, was used instead of potatoes. Some 250 or 300 birds are taken annually on Koltur and Trøllhøvdi, but if you ask how many are caught, the answer is " Nine ! " and a sly smile—for there is an unrepealed law demanding a tithe of one *líri* in every ten ! The young kittiwakes are said to be well-tasted, and are usually fried as a breakfast dish on Mykines. The eggs of the arctic tern are still considered a delicacy in many places, as was the case in Landt's time.

The soft white breast feathers of the auks are extensively used for stuffing pillows and the big quilts which form the only bedcovers in Faeroe houses, and for many years before the war quantities of these feathers were exported to Denmark for a similar purpose. Plucking is a woman's occupation, and a good worker can deal with 300 birds a day. Owing to their very objectionable odour the feathers of the fulmar have no commercial value. At two places only, Kirkjubøur and Sunnbour, the down of the eider-duck is gathered in the large nesting-colonies on the low-lying offshore holms.

3

In considering the methods by which the birds are captured we must deal first of all with the puffin or *lundi*, for he is indubitably the most important of the *fuglabjørg* fraternity. The initial day of his demise, July 2nd, is as important a fixture to the Faeroeman as August 12th is to the sportsmen of Britain. It appears in the local calendar as Fyrstifleygidagur, and from then onwards until the end of the following month, when the birds begin to desert the cliffs, fowling with the *fleyg* is in full swing. This type of fowling begins so late in the season because the greater part of the non-breeding stock which is victimised does not resort regularly to the land until breeding is at its height. These birds do have their " land-coming days " in the early part of the season, but they are irregular and may even be infrequent : on some days thousands are to be seen in the vicinity of the cliffs, and then for many days together they go fishing far out to sea.

The instrument used in their destruction is a large triangular net (see page 150) called *fleyg*, fastened to a pair of ash supports which are bound to the end of a ten-foot pole called *fleygastong*. When assembled it looks like an enlarged lacrosse racquet. This " fleyging " (as we shall call it, for convenience's sake) is a skilled art requiring a special knowledge, the accumulated mental capital of generations of fowlers ; it calls for a high standard of co-ordination of hand and eye, strength of arm and wrist, and a well-nigh perfect sense of balance. The *fleygastong* is a heavy instrument, and an awkward one to wield, and without these accomplishments one can never hope to become expert at this fascinating game. This much I know from a brief and undistin-guished career, although I have the consolation that the species I chose for my initiation, namely arctic tern and Leach's petrel, are not by any means the easiest to catch. With me the glamour of the occasion outweighed economic necessity, so I forfeited the slender prospect of success which might have attended the choice of the commonplace puffin.

The pole is held by closing one hand low down near the end, and the other a comfortable arm's-reach higher up. Guiding the implement with the uppermost hand, and using the lower one as a steadying influence, the fowler sweeps the net upwards in a

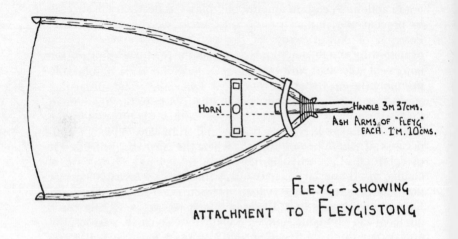

HORN

HANDLE 3M 37CMS.

ASH ARMS OF "FLEYG"
EACH. 1'M. 10CMS.

FLEYG - SHOWING
ATTACHMENT TO FLEYGISTONG

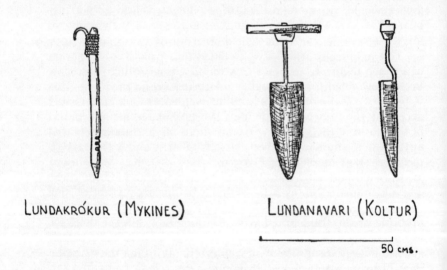

LUNDAKRÓKUR (MYKINES)

LUNDANAVARI (KOLTUR)

50 CMS.

FOWLING IMPLEMENTS.

wide arc, for it must rest inconspicuously on the ground when not in action. A certain amount of " play " is necessary in striking to prevent the impact of the bird breaking the mesh. P. F. Petersen of Nólsoy wrote of the puffin's inquisitiveness being exploited by the fowlers, for it is a general practice to set up the bodies of the first few victims on a pole, or display them prominently on a rock, to serve as a lure.

What are the golden rules of this intricate game ? First among them, I was told on Mykines, is that you must never shift the site of a " fleyging " place or *rók*. You might imagine that an occasional change would be all to the good, ensuring less exploitation of a particular haunt, and giving the colony there a chance to recuperate. The truth is that a colony has never any need to replenish its strength, because the old wisdom of the Faeroe fowlers sees to it that the vital part of the population— namely the breeding-birds—remains untouched. Any bird approaching the land with orderly rows of small fish fringing its coloured bill is allowed to go by unmolested, for a good fowler would no more dream of slaying a *sildberi* (" herring-bearer ") than a rider to hounds would dream of shooting his fox.

You might also imagine that the puffins would become wary of a much-used *rók*, and that catches would accordingly decrease unless new ground were sought. This is not so : the explanation is perhaps psychological, the puffins calmly and philosophically accepting the presence of the man and his net as part and parcel of the world of the puffinry. Apparently they are not aware that anything is amiss with their environment until some radical piece of stage-management changes it, upsetting the familiar scene, as when a man begins to " fleyg " in an unaccustomed place. The older fowlers know how wary the puffin can be under such conditions, and so they impress upon their sons the necessity for profiting by this trait. So it is that the forty or fifty *røkur* along the south coast of the island have been in constant use for many generations—so long that men cannot say how deep into the past their history goes.

As with all outdoor pursuits, wind and weather play an important part in " fleyging." Puffins, for instance, are much fewer at land on a day following heavy rain (no matter how fine a day it may be), for wet weather sends the immature birds far out to sea and some days may pass before they return to the cliffs. The great majority of the catching-places on Mykines lie along the south coast, because the prevailing winds in summer are from southerly points, and the best winds are those blowing lightly at an angle to the coast. A breeze blowing directly offshore is no good at all, for the birds then tend to fly straight inshore instead of laterally across the " fleyging " site. Nor are exceptionally warm, still days favourable to " fleyging," for the immature birds are then lazy and keep much to the land, standing about on the rocks and brows. The fowlers call them *setralundar*, " sitting-puffins."

During my week's holiday on Mykines in 1942 the weather was unsatisfactory for " fleyging " because the wind was mainly from the north, and therefore directly offshore at the majority of the *røkur*. All the catches were very poor except at Núgvunes a headland in the extreme east of the island where the wind was favourable to the lie of the land. On August 3rd, for instance, two hundred birds were taken there, whilst two other parties gave considerable time to catching six and fourteen birds respectively at two colonies on the south coast. When the wind changed to the south-east on August 6th my host's son and a friend succeeded in taking 240 in a day's fowling at Tangi midway along the southern shore. Owing to the distance of some of the catching-places from the village the small and sturdy ponies are used to carry the birds, for they can easily cope with a day's catch, whereas a man's load over a long distance is not more than a hundred or so.

A less hazardous though more toilsome method of catching *lundar* is practised on Mykines in the spring, when a number of adult birds and newly-laid eggs are collected from the Daliđ and Lambi puffinries. A special instrument called *lundakrókur* (see page 150) or " puffin-crook " is used for this work, which is known as *draga* or *dráttrar lundar*—" drawing puffins." It is a wooden stick about two feet in length with an iron hook, usually a bent six-inch nail, at the business end, and the other end bevelled to form a *grev* for digging. On the reverse of the grip three or four deep notches are scored in the wood so that when groping at arm's-length in the darkness of a tunnel the fowler can tell by the feel of the grip which way the hook is pointing, and therefore whether or not his quarry is on the effective side of it. Long burrows are attacked by sinking a shaft to meet the tunnel some three feet from the entrance, and by working with the *lundakrókur* from the new hole. These shafts are carefully filled in afterwards so that the burrow will be of service to another pair.

It is not likely that this type of fowling, since it takes place on one or two days only at the beginning of the season, harms the breeding potential of large colonies to any extent, although P. F. Petersen records that the method was discontinued on Nólsoy in the middle of the last century because it was thought to be impairing the strength of the colonies there. Users of the " puffin-crook " tie a piece of cord, *vevlingur*, round the sleeves of their jerseys to prevent the intrusion of too much dirt and fouled soil—for the puffin's burrow would certainly not inspire enthusiasm in a Brighter Homes Exhibition ! The birds' necks are broken and their heads are slipped under a line, *beltisgyrdi*, encircling the fowler's waist, and at the end of the day the men return to the village with their girdles providing a picturesque and exotic skirt. Normally, on Nólsoy and other islands, the day's catch is carried home on the back, the load being supported by a cloth head-band.

4

There is a prolific folk-lore concerning the sea-birds, especially those which provide food ; I have mentioned something of the fowlers' lore with regard to the puffin, and here propose to consider further items which, based as they are on long experience, may fairly claim the serious attention of the ornithologist as well as the student of folk-culture. The fowlers' belief that the puffins do not begin to breed until they are at least four years old may well be true enough, and the statement made to me on Mykines that the first-summer birds do not come to land at all is borne out by the observations of Niels Fr. Petersen, a fowler-ornithologist, on Nólsoy. Out of nearly a hundred birds which he has ringed as young, he has " fleyged " seventeen at their native colonies in the second and subsequent seasons, but none in the first year. The fowlers believe that the puffin does not mate until its third summer, in which is begun the excavation of the nesting-burrow. This is finished in the following season, and the first egg may then appear.

One may well ask how these men are able to compute the age of a puffin. Abraham Abrahamsen surprised me by claiming that he could estimate a bird's age, with a year's margin of error either way after the fifth season, up to the age of ten or twelve (when, incidentally, a puffin is still young). He demonstrated with

examples taken at random from one of Jákup Nielsen's " bags "
and although I now think I could age puffins fairly accurately
up to the third or fourth year, I would not care to venture an
opinion beyond that. The shape of the beak, the number and
depth of the transverse ridges and grooves, and the amount of
red give the chief clues ; and I can well appreciate that through
long familiarity with the birds the feat may be possible—unless,
of course, there is considerable individual variation between
birds of the same age.

Hr. Abrahamsen told me that a puffin, once the first five
dangerous years are past, might live to the ripe old age of sixty
years ! He based this statement on observation of an albino
bird which came every year to the " fleyging " place at Tangi
during his father's time and his own active fowling days.
During its last ten years or so it was never seen to come ashore—
having doubtless ceased to be capable of breeding—although
warm, sunny weather attracted it to the vicinity of the cliffs.
Cold weather, on the other hand, attracts a different kind of
puffin, one which is known to the fowlers as *grønlandslundi*, and
is a distinctly bigger bird than the one breeding in the Faeroes.
Ornithologists recognise it as the northern race of this species,
inhabiting Greenland, north Iceland and north Norway—areas
in which Faeroe fishermen (whose taste for *lundi* goes with them
on their fishing-trips) are familiar with it too. A few of these
northern birds are always captured in the nets on Mykines and
Nólsoy, and doubtless other islands, in bad summers when the
wind is northerly and cold. Here again, Petersen has shown me
irrefutable proof that the surmise of the fowlers is correct, and in
1945, when an unusually large number of *grønlandslundi* were
caught on Nólsoy, I was able to examine specimens whose
measurements were well within the range for arctic birds. Their
occurrence on the Faeroe cliffs is most interesting : probably
their northward migration is delayed, or stops short, in backward
seasons in this region of plenty and they merely " summer "
among the local puffins, without breeding.

I do not know that the next item would pass muster with the
folk-lorist or the ornithologist, but it is worth telling. A young
sea-bird—puffin, guillemot or razorbill—is called *pisa*. A man
who has gone to a party or dance well provided, and who desires
to sneak out of the room to sample the contents of his flask, will
make the excuse that there is a little *pisa* waiting to see him at
the door !

The arctic-skua is known to the Faeroese as *kjógvi*, " the thief," because of his reprehensible habit of pursuing kittiwakes and other weaker birds and forcing them to disgorge their last meal, which he neatly intercepts as it falls towards the sea. He comes to the isles on April 15th, the day after the puffin, who is always due on Summarmáladagur. The puffin is there said to be *klasseksdrongur* to the skua—in other words, his luggage-boy. The story adds, very neatly, that *kjógvi* rewards his faithful servant by snatching the food out of his mouth !

The puffins leave the land after breeding, usually towards the end of September, to pass the winter far out on the open sea. This fact too has found its way into the folk-lore, and any event deemed to be so unlikely as to appear almost incredible is said to be " sum lundi a jólanátt,"—as rare as a puffin on Christmas night !

The spring fowling on Mykines and other places has given rise to the widely held belief that there are seven puffins to every nest—which means that it is possible in the early spring to kill up to seven birds from the one burrow before the egg is deserted. It may well be that the males are able to draw on a pool of newly-matured and unmated females for replacements, for such a pool certainly exists, if the number of non-breeders in the catches later on is a criterion. The fact that seven is a magical number (and appears as such in other Faeroese folk-lore) at once raises suspicion, but essentially the underlying theory is probably sound enough, though there can surely be no restriction on the number of birds involved. (There may well be an upper limit to the puffin's patience, however !) It is said that the remaining adult will not mate again if one of the pair is killed after the youngster has hatched—one of the reasons why no worthy fowler will slay a *sildberi* or food-carrying bird.

That the puffin's status is not impaired by the constant drain on its numbers is shown by the fact that in many districts the birds can be induced to occupy new ground, suggesting that many colonies are overcrowded. On Koltur I was shown an instrument called *lundanavari* (page 150) which the people use for this purpose : it is a concave wrought-iron scoop, something like an elongated garden trowel, and is pushed into the earth and twisted round several times so that a deep hollow is excavated. These partly dug burrows are a great attraction to house-hunting puffins in the spring, saving them the labour of driving a tunnel-entrance through the root-bound turf. I have been told of a man who built a stone wall at the clifftop, leaving holes at intervals along its base, and had a minor puffinry there the next year ! The puffin is the only species of the *fuglabjørg* which will respond to " farming " of this kind.

Formerly many birds were taken at sea with the gun during the early days of the season, but under a special law passed by the Løgting on November 25th, 1943, the shooting of this species is no longer permitted.

5

The guillemot, *lomvigi*, is victimised chiefly on the Dímunar and Skúvoy, and on the north-west coast of Streymoy in the neighbourhood of Vestmanna and Saksun. Early in the summer the immature birds, called *hellufuglar*, are " fleyged " from boats as they fly to and from the foot of the cliffs. When the breeding season is well advanced these non-breeders move higher up the cliffs and are then " flegyed " by fowlers who are lowered in rope slings. The first method is known as *omanfleyg*, and the second *fygling*.

Fowlers indulging in the latter task often spend several days working the cliff-face for their prey—truly, to borrow from Shakespeare, a " dangerous trade." Lítla Dímun, which belongs to the outfield of Hvalbøur, is visited by men from that village who take water and provisions and remain on the island for a fortnight or so, boats coming out daily from Hvalbøur when the weather permits to collect the catch thrown down into the sea by the fowlers. These bird-catchers must sometimes endure the Troglodyte life for weeks, for on this marine mountain-top there are no dwellings, and those who exploit its rich store of birds must needs live as they live, converting a small cavern into a cramped and uncomfortable nest, where they sleep on rough beds, and cook a portion of the day's catch on an evil-smelling oil-stove whose fumes must make their retreat an insufferably stuffy place. Dr. S. Hansen has told me that when collecting eggs on the precipitous western cliff of Skúvoy members of the party have to spend each night roped together on the open ledges, one man remaining awake to watch over the safety of the others.

Some twenty years ago a method of snaring guillemots and razorbills at sea was introduced (or rather, re-introduced) from

Iceland, and is practised by the people of Sandur and the north Suðuroy settlements in the vicinity of Skúvoy and the Dímunar, and to a less extent by the inhabitants of Viðoy and Borðoy in the north islands. Large boards (some six or seven feet long, and three or four feet wide), on which fifty or more loops of plaited horsehair are arranged, and at one end of which a stuffed skin is mounted on a stiff wire, are floated on the water and visited from time to time by the boats. The guillemots and their relatives the razorbills are attracted to the boards by the lure, and after paying their respects to this inanimate friend become ensnared in the loops when they attempt to take their leave., A boat will usually have ten such boards, and will release five and allow them to float away on the tide whilst the remaining five are being prepared. Then these are released together, and thereafter each group is visited in turn to remove the victims and reset the loops.

Landt records that the fowlers experimented with this method at the end of the eighteenth century, but that the return was considered too poor for the amount of labour involved. Better success seems to have attended the reintroduction, for on a good day a boat can capture up to five or six hundred birds by this method. It is an interesting reflection on the jealousy with which bird-fowling rights are guarded that when *at snara* was first tried by the boats from Sandur, off the cliffs of Skúvoy, the inhabitants of that island protested strongly, and even made representations to the Løgting to get this unwarrantable trespass stopped. Eventually, however, they took the line of least resistance, and began to compete in the trade themselves !

Young guillemots are hunted when they leave the ledges and gather in large companies on the sea below. North of Vestmanna several boats co-operate in herding these flocks together, driving them into a narrow inlet. In this confined space many of the young can be despatched—for they are unable to fly—by a well-directed stone *kast* attached to a fishing line. Sometimes more than a thousand are slaughtered in this manner in a day.

Many guillemots and razorbills are shot at sea in the spring, especially by people from settlements which have no fowling-cliffs, such as Tórshavn and Tvøroyri. A large landing-net is often used to secure the victims. The success of a day's shoot depends largely on the weather : on a fine day the birds are much on the wing and provide difficult and expensive targets, but in calm and misty weather they keep to the water and the discharge of a single barrel will often account for many birds. Shooting within two sea-miles of the fowling-cliffs must cease by March 15th, but it continues outside this limit throughout the summer months.

A bird of the same family as the guillemot and razorbill, and which formerly had a minor food value, was the garefowl or great auk. It has been extinct since 1844, when the last two known birds were killed on Eldey, off Iceland, but for many years before that date it must have been—at most—an exceedingly scarce visitor to the Faeroes. Feilden investigated its local history, but the facts he collated are few and give us little definite information as to the bird's status. So far as I am aware, it is not absolutely certain that the garefowl ever bred among the islands, though Svabo records the capture of a female on Fugloy which was found on dissection to contain a well-formed egg. Being flightless, and clumsy in its movements on land, few places on the coast could have suited its needs, for Faeroe topography very seldom provides the low flat rocks or shelves close to the water up which the great auks could scramble to lay and brood their eggs. Landt, however, speaks of them " climbing up the low rocks," and we know they were sometimes caught by the fowlers when resorting with the *hellufuglar* to the talus at the foot of the cliffs. So perhaps, on circumstantial evidence, the great auk should be given the benefit of the doubt.

Feilden interviewed an old, blind man, Jan Hansen, on Skúvoy in 1872, who claimed to have killed a garefowl on the rocks of Stóra Dímun on July 1st, 1808—the last Faeroe bird for which there is a record. He said it weighed nine Danish pounds, which would be about ten pounds by our reckoning, and at the division of the birds was deemed to be of equal value with six guillemots. Two notable historians, Olaus Wormius and Graba, kept Faeroe captured garefowls as pets—what would an ornithologist give for such an opportunity to-day !

6

The fulmar is taken in the *fleyg* on most of the islands throughout the winter and spring, a recent occupation dating back only twenty years or so. The adults leave the cliffs after breeding, but are back again by the end of November, and are hunted from then onwards to the beginning of May. I was told on Sandoy that there are special " fleyging " places, as for the puffin, but on Mykines, where practically all the fulmar catching takes place along the densely populated north coast (the prevailing winds during this season being from the northerly quarter) a special *rók* is not used. Those who have watched fulmars as they plane with smooth, effortless grace past the cliffs will know what an insatiable curiosity they have, and that time after time the birds will sweep past quite close on rigid wings, their eyes fixed inquisitively on the watcher. The fowlers also know this trait, and take good advantage of it : here, this inquisitiveness proves his undoing, and the fulmar does not often get a second chance to satisfy his craving to gaze.

Formerly immense numbers of the young birds were taken in the late summer, for when the young are fully-feathered they leave the nests and gather on the sea at the foot of the cliffs. They are unable to fly at this stage of their lives, and they were captured from rowing-boats, being lifted out of the water in the same landing-net that is used for retrieving guillemots and razorbills slain by the gun. At least three men were required to a boat, one to row, one to wield the net, and the third to tie cord round the necks of the captured birds—for the fulmar has an objectionable habit of spitting an evil-smelling stream of oil at its captor. By rowing the boat against the stream, which carried the young birds along with it, splendid catches could be made. The young birds quickly disperse on the tides and are borne many miles out to sea, so that their capture in large numbers was only possible for a few days in each year, usually from August 20th to about the end of the month.

The fulmar has been blamed for the expulsion of thousands of guillemots from the breeding-ledges on Skúvoy and Stóra Dímun, and its rapid spread is said to have had a deleterious effect on the sea-fowl generally in the Faeroes. I fancy, however, that this effect has been much exaggerated. In north Streymoy and on Koltur and Mykines the fulmar shows a distinct preference for rocky scarps with a good deal of scattered vegetation, where the birds sit in grassy alcoves at some height above the sea. Comparatively few inhabit the open ledges of the naked cliff-face immediately overlooking the sea, the only habitat which suits the guillemot, razorbill and kittiwake. The species most frequently found in association with the fulmar is the puffin, but as this is able to burrow in the soft ground the fulmar cannot be said to be a competitor for nesting-sites—except, perhaps, in the very restricted *urð* habitat on Nólsoy and elsewhere, where both use cavities in the fallen rocks or talus at the foot of the cliffs. The newcomer, indeed, seems to have stepped into a ready-made and at the time vacant ecological niche—a factor which, I have no doubt, has very materially assisted the tremendous rate of its spread since it began to colonise the islands less than a century ago.

There seems to be no reason why the fulmar should not continue to increase in numbers and in the extent of its breeding-ground. The general topography of the cliffs, with their regular bands of *hamrar* carrying a fairly luxuriant vegetation, and extending upwards to a great height, provide the fulmar with a potential nesting-area far more extensive than that enjoyed by any other coastal species. As illustrations of the possibilities of this environment, fulmars are nesting in the mountain *hamrar* above the lake at Saksun, fully a mile from the coast, and at Kirkjubøur and Mykines they breed in similar situations over-looking the cultivated fields. I have seen them planing past the dark rocks just below the summit of Stiðjafjall, over a mile inland from the mouth of Norðradalur and at a height of 450-500 metres ; whilst to the north of Núgvan at least as far as Skaelings-fjall the species is common in the hillside *hamrar* several hundred yards away from the sea.

For a time the fowling of young fulmars had tragic conse-quences, and it has been prohibited by law since 1936, when an outbreak of psittacosis in the community was traced to these birds. The illness first appeared in Suðuroy in 1933, and its nature and origin baffled investigation, until the mystery was finally solved through the work of Dr. Rasmussen of Eiði. In the early days the affliction was known as *septembursjúka*, because it usually appeared in that month, especially at haymaking time, to which occupation it was thought to be related. A number of the 165 recorded cases proved fatal : for the most part it was the women who were affected, doubtless because the task of plucking and salting the young birds fell to them. The disease appears to be communicated to human beings only by the young and the adults are apparently immune. It is popularly thought that the fulmar first contracted this disease by inquisitively meddling with parrot victims of psittacosis jettisoned at sea by a ship carrying a cargo of pets from South America to Europe !

(*Top*) Guillemots on a crowded ledge

(*Bottom*) Fowler with *fleygustong*

Mykines—the north coast

7

It is curious in view of its popularity in the Westmann Islands, that the kittiwake is never taken in the *fleyg* in the Faeroes, where it is in many places a very abundant bird. According to Landt this method of capturing the adults was used to some extent in the late eighteenth century, but it must have been discontinued long ago. On Mykines, and doubtless some other islands, the fledglings have a minor food value, but are only taken from their nests on days when the weather is too bad to permit of more important work being done. I have been told that in a bad season, however, when other food is scarce, as many as a thousand young may be taken on Mykines. The eggs provide a small food-crop in the early summer. At Sandur numbers of adults are shot from a hilltop over which the flocks from Skúvoy pass throughout the day when on their way to bathe in Sandsvatn. Niels Petersen has told me that in his boyhood days he and his playmates sometimes captured young kittiwakes in a horsehair noose at the end of a fishing line which they dangled over the cliff; but this juvenile fowling was the outcome of a desire to have birds for pets rather than bodies for the pot. Kittiwake chicks are still great favourites in this respect among Faeroe children.

Sometimes in the winter, herring-gulls and the larger glaucous-gulls are shot at sea to provide fresh meat, and I have seen successful hunters walking through Tórshavn with as many as half a dozen slung over their shoulders. The larger gulls, however, have but little food-value, considering their abundance in the islands. A small number of eggs of the lesser blackback are taken at some places, and the fat grey-brown youngsters are shot in the late summer when they begin to wander away from the breeding colonies. When Faeroemen go fishing in Greenland and Iceland waters they vary their diet with the fine meat of the greater blackback and glaucous gulls—the former a species they hardly ever bother to catch at home.

Another bird which was formerly much in demand, but is now fully protected because the fowling (and latterly the " bill-tax ") damaged its status so severely, is the bonxie or great skua. To-day there remain only a few small colonies and scattered pairs, but when the islands were first settled by the Norsemen the species was so abundant that one island, Skúvoy, and a number of hill

L

districts were named after it. Again, only the well-grown, well-fed youngsters were victimised, being knocked down with a stick just before they were strong enough to fly, and it is said that 6,000 a year were taken on Skúvoy alone. Many were pinioned and kept about the houses, being fed on kitchen scraps until they had fattened nicely for the table.

Shags are sometimes taken outside the breeding season on Mykines and other islands by men who go down to their roosting-rocks at night, and catch the birds whilst they are asleep. Juveniles are obtained in the same way when fully-fledged, and probably such methods were also used in capturing the cormorant before this species became a rarity among the islands. The shag is a notorious sleepyhead, as the following charming story shows. The shag, *skarvur*, and eider-duck, *aeða*, were originally con-testants for the right to use down in making their nests, and they agreed that the right should belong to the one who was first to see the sun rise over the horizon. The shag was overconfident of victory, because of her long neck, and sat up all night, quivering with excitement and craning her neck upwards so as to glimpse the sun's rim a split-second before her rival. The eider was wiser, and, knowing there were several hours to go before the dawn, put her head beneath her wing and went to sleep. As time wore on *skarvur* grew drowsier, and when at length the first faint gleam of the false dawn silvered the distant waves she croaked excitedly, " Dagur í havi, dagur í havi ! " The eider was at once awake and alert, watching for the sun, but before it tipped the horizon the tired shag, still muttering " Day in the sea ! " fell fast asleep. If you visit the Faeroes and hear the expression " Skarvur tunguleysur ! " you may be sure that the speaker knows this story well, for it is an epithet in common usage for those who are unable to keep a confidence.

In the early autumn the Kirkjubøur people go to Trøllhøvdi, an islet at the northern tip of Sandoy belonging to their outfield, for the dual purpose of haymaking by day and taking the young of the Manx shearwater by night. Nowadays an electric torch is used to dazzle the full-grown young as they sit outside their burrows trying to pluck up courage for their journey to the sea, for the early life-history of this bird is very much the same as that of the young puffin. Sometimes they are hunted in the day-time by sinking a shaft to the nesting-chamber, but this is a tire-some business as the opening must always be filled in carefully afterwards, or the birds will seek a new burrow in the following season.

Years ago these *lírar* were drawn from their holes by means of an iron hook similar to the *lundakrókur* used in the spring puffin-fowling on Mykines. Although discontinued on Trøllhøvdi this practice is still in vogue on Koltur, where the shearwater's habitat on shelving grassy slopes half-way down the precipitous cliffs renders night-work impracticable. The men descend the cliff to these steep slopes on ropes which are put in position at the beginning of the season, fastened to long wooden pins driven into the turf at the clifftop, and removed when fowling is at an end. Only the young of the year are taken, and as these when fully fledged are indistinguishable from the adults in plumage, the fowlers ascertain the bird's age by pulling out a tail feather. If they are able to squeeze a drop of blood out of the end of the quill, the bird is killed ; if no blood appears, it is a sure sign of maturity, and the bird is set free.

Andrias Weihe records that in olden times, before setting out on the hunt for *lírar*, the men would recite a traditional verse in the belief that by doing so they would ensure an excellent catch. A simple translation of it is :

" In the cliff your grey ones are lying warm and fat,
Often we talk about you as we stand in the hagard,
We are coming now to take and not to buy,
And you must not run from us into your burrows."

This hunt was (and still is at Kirkjubøur) regarded as a festival, and always took place on August 24th, which is called Líradagur. Weihe adds that each of the fowlers kept a single bird, and the remainder were *felagsogn* and were shared among the men in proportion to the value of their holdings.

The Manx shearwater took its name, incidentally, from the fact that a tremendous colony once existed on the Calf of Man. It must have been one of the biggest colonies that the world has known, and annually some three to four thousand young were drawn from their holes by means of an iron hook which must have been very similar to the *lundakrókur*. Many were exported to fashionable English epicures, including the then Lord of Man, the Earl of Derby, and they were considered a great luxury when prepared with wines and spices. In the Island the peasant people as well as the high officials ate them, usually with potatoes, and in the records the fowlers themselves (who must have been veritable paragons of virtue !) are shown as having purchased birds. This tremendous " puffinry " was exterminated at the end of the eighteenth century by rats which got ashore from a Russian vessel wrecked in the Calf Sound. Luckily the brown rat, as much a curse to endemic faunas as to civilisation, is still absent from most of the smaller Faeroe islands, Koltur, Mykines, Trøllhøvdi, Skúvoy and Stóra Dímun among them, so that the *skrápur* and its offspring should flourish in peace. In fact, the rat may be the only factor ever to interfere with the great and varied bird-harvest in the islands, for experience on the Calf of Man has shown that not even the strong-billed puffin can fight against the menace for very long.

8

The only gannetry in the Faeroes is situated on Mykineshól-mur : the colony is very likely older than 1500, when the gannet was first mentioned in the bird-ballad " Fuglakvaeði," and it is also probable that it has been a source of food to the people of Mykines at least from mediæval times. There are not more than twenty gannetries of any size in the world and this is one of the smallest, its numbers being less than one per cent of the estimated world population, which was put at about 167,000 breeding-birds in Fisher's and Vevers's survey of the known colonies in 1939.

Only at two other breeding stations, Sula Sgeir in the Outer Hebrides and Súlnasker in the Westmann Islands, are the birds captured for food. Since each of these " gannet-skerries " must be approached in open boats from the nearest inhabited islands, Lewis and Heimay respectively, the regularity and success with which they are visited depend largely on sea and weather conditions, and in some years it is not possible to land on the stacks during the period when the slaughter should take place. The hunt on Mykineshólmur is much less at the mercy of the elements, and although adverse weather may cause a postpone-ment or add to the difficulties of the hunt, it is in fact an annual event.

The majority of the gannets have their nests on a fairly wide shelf which runs along the precipitous north face of the holm, and on the two offshore stacks Flatidrangur and Píkarsdrangur, which are 81 and 104 feet high respectively, and stand immediately to the west of Bóliđ, the south-west point of the holm, where there is also a small station. A considerable number breed in scattered groups on small ledges above the level of the main shelf, and some of these are fairly close to the top of the three hundred feet cliff. There is also a small and very recent extension of the colony on the north-western corner of Mykines itself.

Only the big shelf and the larger subsidiary ledges, in addition to Flatidrangur, are now visited by the fowlers. They go down the cliff at night, when the gannets are asleep. Because the shelf is not continuous, two men are lowered at each of several points, the eldest enjoying the somewhat dubious privilege of being the first to descend. About two or three in the morning the last fowlers, three in number in this case, are let down to the biggest section underneath the lighthouse at the western end of the holm. The men slip from the rope as soon as they reach the shelf and stalk about quietly, capturing the sleeping gannets and wringing their necks. Although the gannet is a sound sleeper a number are always awakened by this activity, but the alarm is only local and in any event the grey-brown juveniles, which are the only ones taken, are extremely loath to fly away. All unfledged young and adult birds are passed by. The bodies are left where they lie, and when the ledge has supplied the needs of the fowlers they settle down as comfortably as they can to wait for daybreak.

Soon after dawn, if the weather is good, a boat puts out from the landing-place and goes round the holm and under the north cliff. The men on the shelf throw their booty into the sea, whence the boatmen collect it. If the weather is too bad to permit safe navigation beneath the cliff the catch is gathered together and hauled to the clifftop by rope—often a lengthy and difficult business. Finally, after a stay of five or six hours on the ledges, the climbers rope up and return to the top.

Years ago the whole of a preceding day was devoted to catching the juvenile gannets on Flatidrangur and Píkarsdrangur : the first, which can be climbed from the sea, is still visited each autumn and yields between a hundred and a hundred and fifty birds. Six men form a ring round the flat summit of the rock and work towards the centre, driving the fully-fledged young before them and thus minimising the number which escape by flight. The taller stack is unscalable and is no longer visited : until ten years or so ago it was reached by casting a fishing-line over the top of the rock from the nearest and giddiest point of the holm, the razor-edged Bóliđ, to a party of men put ashore on the talus at the foot of the stack. A rope was then drawn over Píkarsdrangur by means of the line, and was held fast by the men on Bólið whilst three fowlers ascended.

Until about 1938 the same tactics as are used in catching the young in the late summer were also employed in April in taking a proportion of the adult birds, and usually from two to three hundred were killed. This part of the hunt was revived in 1943 when food was short on Mykines in the spring, and 210 birds were killed. In former times, before the suspension bridge was built across Hólmgjógv, the party had to cross the chasm on a ropeway, and they took several days' provisions with them in case a deterioration of the weather should delay their return. There are the remains of a stone hut near the south-east corner of the holm, in whose crumbling walls the storm petrels now sing at twilight, which was their headquarters when the men were marooned.

My host on Mykines told me that a young man of sixteen years is considered mature enough to go with the hunting-party to the holm, but in his first year he is not allowed to go down the cliff. Before descending, it is the custom to eat *skerpikjøt* cut from the dried mutton which is taken to the holm to provide refreshment for the party. " You should always eat *skerpikjøt*," Abrahamsen says, " When there is strong work to do," and many a Faeroeman will echo those words !

On the afternoon when we ringed the gannets, and I was safely perched on the cliff taking photographs of Sofus at work below me, I could not but admire the courage and endurance of the men who annually perform this remarkable feat. Until you have seen this towering wall of the holm, with only the main ledges some two hundred feet down to break up its vertical face, you cannot be expected to appreciate the real nature of this exploit. In daylight the descent would be formidable enough : the men who dangle their way down to those shelves in total darkness and move about unroped on the slippery rock have more than ordinary physical fitness and courage. Most of them have done it many times since they turned the age of seventeen, and regard it as one of the greatest moments in the summer routine. Perhaps it is indeed the greatest moment, a co-operative endeavour which binds the villagers more closely than ever in friendship and neighbourliness, and rightly an occasion for joy and quiet festivity when the hunters return, and the worry and apprehension of their womenfolk is dispelled. The feat is a compliment to the healthy and vigorous outdoor life these people lead, and to the intelligence and care they bring to this unique task. It is no daredevil escapade, but a serious job of work, and there is proof of this in what is perhaps the most remarkable fact of all—that no man of Mykines has lost his life, or sustained severe injury, at any gannet-hunt within living memory.

In Mykines, I may say, there is an air of humble pride when they tell you of this splendid record.

References to Chapter Six

FEILDEN, H. W. (1872) ; FISHER, J. and VEVERS, H. G. (1943) ; FISHER, J. and WATERSTON, G. (1941) ; HAMMER-SHAIMB, V. U. (1891) ; LANDT, J. (1810) ; PETERSEN, P. F. in ANDERSEN, K. (1899-1902) ; SALOMONSEN, F. (1935) ; SVABO, J. C. (1781-82) ; VEVERS, H. G. and EVANS, F. C. (1938) ; WEIHE, A. (1928) ; WILLIAMSON, K. (1945a and 1946b).

Chapter Seven

PORTRAIT OF AN ISLAND (2)

1. We arrive at Mykines in time for a double wedding and an old-fashioned dance (*page* 168).
2. We take a stroll in the outfield to Kálvadalur and the summit of the isle, observing the birds by the way (*page* 172).
3. We learn about the island's commonwealth and the way the people share its blessings (*page* 177).
4. We spend an amazing night among the petrels on the holm (*page* 180).
5. We travel hopefully, and in some discomfort, back to the capital (*page* 185).

I

I ARRIVED at Mykines in 1943 just in time for a party. I had an idea that something of the sort might be in the air, for the most distinguished of the passengers (until the boat began to rock in the tideway) was the *prestur* from Miðvágur. This was his second trip to Mykines that year, and during his short time ashore he was a very busy man. Mykines had saved up, pending his arrival, a couple of christenings and a double wedding.

Harra Abrahamsen met the parson at the landing-place, and whisked him away to his plum-coloured house below the church. I spotted Nielsen, my friend of the previous year, among those who had come down to watch the arrival of the boat, and stayed for a few minutes to converse with him. When I arrived at the house the *prestur* had already put on his vestments ; and, whilst enjoying the coffee and cakes which Frú Abrahamsen had set before him, he received the lucky people whose lives he was to bring together, and completed the official documents essential to the proper performance of this office. Then he rushed off to the church to do the christenings, and immediately afterwards joined the two happy couples in marriage.

I would have attended the weddings had not the speed at which events moved in this usually easy-going land taken me

completely by surprise. I had no idea then that the parson had
asked the master of the post-boat to wait for him, fully intending
to perform his several duties in the short space of an hour and a
half. By six o'clock his task was done, his vestments and papers
were packed away, and he said " Farvæl ! " In many respects
life in the Faeroes may be liesurely, but there are times when I
think even the Americans would find it hard to move faster !

I did not fully realise the state of affairs until the wedded
couples left the church to the exultant clanging of the bell, and
walked arm in arm through the village at the head of a procession
of relatives and guests. As I watched them from the window my
first thought, curiously, concerned woman's dress. Here we were,
in an utterly remote corner of the earth, far enough removed
(one would have thought) from the influences of fashion and
fashionable behaviour, and yet these two charming young brides
in their blue silk gowns and trailing lace veils would have created
a stir of admiration even in Westminster. My women readers
will say, " Well, of course !—what else does he expect ? Is not
her wedding-day the one day in her life . . ." and so on, and
doubtless they are right. But it seemed to me to be yet another
instance of the curious but happy mingling of modernity and
old tradition in the outlook of these isolated folk—a quality of no
small account in the fine character of their life and manners.

This lovely vision of young womanhood, in which natural
charm and beauty were enhanced by the subtle art of the times,
threw into striking relief the behaviour of certain young friends
of the brides and their consorts. It was behaviour which, in
comparison, seemed to have stepped out of a past age. These
youths ran before the couples, or sprang into the street before
them from behind the corners of houses, firing shot-guns into the
air. Reloading, they retreated to some new hiding-place, to
repeat the seemingly dangerous procedure on the party's nearer
approach.

The custom intrigued me much, and I made enquiries about
it later, but without getting any really satisfactory explanation
of its origin or purpose. It was once universal in the Faeroes,
and indeed survives at many of the remoter settlements, and it is
said to be a salute to the bride and groom. But what is its origin ?
It seems to have been a widespread custom in Europe, and is
still practised among some peasant peoples on the Continent.
Was the idea, originally, to make a loud noise and so frighten
evil spirits away ? I ask the question because formerly at Faeroe

weddings it was always the custom for the village youths to go before the procession making a loud noise by beating inflated sheeps' bladders. The noise of the shot-guns, whatever its meaning in popular conception to-day, appears to be merely a modern substitute for this.

Except at the homes of the newly weds, where family celebrations were taking place and a good deal of hard work was being done, there was little excitement until the dancing began in the village hall—a mere shed on the outskirts of the settlement. There was little of the carnival spirit abroad, and most of the folk remained in their own houses. The *skeinkjari* went the round of the houses with his bottle and little glass, pouring each person a drink so that he or she could toast the happy couples. He too is an old institution, and no wedding in a Faeroe village would be complete without him.

The real wedding-party, my host informed me, would take place on the following day, and in common with every other soul in the village I was invited. The morrow dawned bright and clear, but something seemed to be wrong with Mykines at my time of rising, which was about nine o'clock. The village was unusually quiet, and the fields, which are generally a scene of brisk activity at that hour of an August morning, were deserted. Mykines, I found, was prepared to take its holiday as seriously as it takes its work. Some menfolk stood idly chatting in a little group on the street, and I noticed they were all wearing their best apparel. The atmosphere was almost Sundayish, except that there was an air of expectancy, of waiting for something to happen, about the place.

Shortly before noon the feasting began. I attended with my host and hostess at three o'clock, and ours was the third sitting. There were five in all, and each one ate its way through a whole sheep. The lamb and beef, with potatoes and a sweet gravy, were excellent, and the meal was beautifully cooked. The final sitting rose about seven, and by that time the *dansuringur* had started again in the little hall at the back of the church. At many times during the evening there must have been well over a hundred people dancing together on a floor measuring no more than twenty by thirty feet. The place was packed tight, but the dancers moved freely nevertheless, the growing ring changing form and becoming a sinuous, fluid, endless chain that wound in and out around and across the room. Newcomers joined in, and those who had had enough (for the time being) fell out as they pleased, and several of the dances went on for well over an hour before the hardy ones decided the time had come for a rest.

The first dance of all went with terrific zest and swing, the men pounding out the *brúðarvísa* in loud but tuneless voices, and skipping up and down with astonishing vigour in accentuation of the more rhythmic passages in the song. The movement is a sideways slithering rather than a step in the dancing sense, and is simple enough to follow : but it can look—and is—very complicated when excitement reaches a high pitch, and the men beat their joined arms vigorously up and down, and prance with the energy of young colts in spite of their years. The *brúðarvísa* is the special wedding-song ; another, *súsonnuvísa*, tells stories with a biblical flavour, and other ballads of Danish extraction have been adapted to the dance. None has much tune, but the Faeroe songs at any rate have some quite indescribable quality which stirs the blood in one's veins and makes one's limbs fidget with the desire to join in. For a time I did not join in, being content to stand in the shadows and watch—a detachment which the Faeroe-man would no doubt consider very wrong ! But it was magnificent to see the shining eyes and the glistening, rapturous faces of the older men and women, as they passed with linked arms and slightly swaying bodies through the yellow glare of the one swinging oil lamp that hung from the rafters. It might all have been happening, I thought, two hundred years ago !

It was soon brought home to me (and I realised this with a good deal of pleasure) that, ancient though it may be, there is no immediate danger of the *dansuringur* dying out. For the most ardent singers and tireless dancers were not so much the men like Abraham Abrahamsen or Hans Pauli Hansen (who is eighty if he is a day), but the young men of the rising generation. The boys of the R.A.F. contingent then stationed on Mykines started dancing to the accompaniment of a piano-accordion at their billet, but it was a very poor opposition. The Mykines folk dropped in and out during their endless tour of the village, and even stayed in some cases for a dance, but in contrast to the rugged virility of the *brúðarvísa*, which ever and anon broke into fresh crescendos of rollicking activity, the piano-accordion and its fox-trots seemed effeminate in the extreme.

I found it difficult to keep away from the tiny hall for long. Even when away at the other end of the village the stentorian saga-voices, clashing here with the restless rowdiness of the kittiwakes and the thud of the surf on the shore, exerted their call.

Sooner or later, no matter what other enticements the village offered, everybody drifted for yet another spell to the interminable dance.

Mykines was on the move all the time : in the dimness, that shadowless half-light of the summer night, the revellers wandered along the few streets on the west side of the stream, calling in at various houses and chatting for a while with friends and neighbours before going off to seek other company. Away from the dance-hall the merrymakers were quiet, and always they were well behaved : there was neither rowdiness nor insobriety, and the enjoyment was obviously very real. From about one in the morning there was an inconstant procession to and from the bridal house, where a breakfast of sandwiches was served. And if at any time of the night you thirsted for coffee (as you very often did) you could always be sure of getting it at any house that showed a light.

I crept away to bed at four o'clock. Dawn's hand was grasping the sea in the east, but the big complex of parties showed not the slightest sign of breaking up. Nevertheless, when I rose, the spirit protesting, some time after nine, and looked out of the window, men and women were at work in the sloping fields. Hans Pauli, who I had last seen doing a waltz to the tune of the piano-accordion, was now doing something to his fowling-net a few yards down the street, and one or two girls were laughing as they came back from milking the cows in the *hagi* beyond the stream. Mykines had had its fun, and seemed to have cast off the previous night as though the celebration had never been.

2

Viewed from the village at the valley's end the Mykines outfield does not at first glance seem attractive. It does not promise to unfold such scenic wonders and ornithological interests as we shall find if we explore farther afield ; nor can one guess at its truly astonishing significance in the economy of the two hundred souls whose destinies depend upon this isle and the seas about—an intricate pattern for living which I shall try to unfold below.

The moorland ascends from the stream-side in a long, uneven series of dark grassy slopes to the craggy *hamrar* supporting Knúkur, the central hill, over 1,800 feet above the sea. On the lower zone of the *hagi*, just across the stream, the cattle graze in summer, and in the morning and the evening the women go out to milk them, bearing pails which hang from each end of a wooden yoke or *dylla*. They are fortunate in that they need not travel very far, for at some villages the *neytakonur* must walk twice a day, in fair weather or foul, a distance of several miles to attend the cattle in the upland pasture. Always, too, on this lower reach of the *hagi*, there is a small area dappled white with countless kittiwakes ; there is no lake on Mykines, so the birds come up from the colonies to bathe in the running stream, and stay on the moor nearby to rest and preen and sun themselves when their bathing is over.

Beyond the kine and the kittiwakes are the turbaries, gloomy with black banks of naked peat and moist sunken areas bright green with sphagnum moss and foam-flecked with the plumed tufts of cotton-sedge, and the whole area dotted with the stone huts where the fuel is stored. About them the whinnying whimbrels and the pied oyster-catchers fly, and in August innumerable sprightly wheatears pass through on their journey from Iceland to the south. At higher levels we meet a few passing curlews, and the sinister shapes of arctic skuas who make a reprehensible living by chasing the coast-hugging kittiwakes and terns, forcing them to disgorge their food. When nesting singly, as they do here, they are quiet and undemonstrative birds, and when we find a dusky brown fledgling crouching in a runnel it is only by the merest chance, for there are no parents anxiously hovering overhead to suggest that he is near.

The small colony of lesser blackbacks inhabiting the stony upper reach below Knúkur produces much more noise, protesting loudly as we cross their domain. They have many grey-brown young who foolishly stick their heads into dark corners and (because they can then see nothing themselves) lie serene in the fancy that they are concealed from prying eyes. It is a habit which reminds one of the fabled idiosyncrasy of the ostrich which thought to escape notice by burying its head in the sand ! Sometimes the village children take a few of these youngsters and keep them for a while as pets, letting them roam about the vicinity of the houses. In late September, when the urge to migrate grows strong, the pets renounce their bondage and fly away to the south. One, which was ringed for me in late August of 1942, was still tame and confiding three weeks later when it let a fisherman take it in his hands on board a trawler in Carmarthen

Bay. In 1943 the fashion in pets had changed, and the children were rearing a number of the larger species, the greater blackback, which their fathers had fetched from a colony on the north coast. Kittiwake " tarrocks " and arctic tern chicks are great favourites in many of the villages, and sometimes hooded-crows, ravens and even young shags are hand-reared.

A few yards beyond the gullery we come to the northern flank of the main hill, and here this amazing island produces yet another of its perpetual surprises. For we stand at the top of a long grassy slope where the moorland takes a headlong plunge into Kálvadalur, surely the loveliest of Faeroe dales. It is a deep half-bowl of a valley, open on the north side where the land sinks to the rocky shore, but completely shut in on the landward sides by this ridge and the precipitous wall of Knúkur towering aloft to south and east. Kálvadalur seems to be accessible only by way of the long slope at the head of which we stand, and the scramble down is difficult enough if you are unused to wandering among the hills. In a wide arc away to the right the rings of mighty *hamrar* and great grassy buttresses, seared here and there by long chimneys of scree, reach upwards in an awesome, perpendicular face. The dark and forbidding grandeur of this massive wall, about whose crags the fulmars soar on rigid wings, makes an unusual contrast with the fertile green of the valley's undulating floor.

No bird-man, standing on this ridge, could fail to be impressed by the sight before his eyes. The picturesque scenery, superb though it is in its grandeur and wild solitude, would seem to him a secondary consideration—for in Kálvadalur the largest colony of arctic terns that I have seen has made its summer home. In their hundreds the white birds flicker against the emerald grass, and although they are for the most part more than half a mile away their shrill voices carry to the ears in a never-ending shimmer of sound. No wonder the grass of Kálvadalur is so beautifully fresh and verdant to look upon, shining even in the shadow of that rugged, overbearing wall ; watered by a network of streamlets, and nourished over many years by the rich guano of the innumerable terns, it is indeed valuable pasture for the isolated flock of sheep which shares the valley with the birds.

One of the island's emergency landing-places is on the rocky shore at the foot of Kálvadalur. Sometimes the villagers must tramp across the rough, rising moorland to the crest of the valley two miles from their homes, and then scramble another mile into the dale and so to the coast—because the south-west wind and a raging sea render the village landing-place unapproachable, and *S.S. Smiril*, the small steamer which serves Mykines once a month in the summer time, must go to the north side for shelter and put a small dhingy ashore. Sofus told me that he and his sister, and other children, had to embark thus on several occasions when returning to school in Tórshavn at the end of their summer holidays.

If we climb the ridge and follow it across the island's summit, looking down over the brink of Knúkur into the beautiful dale below, we soon arrive at another steep edge where the falling moor opens out into the long, narrow basin of Borgardalur. The clean green sweep of this third valley runs away between the rocky peaks of the coastal cliffs to the easternmost point of the island. Although it lacks the formidable craggy wall that encloses its sister-valley, its long and gently undulating floor rising to the serrated clifftops on either side, and dominated by the pinnacle of Árnafjall in the south, creates an effect of great beauty, and serves to strengthen our impression that Mykines must surely be numbered among the world's loveliest islands.

Beyond the end of the valley and the strip of sea are the Vágar mountains, and away to the north the great bird-cliffs of the Norðstreymoy coast gleam in the haze. We look into the vale where lonely Gásadalur sits beneath another and a greater Árnafjall, and see the sun illuminating the coloured houses of Sørvágur at the head of the deeply cut fiord. Away to the south of Vágar are the shapes of other islands—Hestur, Sandoy, Skúvoy, the Dímunar and Suðuroy, the last shape almost one with the distant clouds. It is a splendid panorama, perhaps one of the widest and the best that the islands can afford.

It is rather surprising to find the puffins, whom one always regards as creatures of the coast, flying across these valleys to and from their homes in the hillsides, sometimes several hundred yards from the sea. On my way from Kálvadalur to Borgardalur I sat on the rocky crest just below the summit of Knúkur, and whilst resting there was startled by a flurry of wings beneath me. A puffin, which had come with fish from the sea a good half-mile away, shot into a hole in the ground just over the edge of the *hamrar*, and was loudly greeted by its hungry chick. I mentioned this to Hr. Abrahamsen as a novelty on my return, and he told me that years ago the puffin was a much more abundant inland-breeding bird than now.

Young puffins are called *lundapisur*. When full-grown they are reservoirs of fat, and in the sixth week of their lives the parents desert them, so that they have to find their way to sea themselves. For several days they remain in the burrows, without food, and it is only when most of their fat has been absorbed and they begin to feel hungry that they leave their homes and make their way down the cliffs. They travel by night, which is only natural, since they are born and reared in utter darkness : it is also fortunate for the young puffin, for unless he is afloat by dawn his chances of reaching the sea at all are very slim. Ravens, hooded-crows and the larger gulls are as fond of *lundi* meat as any Faeroeman.

How, then, do these *lundapisur* of the hills manage to complete the long overland journey to the coast in the darkness of a single night ? The question intrigued me, and as always I went to my host and mentor for the answer. These youngsters do not walk, but swim, and every morning in the late summer a number are to be seen sailing along on the stream which flows through the village. The people call them *áarpisur*, " young puffins of the stream," and they often take these voyagers, for they are said to be delicious eating, the best of all puffins for the pot. Doubtless others of the island's streams, especially those in Kálvadalur, have their *áarpisur* traffic on summer nights, and very likely the majority of the young born in the hillsides reach the sea safely enough by this means.

Our way back to the village lies across Líðarhagi, over the high pasture of the ponies and the feeding-ground of flocks of oyster-catchers and Faeroe starlings, towards the still pools that gleam in old turbaries on the moor. Here we can approach the edge of the land and look down on some of the most splendid coastal scenery in a country which is justifiably proud of the wild and rugged grandeur of its bird-teeming cliffs. The characteristic coast architecture of the Faeroes is here at its very best, tier upon tier of narrow and almost uniform basalt bands, the *hamrar* habitat of thousands of fulmars, and dividing the tiers, steeply sloping terraces of grass where the numberless puffins have their homes in the honeycombed earth.

As we continue on our way we see ahead the distant sward of Mykineshólmur glowing in the slanting light of the sun, a fit field for the twenty bullocks whose only task in life is to feed and fatten and die for the fulfilment of the old boast that " Mykines

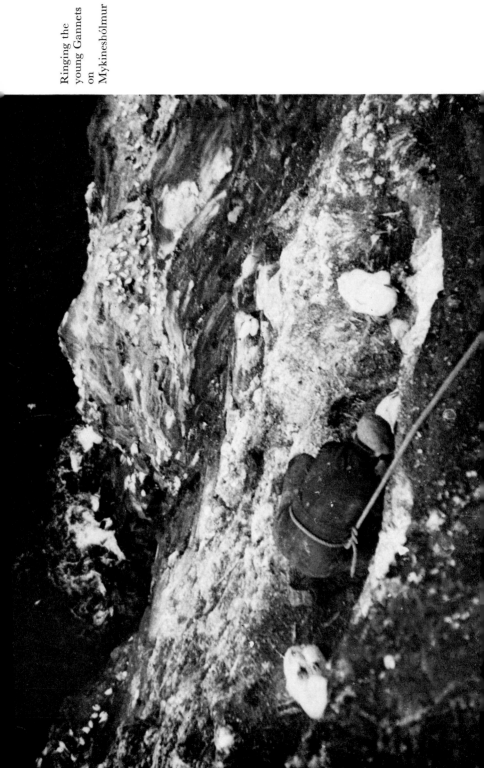

Ringing the
young Gannets
on
Mykineshólmur

A *fuglaberg* with its Kittiwake and Guillemot tenements

beef is best ! " Years ago it was a much harder task than now, for when they went to market in Tórshavn they had a tremendous feat of strength and stamina to perform. The only way to get the herd to the capital was to swim the beasts to Sørvágur—with a rest at Tindhólmur on the way—and drive them across Vágar to the landing-place at Fútaklettur. It was necessary to swim them again from there to the Streymoy shore at Kvívík, and drive them thence over the rough hills to the town.

Soon the turf-bogs and the glassy pools lie behind us. The western headland and the holm point like a long finger towards the sunset on the burning edge of the sea, and the village, nestling cosily in the hollow beneath a bloom of its own blue smoke, begins to take shape among the deep shadows already forming at the valley's end.

3

The exact nature of the people's rights in the Faeroese *hagi* had long been a mystery to me at the time of my second visit to Mykines, and might have remained a mystery had not my host, with infinite patience, explained to me one morning how he and his neighbours live. Shortly after this holiday I stayed at Froðbøur in Suðuroy, and found there quite a different administration of the outfield, and one which is peculiar to that island. So we must examine the question in so far as it affects both communities, but in so doing we should not forget that these represent but two of the varied designs for living which exist in the Faeroes. Although Mykines may fairly represent the system in the north and central islands, and Froðbøur the Suðuroy settlements, the picture varies in detail, according to the local conditions, from place to place.

All the country we have recently seen—hill, holm, dale and towering cliff—is called the *hagi*, and like the cultivated *bøur* surrounding the settlement, it is valued at 40 *merkur*. For every *mørk* and so on of his holding in the *bøur* the Mykines farmer lays claim to an equivalent part of the 40 m. total worth of the outfield. In some parts of the country the *hagi* is treated as common land, except for that attached to the " kongs " holdings ; at other places (as on Mykines) a farmer's share may comprise a definite area of ground which he owns outright himself, or jointly with one or more other members of the community.

The outfield here is in four main parts. Líðarhagi in the

M

south has the value 11 m., the pleasant valley Borgardalur is worth 10 m., the small but rich Kálvadalur 9 m., and the moorland Heimangjógv in the north-west, 10 m. One half of Mykineshólmur is vested in Heimangjógv, a qua ter goes with Kálvadalur, and the rest is part of the 10 m. of Borgardalur. The boundaries of the dales are clearly defined by the coasts and the hill-ridges, and Líðarhagi and Heimangjógv are separated by the stream which flows through the mid-western part of the island to the village landing-place. In some places there is no clear line of demarkation between the outfields of two settlements, and a kind of no-man's-land exists which is common to both, as at Semingsstykki (a usual place-name for such areas) between Kirkjubøur and Velbastaður.

The major resources of all this land, after certain special claims have been met, belong to the ground, and are, in the Faeroese expression, *felagsogn*. This means that they are the property of the community for fair distribution to each farmer according to his wealth in *merkur*, *gyllin* and *skinn*. On Mykines the produce apportioned in this way includes mutton, wool, gannets from Mykineshólmur, and puffins from one particular catching-place. Landt records that in places where much seawrack was washed ashore and used as a fertiliser this was also divided among the farmers in accordance with their wealth. The system does not apply to turf-cutting, and usually the village turbaries are concentrated for convenience in one particular area of the moor.

On Mykines there are some 1,200 sheep, the property of the commonwealth. They run the whole year round in the two dales, where the grass is plentiful and good, and in summer on the upper reaches of Líðarhagi and Heimangjógv, these flocks being brought down into the *bøur* during the winter months. The flocks are tended by four shepherds appointed by the villagers, and to prevent any confusion should they stray, each flock has its distinguishing mark. If it is intended to kill lambs, say, from the Borgardalur flock, each man whose wealth in the *hagi* includes a part of the 10 m. of Borgardalur will supply labour according to the size of his holding. If he has one *mørk* he may be expected, perhaps, to provide one man (i.e. to go himself) for rounding-up and disposing of the sheep ; if he has 2 m. he may have to supply two men, whilst if he holds only 8 g. or half a *mørk* he may have to exchange the duty in alternate years with a neighbour of equal wealth.

The men go out to the valley and drive the sheep into the *rætt* or fold : they will have decided beforehand, on the report of the shepherd, how many lambs per *mørk* can be killed in that year. Before the distribution is begun, a twelfth part of the lambs is paid to the shepherd for his work. The remainder are *felagsogn* and are divided among the men in proportion to the value of their holdings in the 10 m. of the ground. The same arrangements apply equally to the Kálvadalur, Líðarhagi and Heimangjógv flocks ; and when the sheep are plucked of their wool in summer this is distributed by weight in the same way.

If your holding is too small to qualify you for a whole lamb, incidentally, you will receive a portion of the carcass, for there is a definite scale of values covering the various parts of the anatomy of a sheep. Thus the back may be 4 *skinn*, a leg 3 *skinn*, and so on. And if you are not able to supply the amount of labour required of you for rounding-up you must meet your responsibility to the community by engaging a man for the task. As payment you will give him a half-part of the wool or mutton that is your due.

The gannets, when the adults are taken in April, and again when the fledged young are taken in the late summer, are dealt out in exactly the same manner as the lambs. Twenty-four men are needed for the hunt, and the land-owners arrange to provide this labour in accordance with the size of their holdings, so that each *áttingur* sends three men. The *áttingur* is an eighth part of the commonwealth, for the 40 m. is split up into sections comprising 5 m. each for convenient administration. The boat which goes out from the village to collect the catch from below the north cliff, or put men ashore on Flatidrangur, receives twenty gannets as payment for its services. The remainder of the catch is *felagsogn* and division proceeds as in the case of lambs and wool.

Only one puffin catching-place on Mykines is *felagsogn ;* this is on top of the Rógvukollur ridge overlooking the Dalið and Lambi puffinries. Here one half of the catch is kept by the fowler and the other half belongs to the ground. As it is impossible to pay every land-owner in the village from the proceeds of a day's work there is a system of staggering the share-out over a period, each *áttingur* being served in its turn as the summer runs its course. The fowlers take it in turns to work at this convenient and productive site, but may forfeit their turn and go elsewhere if they wish, in which case the choice falls to the next man on the list. At the other catching-places the ground is either owned outright by one family or is shared in partnership by two or more men, and at such places the full distribution of the half-part which goes to the gound can be made at once.

Many years ago this system of the fowler retaining half of his catch was general in the Faeroes, but in the face of changing conditions in the last century a half-part was no longer considered adequate recompense for the work, with the result that fowling was largely deserted in favour of fishing or some bther more remunerative pursuit. Nowadays, in many places, the custom is for a quarter only to go to the ground, the fowler keeping the rest. Birds which have only a minor importance as food, such as young kittiwakes and shags, are not affected by these arrangements : any man may go in search of them and keep all he can take provided he first has the landowner's consent. Nor do the laws apply to the fulmar, for they were in operation centuries before this species began to breed on the Faeroe cliffs, and no provision has as yet been made for its inclusion.

4

Petrels are the sparrows of the sea, abundant little birds who roam far on tireless wings between horizons of uneasy, volatile waves. The sea is one of the richest feeding-grounds on this planet, and they and numerous allied creatures have fitted themselves for a life that has no need of land, except as a place where they can perpetuate the species. So they nest on the fringe of the ocean, often on remote and isolated islets. There may be thousands nesting on Mykineshólmur but you would never know it unless you looked for them at night : for while the sun shines they must reap their harvest far from any land, and it is only when the night comes that they go in the stillness to the lonely shores where their nesting-tunnels are scored in the soil.

A night with the petrels is a remarkable and memorable event. Two kinds nest in the west of Mykines and the holm—the storm, more romantically known as " Mother Carey's Chicken," and the rather larger and browner Leach's forked-tailed petrel. Because of the comparative isolation and inaccessibility of its few known breeding-places, Leach's petrel is one of the special treasures of a bird-watcher's life. How many there are on Mykineshólmur and that western peninsula I do not know and cannot guess with any degree of confidence. Salomonsen recorded that in 1934 the species was a newcomer to the Faeroes and only four or five pairs were nesting. Either it had been previously overlooked, or its increase since that year has been phenomenal, for its population to-day cannot be less than as many thousand pairs.

The summer night is alive with these elfin birds, shadows a shade darker than the sky flitting to and fro in a whirl of giddy movement. They electrify the air, dancing around like strange, nocturnal butterflies, and with the same wayward flight as big-winged, exotic butterflies. One moment a dozen are visible whilst you watch, and the next moment they are gone with the gloom. They swirl and eddy about your head, sometimes brushing past your face with a soft, ghostly touch. The night is feverish with brisk, excited movement and their clear staccato cries ; for they are constantly calling, and their eerie voices are flung against the murmur of the wave-roll on the shore and the soft sweep of the wind through the long grass. It is an unreal and fascinating world which any naturalist would feel pride and joy in visiting for a while.

When the last pale wash of sunset is in the sky the storm petrels come to the isle. They are the first to arrive. The path on the northern side of Rógvukollur is a good place to see them, and in parts of west Mykines they outnumber the larger kind. The old ruin on the south-east corner of the holm is another of their strongholds, and here they fly in wide circles, fast and fairly direct, and in the gloaming their quaint conversation and mysterious love-making begins. Their song rises out of the earth or comes from among the stones of the ruined walls ; it is a thin, whirring song reminiscent of the hum of a spinning-wheel. The Leach's petrels are later in their arrival, but soon after dark they are to be found fluttering in scores above the sloping brow where the pasture descends to the south side rocks, whilst one can also find them, though not in the same large numbers, on the brink of the great northern cliff. One of the finest vantage-points for watching both species, and the Manx shearwater as well, is on the lower side of Klettur. On Mykines itself the Leach's flies thickly above the Lambi *lundaland* and extends as far eastwards as Daliđ and the north-west cliff behind the village *bøur*.

We " fleyged " the petrels with the fowling-net ; or, it is more truthful to say, my companion " fleyged " and I watched, and was kept amused by his antics whilst awaiting opportunities to use my rings. Sofus Sivertsen has great skill with the *fleyg*, but he met his Waterloo that night on the teeming holm. He danced and shouted like a Dervish in the dusky light, his accustomed calm and quiet confidence completely shattered by the will-o'-the-wisp tactics of these astonishing sprites. When the net was passed to me for a spell I merely floundered to little purpose, breathing heavily from the unusual exertion, and feeling much pity for the aching muscles of my arms. I too loudly deplored the birds' nimble ways, their loud cackle of a cry that seemed to mock my clumsy efforts, and their covering cloak of night, an ally and impervious retreat.

In actual fact we both caught more than we were able to hold in the net, for the birds are so quick and sprightly on the wing that the net never seemed to strike them with any force, and only a few became sufficiently entangled to find escape impossible. Many merely brushed against the strands and shot away again before we could effect their capture. The *fleygastong* was much too heavy for the fast, close work required ; something lighter and easier to wield, say a ten-foot bamboo rod attached to a net of a smaller mesh, would be a great improvement. When I went home to breakfast later that morning my host grinned widely and said he supposed we had made history, for it must surely be the first time that *drunnhvíti* had been " fleyged " in the Faeroe Isles !

A simple translation of *drunnhvíti* is " white rump," a feature common to both species, but having in the Leach's an ad-mixture of brown feathers extending downwards from the middle of the back. The name really belongs to the storm petrel : few of the Mykines people are able to distinguish between the two, which is not surprising if the species now dominating the holm has only nested there since 1934. Because of this uncertainty I could learn nothing definite about the status of either species until the night when I stayed on the holm and found out for myself. All I knew was that the Leach's certainly occurred, for on the second morning of my stay I found the sooty-brown wings and deeply-notched tail of a slain bird lying on the Rógvukollur path.

This discovery introduced me to the one man on Mykines who probably knows more about the habits of Leach's petrel than most ornithologists. Although past the three score years and ten, which, rumour has it, mortal man is allowed, he is still one of the most active figures on the island. His name is Hans Pauli Hansen. When I turned the corner of the Rógvukollur path I saw him climbing up the Lambi slope with his *fleyg* raised on high like a

banner and a number of defunct puffins dangling from his belt.
It was then only nine o'clock, and Hans Pauli had already caught
for himself and family a very substantial lunch.

He showed me the remains of a dead storm petrel he had found
(there were several on the Dalið and Rógvukollur paths that
morning) and asked me to return with him to the ridge, where
he picked up the remains of the Leach's petrel which I had
examined a few moments before, and illustrated scientifically by
means of dumb show the diagnostic characters of each, for he
understands but little English, and I but little Faeroese. He
managed to make me understand that the birds are active until
well on into the winter months, and that he has found young so
late in the year as December. At first I felt that a possible reason
for this protracted breeding-period might be that these nocturnal
species, for protection against gulls and other predators, do not
begin their domestic cycle in this northern latitude until the light
midsummer nights give way to a few hours of comparative darkness in mid-July. The theory can hardly be applied to Leach's
petrel, however, as my friend Petersen, who visited the Mykines
colony in 1946, found hard-set eggs in mid-June. But it may
well fit the storm petrel, for his long experience on Nólsoy and
my own slight acquaintance with the bird on Koltur show that
it is unusual for the chicks to hatch before the third week of
August. Hans Pauli, by the way, attributed the presence of the
wings, feet and tails of slain birds on the paths to the hunting
prowess of the village cats.

The amazing nights I spent on the holm resounded with the
clear, distinctive cries of the birds. It is a difficult call to set down
on paper, but after much careful listening in 1942 and 1943,
during which I realised that there is a very considerable range of
variation (probably sufficient for the partners to recognise each
other by voice alone) I wrote it as " tak-too-*wak*-oo, kuk-uk-uk-
uk," the latter part a hasty series of emphatic notes. It was to
be heard every few seconds on every hand, a wild and uncanny
cry in the all-pervading gloom, and muffled versions of it rose up
from the burrows at one's feet. There is a thin reeling song
similar to the storm petrel's, punctuated at intervals by a wheezy
sound that suggests a deep intake of breath : this song I heard only
from the burrows, and it is often interrupted by the normal call.

During watchings in these two years a curious habit, which I
find it difficult to interpret, was noted on many occasions. Birds
flying above the nesting-area were often seen or heard to collide

in mid-air. This was observed twice within a few minutes one night on the southern shore, at very close quarters and in perfect silhouette against a fairly light sky : in both cases the birds fell to the ground immediately after the impact, but could not be found a few seconds later when I arrived at the spot and made a search. Without doubt, for none was seen to rise again, they had gone into one of the many burrows. Owing to the poor light and the distance at which the many other collisions occurred I could not observe the subsequent behaviour. Certainly, however, these collisions are not accidental : admittedly the birds fly thickly above the burrows, but no creature so light and agile on the wing as to avoid the sweep of a fowling-net with comparative ease would blunder so often into its fellows, and it seems to me that the collisions must be a regular and important feature of the sexual behaviour. Perhaps the sitting bird, recognising the voice of its mate above, leaves the burrow and the two join in an ecstatic aerial dance or sexual chase which culminates in this impact and the immediate descent of the pair to the burrow. There, to the accompaniment of the reeling song, further ceremonial, possibly connected with mating or the change-over of sitting birds, takes place. This is merely a suggestion as to the possible nature of the pattern, for more observations on this fascinating species, particularly earlier in the season, are needed to explain the curious phenomenon.

The storm petrel is an even duskier beauty than its cogener. Jákup Nielsen showed me where to find one on the first afternoon of my stay, when we took a bird from the walls of the old ruin, where it was sitting quietly and demurely on a solitary white egg. Two days later I took and ringed its mate—sometimes a bird will remain on the nest for forty-eight hours or more before being relieved. One wonders if the tremendous increase in the larger species on the holm is pushing the storm petrel farther to the east, to the high Rógvukollur and the broken ground of the Dalið beyond. It is in fact probable that the Leach's petrel is gradually ousting the smaller bird in the competition for nesting-sites, for one sees very few indeed in those areas where the newcomer is abundant. Certainly the storm must have been a far commoner species at one time than it is now, for until the middle of the seventeenth century the Mykines folk collected a considerable number of the very fat and oily young, plucked, decapitated and dried them, and by the simple expedient of threading a wick through their bodies used them as candles in the wintertime. It is said that the nightly *kvøldseta* in the *roykstova* lasted just so long as it took a fresh storm petrel candle to burn out.

I had hoped to find the Manx shearwater breeding on Mykines, but on making inquiries soon after my arrival I was told that *skrápur* did not nest on the isle. The pleasure of the first night was therefore enhanced when, among the noise of the Leach's petrels, I heard the louder, weirder voices of shearwaters as they came in from the sea, passing high over the shore with fast, straight flight. They appear to inhabit for the most part the Lambi puffinry and the eastern portion of the holm below the Klettur rock, though some could be heard crooning their unmistakable " kuk-kuk-koo-*quark*-oo " and its many variations in burrows among the puffin-holes on the southern slope. There are not a great many, perhaps about a hundred pairs in all.

Long before the first light I left the mad whirl of night-life on the holm and made my way over Lambi and Dalið to the village. Arctic terns were bickering over their colony and the coastal rocks below ; under Klettur the gannets cackled drowsily, and the voices of the kittiwakes rose in subdued chorus from the cliffs below the Dalið slope. No matter what other activity claimed attention, however, it was impossible to forget for a moment that the night belonged in spirit and in fact to these dusky adventurers of the deep. The shearwater and the storm and Leach's petrels give by night to this bird-watcher's paradise a life as intensely vivid and dramatic as the quite different life it has from its many other inhabitants in the bright light of day.

5

The way back from Mykines was a nightmare that will live long in my memory, and my only reason for bothering the reader with the details is that they provide a commentary on what travel can be like among these far islands. It was one of those grey days when the south-west wind and the sea combine to shut off Mykines from the rest of the world, and I was really lucky to get away. The post-boat arrived at 7 a.m.—exactly seven hours before the scheduled time—and at that hour I was fast asleep and dreaming of the petrels I had but lately left in the darkness of the holm. I had a rude awakening, and was told the skipper would wait exactly ten minutes for me—not a moment longer !

For the first half-hour conditions were none too bad. We sailed close in to the coast, and I found time to eat my breakfast of *skerpikjøt* (a vain gesture, as it proved) and admire the towering mist-topped crags above us and the swirl of bird-life about the rocks. Then we turned the eastern corner of the isle, outside Núgvunes, and ran for the opposite coast. The little boat twisted and strained, leapt and lurched and did everything but dive under the waves. I propped myself up between the door-posts of the skipper's cabin and, if only I had dared to leave go, would have hit him hard for his incurable cheerfulness. Nevertheless, although I have an unwilling stomach for sea-travel, I would rather have the temporary discomfort of sea-sickness than the gnawing cancer of boredom at any time. And boredom is the great bugbear of travel among these scattered isles.

There are three ways of travelling from Vágar to the capital, although usually only one of these is available, according to the day. You can go by sea from Sørvágur, which takes five or six hours, by sea from Miðvágur, which takes about three, or you may have to go by what is called, out of courtesy or jest, the "overland route." This takes you across Vágar to Fútaklettur by car, across Vestmannasund to Kvívík in a small boat, from Kvívík to Kollafjørður by road, and thence to Tórshavn by the local ferry. This is the way I was obliged to go.

It will soon become obvious to any traveller attempting this or almost any other journey that his movements are largely dependent upon the whims of local car-proprietors and skippers of small craft. This, I should make clear, is not an aspersion on their willingness to collaborate—for they are helpful and courteous enough—but a reflection on the numerous factors and circumstances which attend their tasks. "Plans" and time-tables are available for most of the regular services, but if the hours of departure and arrival detailed therein coincide with your anticipated geographical position, then you may congratulate yourself on having picked a day when every conceivable circumstance—tide, wind, mists, postmen, internal combustion engines and the rest—behaved in an exemplary manner.

The post-car does not always leave at the stipulated time, but this matters little, as I have yet to learn of one which failed to make its connection with the boat. It may wait for other cars, for the mail, for items of general merchandise (to be delivered by the driver on route), or for those occasional passengers who have a deplorable " it won't go without me ! " type of mind. If there are many voyagers a variety of automobiles, ranging from limousines to tradesmen's vans, will be pressed into service— everything possible is done to find accommodation for all. When the shuffling and reshuffling of the passengers is complete we set out, and, on this particular route, enjoy a speedy and comfortable run round the lakeside of Sørvágsvatn to Miðvágur, along an excellent road which was constructed during the war by British Engineers and Pioneers. They also built a landing-field above the lake, and, with the R.A.F., established a Coastal Command seaplane base at its northern end.

There is a short run from Miðvágur to the next centre of population, Sandavágur, a pleasant little village of diligent and successful farmers and fishermen, with a picturesque church standing almost on the sandy shore of the bay. We then turn inland and climb a rough upland road which, after passing through the hills, coils like a gigantic snake down the steep coastal slope to Fútaklettur. This is not a village, and indeed there is practically nothing there at all except (as its name implies) the foot of the cliff, the end of the road, and the probability of another long wait before we set out for the opposite shore. All my journeys by this particular route were made much worse than they might have been by the prevailing weather, and indeed my experience of Vágar is that it is one of the wettest places on earth. There is no shelter within several miles of Fútaklettur, except within the cramped space of the cars. At length the post-boat is seen southward-bound in Vestmannasund, hugging the far shore as though ashamed of itself. Finally it dashes boldly across and with spluttering apologies ties up at the concrete platform which serves as a landing-place, the end (or the beginning) of Vágar's one arterial road, and the object which assigns to this bleakest of spots the merit of an honourable mention on the map.

Within the half-hour the little boat, a ten-ton former fishing-smack, is skilfully piloted alongside the quay at Kvívík, and there is a rush for the best seats in the motley array of motor-cars lined up on the road. Luggage of assorted kinds, from bags and boxes to babies' prams, is roped to the roofs, running boards and radiators, and we are soon ready to proceed on our way.

We skirt the coast, not without some anxiety, for (as with many Faeroe roads) the offside runs along the edge of a precipice, to Leynar, a pleasantly-situated village with a little sandy shore and a magnificent view of the towering height of Skaelingsfjall—

beyond question one of the finest of Faeroe mountains. Then we climb into the hill-pass which takes us past the lakes of Leynarvatn and Mjávøtn into Kollafjørðsdalur, and brings us to the grassy head of the long fiord. As likely as not, if there is any room, our driver will stop somewhere or other on the road to offer some weary farmer or villager a lift.

It is too much to expect that the ferry will be waiting at the village when we arrive, and so we pay for the ride (the charge is very reasonable on the more regular runs) and resign ourselves phlegmatically to another long wait in the cold and the rain. Sooner or later peering eyes, hopefully scanning the horizon, see the ferry emerge from the curtain of Scotch mist at the mouth of the fiord ; and in a few minutes we embark, together with the usual merchandise and a few sheep (which however, travel steerage) on the last lap of the long journey to Tórshavn. Now indeed we travel hopefully, for this little boat is fast, making at least seven knots, and offers a certain amount of warmth and shelter below the deck.

Mykines, at the least, is a six hours' journey from Tórshavn by the "overland route," and not very much less by either of the sea-routes linking Vágar with the capital. It can be, and not infrequently is, much more. Movement in the Faeroes can be a long, dreary and tiresome business, and although it is impossible to control the weather or the tides, there are aspects of travel which ought to be taken up by the Løgting with a view to improvement. There is a real need for waiting-rooms at the termini of the most-used routes, and such places between as Kvívík and Kollafjørður where the change-over from land to sea, or vice-versa is made. Here the traveller, especially if he is a stranger to the land, can search in vain for shelter, warmth and sanitary facilities, as well as for refreshments. The need for some attention to these matters is urgent, not only for the comfort of the Faeroe people themselves, but for the visiting tourists who will always be attracted by the strange beauty and enchanting unusualness of the Faeroe life and scene.

References to Chapter Seven

LANDT, J. (1810) ; SALOMONSEN, F. (1935) ; WILLIAMSON, K. (1945 a and b).

Chapter Eight

HOLIDAY AT FRODBØUR

1. The legend of Frode, some notes on rock-formations and Suđuroy coal, and a walk up the hill behind the village (*page* 189).
2. The administration of the Frođbøur outfield—an interesting comparison with Mykines (*page* 192).
3. Some remarks on sheep-rearing in the Faeroes (*page* 195).
4. The business of hay-making here and on other islands (*page* 198).
5. The " harvest home " in which it culminated in days gone by (*page* 202).

I

FRODBØUR, so the story goes, was first settled in Viking times by a Danish chief called Frode. He sailed from Denmark with his house-karls, womenfolk, cattle and goods intending to go to Ireland, but when a few days out from land his ships encountered calm and misty weather. The fog hid the stars at night, so that navigation was impossible, and the boats drifted helplessly on the ocean tides and currents. Then one day the men saw a great flock of birds, and knew that land was very near. Suddenly the mists lifted, to reveal the great cliff of Frođbiarnípa looming high above, and, sailing southwards close in to the shore, Frode searched for a landing-place.

So the ships came to the low beach near Skarvanes, a long spit of rock jutting out into the mouth of Trongisvágsfjørđur, and there the men took the cattle ashore. The beasts ate greedily of the fresh green grass, and afterwards, as he watched them ruminating with obvious relish, Frode remarked that land which the cattle found so good the womenfolk would be sure to appreciate too ! So the fateful decision was made, the women were disembarked and the household goods and chattels carried from the boats. To-day the Frođbøur villagers will show you the roughly-hewn steps in the low cliff against the beach which the *húskallar* made to ease the landing. The voyagers made their homes on the wide shelf of fertile soil, called Ásdalur, which rises westwards from the shore, and where that part of the modern village called the Hamar now stands below the steeply-rising hills.

Neither this nor the lower section of the village, Undir Skorðum, which occupies a flat area on the shore of the fiord itself, can be called picturesque, but the Hamar is certainly full of interest, and its setting is pretty enough on days when the weather is kind. The most striking natural feature of the district is its geology, for the *hamrar* between the village and the coast of the fiord are composed of vertical prismatic columns of the latest of the Faeroe rocks, an intrusive basalt much younger than the dolerite which forms the mass of all the islands except the two most ancient, Suðuroy and Mykines. This feature is at its best on the coast just to the east of the fine old farm, Niðri á Bø, of which I shall have something to say in the next chapter. There is a promontory called Sigmundsnæsi, " Sigmund's Nose," made of these upright hexagonal prisms, and half-way along it a curious fan-shaped formation that gives abundant evidence of the volcanic upheavals which, in the dim and distant past, created these Atlantic Islands. Similar volcanic vents are to be found on other parts of the Faeroe coasts, but this great inverted fan at Froðbøur is the best. The cliffs on either hand are fluted with the picturesque plinths, and on the low shore nearby one can walk for several yards on a crazy-pavement of their exposed tops.

Whilst on the subject of rocks I must mention another feature of this part of Suðuroy—its coal. The island is constructed mainly of anamesite basalts, older again than the dolerites, and between these are some coal-bearing strata. If you look out to the great hills across the head of the fiord you can see the pylons supporting the overhead ropeway down which the tubs of coal are sent to the coast from the surface-mine high in the hills between Trongis- vágur and Fámjin. At the lower end of the ropeway is the big, ugly receiving and sorting establishment—one of the few buildings in the Faeroes to have suffered partial demolition by German bombs. There is another mine at Hvalbøur, the seams almost at sea-level, and although there is coal in plenty at these two places it is hardly likely that the mining has a bright future before it as a live industry. On the whole the fuel is of poor quality, and although it could be bought in Tórshavn before the war at 20-25 per cent less cost than English coal, many people consider its value to be only half that of an equal weight of the imported fuel. Its usefulness to the north Suðuroy settlements, however, cannot be over-estimated : not only is it easily procured, and therefore cheap, but its existence reduces considerably the protracted labour of turf-cutting and the consequent spoiling of the moors for the sheep.

One afternoon I climbed the long hill-road behind the Hamar to the great headland of Froðbiarnípa, where the Viking Frode is said to have been buried. I was not in search of his grave, but of the view, which is truly magnificent. The hills of Suðuroy unfold to the west and south, reaching their limit at the peculiarly shaped eminence called Beinisvørð, beyond which is Sunnbøur, the most southerly village in the Faeroes. It is to the north, however, that one must look for the finest panorama, for the sparkling sea stretches away to Skúvoy and Sandoy, and beyond to the dim blue mountains of the Norðuroyar. Nearer at hand the waves lap in whiteness against the great, green-topped crags of the Dímunar. In the sunlight the inclined plateau atop of Stóra Dímun shines vividly green, and through binoculars one can see what must surely be one of the loneliest, and perhaps one of the oldest, farmsteads in the world. It is no wonder that mediæval law and order used it as a penal settlement : banishment to Stóra Dímun, there to work as a húskallur, was at one time the harsh sentence imposed on wrongdoers in other islands. Indeed, it is still said of a bad character that he or she ought to be put on Dímun—" hattar átti at verið sett úppa Dímun ! " Its lesser neighbour rises almost in the shape of a house with a hipped roof, and the cliffs gleam with the guano of its countless birds. Formerly it was the haunt of a peculiar breed of wild sheep, of small stature, dark flesh, black curly wool, and the agility of goats—which, one imagines, they must have found an invaluable asset in such a home. How they came there must remain a mystery ; perhaps they were the original sheep introduced by the earliest Viking settlers, reverted to the wild ancestral type through centuries of isolation and in-breeding. Now, alas, they are all gone. It is said that the survivors of a shipwreck killed most of them to eat the meat and drink the blood—for Lítla Dímun is a waterless isle—but perhaps it is more likely that the Hvalbøur people exterminated them to save the grazing for their own animals.

Beneath Froðbiarnípa the sea breaks in white frenzy on a low

shore at the mouth of one of the most inaccessible valleys in the
Faeroes. Beautiful as the day was when I first looked down into
Froðbiarbotnur, this deep scoop in the hills was a steaming
cauldron of steely-grey mists ; but occasionally, as I walked
inland along the rocky rim where the moor ends abruptly in a
precipitous scarp, the mantle was rolled aside for a few moments
to expose a bright grassy floor, sheep-dotted, and watered by a
winding stream. It looked an interesting and inviting valley—
perhaps the more so because I knew it was beyond my reach. As
I scanned the rim and the *hamrar*-ringed walls below, they appeared
to be everywhere impossible of descent. At the village they had
told me that there is only one way down, far over on the northern
side. Nor do I think they were over-solicitous for my welfare
when they suggested I should not try to reach Froðbiarbotnur
without a guide.

2

At Froðbøur and in other parts of Suðuroy the administration
of the outfield is quite different to that obtaining on Mykines
and in most parts of the northern and central islands. The sheep
here are privately owned, not a part of the village commonwealth
—a system which, the northerners say, has grave disadvantages.
For one thing, any losses suffered by the flock must be borne
by the individual, and not shared by the whole community, as
they are where the sheep are *felagsogn* ; for another, the shepherd
is also a sheep-owner, and he sometimes has a natural tendency
to care for his own sheep first, and those of his fellow men afterwards. His position is not a neutral one, and even though he be
an impeccably honest and conscientious man, there is not the
same incentive for him to give of his best in the interests of the
community.

Each owner has a special mark allotted to him, which he
makes by clipping a piece of a certain shape from one or both ears
of his sheep. A record-book of these earmarks and their owners
is kept by the *sýslumaður*. Similar earmarks, each having its
distinguishing local name or description, as in the Faeroes, were
used years ago in parts of Britain where the flocks were grazed
on common land. They are also used under the *felagsogn* system,
not to denote ownership, but to earmark the flocks belonging to
certain sections of the *hagi*, so that the animals may be easily

sorted out if two flocks become intermingled. Where the marks are used as a means of recognition by definite owners the system has the name *kenning*—i.e. " to know." I have heard of only one exception to it in Suđuroy ; at Øravík, a small " kongs " settlement on the opposite shore of the fiord to Frođbøur, the sheep are *felagsogn*. The *kenning* system, on the other hand, obtains at Strendur and one or two settlements in eastern Eysturoy.

The outfield belonging to Frođbøur and the comparatively new town of Tvøroyri is an extensive one, and as the far-seeing villagers do not cut much peat on the *hagi*, preferring to buy cheap coal from the nearby mine in the hills above Trongisvágur, the ground is always in the best possible condition for the flocks. It is divided into six sections and as it is common land private owner-ship of the stock had necessitated a somewhat complicated plan for the distribution of the grazing-rights. On Botnskarđhagi land-owners are entitled, in theory, to graze 3½ sheep for every *gyllin* of their wealth, a right which is termed *frælsi*. On Kambhagi, Líđarhagi and Tvørahagi this *frælsi* is 3 sheep per *gyllin* ; and on Hvannhagi, a much smaller but very rich pasture of the kind known in the islands as *feitilendi* (" fat land "), which has room for very few sheep, a villager has the right to graze one animal for every 6 g. of his wealth.

The men provide labour for rounding-up the sheep in proportion to the size of their holdings, in the same way as on Mykines, but the shepherd, instead of taking his reward in meat and wool, takes it in grazing-rights. Although the *frælsi* for Botnskarđhagi is 3½ sheep, in actual practice the landowner may graze only three animals, the right for the remaining half a sheep being his contribution to the wages of the shepherd. Thus the Botnskarđhagi shepherd may have one sheep on the *hagi* for every 2 g. of its worth. In the same way, owners pay to the *seyđamađur* on Kambhagi, Líđarhagi and Tvørahagi the grazing right for half a sheep, so that actually they have five sheep on each of these grounds for every 2 g. and the *seyđamađur* has one. By the same rule a villager must own 12 g. before he qualifies to put a single animal on the rich fattening land of Hvannhagi.

Húshagi, the section of the outfield lying nearest to the village, is used as summer pasture for the cattle. The cows remain there between April 14th, traditionally the first day of summer, and July 29th, Ólavsøka Day. After that they must be tethered in the *heimabeiti* or home-field about the houses, and later in the

N

bøur when the grass has been mown. From Ólavsøka until October 25th, when all beasts are brought indoors for the winter, only the heifers and bullocks are allowed the use of Húshagi, their owners paying a small sum to the *komuna* funds in respect of the privilege. There is only one bull at Froðbøur and he is *felagsogn*, the only charge being one *byrða* of hay for winter fodder from every owner of a cow that he has served. The man who looks after the bull also gets a small payment in respect of

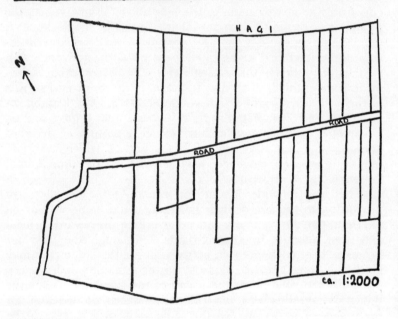

PLAN OF NEW FIELDS AT FROÐBØUR TO SHOW STRIP-CULTIVATION.

calves born, and his wages are made up to a fixed sum from the *komuna* funds.

A man may keep one cow for each *mørk* of his holding, an arrangement which does not prevent joint-ownership or deny the owner of one or more *merkur* the power to delegate his right to a poorer neighbour if he so desires. It does, however, restrict the number of cows in the settlement to twenty-four, the total value in *merkur* of the Froðbøur land. Similarly one family of geese is permitted for every *mørk* : as with the sheep, geese are brought into the *bøur* in the winter time, but must leave again for the outfield on or before May 14th. The wings of geese must be properly clipped to keep them within bounds, and a man has the right to shoot or otherwise take any unpinioned birds he may find despoiling his land.

Formerly there was no restriction on the ownership of cattle, but so much of Húshagi has been taken under cultivation as *trød* by this very busy community that a law limiting the number of cattle became essential. I was shown a plan (see page 194) of an area of Húshagi earmarked for cultivation after the war, and it was interesting to note that the ancient system of field division has not changed one whit. Each farmer will have an area corresponding in size to his holding in *bøur*, and his field will lie in a narrow, attenuated strip on either side of the roadway which will traverse the middle of the *trød*, joining the Hamar and the footpath to Tvøroyri, when the scheme is complete.

3

A few general remarks on the sheep-rearing may not be out of place, for the wealth of many a farm and community is measured by the number of sheep its outfield will support, and the number of lambs the flock will produce each year.

The year's lambs are marked when the flock is driven into the *rætt* or fold for plucking, and any man finding an unmarked sheep after that time may claim it as his own. The sheep are not actually shorn, owing to the shortness of the wool, their coats being pulled out by hand late in the summer when the wool is comparatively loose. Often the animals are dipped at the same time. As elsewhere, a certain amount of liver-fluke is rampant in the Faeroes, and the farmers use modern scientific methods to combat it. It was formerly believed that this disease arose through the sheep eating pondweed, *Potamogeton*, in the moorland pools : in the Isle of Man another plant, the marsh pennywort, was held to blame before scientific discovery revealed the truly astonishing life-history of this parasite. Both races seem to have come close to the truth, at any rate associating the disease with marshy ground, where the water-snail that is the fluke's intermediate host is to be found.

When the sheep were herded into the fold for plucking it was general in former times to sell the best ewe lamb and buy *brennivín*, a potent drink distilled from flour, and popular in the Scandinavian countries, with the proceeds. This valuable liquid was kept until the dancing season in the winter, when it was the guest of honour at a celebration called *garðarœrsgildið*, at which there was dancing and singing throughout the night, following a good meal provided by the richest *bóndi* in the village. The rams are killed at the end of September or in early October, an occasion known as *í skurð*, and the ewes about a month later, *í klipping*. At such times, when the menfolk go out into the *hagi* after the sheep, they are said to go *á fjall*—which, although it means simply " to the mountains," is used only of excursions in which work among the flocks is concerned.

Sund in south Streymoy, Dalsgarð in Sandoy, Kirkjubøur and Stóra Dímun are often cited as four of the richest areas in the Faeroes, their outfields producing some four hundred lambs a year—a very high yield of over thirty to the *mørk* in some cases. In these places there is excellent grass and the sheep feed well throughout the winter, and bring forth a large number of twins, and even triplets, in the spring. In most parts from twelve to fifteen lambs per *mørk* is considered a good yield, and it is believed that the islands produce some 30,000 to 35,000 a year, which is an average of between eight and ten lambs per *mørk*. It is said that the best mutton comes from sheep feeding at the highest altitudes ; and as the rough grazing remains good up to the turn of the year the sheep keep their fat up to that time, although the year's lambs lose weight more quickly than the adults. Owing to the hardy life these half-wild creatures lead, care is taken in many places that the ewes do not carry lambs until they are two years old, for there is then a much better chance of ewe and lamb surviving as healthy animals.

On the whole sheep-rearing in the Faeroes is a rather haphazard affair, a remarkable fact considering the vital importance of the flocks to the well-being of the community. " Faeroe wool is Faeroe gold " may well be a good proverb, and one cannot avoid the impression that much could be done to achieve a better return. The number of sheep that can be brought into the *bøur* between the end of October and the middle of May is naturally limited by the very small extent of the tilled area, and the greater part of the flocks has to run in the *hagi* the whole year round. In mild winters the sheep come to no harm, but if long periods of cold and snow precede the onset of spring the flocks suffer greatly. February and March are the danger months, for the grazing is then at its poorest and the cold and snow are usually most severe. Many sheep, physically weakened by these conditions, sicken and die when the new grass comes up in the spring, whilst others are too weak to give sufficient milk for their lambs, with a consequent mortality among the season's young. When snow covered the ground during practically the whole of January in 1945, the damage to the hill-flocks must have been considerable. One heard of farmers being obliged to slaughter their cattle so that they might use the hay to save the stricken sheep ; even those animals which were fortunate enough to be in the *bøur* were driven to the shore to find sustenance on the stranded seaweed. Not infrequently the whole stock in certain districts is irreparably damaged by a hard winter.

It is surprising that so little provision is made for the winter feeding of the flocks, for a little energy and foresight in this respect would mean not only an increased crop of lambs, but a general all-round increase in the size of the flocks—for the capacity of the *hagi* is at present determined largely by the numbers which can be supported in the winter months. Moreover, earlier and better hay-crops could be taken from the *bøur*, for it would not be necessary to keep the sheep in the infield until so late in the spring if some alternative winter feeding were available. A few farmers only have enough hay to give to their flocks in the winter, and they find that this helps enormously in keeping the animals fit. But in villages where the sheep are *felagsogn* little or no provision of this kind is made for their welfare.

The problem is an urgent one and presents many difficulties in so poor a countryside as this, and it is a question which is perennial at the *grannastevna*, the spring meeting of the farmers. The backward system of land tenure militates against the cultivation of additional ground in the *hagi* nearest to the village, either for grass or swedes and other root-crops which might be fed with advantage to the hungry sheep. In many places there are parts of the outfield where the grass grows long enough to provide a valuable crop if only the trouble were taken to cut it. It need not be necessary to spend time and trouble over the protracted business of making it into hay, for such grass could be quickly and easily prepared as silage and given to the flocks with hay and other food in the winter. Silage has been adopted by one of the best farmers in the Tórshavn area with singular success, and despite the more than usually conservative outlook of Faeroese agriculture, this manner of saving the grass crop ought to have a bright future before it in this country, where the climatic conditions admit of only a limited amount of hay being made.

4

When the Ólavsøka celebrations are over the time is ripe for the greatest harvest of the year. Haymaking—*hoyggja*, it is called —usually begins in late July and continues throughout August, for it is a protracted task ; but the start may be delayed if sheep have remained in the *bøur* until late in the spring, and in some places the last load is not home until early October. For this reason (although work in the fields had been much impeded by rainy weather) the harvest at Froðbøur in late September, 1943, was only so far advanced as I had found it on Mykines five weeks before, and it was really touch and go whether or not the greater part of the crop could be saved.

Except at Kirkjubøur and Syðradalur, where the fields are fairly large and flat, and the farmers rich, I have seen nothing of the mowing-machine whose toneless rattle and whirr gives such pleasant character to the English harvest scene. The grass is felled by scythe, *líggi*, and the act of mowing is *at sláa*. The old Faeroe scythe is shorter and lighter than its English counterpart, and the haft is straight and the blade smaller. The Norwegian and Icelandic type seems to be the most favoured nowadays : this has a long, straight haft of light wood and is held with an underhand grip, the upper arm passing beneath the shaft and the hand gripping a projecting " T "-shaped handle on the underside. The upper reach of the shaft rests in the crook of this arm, and the lower arm holds and guides the scythe in the normal way as the sweep is made by a half-turn of the mower's body.

Froðbøur has the reputation of being one of the windiest corners of the Faeroes, and for this reason there is a different tradition in haymaking to that on Mykines, and among the more conservative farmers of the Tórshavn district. Let us take the Froðbøur method first. When the grass has been cut the swathes are taken up and shaken out by hand, *at rista*, so that the grass is spread loosely and evenly over the field and will dry uniformly. Then it is turned over with the rake, *at breiða*, so that the underside will also dry. When drying is well advanced the grass is put into small hand-cocks, *kyllingar*, and these are secured by a single band of hay-rope which passes over the crown and is tucked beneath the stack on either side. These *kyllingar* are usually made in the evening and allowed to stand overnight.

After they have been broken down and the grass spread and turned once more the hay ought to be " made," and ready to put into *sátur*. The *sáta* is a fairly large and well-made tramp-cock which will stand until the farmer is ready to carry the crop home, or may even stand in the field during most of the winter months. The hay is raked together in a loose mass called *hoyrúgva*, and whilst his wife and children are busy doing this the farmer lays down the foundations of his *sáta* nearby. When it is two or three feet high he gets on top and takes the grass handed up by his wife from the *hoyrúgva*, distributing it evenly round the stack and trampling it down with his feet. As the area on top diminishes— for the cock is beehive-shaped—he kneels, pressing the grass into place with his knees. Occasionally his wife or other helper works round the tramp-cock with the wooden rake, combing out the loose grass, and so improving its solidity and appearance. It is most important that man and wife should produce a perfect *sáta*, for there is a saying in the Faeroes that those who make ugly ones will beget ugly children !

Having been well-made, the *sáta* must be well-secured, for it must stand for some time, and may have to survive heavy weather. Again hay-bands, made on the spot, are used, the man walking backwards and twisting the rope with his hands whilst his wife feeds the grass into the loose end from the *hoyrúgva*. Usually one end of the rope is pegged into the ground at the foot of the *sáta*, the rope being drawn taut over the crown and a loose stone, *kliggjagrót*, tied to the free end, below the middle of the opposite side. Two such ropes, crossing at right-angles, give the best security in the case of large *sátur*. It would be unwise to peg down both ends, of course, because in a short time the stack shrinks ; and the rope would then become very slack, with the result that a strong wind would loosen and scatter much of the hay.

All this, I should say, is the theory rather than the practice of haymaking, for if the weather is bad (and not infrequently it is) the making of *kyllingar* and the twin processes of *at rista* and *at breiða* may go on for many days until the hay is ready, or, if the worst happens, is spoiled. The *hoyrúgva*, too, is not only a necessary preliminary to the building of the *sáta*, for it is used to afford the crop protection from sudden heavy showers. At Frodbøur, in fields where *sátur* were not yet contemplated, I saw many a *hoyrúgva* frantically flung together when a dark cloud gloomed the western horizon, sweeping with evil intent out of the hills.

To turn now to other districts. When the grass is cut on Mykines and in other places among the central islands it is first spread, and then turned, in the same manner as at Froðbøur. Next the grass over an area of one or two square yards is raked together with a few deft strokes of the *hoyríva*, and the field is soon covered with numerous small mole-hill mounds of grass called *klúkar*. Later these *klúkar* are turned completely over, *at venda*, so that the sunshine can dry the undersides. When the crop is ready, hand-cocks called *sátubørn* (" children of the *sátur* ") are made, and when these have stood for a short time the hay is spread for a final drying before being carried in, or built into the more permanent tramp-cocks. In Tórshavn, Vestmanna and other places the whole process may be simplified by wrapping the swathes on a specially made wire fence or frame in the Scandinavian manner. This method is of quite recent introduction : it was first brought to Kunoy in the north islands about 1911, and has been generally adopted there and at the villages on the opposite shore of Kallsoyarfjørður. In good weather it is speedy and efficient, but it can also be wasteful in this land where high winds and sudden gales are likely to occur.

In former days it was usual to begin the haymaking by taking up the swathes and " lapping " (as the Irish term their not dissimilar method) them into small, compact bundles called *nulvingar* or *ballingar*. This preliminary, which was taken primarily to clear the ground so that the surface would dry, is now hardly ever used, although *nulvingar* are still made from the loose wisps combed out of the *sátur* when the final touches are being applied to these lovely creations !

The use of hay and straw rope has a long history in western Europe, and it was formerly made in many country districts in Britain, special twisters of a variety of patterns being used in its manufacture. These twisters have been the subject of a very thorough study by Mr. R. U. Sayce, one of our foremost ethnologists, and examples have also been figured by Dr. E. Estyn Evans for Irish districts. In Celtic countries the rope was used for a variety of purposes, such as tying down the thatch, making harness, creels and chair-seats, and as a foundation for mud-and-daub chimney canopies. Evans says it is on record that the men of Co. Wicklow descended the cliffs on these " sugan " ropes, but

HOYGGJHÚS dated 1831 at BØUR, VÁGAR.

I have not heard of the Faeroe fowlers taking such foolhardy risks ! Twisters of the types employed in Britain do not appear to have existed in the Faeroes. This rope, *bendil*, is to-day made almost invariably by hand, although formerly a small wooden instrument called *bendlasneis*, consisting of two cylindrical pieces, one turning inside the other, was used.

At the present time most of the hay is garnered in a barn or *hoyggjhús*, a splendid early example of which I have figured from Bøur in Vágar (see above). But the *hoyggjhús* is of comparatively recent institution, and in olden times it was customary to carry the crop to a handy place near the farm-buildings, and there build a large storage rick or *des*. The largest of these *desir* would contain a winter's supply of fodder for several cows and would stand about twenty feet high. The rick was often much smaller, for the usual *óðalsbóndi* seldom had more than two or three animals, and small *desir* up to ten or twelve feet in length and height are to be found in many villages even to-day.

5

It was with the building of this rick, the final phase of a long and anxious task, that the haymaking ceased to be an affair in which individual families were concerned, and became a communal event of the kind so important to the lives of peasant folk. Storing the hay in this manner required more labour than one farmer and his *húskallar* could provide, so mutual help was readily given on these occasions, and the work was accompanied by feasting and good cheer. The farmer would invite his neighbours to lend a hand, and on the great day the men would come with their families to the fields. Whilst the men were busy carrying the hay the women would gossip and make *bendlar*, and the children's play would be interrupted by the more serious business of searching for stones suitable as *klíggjagrót*. The host would have slaughtered one or more sheep specially for the occasion, so that there would be no lack of food for his willing helpers, whilst there was always a sufficiency of *brennivín* for the thirsty men. There was dancing and singing throughout the evening after the big meal which followed the completion of the task, and the celebration, *desasneið*, appears to have had much in common with the English harvest-home.

The men broke down the *sátur* standing in the fields and packed the hay in large bales, securing each with a horsehair rope that is not unlike the Irish burden-rope, even to its horn " eye." A good *byrða*, as such a bale is called, would fill a seven fathom rope, doubled around it with one lengthwise and one crosswise turn (as though it were a rectangular parcel tied with a double strand of twine), and its weight would be about 120 lbs. Raising it was no mean athletic feat—and indeed, still is, for even in Tórshavn to-day most of the hay is borne home on the backs of men. The man lies on his back on top of the bale, gripping the crosswise turn of the rope with both hands, just above his head. Then, whilst another man heaves the burden upwards and forwards to its point of balance, he comes forward into a kneeling position, and then rises, balancing the awkward load, to his feet. I have been told—and well believe—that the men spent most of the evening of the *desasneið* in shaking their heads to get the stiffness out of their necks !

At first each man would arrange his own bale on the rick and go back to the field for more, but as the *des* grew in size fewer men could be spared to carry the hay. Two men were required to stand on top and take the *byrður* handed up to them, and build the hay into the stack ; three or four were needed below to throw the hay up ; another went round the stack combing out the loose grass with the hay-rake, and occasionally still another had to find long spars of wood to set against the sides of the *des* to keep them from bulging outwards. An old and experienced hand, or the *bóndi* himself, would always keep a watchful eye on the work to see that building was proceeding in the right way. Eventually the rick would be built inwards, to give it a sloping roof like the roof of a house, and the men on top would have to kneel to their work, and finally pack the hay down whilst sitting astride the ridge. The last thing, before they descended, was to take the hay-ropes thrown over the *des* from below, and place them at short and regular intervals along the ridge, and then peg into the roof above the " gable-ends " those ropes which secured these sides. A *belti* of rope was carried right round the walls of the *des* to provide greater security, and sometimes a rough stone wall was raised about the stack, a yard or so away, so that the animals would not be able to get at the hay. Year after year the *des* was built on the same site, usually on a platform of rocks to give it better ventilation and drainage, and it was customary to put some of the year-old fodder in the middle of the rick to counteract the " sweating " of the new hay.

I passed one or two days very pleasantly in making hay during the Froðbøur holiday. Most of the time seemed to be spent in going from one plot to another, turning the grass here, making or breaking *kyllingar* there, or building a beautiful *sáta* somewhere else. I was taught many little points in local technique—such as that, in turning the spread hay, one should stand to the windward to use the rake, merely lifting the grass and letting the breeze do the rest. At one time I was in disgrace because I left my rake lying on the ground with the tines pointing upwards, for to do that, they say, is to invite rain ! My retort that it was sure to rain anyway, this being the Faeroes, was thought to be in very poor taste !

This was the first reasonably fine day for some little time (except for the previous Sunday—but no good Faeroeman will break the Sabbath even if his crop is in imminent danger of ruin) and every villager was fully occupied in the fields. There was no school for the children, since they and their school-mistress had much more important work to do. When the people are working against time and the weather, as is so often the case when the harvest is left so late, they have no thought for anything other than the vital importance of saving the grass. There is no attempt to prepare the usual meals at the usual times, and all housework is left in abeyance. The children bring tea and sand-wiches to their parents, and give what other help they can. One of the pleasantest moments of the day was when we sat down in the lee of a *sáta* during a shower for which I was deemed to be personally responsible, and drank hot tea noisily out of bottles, to wash down a frugal lunch of white bread and cheese.

The fields are raked clean, and not a wisp of hay is wasted. Even hay spoiled by the weather is saved for its usefulness as bedding for the cow. The loss or partial loss of the crop is a major tragedy which may have far-reaching consequences to the community, and indeed we have seen that the successful harvest-home was here, as in other countries, a matter for celebration and rejoicing among all the people. I used to imagine, in England, that haymaking was a very simple process of sending a succession of machines round a field, and taking the finished article away on a wagon. I suspect that this may be an exaggerated view, for it is very obvious that haymaking by hand is a long, tedious and intricate business which plays a truly astonishing part in the country's spiritual life. Consider, for instance, the many qualities it demands—the art of swinging a scythe with an unvarying, unflagging rhythm through the sometimes wet and heavy grass, the art of twisting a good strong rope with your hands, and the supreme joy of building a *sáta* that will scorn a tempest and (which is more important !) give your neighbours no cause for levity concerning the generation to come ! There is, too, the athletic prowess of lifting and bearing the shaggy *byrða* on your back, the ability to judge the weather and make the right decisions for the safety of your crop, and the final display of science and skill in the construction of the *des*. Haymaking, simple though it may seem to the unitiated, is indeed a glorious spotlight on the achievement of rustic culture ; and although the machine-age may have made it, for better or worse, a subject in agricultural science, its proper place among these far islands remains in the proper study, ethnology, man's study of mankind.

References to Chapter Eight

EVANS, E. E. (1944) ; NICLASSEN, P. (1938-39) ; SAYCE, R. U. (1939) ; WALKER, F. and DAVIDSON, C. F. (1935-36) ; WEIHE, A. (1928).

HESTUR CHURCH.

Chapter Nine

CORN HARVESTING AND MILLING

1. A description of how barley is grown and harvested, and of the *sodnhús* where it is prepared for milling (*page* 206).
2. Notes on the process in former times, and the place of the *sodnhús* in village life (*page* 212).
3. The fine old farm Niðri á Bø and its setting, with some remarks on building methods (*page* 214).
4. The little water-mill at Niðri á Bø and how it works (*page* 217).
5. A brief history of the horizontal water-mill in north-west Europe (*page* 221).
6. Some other Faeroe mills, with notes on the miller's life and the Faeroeman's daily bread (*page* 225).

I

WHEN THE HAY has been gathered in the people's attention turns towards the standing corn. Even so late in the year (for it is now September) the fields are still green and far from ripe. Nevertheless, it is high time the crop was harvested and carried to the village for treatment in the special kilns called *sodnhús* which prepare the grain for the mill. Only the hardy six-rowed barley or bigg is grown in the Faeroes, and even under the comparatively mild and sunny conditions which prevail in Suðuroy, where more grain is produced than in the rest of the islands together, this artificial drying is always necessary.

Our week's holiday in Suðuroy gave me splendid opportunities for studying the manner in which this last harvest of the season is made. Shortly after our return I came across the excellent account given by the Rev. G. Landt, and it is remarkable how little the method has changed in the course of a hundred and fifty years. Almost the only difference lies in the fact that men now replace women in the work in the *sodnhús*. I have thought it worth while quoting freely from his book to provide a historical

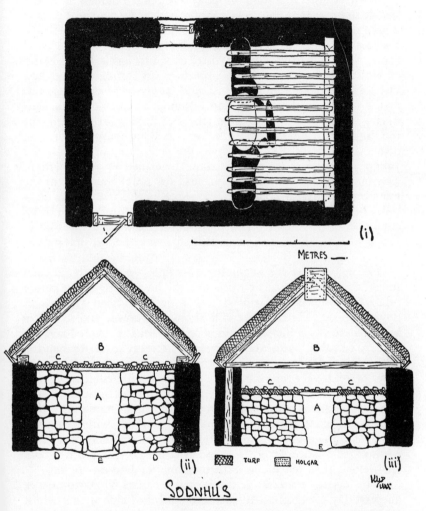

<u>SOÐNHÚS</u>

Plan and sections of examples at Froðbøur (i & ii) and Koltur
(iii)   A, Soðnker; B, Soðnur; C, Soðnspølur; D, Munni; E,
Munnhella.

background for my own notes, and to give this important phase of Faeroe folk-culture the completeness of record it deserves.

Corn is still a regular crop at Froðbøur, though it is not nearly so important now as was formerly the case, when (it is said) a greater quantity was grown than at any other settlement in the Faeroes. Sunnbøur and Fámjin, also in Suðuroy, have good reputations as barley-growing districts, whilst formerly the island of Koltur and village of Kollafjørður had probably the best yields in the north and central islands. Only one *sodnhús* remains at the Hamar in Froðbøur, and although it had not been used during the war I was assured that it would most certainly be required again afterwards. I examined it in company with its owners, Olaus and Emil Hammer, my wife, and our host Daniel Jákup Jensen, and from all of these I gleaned my information. The building was full of cobwebs and the usual *bric-à-brac* of the Faeroese outhouses—spades, rakes, ropes, nets, *leypar* and so on— but when my eyes grew accustomed to the semi-darkness and the confusion of its contents, and the story of the *sodnhús* was told to me, it took on an interest its forbidding aspect had at first belied.

Let us begin at the beginning. Sowing is done by hand, and in common with the turf-cutting and the haymaking it is a family affair. On the large farms it was done by women servants in days gone by. Harrows are still almost unknown, and in places where there is a sufficient depth of soil the seed is covered and the clods are broken by means of a special broad rake, called *kornríva*, which has a double row of iron tines (see page 210). Where the layer of soil is very thin the family may stab the earth instead with light spades such as are used for cutting the turf, this treatment serving the same ends, and going by the same name, *at mylda*. Finally, in place of rolling, the earth is pounded with a wooden *klárur* (see page 210), a heavy board set at one end of a long, low-angled shaft. Apart from an occasional visit for weeding, the field is then left alone until the time for harvest comes.

This event, *kornskurátíð*, traditionally begins on Bartolsmessa, the first day of autumn, August 24th, and the fields are cut whilst the barley is still green. A reaping-hook, *akurknívur*, is used, or sometimes a scythe-blade with a cloth binding or wooden grip fitted to the wider end. The mower cuts a handful of corn at a time, and several of these are laid down together to form a sheaf, which is taken up by a woman following him. When there are sufficient to form a man's load she binds these sheaves together

(*Top*) Niðri á bøur farmstead and watermill

(*Bottom*) Nólsoy—a group of *hjallar*

Haymaking at Frodbøur   (*Top*) Building a *sáta*

(*Bottom*) Carrying *byrdir*

with a piece of hay-
band wound two or
three times round the
middle, and the *bundi*
thus formed is ready
to be carried home.
Landt says of this
toil, " the sheaves are
placed on the highest
side of the field above
each other, in such a
manner that the ears

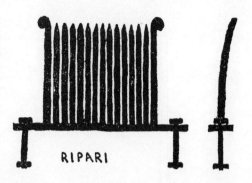

RIPARI

hang over the brink " (i.e. the edge of the drainage channel in
the old *teigur*) " that the water, in case the corn has been cut wet,
may run off, and that it may be better dried by the wind."

" After being exposed in this manner for a few days," he
continues, " it is carried home ; and the ears are separated from
it by picking them off with the hands ; but a machine invented
for this purpose by a person named Debes, has lately been introduced into these islands, and is now almost generally used." This
device is doubtless the one shown to me by our host, a smithy-
made comb having a single row of about a dozen close-set iron
teeth, and called *ripari* (see above).   It is bolted to a firm wooden
base, such as a bench-top or doorpost, when required for the
process *at ripa*.   One man takes a handful of barley from the
loosened *bundi* and presses the straws into the comb, the ears
pointing away from him, and with a sharp tug towards the body
he brings the straws through the long teeth, so that the ears are
wrenched off and fall into a tray or other receptacle below.   He
drops the handful of straws behind him, where a second person
removes from it any grass or weeds that will make green fodder,
and with a single straw ties the remainder in a small bundle
known as *hólgi*.

Corn and *hólgar* are taken to the *sodnhús* for drying.   This is a
rectangular stone building divided into two unequal sections by
a stone partition-wall, *munni*, beyond which is a little-used section
called *sodnker*.   The bigger compartment, as we shall see, is used
as a threshing floor after the ears have been dried.   In the opening
between these two sections a rude hearth, *munnhella*, occupies a
depression in the earth floor.   The half-loft above the smaller
room, *sodnur*, has a floor of wooden poles, *sodnspølir*, set at
intervals of three or four inches.   At one end they rest on a turf

o

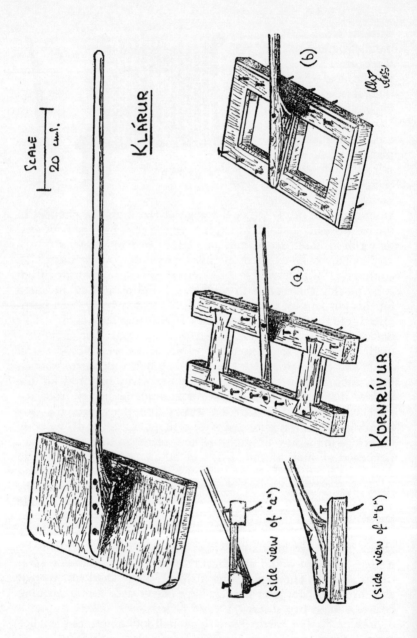

SCALE
20 cms.

KLÁRUR

(a)

(b)

(side view of "a")

(side view of "b")

KORNRÍVUR

packing along the top of the partition-wall, and at the other on a wooden beam which rests against the gable-end. I made measurements of the existing *sodnhús* at the Hamar, and a plan and section are given on page 207.

Numerous *hólgar*, packed tightly together, are placed across the poles to form a floor, and the broad and narrow ends of the sheaves are laid alternately so that a close fitting is assured. On top of this floor the ears of corn are scattered to a depth of an inch or so. A turf fire is lighted in the hearth and is kept burning, not too fiercely, day and night. Usually there are four men working in the *sodnhús* and they sleep in the building whilst it is in use. At times they must find this very uncomfortable, for there is no chimney or hole in the roof to provide an outlet for the smoke, although sometimes, if this gets too dense, a wooden hatch in the rear wall is opened and the draught from the door soon clears the smoke away. This draught can also be used if necessary to regulate the temperature : a chimney, I was told, would permit most of the heat to escape, with the resultant loss of time and efficiency in drying the corn. The men work in watches so that there is always somebody available to tend the fire, and climb to the loft at intervals to turn the corn, so that the ears will dry uniformly.

When the ears are dry they are collected and the *hólgar* are removed and made into a stack, *hólgasáta*, outside. A fresh floor of straw is made and more ears are dried whilst the corn from the first lot is threshed and winnowed in the larger room. The grain is cast on the earth floor, which is hard-baked owing to the constant heat of the fire, and is beaten with wooden bats called *treskjur*, which have short handles and are flat on the underside. The four men do the threshing, kneeling one at each corner, facing inwards : those at opposite corners synchronize their strokes so that two bats descend as the others go up. Afterwards the corn is put into a wide, shallow tray and vigorously shaken so that the chaff rises and falls away. This *dumbur* was often saved and used as fodder, being boiled in water to make a kind of gruel. The *hólgar* are employed in roof and chimney construction, as is described in connection with the farm Niđri á Bø, but in hard times the straw was also fed to the animals, mixed with more palatable food.

2

Such is the method employed at the present day. For comparison, I give in full Landt's account of how it was carried out at the end of the eighteenth century :

" The operations of drying, thrashing and cleaning the corn, is performed in Faeroe by women ; and it would be considered, particularly in some places, as very indecent if men should perform that kind of labour. When the woman who attends the drying-house, or kiln, thinks the corn is sufficiently dry, it is taken off ; and if there be a large quantity of it, she is assisted on this occasion by one or two girls. A door is then placed lengthwise on the floor, and in a somewhat sloping direction, with one end of it resting against the wall, and on this door a certain quantity of the ears are deposited ; the three females then get upon the door with their backs turned towards the wall, and with their feet tread upon the ears till they are pretty well bruised. Some extend a rope before them, which they lay hold off with their hands to assist them in this labour, and to enable them to jump up with more facility.

" The women then place themselves on their knees, and with a piece of wood shaped somewhat like a bat, thresh or beat the corn in measure, and then it is cleaned. One of the girls holds a kind of tray, by means of which she separates the chaff from the corn ; and the other has a sieve consisting of a skin, stretched over a hoop, but without holes, into which the winnowed corn is thrown by the first girl. This sieve is then whirled round in the hands in order that the dirt and bad grains may rise to the top, and these being picked out, the corn is put into another tray, where it is winnowed for the last time.

" The labour of drying and cleansing the corn is not entrusted to unexperienced girls, but to such as are fully acquainted with the whole process, and capable of performing it in a complete manner. The woman who attends to the drying-house, and superintends the whole operation, receives, besides her victuals and a live lamb, what the inhabitants call *turkagiekn ;* that is, as much corn of each drying as she can hold between her hands ; also *sodnkieiakodn*, the ears which in drying fall down between the laths, and are either over-dried or half-burnt ;

and *lattukodn*,* or the chaff which remains after winnowing, and which she divides with the girls who have assisted her to winnow and thresh."

This description, obviously the result of careful personal observation, forms a valuable historical record. When I was in Froðbøur I was introduced to a dear old lady of eighty years or so, who, I was assured, had dried and threshed more corn than any other person in the village—so that little more than a quarter of a century can have elapsed since men replaced women in this work.

When we visited Fámjin—a village with one of the loveliest settings in the Faeroes—we saw on the wall of our host's parlour an oil-painting of the interior of the *sodnhús* at Nes, which lies between Porkeri and the port of Vágur. Four women, in long black dresses and white caps and aprons, are kneeling near the four corners, belabouring the corn-strewn floor with their *treskjur*. A *kola* light hangs from a beam, and—ingenious touch!—a kettle lies ready to hand against the wall. The most interesting feature of this kiln (and I was told there were others like it at Fámjin and elsewhere) is that not one, but two fires, burn in evenly-spaced hearths which break up the dividing wall.

Corn from the first drying (*einnáttarsodnur*, " one night's drying ") was very often set aside for the following year's seed. The remainder, incidentally, was usually stored in the loft or the *hjallur* for a year before being milled, partly to create a reserve as an insurance against famine, and partly so that the smoky taint would disperse. Latterly, in some places, corn was actually wind-dried in the *hjallur* in preference to the *sodnhús*, so that the grain would not have the disagreeable smoky taste.

Olaus Hammer told us that Froðbøur latterly produced some eight or ten barrels of corn per year, but that half a century ago between forty and fifty was the regular output. From two to three days, treatment, depending upon the condition of the crop when it was cut, was normally required to prepare one barrel for milling. He estimated that the *sodnur* would hold about ten bucketfuls of corn at a time. In Froðbøur's hey-day there were no less than five kilns in the Hamar, one very old one being contiguous to the present building, whilst another, the exterior of which is in much its original state, still stands against the *hagi*

* Jacobsen and Matras spell the words as follows : *turkageykn*, *sodnkerakorn* and *lættikorn*.

wall behind the houses. These were kept working at full pressure in the late summer, preparing the grain for as many mills.

It was evident that the people of Froðbøur cherished many happy memories of the times they had spent at work in these dark ill-ventilated places ; and that to them, as doubtless to many among the islands, the *sodnhús* stands for something bright and cheerful in the old folk-life that is slowly but surely fading away. For the men and women gathered here in the evenings, and in the daytime too if there was much rain and little work could be done in the fields, and told long-remembered tales and sagas that had come down to them (perhaps through their fathers, beneath this self-same roof) from olden times, or indulged in the daily exchange of gossip with those in charge. During those September days the building was the centre of the village social life, for the people met in its warm and smoky fug in that communion of brotherhood which is possible only to those who enjoy similar interests and outlook, the same cultural antecedents, and who take their gladness and disappointments together in the hard toil and varying fortune of the village life. Unquestionably such meetings played no small part in breeding in this race of men an awareness of their distinct historical background, and so kept alive those cultural attributes which are marked features of the Faeroe way of life.

We see, therefore, that the *sodnhús* is much more than a rude stone outhouse with the green grass growing from the roof. It is something more, even, than the heart of a rustic industry, for beyond its immediate purpose and reason for existence it has stood for many centuries as a monument to the peasant culture of the tiny Faeroe race.

3

In the palmy days of the Froðbøur corn-growing industry there were at least four small mills serving the Hamar. Two, Kristnahús and Óman Tún, stood a little apart on the same stream behind the houses, and a third, Laðnum, was also situated in the village area. A very old mill was sited below a waterfall, Millufossur, between Froðbøur and Tvøroyri. All trace of these has vanished and nowadays the only water-mill in the district is at Niðri á Bø, a farm on the coast below the Hamar.

This is unquestionably the finest group of farm-buildings I

have seen in the Faeroes, and it was a constant source of admiration to me during our stay. It is a beautifully compact group, in a most picturesque setting, and its splendid condition is a tribute to the pride and care bestowed upon it by the present occupiers, who have maintained it in excellent repair without destroying any of its pristine glory. Niðri á Bø is more than a farm : it is a valuable historic possession of which Faeroe people should be proud. It belongs to the same class of monument as Dúgvugarður at Saksun, which has the nominal protection of the Museum authorities, the fine old farm on Koltur, the stone mills at Sandavágur and the old barn at Bøur, all of which, as yet, have not. In a country whose government has still to realise it has a duty to preserve such manifestations of the people's culture for posterity, it is a matter for satisfaction that a place like Niðri á Bø is in good hands.

The farm is a subject no student of folk-culture could possibly resist, and it is worth describing in some detail as a gem of Faeroese farm-planning and peasant architecture. It stands a little way back from the low shore, the majority of its infield (for it is a " kongs " estate) extending along the coast on either side and the hill-slope behind. The land has a gentle slope, and a stream, which feeds the mill, descends from the Hamar through a pleasant grassy *gil* and runs past the farmhouse to the shore. Behind the buildings the motor road from Froðbøur to Tvøroyri curves underneath the *hamrar*, with its gay flowers and picturesque outcrops of six-sided basalt columns, and is carried across the stream on a new concrete bridge that made sharp contrast with the centuries-old settlement below.

The house is a black walled, wooden building, rectangular in plan, with a big stone-flagged *roykstova*, a kitchen and living-room combined, at the western end, and the spotlessly clean and airy *glasstova* or sitting-room in the east. The roof is of characteristic sod construction and an important detail, now rarely observed in the Faeroes, is the straw-thatched chimney—a feature reminiscent of the chimneys of early Manx and other Celtic dwellings, and one which I have also seen at an old black house near the church in Norðragøta, on Eysturoy. Water is drawn from a spring in the field rising from the eastern bank of the stream, and in the middle of the haggard before the house there is a huge flat boulder where, I was told, the farm-workers used to gather in the evenings to sit and smoke and yarn.

Across this yard is an old walled cemetery. Many years ago,

before the rise of Tvøroyri as an important port, the Froðbøur parish church was located here. Later it was removed to the lower village farther west, and finally to Tvøroyri itself, since when it has been replaced by the fine new wooden church which dominates the town. With its cream-painted walls and bright red roof, western bell-tower and imitation buttresses enhancing its lofty appearance, it is to my eye more pleasing and sympathetic to Faeroe traditions than the more ornate and ambitious church in the Danish style at Vágur, Suðuroy's other important town.

The barn at Niðri á Bø, a large erection in masonry and wood standing a little above and to the west of the farmhouse, is a noble example of Faeroe peasant architecture. It has double gable walls of impressive width, consisting of an inner and outer face of basalt blocks with a rubble filling between. The rear wall is also of stone, but the front consists of wooden planks loosely joined so that the wind can penetrate and help to dry the hay. Above the low cliff a hundred yards to the east are the remains of two older *hoyggjhús*, as well as those of a meat-drying *hjallur*, built on the edge of the cliff so as to get the best advantage from the continual up-draught of air. The *hjallur* is an interesting outhouse in that the loose stone construction has required an oval rather than rectangular plan, dispensing with corners : the stones are rounded and water-worn and obviously from the nearby beach, whereas those used in the farm-buildings appear to have been quarried from the *hamrar* above. The present *hjallur*, a wooden one with a sod roof, stands on the bank of the stream near the white-washed byre or *fjós*—again carefully sited so as to intercept the continual currents of air moving along the course of the stream.

Below the barn and beyond the walled-in flower gardens (for in such a situation walls are necessary to protect the plants from the strong winds) stands the *sodnhús*, in common with the barn and boathouse a grass-roofed building, and in very much its original condition. At a glance it does not appear to differ from the *sodnhús* in the village, but owing to the fact that the present tenants, the ducks, had made of its once-hard earth floor a quagmire much more to their liking than mine, I did not examine the interior closely. Cheek by jowl with the *sodnhús* is the *neyst*, another double-walled structure where the men of Niðri á Bø keep their boat. Before it a slipway, with loose wooden rollers for the keel, runs down to the rocky shore.

Roof-construction in these Faeroe outbuildings is interesting and worth a passing reference. The rafters rise from a wooden beam lying along the outside edge of the thick stone wall, and each is mortised into its opposite number at the gable by a simple tongue and slot. There is no roof-tree, nor (except in large buildings) are there any ties. Flat boards, unevenly spaced, are nailed to the rafters to fill the spaces between, and usually the uppermost of these will form an inverted " V " at the apex of the roof. The apex is called *møna*, the rafter *sperra*, and the short boards which join the rafters *tróðr*. In the older buildings, especially in good corn districts, the roof has a thatch of closely packed *hólgar* outside the *tróðr*, but more usually a layer of birch bark, imported from Norway, takes its place. The covering of sods is supported at the eaves by a narrow plank running the full length of the roof, called *flaghaldi*, and on larger roofs the sods are held down by a pair of narrow planks, called *vindskeið*, which reach from the eaves to the gable and are mortised at the top. In small buildings there is no need for these boards, and in some cases large stones placed on the roof serve the same purpose (see page 69).

4

The building which interested me the most was the little mill, a perfect gem of its kind probably unique in the Faeroes to-day— for, although other mills exist (as we shall see), they are of more recent and much poorer construction. With the permission of the owners I was able to examine this example closely, and from my notes have made a diagram of the working parts (see page 218), which, with a brief description, will serve to explain how this primitive engine works.

As to the mill itself, the double side-walls seem massive for so tiny a building—it is only two metres in length and height, and less than that in width—and they taper from 80-90 cms. at their base to less than half that thickness at the eaves. As with the *sodnhús*, the roof is thatched with straw underneath the sods.

To set the mill working it is first of all necessary to dam the stream and so divert the water into the earth trench which serves as a race. This is done by dropping a stout wooden board, *slúsa*, which slides up or down grooves cut in a wooden framework, and thus controls the flow of water along the stream. The diverted water rushes down the race and is directed by a wooden trough, *rennustokkur*, against the eight flat paddles which form the spokes or vanes of the wheel in the cellar. In cases where the

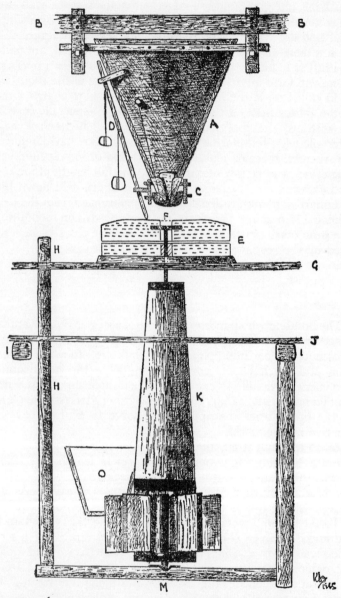

HORIZONTAL WATER-MILL based on example at NIBRI A' BØ, SUÐUROY.

rennustokkur has a shallow inclination these vanes are often mortised obliquely into the bottom of the upright shaft, the better to catch the full force of the descending stream. The shaft is a long wooden cylinder, often tapering outwards towards its base. It is called *kvarnkallur*, or, together with the wheel, *mylnuspael*—a poetic name, since the verb *at spaela* means "to play!"

At the centre of the axle-base an iron gudgeon pivots on a hollow iron plate at the middle of a stout cross-beam which rests on the cellar floor. At the top of the shaft a vertical iron spindle enters the mill through a cavity, called *grotti*, at the centre of the nether-stone, and is made fast in grooves in the eye of the upper stone by means of a " T "-shaped piece called a sile or *sigli*. Thus any motion given to the wheel is at once transmitted by means of the spindle and sile to the upper millstone.

In most of the north British and Scandinavian mills there is a simple wooden lever affixed to one end of the big cross-beam below the wheel, and this rises perpendicularly into the mill, where it terminates in a sword-hilt handle called *laettitrae*. By raising or lowering this handle, and jacking it up at the required height by means of wedges, the miller can adjust the space between the two stones, or, if he wishes, separate them for cleaning. This cross-beam is called a sole-tree, and the lever is known as the lightening-tree, the Faeroe name for the latter being *lyftustong*.

The *kvørn* is mounted on a wooden bench or *lúður* which is raised some eighteen inches or two feet above the floor of the mill. The nether-stone has grooves chipped in its base and these fit over pieces of wood nailed to the bench in such a way that the stone is firmly held. The grinding surface of the upper stone is not grooved in any way, but the Faeroese recognise three distinct tracks through which the corn has to pass—an inner one called *kornfari* surrounding the *grotti*, a middle track called *mellingi* and an outer one *fellingi*.

Key to diagram opposite.

A, Hopper, loosely supported by struts attached to roof-timbers, B; C, Shoe, attached by wooden bracket and pins to hopper; D, *rystari* weighted with stones; E, Quern; F, Eye of quern, and sile; G, Bench or *lúður*; H, Sword or *lættitræ* at top of lightening tree; I, Timbers supporting floor, J; K, Tirl or *kvarnkallur*; L, Wheel; M, Ground-sile in middle of sole-tree; N, Bolster-head; O, Position of *rennustokkur*.

Corn is fed to the eye of the quern from the spout of a " shoe," usually called *fótur*, but at Kvívík known as *svíni* because of a fancied resemblance to the snout of a pig ! This is suspended, usually by string (but at Niðri á Bø by wooden brackets and pins), from the corn-box or hopper, which is itself supported loosely on a framework affixed to the roof-timbers.

Thus far the mechanism is in no way different from that of the Shetland and Hebridean mills described by Goudie, but the manner in which the grain is induced to fall from the spout of the shoe to the eye of the quern is distinct. In the north British mills a "clapper"—usually a block of wood, but sometimes a stone —is tied to the shoe by a leather thong and allowed to trail on the revolving upper stone, so that its continuous vibration is imparted to the shoe, causing a steady flow of corn. The same principle is adopted in the Faeroes, with a different application. A long thin stick, attached to both hopper and shoe by wooden brackets, and with its lower end standing on the upper stone, takes the place of the " clapper." This stick is variously called *rystari* (heard at Tórshavn and in Suðuroy), *stiltari* (at Kvívík), and *dartari* (at Skálavík in Sandoy), the name in each case being descriptive of the shaking or jumping motion of the stick when the mill is in operation. Hr. Karl Ervik, who remembered the form of several mills in South Brundal, near Aalesund in Norway, told me that an identical device was used there.

The rotary movement of the quern throws the ground meal on to the bench, whence it is gathered up by wooden scoops, or swept with a special brush, *sóbil*, into a deep bin standing below. The brush is made of two goose-wings sewn together : similar dusters are also used in the house, and are called *kvastrar*, the other name being specially reserved for the miller's brush. Before the brown meal is ready for use it must be put through a sieve, which is in the form of a small rectangular box having a piece of the stomach-skin of the caaing-whale, punctured with numerous holes, stretched across the bottom.

This final sifting and cleaning marks the last of the many operations necessary for the transmutation of the green ears of barley into the brown flour from which *drýlur*, the Faeroe bread, is made. It is a long and varied, and perhaps tedious process ; and no matter what its eventual fate in the islands may be, it will remain a story of undying interest to those who find pleasure and instruction in the social and economic history of mankind.

5

The water-mill with the horizontal wheel is the most primitive power-mill in the world, and although much has been written about it, its origin, and the route or routes by which it came to north-west Europe, remain wrapped in the mists of antiquity. The genius who first conceived the idea of harnessing a stream to drive the rotary quern must be reckoned one of the greatest of forgotten human benefactors, for the emancipation from drudgery which followed its discovery was immense. Antipater of Thessalonica sang an enthusiastic paeon of praise in its honour as early as 20 B.C., very soon, we may suppose, after its introduction to Greece . . .

" Cease your work at the querns, ye grinding-maids ; sleep long, even if the crowing of the cocks proclaim the dawn. For Demeter has laid the toils of your hand upon the water-nymphs, and they, leaping down upon the top of the wheel, turn the axle which by its whirling spokes causes the heavy, hollow Nisyrian mill-stones to revolve . . ."

King Mithridates of Pontus, on the shores of the Black Sea, had among the wonders of his city some such " water-grinder " as this—so we are told by the historian Strabo. Pontus fell to the Roman Pompey in 65 B.C., and with that conquest the horizontal mill perhaps began its wanderings through the western world. Later it spread all over rural Italy, to north Spain and south-west France, and doubtless from there to Ireland, whence the Dalriadic Scots may have carried the idea to the Scottish mainland. Abroad, the principle is or was known in Roumania, Norway, Sweden, Asia Minor, Syria, Turkestan and far away in China : and indeed, it has been pertinently suggested that the invention may have arisen in the fertile minds of the Chinese, and have reached Europe along the great caravan route through Turkestan to the Near East.

Whether or not the Vikings took the idea home with them from their forays in the Irish Sea, as E. C. Curwen has suggested, is a debatable point. Certainly the horizontal water-mill is widely used in the vast rural areas of Norway and Sweden, and has been in use formerly all along the line of Norse occupation in the west of Britain, from Shetland (where Sir Walter Scott estimated their number at five hundred in 1814), through Orkney and the Outer Hebrides south to Ireland and the Isle of Man.

There is clear evidence, however, of the existence of two quite distinct families of horizontal mills, having important structural differences, in these regions. It is obvious from the detailed descriptions of Goudie and others that the Shetland-Hebridean type has close affinities with the Faeroe and Norwegian mills, whilst the Irish-Manx-Scottish mills form an inter-related group. In the former the wheel usually has from six to ten flat paddles, whereas in the latter it is made up of a larger number of long, narrow, spoon-shaped vanes. In these mills the quern was apparently on the floor, whereas in Norway and the Faeroes, and some Shetland examples, it is on a raised bench called by the same name, " ludr " or *lúður*, in each area. In the northern mills one finds the lightening-tree and sole-tree lever system, but there is as yet no clear evidence that it existed in the southern ones. The key to the distribution of the mills in north-west Europe may lie in the origin of this mechanism or its adaptation to the water-driven quern : it was certainly a part of the Shetland hand-mill, and it has been suggested that some such lever was associated with late Bronze Age rotary querns in ancient Ireland.

The differences were remarkably constant in the two areas, and this strongly suggests the possibility of an independent origin for each type. Curwen is doubtless right in believing that the Irish-Manx-Scottish type was introduced from the Mediterranean area along the line of the ancient sea trade route which followed the Atlantic coast ; but it seems equally probable, on the present evidence, that Shetland, Orkney and the Outer Hebrides derived their mills from Norway and not from the south. The principle may well have been brought to the Scandinavian peninsula by the Swedish Vikings, who are known to have penetrated along the Volga and its tributaries to the Near East, where such mills existed in the earliest centuries of the Christian era.

I cannot believe that the horizontal mill has a long history in the Faeroe Islands : if it has, then it must have been an exceedingly rare object until the nineteenth century. The mill is not mentioned in the work of Lucas Debes, dated 1673, and the first references to it appear to be those in the MS account of the Faeroes written by J. C. Svabo following his visit in 1781-82. According to the published extracts from this very thorough study of the life and manners of the people, most of the milling was done in hand-querns, a servant-girl being employed specifically for this task on the bigger farms. Svabo describes how she sang hymns to the rhythm of the quern, in order to lighten the drudgery. At that time the ruins of old mills were to be seen at Eiði, Froðbøur and Kunoyarbygd, and nine extant mills were known to him, including two which housed two querns. Four of these were owned by farmers, and two by clergymen : three of the mills, the oldest dating from 1740, were at Tórshavn, where there lived a builder of mills, one Johannes Poulsen.

The Rev. Jørgen Landt, who was resident in the Faeroes for a number of years at the end of the eighteenth century, gives the impression that the water-mills were just then coming into favour. There were about twenty in existence, and the number was increasing. His description of the mill and its mechanism is very complete and might well apply generally to the examples (some of fairly recent construction) to be found to-day. The place-name Myllá (" the stream of the mill ") occurs on five islands—at Kunoyarbygd, near Húsar on Kallsoy, on Nólsoy and Hestur, and at Froðbøur in Suðuroy.

It is obvious from a study of the mechanism and the nomen-clature of the various parts that the principle was introduced from Norway, although a ninety years' old mill at Bøur in Vágar may have some Shetland influence. It is a large and entirely stone-built example, with small lintel-covered apertures for the waterflow, almost identical with the Shetland mills. During the eighteenth century, when it seems possible that the mill was introduced to the islands, Faeroemen sometimes sailed to Shetland in their twelve-oared boats. A plan of this site is given on page 224.

In the Faeroes these buildings are usually small and nearly square wooden sheds, as was the case in Landt's time : the walls are of planks, not logs as in the Norwegian mills. Many of the older examples, however, have two and sometimes three of the walls built of undressed local basalt stones. The roof in both types consists of grassy sods laid on a thatch of *hólgar* as at Niðri á Bø, or more usually a layer of birch bark, *naevur*, imported from Norway. In recent buildings, however, the roof is often of wooden boards or corrugated iron sheets. The cellar or underhouse is always of stone and is usually open at two sides to allow the stream unrestricted passage.

There are two major reasons for their steady decline as an economic proposition in recent years. Firstly, the potato has widely increased its popularity since the beginning of the nine-

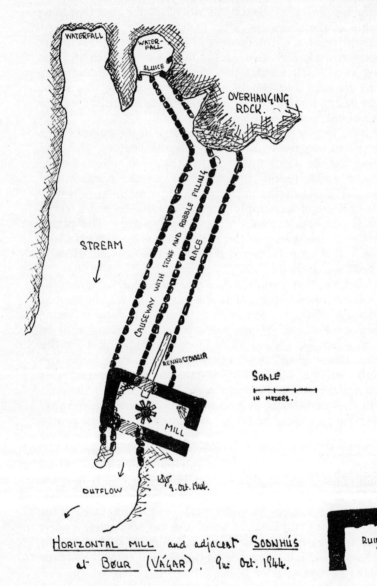

WATERFALL

WATER-FALL

SLUICE

OVERHANGING ROCK.

STREAM

CAUSEWAY WITH STONE AND RUBBLE FILING

RACE

RENNUSTOKKUR

SCALE

IN METRES.

MILL

OUTFLOW

9. Oct. 1944.

HORIZONTAL MILL and adjacent SODNHÚS at BØUR (VÁGAR). 9ᵘ Oct. 1944.

RUINS OF SODNHÚS

Faeroe village and fields

The Klakksvík—Arnafjørður road-tunnel

teenth century, and has now largely replaced the barley crop ; and secondly, the increase in sea traffic between the Faeroes and Denmark within the present century has encouraged the importation of flour. Villages which supported several mills even within living memory now maintain only one, or have found it more convenient to revert to the old hand-querns for grinding the little grain they grow. So the horizontal mills, perhaps the earliest and most romantic machines in the world, which took more than a millennium and a half to cross Europe to their journey's end in these Atlantic islands, are here as elsewhere slowly disappearing from the human scene.

6

When we left Froðbøur a few days of our holiday remained, and we decided to spend them at Saltangará, near the mouth of Skálafjørður, that long arm of the sea which reaches to the heart of Eysturoy. A dormant interest in the history and distribution of the horizontal water-mills had been aroused by my visit to Niðri á Bø, and I remembered having seen a pair of these buildings on a previous excursion at the corner of the quiet bay where the stream from Toftavatn enters the fiord.

I found that the mills were very young : from dates incised on their central beams they appear to have been first used in 1895 and 1904 respectively. Nevertheless, young or old, such relics of a passing age are to me irresistible, and on going down from the road I found my curiosity amply rewarded, for the lower mill was actually hard at work. The sparkling water rushed through the cellar, spinning the shaft at a tremendous rate, and the clatter was almost deafening. I was instantly reminded of a children's rhyme which Rasmus Rasmussen wrote out for me one night when we were discussing the Tórshavn mills of his younger days :

> *The short stick is dancing*
> *The axle sings away*
> *In comes the water splashing*
> *And says " Good-day ! "*

It struck me as a very happy rhyme as I watched the wheel twirling madly and the water bouncing off the shining blades —a charmingly poetic expression of the mechanism by which the Faeroeman, years ago, won his daily bread.

P

I pulled open the little door and was almost assaulted by the atmosphere, for the brown flour-dust was everywhere, coating the woodwork and the rattling quern and hanging like a London fog in the gloom of the shed. There was no miller present, and the fact did not surprise me, for the interior was quite intolerably dusty and dark. Very likely, I considered, he comes occasionally to refill the hopper and sweep the meal off the bench, and then beats a hasty retreat, taking in great gulps of good fresh air ! Yet Poul í Geil, one of the last millers in Tórshavn, assured me that he often sat in this murky fog whilst the grain trickled into the quern, assiduously knitting himself a pair of stockings or sewing sheepskin shoes, the light of the single *kola* lamp a faint golden glow in the hazy gloom. And he would have done so more often, he said, had not his contract with the merchants bound him to collect the grain from their warehouses, and deliver the flour after milling. At busy times he spent a large part of the day going to and from Tinganes, nearly a mile from Geilamilla, with a heavily laden *leypur* on his back ; and he must often have envied the Sandagerði millers whose establishments were so situated that they could always collect and deliver the corn and meal by rowing-boat !

Poul í Geil used to earn 1 *króna* 32 *oyrir* for every barrel of corn he put through the quern, and he was " glad of it ! " It does not seem much of a sum judged by modern standards, being worth about one shilling and threepence ; but in those good old days it went more than ten times as far and was in fact equivalent to two-thirds of a workman's usual daily pay. He also milled corn for the policemen quartered at the Skansin fort, for their wage from the Danish government was about 7 *krónur* and 30 lbs. of corn each month. The drawing of the mill on page 227 is from a photograph given to me by Erling Isholm, taken by his father about 1900.

The Geilamilla was a fine example of the old wooden type of mill, and was one of five which ground imported grain in Tórshavn in former days. Three others stood at Sandagerði near the mouth of the stream which comes down Havnadalur, and one of these was last used for grinding sugar during the first great war. Another stood near the west harbour, Vágsbotnur, and is now commemorated by the street-name Mylnugøta ; it was an ambitious enterprise which housed two big querns, each with its own wheel. There was formerly a similar " double mill " at Skálavík on Sandoy.

The horizontal mill in Tórshavn was purely a commercial proposition, but in the outer settlements it was (and in a few remains) a characteristic feature of Faeroe peasant culture, as indispensable to the economic structure of the village as the *sodnhús*, the *hjallar* and the turbaries in the hills. Although most of the mills were formerly the property of the bigger farmers, it appears to have been a general rule that any one could use them, with the owner's permission, without payment of a fee. None but a scoundrel, Mikkjal á Ryggi inferred, would stoop so low as to demand money for so small a service ! Sometimes mills were owned by several *óðalsbøndur* in partnership, and one on Kunoy was shared by six men each of whom had his appointed day of the week for using it ! The present mill at Kvívík is owned by .

GEILAMILLA ca. 1900

four villagers. In Shetland too, five or six families would often collaborate in building and working a mill.

Apart from Niðri á Bø, the oldest and most picturesque of these tiny buildings are to be found at Kvívík and Sandavágur. There is a splendid pair in the valley behind the latter village, made of rough stones, and with sod roofs and earth-banked races : they must be at least two hundred years old, and are in an incipient state of decay. The fact that they make useful store-sheds for turves has doubtless postponed their impending doom, but they are worthy of a better fate and I hope some generous citizen will come to their rescue whilst there is still time.

Hellumilla, the older of the two at Kvívík, is unique among those I have seen in that it lacks the usual lifting mechanism. The shaft is a piece of ship's spar found as driftwood on the shore, as the innumerable *Teredo* tunnellings testify, and it has a small iron cup at the centre of the base which sits on an iron spike protruding from the bed of the stream. Another distinctive feature is that it is slotted for twelve blades instead of the customary eight, and these were narrower than usual and canted at a sharp angle to the water-flow. Efforts were made by Hans A. Djurhuus, on my instigation, to have this unique mill restored, and I was glad to hear shortly before leaving the islands that its owner had agreed to repair it and preserve it *in situ*. He is to be heartily congratulated on his public-spirited act.

The present mill is a fairly new one, but there has been a mill on the site for a hundred and fifty years. Nicolas Jacobsen and Hanus á Skælingi, who showed me the mills, told me that the original one was erected by a parson named Holm on land belonging to a farmer at the nearby village of Leynar, and that Holm got the use of the ground on the tenure of milling one barrel of corn each year for his landlord !

My friend Niels á Botni told me that there were no less than six mills on Nólsoy a century ago, when barley (as witness the place-name Korndalur) was a very important crop. There is no sign of even the ruins of a mill to-day—evidence of the rapidity with which these little structures vanish once the community has ceased to have further need of them. He recalled the names of two of the six : one was Tvistur, because there was always a good deal of dissension about the ownership of the site (*tvistur* is archaic Faeroese meaning " argument ") ; and the other, Sallarin, was so named on account of the coarse meal it ground. Other mill-names are not so picturesque, and the majority appear to have been called after the farms that owned them, or the streams on which they stood.

Finally, we must say a word or two concerning *drýlur*, the daily bread of the Faeroe people years ago. It was made on an iron griddle supported over the open fire, and was a dark brown in colour owing to the fact that the barley became smoked during the drying process in the *sodnhús*. Indeed, Hans A. Djurhuus told me that it had a smoky taste which, in the opinion of many, increased rather than diminished its excellence. The loaves were small and oblong, rather like the small griddle-scones made in Scottish homes, and were turned on the iron plate until all the sides were well browned. They were always eaten fresh, being made daily, and the warmer they were, the better they were liked. The finest was that which was removed from the griddle when it began to get brown, and was pushed beneath the ashes of the turf fire and left to bake there for an hour or so. Niels Rein gave me an old saying to the effect that every year a man eats half a kilo of mould (on his *skerpikjøt* and *raestur fiskur*), half a kilo of feathers (on the carcases of the sea-birds), and half a kilo of turf ash adhering to the *drýlur* baked underneath the fire ! Often a hollow would be made by pushing a finger into the loaf lengthwise, whilst it was still hot, and this recess would be filled with saithe liver or tallow : children were very fond of this curious sandwich, and it was considered highly nutritious food. *Rognadrýlur* was some such sandwich as this with fish roes on top, and was a favourite at breakfast time. *Rómi*, or sour cream, was often taken on *drýlur*. Only on Sundays and holidays would bread be bought at the baker's ; or if *drýlur* were made instead it was baked as a long, cylindrical loaf and a little pattern was stamped on it to improve its appearance in honour of the day.

References to Chapter Nine

CURWEN, E. C. (1944) ; DEBES, L. (1673) ; GOUDIE, G. (1886) ; JACOBSEN, M. A. and MATRAS, C. (1927-28) ; LANDT, J. (1810) ; SVABO, J. C. (1781-82) ; WILLIAMSON, K. (1946 a).

Chapter Ten

CUSTOMS AND FOLK-LORE

1. The celebrations at Christmas and the New Year (*page* 230).
2. Two " Thirteenth Night " legends (*page* 233).
3. A review of the more important calendar customs and festivals (*page* 236).
4. The great celebrations of Saint Ólav's Day and their significance (*page* 240).
5. Ushering in Lent—mainly a consideration of children's games (*page* 246).
6. Births, marriages and deaths in Faeroe folk-lore and story (*page* 251).

I

IN OLDEN TIMES the preparations for the Christmas holiday occupied the four weeks of Advent, and there was much work for men and women alike. The house was thoroughly " spring"-cleaned, and this is still done to-day. New clothes were made for all, for it was customary to have a new outfit every year about Christmas time, and the materials from which it was made were given by the *bøndur* to their servants as part of their pay. The sewing, weaving and knitting kept the womenfolk very busy throughout this period, and because of their preoccupation with such tasks a large part of the house-cleaning fell to the men. Andrias Weihe says that once a year, customarily at Tollaksmessa, it was the duty of the *húskallar* or " house-karls " to scrub the ceiling of the *roykstova*. Towards the end of this period the men would also lay in sufficient turves to tide them over the festive season, and visit Tórshavn to buy sugar, *brennivín* and other goods for the celebrations.

The preparatory work was completed on Tollaksmessudagur, " the Little Christmas Eve," which falls on December 23rd. On that day the candles were made and the final baking was done. Any items of sewing or knitting which had not been completed by the womenfolk were most cunningly hidden away by their owners. It was necessary to hide them well, for the men showed great tenacity in seeking out such trifles, which they called *jólatrøll*. Such unfinished work as came to light they hung over the fireplace for all to see and ridicule, and the exhibition was considered to bring great shame on the persons to whom the items belonged.

The actual celebrations began on Christmas Eve, Jólaaftan, and in the Faeroes to-day this, and not December 25th, is the most important day of the holiday. Nowadays work ceases in the early afternoon, and at six o'clock the people go to church. They eat their Christmas dinner on returning, and spend the evening in a family exchange of greetings and gifts, afterwards singing carols as they walk with joined hands round and round the brightly-lit Christmas tree. The church is also attended at midday and in the early evening on Jóladagur itself, and friends and relatives are visited with presents and seasonable wishes. Following supper there is " dancing " and singing round the lighted *jólatrae* as on the night before, and there are games for the amusement of the children. There is a midday service in the church on the " Second Christmas Day," Annar Jóladagur, and in the evening the dancing season begins. It continues until Føstu inn Gangur, the first Monday in Lent, when it ceases for the duration of the fast. At this last dance, as on the first of the season, the men were hatless in former times. Although it is usual in Tórshavn for men to dance bare-headed to-day, it was not so formerly, except on these two special occasions, and the custom of wearing a hat still survives at some of the remoter settlements.

The Christmas tree, in common with the Christmas pork and goose, is of comparatively recent introduction, but in earlier times most of the families made a wooden framework and covered it with moss and ling to make it green and tree-like. A true story is told of a Tórshavn miller who lived in the early part of the last century. He was very proud of his garden, and especially of a flourishing young fir sapling which he had had brought from Denmark, and which was the only one in all the islands. One Christmas a man came to Tórshavn from an outer island to buy provisions for the holiday, and in particular a *jólatrae* to delight his children. But he was too late, for the few imported Christmas trees had been sold by the time he arrived. He met the miller, and told him of this misfortune, whereupon the miller uprooted the fine sapling fir that was his pride and gave it to the happy father to take away. It is a lovely, simple story of the kindness and goodwill proper to this season, and a story likely to live long in the memories of the Faeroe people.

A candle was always kept burning in the window of the living-room on Christmas Eve, and indeed Hans A. Djurhuus told me that it was customary to keep a light burning in every room in some houses on that night. To-day the custom survives in having one or more lighted candles on the table at meal-times throughout the Christmas period. In former days a light was also put in the *fjós* or *kjallari* where the animals were stabled. The old legend that there is peace and goodwill among all dumb creatures on this night is current in the Faeroes as in other countries.

The food at the Christmas dinner on the evening of Jólaaftan was traditionally *raestur fiskur*, with potatoes in later years, and *sperðil*, and this menu is not by any means out of date. The last named corresponds to what is known in the turkey as "the parson's nose," but it is derived from the sheep ; it is salted and filled with melted tallow, and boiled. On Christmas Day the dinner con-sisted of some kind of meat, such as *raest kjøt* or, with well-to-do families, fresh mutton. The farmers often killed a sheep a week or so before the holiday, and this *jólaseyður* provided food for themselves and their servants. For the children there was usually a kind of shortcake, made in small pieces having the likeness of little men, with currants and raisins for their eyes and the buttons of their coats. Very similar cakes, called " fairings " and repre-senting horses, hens and other creatures as well as men, were formerly a feature of the Manx Christmas-tide.

In olden times *raestur fiskur* and *sperðil* were again eaten on Saint Stephen's Day, New Year's Eve, and the Thirteenth Day, January 6th—when the festivity ended and the decorations and *jólatrae* were removed. Weihe records that on Gomlu Trettandi, the old-style Thirteenth Day on January 13th, it was usual to have *ræst kjøt* and *ræst súpan* for the evening meal.

As in Britain the coming of the New Year is celebrated heartily, but there is no custom of " first-footing " such as is widely known in England, and more particularly in Scotland. There is a Watch-night service in the church and afterwards the people call on their neighbours with greetings and wishes for a " Happy New Year ! " It is always good etiquette to add a word of thanks for the hospitality and kindness shown towards you in the past by saying, " Tøkk fyri tað gamla ! "—literally, " Thank you for the old one ! "

Following the round of visiting, most of the residents of the neighbourhood go to high ground nearby and light a bonfire which the children have built of wood, old straw, old mattresses and clothes—and in fact anything that will burn—collected in a house to house hunt during the previous week. Sometimes Christmas trees from the season before are saved all the year and handed over to the children for the bonfire on this night. The people join hands and sing and dance in a circle round the fire, and when the flames die down they usually repair to someone's house for coffee and cakes before dispersing, very late, to their own homes. This manner of ushering in the New Year was quite the fashion until the first year of the war, when black-out restrictions, of course, put a temporary stop to such proceedings. The young men formerly went about the town or village firing shotguns to herald the New Year.

The people believed that if they remained wide awake throughout the first night they would always be active and energetic during the year. A candle was kept burning in the *roykstova* window all night, and if this light went out before the morning it was said to be a sign that somebody in the household would die during the coming twelve months. If those gifted with " second-sight " remained in the church when all the others had gone, they would see pass before them the faces of all those in the village who were destined to die before the year's end. It is said that any man standing with arms akimbo, or his hands in his trouser pockets when he first sees the New Year's moon will be ill ; and that if he is carrying anything in his hands, the nature of the object will indicate the kind of work he will follow during the year.

2

The Christmas and New Year festivities end on the Thirteenth Day. Trettandi is a half-holiday and the afternoon is often set aside for a visit to friends or relatives in outlying villages. No fishing or work on the land was done in olden times, and no spinning or weaving in the house. The midday meal was again *raestur fiskur* and *sperðil*. The night of the old style Thirteenth Day was one of great activity among *trøll*, witches, ghosts and the like, and in " Sagnir og Ævintýr " Dr. J. Jacobsen, a great student of the Faeroe language and folk-lore, recorded these two stories of events on Gomlu Trettandi *nátt*.

The ghosts rose after midnight to dance and sing in the neighbourhood of the burial ground. If a man wanted to earn great riches he should go with an axe and a calf-skin and sit at a cross-roads near the cemetery, the calf-skin spread out behind him with the tail pointing away from the graves. There he should sit, assiduously sharpening the axe and repeating aloud " Eg hvøtji, eg hvøtji," whilst the ghosts sang and danced about him. They would heap treasure on the calf-skin, and would do their utmost by taunts and jibes to make him look up from his work, or say something other than " Eg hvøtji." But if he were to look at the treasure, or at them, or any other sound were to pass his lips, he would be lost forever. Finally they would take the calf-skin by the tail and try to drag it away. That was the time for action. Without looking up, he must swing the axe behind him and sever the tail at its base. If he succeeded the riches were his ; if he missed his aim, or in striking damaged the edge of the axe in any way, the ghosts would take the riches and himself too.

The word " hvøtji " is an archaic form of *hvessi* (*at hvessa*, to sharpen). The act of putting an edge on any sharp instrument, such as an axe or knife, would prevent supernatural beings from exerting any power over a mortal. A better story tells of the Kópakona : it is said to belong to Mikladalur on Kallsoy, although a variation of it is recorded for Skálavík on Sandoy, and a very similar tale exists in the Shetland Islands.

The seals come up on shore on Gomlu Trettandi *nátt* and, putting aside their skins, take on human shape and dance and make merry for a few hours. Once upon a time a young man hid behind a rock and saw the seals come to land, take off their skins, and become as men and women. Among them was a very beautiful seal-girl, and he fell in love with her at once. All the time the dancing went on he watched her with covetous eyes, and when the merrymaking was at its height he crept unseen to the place where she had lain her skin, and took it. Then suddenly the dance came to an end and the seal-people put on their skins and slid back into the sea, leaving behind them the beautiful maiden, who could not find her skin anywhere, and so was locked in human shape.

The young man took her to his home and married her, and he locked the skin away at the bottom of a big chest, the key to which he was always careful to carry in his waistcoat pocket. They lived happily together for several years, and had children, and the Kópakona was well spoken of everywhere as a good and clever wife. Then came a day when her husband went out fishing, and after he had been away an hour or so he remembered, to his horror, that he had taken on another waistcoat, and had left the key to the chest in the pocket of the one at home ! He turned at once to the oars and pulled for the shore with all his might ; but alas ! as he came to the land he saw a dark shape slipping into the water from the rocks.

His wife had gone. When he reached the house only the children were there to welcome him. The big chest stood open and its contents were scattered about the room. It is said that the Kópakona, a faithful mother to the last, had put out the fire and locked away all the knives and sharp things so that the children should not come to any harm. . . .

Time passed by, and there came a day when the men of Mikladalur said they would go to the caves on the morrow to kill seals for their furs and for oil to fill the *kola* lamps. At night, in a dream, the seal-wife came to her former husband and begged him to spare her seal-husband and their children. She told him where he would find them : the first would be guarding the entrance to a certain cave, and the others would be lying in the darkness beyond.

The men set out on the hunt in the morning, and soon they came to this cave, and there was a bull seal at the entrance as the Kópakona had said. They disregarded her behest and killed him. Then they entered the cave and killed the two calves which they found at its end. When the hunt was over the man who had had the seal-wife received as his share the head of the bull and the flippers and tails of the two calves ; and that evening when he and his children were sitting at the table eating this meat they heard a scuffling on the roof, and knew that the Kópakona had come. She cried out in anger and distress, upbraiding the man for his faithlessness, and she put a great curse on the men of Mikladalur, saying, " So many men shall be killed on the cliffs, or lost at sea, as would encircle the whole island if they were to stand with hands grasped and arms outstretched ! "

They say nowadays that so great is the number of men from Mikladalur who have fallen from the cliffs whilst bird-fowling or have lost their lives whilst fishing that the Kópakona's revenge has been satisfied and her curse has ceased to be.

3

Candlemas, called Kyndilsmessa or Ljósamessa (" the festival of the light ") ushered in the month of February. It seems to have been associated only with a variety of omen-seeking rites. If you were an unmarried girl, and Candlemas Eve found you in a romantic mood, you would mix the white of egg and water in a glass and put it on the window-sill before you went to bed. The following morning you would rush from your room, full of eagerness to see the result, for the white of egg would have coagulated overnight, and its shape would suggest some object associated with the man who was destined to claim your heart. It might have the form of a ship, for example, in which case he would be a fisherman or sailor ; or it might conjure up the picture of a cow or sheep, in which event you would become a farmer's wife.

This custom, which was also known in Scotland, was very much alive in the Faeroes in quite recent years, and indeed it is so still. The commercial age fostered an interesting and speedier variant in which molten tinfoil was poured into a glass of water, giving an immediate and more permanent token of your fate. My friend C. I. Paton has recorded a not dissimilar quest for matrimonial information for May Day Eve in the Isle of Man. The Manx maids imprisoned a snail between two pewter dishes, and on the following morning expected to find the name of the husband-to-be scrawled by the snail's trail across the bottom dish.

Not content with the evidence provided by the tinfoil or the white of egg, our maiden sought a further omen on Kyndilsmessa morn. She went out before breakfast, armed with a stone, a bone and a piece of turf, to look for a hooded-crow. When she found one standing on a rock or in a field she threw at it in quick succession the stone, the bone and the bit of turf, reciting as she did so :

Eg kasti stein,	*I throw a stone,*
Fá ikki mein !	*Don't hurt yourself !*
Eg kasti bein,	*I throw a bone,*
Berð tað heim !	*Carry it home !*
Eg kasti torv,	*I throw a turve,*
Nú er krákan horvin !	*Now the crow has gone !*

She watched the crow closely, for her fate depended upon its movements. If it flew to the shore, then her husband would come to her over the sea ; if it settled on a house or a man's property, she would get her husband from that family ; and if it was disobliging enough to stay where it was, then she would be an old maid ! Another version says that the husband will come from the direction in which the crow flies.

Another picturesque ceremonial of the same kind was connected with Jóansøka, June 24th. On the eve of this day the women would gather the flowering heads of ribwort or lamb's-tongue plantain, rub off the white stamens, and put the flower heads under their pillows, making a wish, when they went to bed. If fresh stamens had come on the spikes by the morning then the wish would be fulfilled. A very similar item, collected by Mrs. Banks, the well-known authority on British folk-lore, and communicated to me by Mr. Paton, comes from the Shetlands, where heads of ribwort were stripped of the white stamens and buried, wrapped in a dock-leaf, in order to get an omen as to the happiness or failure of a marriage. The marriage would be a success only if fresh florets had appeared on the heads by the next day. Landt says that the young men enjoined in the Faeroe version in his day, a hundred and fifty years ago, in order to know if they would win their sweethearts. The meadow cat's-tail grass is called *syftunsøkugras* because the flower-heads were used in a similar omen-seeking rite on the eve of Saint Swithin's Day.

On the night of Jóansøka, according to the old style calendar, a picturesque festival was held at Varmakeldueiði, a fairly flat shore on the east side of Eysturoy, almost equidistant from Lorvík, Norðragøta and Fuglafjørður. Many people went there in the evening from all over the islands to drink from a warm spring in the neighbourhood and spend the night in singing and dancing on the shore. The spring, which is said to have a temperature of 19 degrees centigrade summer and winter alike, had the reputation of restoring to good health those who were feeling unwell, but perhaps the dancing and *brennivín* were actually the better medicine ! This interesting social gathering was declining when Landt wrote his book, although the spring was still being visited by believers in its healing properties. Recent attempts have been made to revive this festival.

Another medicinal matter was connected with Jóansøka. Sufferers from *eldkast*, a skin disease, must take *jarðarsípa*—an infusion made from a greyish-brown lichen common in the *bøur*—

on this night. But it would be effective only if the invalid wore gloves when gathering the lichen and brewing the drink, for its curative properties were destroyed if it was touched by the bare hands. Any person suffering from scrofularia would likewise benefit if he or she rose early and bathed in Jóansøka dew—a practice which recalls the healing properties of May Day dew in England.

May Day, that great day in English and Celtic social life, has no meaning for the Faeroeman : its place seems to have been taken by Summarmáladagur, April 14th, the first day of summer. Though not regarded as a holiday, as it is in Iceland (where people wish each other a prosperous summer, and exchange " summer gifts "), Summarmáladagur is nevertheless an important day in the Faeroe calendar. For one thing it marks the return of the puffins, bounteous store of food, to the cliffs, and the wheatear also arrives traditionally on this day. Between Summarmáladagur and Líradagur (August 24th) no light was used in the house in the evenings. If the maidservant did not have the supper on the table before darkness fell on Grækarismessa, March 12th, she would get no wages for the summer months. There was a similar forfeiture of pay on the part of erring menservants, although it had no connection with this day. By old custom the first three ribs of a sheep on either side of the body (called *válgari*) belonged to the manservant who undertook the task of butcher in the autumn ; if he cut four ribs instead of the lawful three, then he was deprived of his wages for the winter.

On no account must you eat eggs on the first day of summer, or you will suffer from boils for the rest of the year ! So my friend Owen Evans and I were warned by the good lady of a tea-room which we visited on the afternoon of April 14th, 1942. She did her utmost to dissuade us from having two boiled eggs apiece as a change from the tinned herrings usually provided by the Government, but to no purpose. For we insisted on having them, and in spite of her gloomy forebodings suffered no ill effects. There are very many families in the Faeroes where no egg is eaten on April 14th, and I would give much to know what quaint superstition lies behind this taboo.

There is another unexplained mystery connected with May 3rd. This is Krossmessa, and Weihe records that the menfolk used to rise early and scrub down their boats with seaweed. He gives no reason, nor could any of my friends satisfy my longing for an explanation, although Neils á Botni told me that Nólsoy men, when they had finished transporting the turves from Borðan to the village, scrubbed the craft clean in this way. This was the day for hiring men and maidservants on the larger farms, and a memory of this is to be found in the word *krossmessuposi*, used to describe a bag containing many varied articles—like the bags in which the servants carried their belongings when going to their new masters.

In the Faeroes, as elsewhere, there is much weather lore associated with the calendar. If the sun shines on January 25th it promises a good year for the corn—and the sun need shine only for so long as it takes a man to saddle a horse ! Pætursmessa, February 22nd, is the first day of the spring, and " if water is dripping from the roof " it is an omen of a good season ; but if snow falls, the spring will be a bad one. The Faeroese equivalent of Saint Swithin's Day is March 9th, called Fjøruti Riddarar (" the forty knights "), for rain on that day means rain for the forty days following, whilst a good day will ensure fine weather for a similar period. If the weather is fine on Summarmáladagur it will be good throughout the summer. It is believed that there will be no big snowfall after Halvarðsøka, May 15th, which is the day on which sheep and geese are turned out of the *bøur* for their summer pastures in the hills. Haymaking customarily began on the first of Hundadagar, the " Dog Days," July 23rd, and if it is fine on that day there will be good weather for a full month.

We have seen how *røst kjøt* and *røst súpan*, and *sperðil* and *raestur fiskur* are special food for certain days. In summer we find days on which buttermilk, *rómastampur*, and cream figure on the menu, such as Jóansøka and Syftunsøka ; and others, in the late summer, when some kind of milk pudding is traditional fare. It was usual to have a milk pudding on August 23rd, the last day of summer, and Weihe says it was believed that by eating it as hot as possible the people would enjoy a warm winter ! Líradagur, when the young Manx shearwaters were captured, is another milk-pudding day, and so also is Mikkjalsmessa, September 29th. A sweetmeat specially associated with Jóansøka is *hvonn* or *heimahvonn*, a domesticated form of the wild angelica which grows profusely on the bird-fowling cliffs. The stem is chopped into small pieces and served with sugar and cream. Another minor festival was Dilkadagur, when the special dish was a sheep's-head, *mørur* (comprising the heart, liver and lungs of the sheep) and *keppur*, which is a large variety of sausage.

The most recent of the Faeroe holidays is Markusarmessa, April 25th, which has been observed since the outbreak of the recent war as a national flag-day. Faeroe vessels were not allowed to fly their own flag prior to the war, and indeed the right to fly it on land was only granted to them a few years ago. After the German occupation of Denmark and the British occupation of Iceland and the Faeroes in 1940 Faeroe ships were instructed by the British authorities to hoist their national flag in place of the Danish, so that allied aircraft and warships would recognise them as friendly craft. So much had this small but proud race longed for this expression of their nationhood that they made Markusarmessa a day for celebrating the event, and what began as a necessary war-time expedient will doubtless continue in the years to come if the enthusiasm accorded to Flaggdagur is to be taken as a criterion. The Faeroe banner is a blue-bordered red cross on a white ground, conceived as a combination of the flags of the two most closely related countries, Norway and Iceland, by Faeroese students in Denmark as long ago as the spring of 1919.

Jóansøka is kept up in Suðuroy more than in the other islands, and there it is the occasion of a summer sports meeting and social festival on much the same pattern as the celebrations which take place in Tórshavn at Ólavsøka, and which are the subject of the next part of this chapter. The games and other competitive events which form the main feature of the holiday take place in alternate years at the two ports, Vágur and Tvøroyri, and although the event is primarily for the benefit of the Suðuroy people a number of visitors always arrive from other islands for the festival. In recent years a similar *fête*, for the benefit of the scattered residents of the north islands, has been held at Klakksvík on the first Sunday in June ; and the youngest of these miniature Ólavsøka festivals was instituted during the late years of the war on Vágar Island.

4

" You have done well, Sigmund, that you did not lay this journey under your pillow."

So (the saga tells us) did king Ólav Tryggvesson greet Sigmund Brestisson, whom he had asked to come to Norway to be his guardsman. He had asked him for another and a greater reason, for he wished Sigmund to become Christian, and to carry the new faith home to the Faeroes and spread the gospel there as energetically as he himself was working for its acceptance in Norway. " Sigmund was then baptized, and all his followers, and the king had him taught holy knowledge. Sigmund was with the king during the winter in great honour."

In the following spring Sigmund returned to the Faeroes, and he summoned a *ting* at Tórshavn, at which he gave the people the message from Ólav the king. But Tróndur, the proud and independent chieftain, was opposed to the change of faith, and persuaded the majority of the landsmen not to pay heed to Sigmund's words. "And we shall go against it in every way, and will attack you here at the *ting* and kill you, unless you promise faithfully never more to set this offer here in the islands." So the *ting* broke up, and Sigmund stayed at home at Skúvoy all the winter, nursing his grievance.

In the spring of 999 he sailed to Gøtuvík with thirty men, took Tróndur and his household unawares, and gave the heathen chieftain the hard choice of accepting the Christian faith, or forfeiting his life. Tróndur accepted baptism for himself and his followers, and went round the islands with Sigmund until all men had been made Christian. But he liked it ill that he had been tricked in this way.

So Christianity gained a footing, albeit an insecure one, in the Faeroes. In Norway Ólav Tryggvesson fared no better in his efforts to spread the new faith, and he was killed in battle at Svolder in the year 1000. His work for the unification and christianising of Norway was pursued, with better success, by Ólav II Haraldsson, but the Saint King (as he was afterwards called) also fell foul of his enemies, and died in battle at Stiklestad on 29th July, 1030. Years later this day became the greatest feast-day in the northern lands. For many years the festival was kept up in Norway and in the Faeroe Islands, but only in the Faeroes did it manage to survive the vicissitudes of time. So important is the festival to-day that other events are spoken of as so long before, or after, Ólavsøka, for this is the very hub of the social year.

Signs of the approaching festival are apparent long before the day. Houses are painted and cleaned, and the little gardens tidied up, for with so many visitors due to arrive from the outer islands the townsfolk rightly desire that Tórshavn shall look its best. A few days before the holiday the influx of visitors begins :

Q

the little inter-island boats become ever more crowded, and the atmosphere on board them increasingly jovial, until, throughout the whole of the 28th, every boat that can be pressed into service is on the water all day long, and literally hundreds of people are landed at the quay. Many of the townsfolk go down to the harbour to meet and welcome friends, or merely to gaze upon each succeeding batch of new arrivals and capture a little of the holiday spirit that is already abroad.

Where all these people go is a mystery. Tórshavn is crowded enough with its five thousand inhabitants, accommodation being stretched almost to the limit, and yet somehow the place manages to absorb almost as many people again for this brief period. The town keeps open house. Every family has its guests and visitors, relatives and friends from distant villages who may be making their first visit for one or even many years. Every divan in Tórshavn becomes a temporary bed—and there are many people, I feel sure, who do not sleep at all between the 27th and 30th of July !

There are knockings at the door, new faces behind them, all day long. One household I know received its first visitor, a friend from Fugloy, at half-past six in the morning—but nobody was really surprised, for in summer on Fugloy 6.30 a.m. is getting on towards dinner-time ! However, such an early start to the day is unusual, but from mid-morning onwards the coffee-pot is never off the stove, and the housewife is perpetually plagued by the fear that the great store of cakes—the product of nearly a week's baking—will fail to finish the allotted course. Long-hoarded bottles of *brennivín* see the light of day : for those who fancy a drop on great occasions, there could be no Ólavsøka without a bottle ! In the cinema, the dance-hall and the street one will often see a fellow nudge his friend and wink, and the two will fade away into an obscure corner to wish each other health and happiness at the expense of a *pisa* from the flask carried at the hip !

By midday on the 28th, when the little ships are still discharging their human cargoes, Tórshavn is full of the gaiety of the holiday mood. The streets are crowded as the people walk up and down, down and up, just to look upon each other and feel themselves a part of the holiday throng. Flags fly over the housetops, and in the town centre, near the Tinghús, a fountain plays over the stream. Nearby a band plays music, and does it well. It is already obvious that everything that man can do to make this the perfect Faeroe holiday has been done ; and the only thing lacking which could conceivably improve matters at all is a *grind* !

Many of the people, of course, wear their national dress ; nevertheless, this most handsome ensemble is never so much in evidence as one could wish. The young men wear a bright red waistcoat, with an embroidered flower-pattern border, and fastened with silver buttons ; dark blue knee breeches with silver buttons at the knee, and light blue hose below, held up by a garter of coloured cloth. The older men prefer waistcoats and stockings of more subdued shades, usually a dark blue. The black leather shoes, *spenniskógvar*, have large silver buckles, and often an ornamental *knívur* is worn at the waist, its wooden sheath inlaid with silver effigies of the *grindahvalur*. The dark blue jacket sometimes has silver buttons down the front, but fastens only at the throat, and during inclement weather a brown woollen coat of similar cut is often worn over it. The hat is hand-loom woven like the rest of the apparel, and with the younger men is red with a narrow black stripe. Old men and widowers customarily wear a hat of dark blue, and very rarely one sees the peculiar *stavnhetta*, which is built up to a high peak on either side, and is used only for weddings and other great festive occasions.

The women have a long and heavy skirt of dark blue with thin red stripes, black stockings, and a dark patterned bodice laced across the bosom, revealing beneath a hand-knitted red and dark blue jumper. They wear an embroidered shawl and apron of white or green or some other light colour, and have a small close-fitting bonnet, tied with ribbons under the chin, to match. Sometimes the *stakkur* is worn : this is a long flowing gown of heavy silk, and is more usually a wedding-dress, and so (one might think) inappropriate wear for this occasion. Perhaps that is not altogether so, however, for probably more heads and hearts are lost at Ólavsøka than during the rest of the year. It is at Ólavsøka, too, that budding womanhood is permitted its first fling : girls of fourteen or fifteen are allowed to stay out late together for the first time, enjoying the fun of watching and mixing with the cheerful crowds and the great thrill of their first dance.

On the evening of the 28th the official programme starts with the boat-races, the crowds thronging the historic point of Tinganes and the shore on the west side of the little bay in order to watch the finishes and cheer the winning teams. There are races for all types of craft from the *fýramannafar* to the *seksáringur*, and women's teams take part as well as men's. There are some close finishes at the end of the long and arduous row down the fiord, and often it is touch and go as to whether the Klakksvík or Tvøroyri boat will get home first, or the stalwart ladies of Vestmanna retain the title they won in such brilliant style last year ! Afterwards the populace surges back to the town to parade Niels Finsen's-gøta and listen to the band playing from the stand below the Tinghús. Soon the dusk falls and the lights go on—coloured lights of blue and green and yellow and red, shining in the trees, reflected in the stream, scattering warmth and cosiness along the road. The fountain too is illuminated, a fantasy of shimmering, sparkling hues, and a wonderful centre-piece to the brilliant scene.

The peculiar Faeroe dance goes on until the small hours, and the people throng the street outside the open windows of the hall to listen with pleasure to the rousing ballads that accompany the stamping feet within. Many invade the dance-hall merely to watch the dancers and listen enraptured to their lively singing, and they enjoy the experience just as heartily as the more active celebrants. On Ólavsøka night itself the dance continues until the dawn, and there are not a few who go straight from the hall to the quay to join their boat and sail away, still hoarsely singing, for home.

On the morning of Ólavsøka day the members of the Løgting go in procession, with as many of the islands' clergymen as are able to attend, to the church near Tinganes, where the Dean conducts the service. After praying to God for His blessing and guidance in their work during the coming year, the procession returns to the Tinghús with the Dean at its head, and parliament is solemnly opened before a tightly-packed mass of interested onlookers who fill the public gallery and even overflow through the entrance door.

In the early afternoon the town streets witness another procession, this time a motley one composed of respresentatives of almost all the organisations that have anything at all to do with the festivities. The town band marches tunefully in front ; Boy Scouts, Girl Guides, sportsmen and gymnasts, schoolchildren, ponies and their riders, and members of the Merkið and other societies follow on behind. Afterwards there are fine speeches by the cultural leaders and the more fervent nationalists in the shadow of the Tinghús, and the crowd listens appreciatively to this oratory.

Beyond the town, the sporting events are in full swing on the edge of the moor. The best inter-island teams contest the cup final on the football ground, the girls are equally energetic on the handball pitch, and the swimming and tennis competitions go on simultaneously. At the other end of the town the band marches out into Havnadalur, leading the well-groomed ponies and their riders to the starting-point for what is perhaps the best attended sporting event of all. The road is too narrow for more than two ponies to race at once, so, when the stop-watch has done its work, the two fastest return to the starting-point and decide the issue in a thrilling final event. The winner, and the band, lead the long procession of participants and onlookers back to town.

Apart from the dancing, the endless parading up and down, down and up the main street under the fairylights and by the stream, the holiday is practically at an end. It has been the finest, the most crowded, and most enjoyable Ólavsøka for many years— or so they say ! But we should do wrong to leave the festival at that, for it is not only the people's holiday, a time for merry-making and the meeting and making of friends. We are perhaps inclined to forget in the fun and thrill of it all that it is something very much more than that, an occasion in which almost every single happening is historic, and an expression of the intensely real, age-old culture of the Faeroese. As we have seen, its roots strike deep into the past, and they go deeper even than Stiklestad. The significance of Ólavsøka is as much political as social and religious.

Sigmund Brestisson first taught Christianity at the summer *ting*, the one meeting which all the landsmen in Scandinavian states were in duty bound to attend, and at which it was customary for all important political and judicial business to be decided. Some time after the firm establishment of Christianity in the islands, the summer *ting* which was held at Tórshavn in the early saga days must have been set to coincide with Saint Ólav's Day. Ólavsøka remembers the coming of Christianity ; but, as with the ancient Althing of Iceland and present-day Tynwald of the Isle of Man, it remembers also the coming of law and order to the land, and through all the modern trappings the Viking theme of equal rights and liberties for every man shines like a light. These three great assemblies are first-cousins : to them men and their families, strong or weak, rich or poor, came from the far corners of the country to know what laws had been made during the year for their guidance and benefit ; to discuss matters of great moment affecting their communal lives, and to listen to words of wisdom from their learned men. They came in their boats, on ponies, or afoot, and pitched their tents on the crowded plain. They met old friends, made new acquaintances ; exchanged ideas and merchandise ; engaged each other in trials of strength and athletic prowess, and listened to the sagamen recounting their vivid tales of great warriors of the past. If a man had a grievance, he sought and found a hearing at the *ting ;* if he were a wrongdoer, he was given fair trial and gained his just deserts ; if he were an outlaw, he could come with impunity and ask that his outlawry be removed. The present-day procession of the *Løgtingsmenn* to and from the church, and the opening of the parliament in the crowded Tinghús, is the shadow of the landsmen's *ting* flitting across the time-hallowed ground. The tennis and football and rowing are not so very modern, after all ; and when a gentleman from Fugloy calls to pay his respects at 6.30 a.m. he is only doing as his distant forefather did on the day that Sigmund, the son of Bresti, was driven from the *ting* because he had not lain a certain journey under his pillow.

5

Two picturesque customs associated with Føstu inn Gangur, the first Monday in Lent, would doubtless have been long obsolete had they not been carried on by the children after grown-ups had allowed them to lapse. (This, incidentally, is the first of the Devil's birthdays : I am told that he has two each year, the second being the day on which the " Final Demand " for the rates and taxes expires !) The first custom was a cruel one in its original form, and seems to have been confined largely to the employees of the merchants and monopoly establishments in the townships. There can be little doubt that its introduction was due to Danish influence during the period of the trade monopoly, for a parallel existed on Amager Island, and probably in other districts of Denmark : it was also practised years ago in Scotland. A cat was put into a barrel, which was then hung up and beaten with a heavy club, the men taking turns in belabouring the wretched creature's prison until the staves were smashed asunder. The man who struck the blow which liberated the demented cat was supposed to give chase and capture it, whereupon he was acclaimed *kattakongur,* the " Cat's King," and received a prize of two litres of *brennivín.* In later times the cat was dispensed with and sometimes a bag stuffed with hay was used instead, or the barrel remained empty, *kattakongur* being he who struck the last piece to the ground. This modification of the custom is indulged in, with great glee, by Faeroe children to-day.

The evening of the first Monday in Lent is called Grýlukvøld and in former times the poorer folk dressed up in bizarre fashion and visited the farmers' houses, receiving small gifts of food. Weihe says that the first *grýla* to enter a house was given a *bógvur* or shoulder of *skerpikjøt*, and this she proudly displayed at all the other houses as an inducement to the people to provide further gifts for her bag. Nowadays it is the children who dress up, as Redskins or anything else that takes their fancy, and they go from house to house receiving small gifts of cakes, chocolate or money.

The *grýla* itself is a rather mysterious creature which appears to be a " fikt " of much the same order as the English " bogey-man "—a " fikt " because no grown-up really believes in its existence, but cherishes it as an invention which prevents children from doing harm. Often, in my own childhood, I was told that if I did such-and-such a thing, the " bogey-man " (or sometimes, in later years, the policeman!) would take me away! Similarly Faeroe children are warned that if they misbehave the *grýla* will get them. The monstrosity has a special connection with Lent, however, and below I give two versions of a current rhyme in which the *grýla* is depicted as a horror waiting to pounce on disobedient bairns—an obvious fabrication to frighten them into accepting the meatless period without demur.

One version, from my friend Jóanes av Skarði, is :

Oman kemur grýla frá gørðum
við fjøruti hølum
bjølg á baki
skølm í hendi
kemur at skera magan úr børnum
sum gráta eftir kjøti í føstu

Down comes a grýla from the mountains
with forty tails
bag on the back
sword in hand
comes to cut out the stomachs of the children
who are crying for meat in Lent

The other, from Hansina Rein, is less blood-thirsty, the horror being armed with a staff in place of a sword, and desiring merely to take the children away :

Oman kemur grýla frá gørðum
við fjøruti hølum
bjølg á baki
stav í hendi
kemur eftir børnum
sum gráta eftir kjøti í føsti

Quite apart from the religious aspect, Lent would normally be a period of meat scarcity in the Faeroes, coming at the end of the winter when most, if not all, of the dried and salted stock had been consumed. The *grýla* has been described to me as having a sheep's body, but walking upright like a man—a picture which one is sorely tempted to ascribe to a yearning for mutton and lamb ! This myth which once gained much in stature (like Father Christmas !) from the personification of its subject by adults, provides a classic example of how a superstition can degenerate to such an extent that its final unconscious expression is in children's play.

A jesting " fikt " of another kind, which has many parallels in other countries, has also enjoyed a considerable vogue in the Faeroes. There is a boulder on the shore south of Glivursnes, near Tórshavn, which is said to turn completely round when it hears the cock crowing on Nólsoy, nearly five miles across the fiord. The best parallel is perhaps the story of the Cloven Stone at Garwick, in the Isle of Man, the two parts of which clap together whenever they hear the bells of Kirk Lonan pealing across the fields. Here are two almost identical yarns which no grown person really believes, and which doubtless originated as tales told to young people in order to mystify them a little—for the undeveloped mind easily misses the point, which is, of course, that stones are physically incapable of hearing. Londoners will be well acquainted with their own version of this jesting " fikt " —Gog and Magog of the Guildhall, who " dined on hearing the clock strike " or, as my friend C. I. Paton was told when a child, " danced round the hall ! "

The *grýla* has something in common with the *huldufólk*—a shadowy existence in the mountain fastness, and a capacity for striking fear into the hearts of timid people. You can call them the " hill-men " or " grey-men," but, if you do as the Faroesee (or as other country people in regard to their fairies) you will refer to them respectfully as " they." At Kaldbak and other villages there are huge rocks or prominent knolls which, no matter how inconveniently situated, are never excavated or blasted away, because it has been told for generations that these are " their " homes. Similar traditions surrounds trees in Irish fields, and prehistoric tumuli and old wells in the Isle of Man. Ill would most assuredly befall those who interfered with these fairy properties. It was said of a Manx farmer who filled in the Chybbyr Unjin, the " well of the ash," that "Kewish wasn't himself when he came for to die ! "

Sometimes the hill-men went fishing in the fiords : if you saw them, and rowed out to the place afterwards, you would land a very good catch. The Manx fishermen would sometimes see the lights of the fairy fleet, and if they waited until the fairies had gone, and then shot their nets on the same ground, they would soon be returning to port (as their prayer says) " with the living and the dead in the boat." The hill-men sometimes carried small children away (people to-day are very definite about this, and dozens of cases are cited) but were always kind to the little ones, and usually brought them home after a few days. Sometimes wanderers vanished mysteriously among the mountains, and it was said that they had elected to join the *huldumenn*.

" They " were certainly a good deal kinder to children than *nykur*, another horrid apparition. This is the Faeroese equivalent of the river-horse, a common supernatural beast in most of the north European countries and in Iceland. In the Faeroes, however, owing to the absence of large streams, *nykur* inhabits the lakes. Eiðisvatn and Toftavatn each has its resident water-horse, I am told, and so doubtless have other lakes. It is described as a small horse which induces children to ride on its back, whereupon it rushes away into the water and drowns them.

In conclusion I propose to say a few words on children's games. Faeroe boys and girls to-day play a good many imported games, most of which have come from Denmark ; nevertheless, the peculiar Faeroese pastimes die hard, and I have seen them even in the capital from time to time. The reader will notice that they are closely associated with the farming, and that,

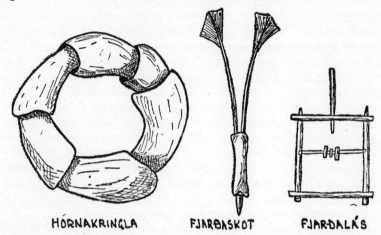

HÓRNAKRINGLA   FJARÐASKOT   FJARÐALÁS

inasmuch as they require objects only available at certain times of the year, they enjoy a seasonal vogue.

Two simple games, *fjarðaskot* and *fjarðalás*, need toys made from goose feathers. For the former, two feathers are inserted in one end of a sheep's shin-bone, and a piece of sharpened wood is put into the other. The toy is thrown into the air; the feathers act as a tail-fin, and the *fjarðaskot* twirls about in the air as it descends, to stick upright in the ground. I watched children indulging in this amusement at Sandur in October, 1944. To make *fjarðalás* long goose feathers, with the vane stripped from the quills, are inserted into each other so that a square is formed, one side of which should extend outwards so that the protruding quill serves as a handle. Parallel with this, a hairpin is fixed between two sides, and a cross, X-shaped, consisting of two short pieces of quill, is fixed on the middle of the pin so that it will revolve freely. The instrument is whirled round in the hand, so that the air causes the cross-piece to revolve rapidly with a loud whirring sound. A slight variant of this, sketched in the Tórshavn Museum, is shown above.

Two kinds of hoop are made, *fjarðaringur* and *hornaklingra*. The first is a large and very light one constructed of feathers, the tips of successive feathers being pushed into the hollow bases of their neighbours. The *hornaklingra* is made at the time of *í skurð*—in October, when the rams are killed—and the hoop is formed on the same principle, the pointed tips of carefully selected horns being pushed into the wider, hollow ends of others, as shown in the diagram.

6

The most important functions in human existence (at any rate, to human beings) are unquestionably being born, getting married, and finally departing this life. And if they are of prime importance to each of us personally, they are hardly less important to us in their relation to our neighbours. That is why the value of gossip and scandal as a pillar of man's sociability cannot be over estimated—and also why the " Births, Marriages and Deaths " column in the local newspaper is the most avidly consumed of the whole sheet ! It is not surprising, then, that there should be a great accumulation of folk-lore and fantasy about these phenomena in all forms of human communities, and it may be of interest to close this chapter on customs and folk-lore by seeking out some of the material which untold generations of births, marriages and deaths have left on record.

Even to-day some people will not divulge a baby's name to any one until the christening. If it is born on a Friday the child is often given a name beginning with " F " in honour of the day, whilst Sabbath children are sometimes called Svanhilda, Sunneva, Sophia or Súsanna for a similar reason. It will have become obvious already to readers of this book that a large percentage of Faeroe Christian names—and patronymics—are of biblical origin : Páll (Paul), Jákup (James), and Jógvan (John), which are regarded as special Faeroese names, are good examples. Others are derived from the sagas—Sigmund, Tórur and Tróndur for boys, and Ragnhild, Turið and Tóra for girls. Still others have their parallels in Norwegian and Icelandic, having sprung from the Old Norse tongue, and we may cite Kári, Heri, Sverri, Bogi, Finn, Egil, and Eyðun for boys, and such names as Hervør, Gunvør, Hjørdis and Tordis for their sisters.

If the family had a long way to go to church for the christening in former days the baby was carried on the back of the strongest and most active man, being supported and kept warm by a woman's skirt which was passed over the man's head and tied beneath his armpits and round his waist. " He should go as quickly as he could," my informant said, " and then the child would grow up strong and energetic like the man ! " Hansina Rein told me that on journeys by sea the babe would be well-clothed and wrapped in a fleece, turned woollen side inwards, and would be supplied with a comforter comprising a small linen bag filled with sugar.

A good christening story is told of a party from Fugloy who, hearing that the parson was at Viðareiði, set out for that village with the mother and child in the boat. On their arrival they learned that the *prestur* had gone on to Klakksvík, whither they followed him. Once more they found that the parson had left an hour or so before, to return to the parsonage at Nes, at the mouth of Skálafjørður. So the next day the men rowed to Nes, only to discover that the parson had gone that very morning to Tórshavn. Nothing daunted, the travellers set off in pursuit. They caught up with the elusive cleric at last, got their baby christened, and rowed home to Fugloy on the *eystfall* the same evening.

Another christening story comes from Mykines. The parson was about to leave the isle at the end of one of his biennial visits when a man came running down to the landing-place, and begged him to stay a little longer to christen his child. " Of course, I will ! " said the parson, " Bring the baby to me at the church." The man then explained, apologetically, that the baby wasn't yet born, but that it would not be half an hour at the most, if he didn't mind waiting. The parson stayed to do his duty, so the story goes, and was marooned for several days in consequence.

Fugloy, like Skúvoy and Mykines, is one of the most isolated islands, and receives visits from the *prestur* only a few times in the course of a year. Years ago his visits were doubtless a good deal more infrequent than they are to-day. Once, long ago, a wedding had been fixed for a certain date, but for some time prior to the date the weather was shockingly bad and no boats could reach the island. Three days before the appointed day, however, there came a sudden lull, and the parson decided to take advantage of it in his anxiety to ensure that the couple should not be disappointed. His arrival was unexpected, and although the couple agreed to be married right away, their families and friends insisted on holding to the original arrangements so far as the celebrations were concerned.

Immediately following the ceremony, the parson departed. When he was some way out from the village he was surprised to see a big *áttamannafar* put out from the landing-place and race after him. He rested on his oars, and as the big boat came nearer he made out the figure of the bridegroom standing in the bows. Soon the boats came within hailing distance, and the bridegroom shouted to the parson to ask whether or not, as the wedding party would not be held for another three days, he was allowed to sleep with his bride before that time ! At a Kallsoy village—again long ago—it is said that the parson, who was a rejected suitor of the bride-to-be, failed to put in an appearance on the appointed day. But the people held the wedding celebrations as arranged, and considered the bride and bridegroom as lawfully wedded man and wife ever after. Both stories have one interesting point in common—they give evidence of the great and solemn significance which was attached to the social side of weddings years ago.

Let us leave weddings, and consider for a few moments their prelude, courtship. I have heard of a Sunnbøur stalwart who often rowed fifty miles in his *fýramannafar* to court a girl on Fugloy. That was a voluntary gesture, but men who courted girls on Vágar were sometimes called upon to prove their fitness by leaping across a deep chasm, Leyphannagjógv, on the eastern coast. I used to see daily in Tórshavn one old man who had performed this feat, to good purpose, over fifty years before.

In former days, when a suitor went to ask for the hand of a maid, he donned his best clothes and hat, and took his *frýggjarastavur*, a long staff similar to the *fjallstavur* carried when going about the hills, but beautifully carved. On entering the maiden's home he would be given the *krakkur*, a three-legged stool, to sit on if she made up her mind that the answer was " No ! " Then he went away, and the girl called her friends together and they took the *krakkur* to the nearest hilltop and burnt it. This custom was known as *brenna krakk*. In later times the stool was spared and its immolation symbolised by the burning of old hay, ling or wood. It was considered great scathe to see the stool burning on the hill behind you as you rowed away down the fiord ! It is still said of a man whose proposal is rejected that " Hann fekk krakk ! " (" He got the stool ! "), or " Hon gav honum krakk ! " (" She gave him the stool ! ").

I am indebted to Jóanes av Skarði and Rasmus Rasmussen for this fine story, and for parallels from Iceland and Norway. The equivalent saying in the first of these countries is " Han fekk ryggbrat ! " which implies that the disappointed suitor " got his back broken," though whether this is a picturesque way of describing his crestfallen appearance and despondent stoop on leaving, or whether he actually got the Icelandic equivalent of the *krakkur* thrown at his retreating back was not explained !

In Norway they say the girl " Gi han pa baten ! "—that is, gave him something for the boat. For the custom there, it seems, was for the girl's friends to load his boat with manure !

The *krakkur*, incidentally, was made from the stem or stern thwart of an old boat when it was broken up, and was roughly triangular in shape. It is very like the three-cornered " creepie " of old Irish homes, which was cut from a section of tree-trunk. Similar three-cornered stools were also common in Manx cottages years ago, but I do not know if they had any association with courtship.

Let us turn now to the subject of deaths. When any one from the outer villages died in the hospital at Tórshavn, the relatives and friends of the deceased went to fetch the body home by boat. When leaving the shore, with the coffin on board, they rowed round three times in a circle, sunwise, singing a hymn, and then, still singing, proceeded on their way. The mourners also walked three times round the church with the bier when the burial took place, the three movements representing observance of the Holy Trinity. Good folk were buried facing the east, as in other Christian countries, because it is in the east that Christ will rise on judgment day ; but when wrongdoers were interred, Nicolas Jakobsen of Kvívík told me, they were laid facing towards the west. There is a place on the coast north of Kvívík called Hálendarheyggjurin, where some of the crew of a Dutch ship which foundered west of Mykineshólmur were washed ashore, and were buried. Hr. Jacobsen said it was the general practice in former days to inter the victims of shipwreck at the place where their bodies were cast ashore, and not in the churchyard, for the people had no means of knowing whether or not such foreigners were of the Christian faith. It is a striking reflection on the almost entire absence of contact between the Faeroe villages and the outside world.

A burial is *gravarferð*, the " earth-going." I think the finest of all the paintings by Faeroe artists is a gloomy but powerfully emotional canvas in oils by Joensen Mykines which depicts a burial party coming to an island by night. It is impossible to describe adequately the depth of sadness implicit in the pale faces of the men and women sitting in the boat : it is to me a most beautiful and touching picture, and the most inspired that this splendid artist has done.

Niels á Botni told me on one occasion, " The old people said, when they heard *lómar* crying above their heads, that the birds were following a soul to heaven." And here, to close the chapter, is a true story from Nólsoy which he relates. One Louisa, a kindly but simple woman, was walking in the *hagi* one day when she came across seven swans on a moorland tarn. She was watching them when a man came along on his way out to the turbary : he remarked what fine birds they were, and how good it would be to shoot one or two, and he turned back to the village to get his gun. The woman, thinking it a great pity that the swans should be shot, drove them away from the pool as soon as the man was out of sight. Years later, when she was being laid to rest in the *kirkjugarður*, seven swans appeared and circled overhead whilst the coffin was being lowered into the grave. Niels á Botni, who was a boy at the time, remembers this last incident well. Coincidence ? Perhaps ! But in any case it is a pleasing story, and it provides an excellent illustration of one way in which local legends could arise.

References to Chapter Ten

JACOBSEN, J. (1898-1901) ; LANDT, J. (1810) ; PATON, C. I. (1940-41) ; PRESS, M. (1934) ; SAYCE, R. U. (1943) ; WEIHE, A. (1928).

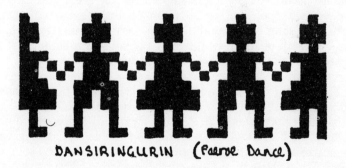

DANSIRINGURIN (Faeroe Dance)

Faeroese knitting pattern.

Chapter Eleven

THE FAEROE LAKES

1. We go to Toftavatn for a bird-watching week-end, and see the ducks, the divers and the grebes (*page* 256).
2. We make a journey along the Sundalagi to Eiđi, and watch the kittiwakes' bathing-parades there and at Saksun. We find a bonxie colony, and climb a *fuglabjørg* (*page* 259).
3. We find a good house at Hvalvík, and ascend to Mýrinar by an ancient track in quest of phalaropes (*page* 264).
4. We go on holiday to Sandur and explore the life of the settlement (*page* 270).
5. We go birding once more by the shores of its lakes (*page* 275).

I

TOFTAVATN was a good choice for a brief birding week-end at the end of April in 1942. You could feel the spirit of the new season trembling around you in that sheltered bowl below the hills. The early insects, Tipulids and an objectionably abundant black fly were on the wing, the yellow kingcups were coming into bloom, and the cattle were being taken to their summer pasture on the upper slopes between Toftir and the lake. The vanguard of the wheatears, pied little birds with bright snatches of song, were going through, and on those two days, the 27th and 28th of April, whilst snow yet lay on the summits of the higher hills, the first whimbrels cried with liquid voices as they forged northwards through the cold, clear sky over the lake.

Tjaldur and *mýrisnípa* were already feeling very much at home, and seemed full of plans for getting down to the chief business of the year. Loud as ever in colour, form and voice, the oyster-catchers were everywhere, standing on the knolls and gravelly patches, or gathering in noisy groups on the rock-littered southern shore. For a short time I watched them, marvelling at the high speed and the sudden whoosh of air with which the birds flew in from the moor—obviously a type of display flight, for on

Couple in national dress

Church interior

(*Top*) Velbastaður

(*Bottom*) Tórshavn—a modern fish-processing plant

alighting such birds very often began to pipe, and set all the others piping too. This sensational full-tilt flight into the middle of the throng is a form of behaviour I have not seen away from the spring assembly places, and there can be no doubt that it has a stimulatory effect on the birds which come together there.

Toftavatn had character too from the meadow-pipits, one or two of which were already gathering material for their nests, whilst other lifted up and down in the ecstasy of their songflight until eventually one was aware of their antics only as something essentially, and almost abstractedly, a part of the quickly-stirring scene.

On the rising land to the west of the big peninsula which juts out of a marshy tract into the middle of the lake numerous small gulls, gathered in white dots against the old dark heather, rose angry and excited whenever one came near their haunt. They were the so-called black-headed gulls which first immigrated to the Faeroes only half-a-century ago, and their jealousy of trespass in this area seemed to presage breeding. Some visited the lake, where there were others of the family—a few common gulls and lesser blackbacks from the hills, a few herring-gulls and one handsome greater blackback apparently visiting from the nearby fiord.

When you stand in the hills above the head of the lake, and look down, it is not difficult to guess how Toftavatn was formed— to see how, were it not for the accident of the low heather-covered mounds on the northern side, this would be merely a secondary arm of Skálafjørđur. It is almost a sea-level lake. It gives life to a little stream which winds between the brown knolls and the black turf-hags to the bay inside the narrow gate of the fiord, the sheltered Kongshavn. Along the shore of the fiord spreads the attenuated cluster of coloured cubes and prisms where the hamlets of Saltangará and Glyvrar coalesce ; and ranged above, proceeding towards Tíril in the north, are the great hills of the south-eastern arm of Eysturoy—Glyvrarfjall, Stórafjall and Stólafjall. The sun shone agreeably on the houses and the hills : how different, and how much kinder they looked than the dead-white battered pyramids of a month before !

There were birds to remember, and birds which themselves brought back memories on this quiet water on those two fine end-of-April days. There was the single redshank feeding at the sandy margin of the south-western shore ; the pair of pintails who persistently refused to oblige me with a close-up view ; the

R

querulous dusky-headed gulls; the spruce "tufties" and Slavonian grebes at the northern end of the lake; the red-throated divers who swam with a finer grace than swans; and the three widgeon cropping the grass with bowed heads far over on the eastern bank. There are few birds more handsome in mature plumage than this little drake of the arctic north, and the widgeon was one of the species I valued most among the birds of Toftavatn—not so much for the present occasion, as for the memories of rare moods of watching in other places, alone or with my friends, in days gone by.

It was pleasant on those two days to sit idly at the northern end of the lake, sheltered by the low peninsula from the cold wind that raised tiny spray-tipped peaks on the surface of Toftavatn, and watch the birds on the unruffled water there. For this end is shut off by a narrow causeway from the main lake, and the birds swam in shelter and solitude, the still water reflecting their sun-touched plumage and lovely forms. They made a splendid group of Faeroe rarities. The Slavonian grebes were the only two in the islands, a pair which has nested at Toftavatn since 1935. The red-throated divers, *lómar* of the Faeroese, kept for the most part to the larger section of the lake, but they could always be seen from the causeway. The three tufted-drakes, accompanied by an equal number of tufted-ducks and a single female scaup, were something in the nature of a surprise, for the species was listed by Salmonsen in 1935 as a very scarce vagrant—an opinion which, I later found, needs to be revised.

Beyond the mere fact of their presence there was nothing particularly exciting about these birds: they were not engaged in any interesting forms of courtship display or other behaviour such as delight the field biologist. They spent the hours in swimming to and fro, or in diving for food, and—which was the most important—in investing this small corner of the Faeroe Islands with unforgettable decoration and charm. Tufted-ducks and Slavonian grebes, when they die, probably become the ornamental waterfowl of the gods. The grebes are graceful, slender birds with the gleam of white satin on their breasts, and in this particular species yellow plumes sprout like strange, elongated ears from their rust-coloured heads. This pair seemed to be very attached to a growth of bogbean which filled a little bay in a corner of the lake, and on a later visit in July my impression that they would nest there was confirmed. By that time the widgeon and pintail and tufted-ducks were doubtless busy on some Icelandic lake, and in their stead on Toftavatn were only a few female eiders and harsh-voiced arctic terns.

The *lómar* remained, and by that time had produced a youngster in a nest at the end of a miniature slipway on one of the tiny islets. This species was formerly much commoner in the Faeroes than it is now, and in 1800 Jorgen Landt wrote entertainingly of the manner in which people used to take the birds for food—for according to him they were fine eating, especially at the beginning of the breeding-season. The men would go to the lakes, and with a loud shout so frighten the *lómur* that he would fall out of the sky! He was easy prey if he fell to the ground, for his legs are set so far back in his body that he was unable to rise from the grass!

In July I had close views of these divers for the first time as they patrolled to and fro near the shore, calling in the dusk, their single " ugly duckling " with them. Most young birds, if they are not actually beautiful, at least have some saving grace from ugliness—but not so the young red-throated diver, who is one of the most ungainly creatures I have seen. He was more like some nightmare trick of heraldry than a natural fact, with a brown box of a body, a straight, thick neck and a whitish spectacle-mark which lent a curious reptilian appearance to his head. It was hard to believe that this unlovely creature, by some Cinderella-magic of the wild, would one day achieve the stately beauty of its parents, and slide across the water with the sun fondling its patterned wings and pearl, black-pencilled neck, and shining on the bright red oval of its throat.

2

The long journey to Eiđi, through the Sundalagi, must be accomplished when the tide-race in the narrows north of Oyri and Streymnes permits, and for this reason you may have to leave Tórshavn at some unearthly hour like 3 a.m. if you are going all the way by small boat. Usually, however, it is possible to take the ferry service to Hvalvík, and go by the smaller post-boat from there ; or you can disembark at Oyri, and travel to Eiđi by road. This is much the quickest and most comfortable way, and the most costly.

If we go by ferry we soon discover that, like a slow local train in rural England, the boat intends to stop at every station along the line. The first two ports of call, Kaldbak and Kollafjørður, are the chief settlements in the two finest of Streymoy's fiords. If you have an interest in geology the first fiord is the better, for it cuts deeply into the hills, and the regular alternation of unbroken rows of *hamrar* and thin grassy slope running the full length of either shore is pleasing to the eye. Kollafjørður is shorter and less picturesque, except at its head, where the flattened pyramid of the highest of the south Streymoy mountains (and the most difficult in the Faeroes to climb) dominates the scene. This is Skælingsfjall, rising to a tiny summit-plateau of rocks and grey-green *Grimmia hypnoides* moss at nearly 2,500 feet. People will tell you that there is only one way to get to this plateau, by an ill-defined track up the south-western face. I tried to find it one winter's day, but without success ; a quarter of the way up a corner of rock put a stop to further progress, so I tried again on the face overlooking the fiord and gave up after starting a minia-ture avalanche on a bed of snow-covered scree. This splendid mountain should be worth climbing if only for the view—which must embrace practically the whole of the Faeroes—to be had from the summit. For long years it has been the custom of south Streymoy folk to scale the mountain on midsummer's eve, and watch the midsummer sunrise from the top.

The next stop is at Selatrað across the sound, where a large white church and a small, darkly-brooding plantation are the only features of interest. Then we cross to Hósvík on the Streymoy shore, situated in one of the round-valleys so typical of the Faeroe scene. At both places there is insufficient depth of water for the ferry to close the shore, so a rowing-boat comes out to exchange passengers, goods and the all-important mail. The hills close in steeply to the sound beyond this village, and as likely as not one of our fellow-passengers will point out the sagging telephone cable which droops overhead like a thin thread, linking the two islands. So we come, after a few miles, to what at first seems to be the end of the sound, but is really only the beginning of its hidden upper reach. Here are Hvalvík and Streymnes on the western shore, and Oyri on the other, and when we reach the first-named settlement we must transfer to the waiting post-boat, for the ferry can go no farther.

The little fishing-vessel enters the narrows, as though entering a barely navigable inland stream, and chugs along past the pleasant village of Norðskála, which takes a long time to fall astern. Here the tide-race reaches something like eight or nine

knots, and a hundred yards width of water little more than two
fathoms deep prevents Streymoy and Eysturoy being a single
island. Now and then, beyond, there is a halt off this or that
group of houses whilst the boat's pram is put ashore to receive
and deliver bags of mail. Soon we near Haldorsvík, occupying
another ill-defined bowl at the foot of the hills, and proud of its
curious octagonal church ; and on leaving we forge diagonally
across the widening Sundalagi towards Eiði, now clearly visible
almost at the mouth of the strait.

Eiði is one of the first villages I visited outside the south
Streymoy area, and I shall always remember the smiling
friendliness of its people. It is a large village of about eight
hundred inhabitants, and by reputation a very busy one on both
land and sea. Its situation on a long slope rising from the sound,
with the tremendous hill of Eiðiskollur at its back gives it a
picturesque approach. Its pride is the church, built in the 1880's,
in which the characteristic style of the old wooden church has
been skilfully interpreted in stone. The good impression formed
from the clean and well-proportioned exterior increases in warmth
to frank admiration when one steps inside, for the atmosphere has
a freshness and charm that is quite unusual. The cream walls,
tastefully decorated with green, yellow and brown ; the painted
pews and fine pulpit ; the arched ceiling of pale blue dotted
with golden stars, and the highly-polished candelabra hanging
in front of the shallow apse, create a light and sunny effect which
cannot but enhance the joy of worship and praise. There is a
carved wooden altarpiece of intricate and beautiful workmanship,
made by a craftsman in the village. For brightness and charm
in interior decoration I would give second place to the church
at Tórshavn, but this is not nearly so fine a building when viewed
from the outside.

The great eminence of Kollur sweeps skywards on the north
side of the village, and it is well worth climbing for the impressive
views down its precipitous face to the mighty stacks of Risin and
Kellingin below, and across to the deep dark bay of Tjørnuvík
near the northern tip of the neighbouring island. Risin and
Kellingin, so fable says, are a giant and giantess who were
towing the Faeroes north to Iceland, when the rope broke asunder
and left the islands in the middle of the sea. From the top one
can see Suðiravatn on the high land south of the settlement, and
the highest of the Faeroe mountains, Slættaratindur, rising to the

east of it. The lower portion of the narrow isthmus below—for Kollur is really an immense peninsula—holds the smaller lake Eidisvatn, whose prettiness adds much to the charm of the village setting.

I had come to Eidi mainly in quest of birds, but apart from a scattered ternery on the lower slopes of Kollur and some arctic skuas on the moors to the east, the only interesting creatures were the kittiwakes. All day long the small gulls passed over the village and the little lake in a never ending procession, coming from their bathing in the hill-lake five hundred feet above. The loose flocks invariably followed the same flight-line, from Sudiravatn down to the Sundalagi, then northwards to the village, turning there to rise through the gap and pass over Eidisvatn to a wide, sloping shelf of rock below the eastern cliff. In the early afternoon this cliff and a nearby promontory were gleaming with thousands of the birds and more were arriving every minute to rest and preen. At Sudiravatn there was a flock of well over a thousand constantly at the lake until late in the day, when the number decreased, thrashing water over themselves and their neighbours and crying interminably. The new arrivals came in at the south, alighted at the rear of the flock, were gradually pushed forwards as more and more arrived, and eventually joined the stream of birds rising and leaving from the front. The whole procedure was amazingly regulated considering the vast number of birds involved, and at the peak period I estimated the passage through the Eidi gap at about 170 birds a minute, an average of over ten thousand an hour !

A few days later I went to Hvalvík, and from there visited Saksun, one of the best-known beauty spots of the Faeroes, and renowned for its fine sea-trout fishing. There is a small lake some distance from the coast, and here very much the same sort of thing was happening. A flock of at least a thousand birds was bathing in the water or occasionally rising to perform aerial exercises with beautiful precision above. Round the shore of the lake, as at Sudiravatn, was a mass of white feathers at least a foot in width, washed there by the tiny waves. The birds were coming and going in continual streams on parallel courses between frowning walls at much the same rate as at Eidi. These immense bathing-parades give one some idea of the plentitude of birds on the Faeroe cliffs, for each must absorb well over a hundred thousand birds a day. And the kittiwake is not by any means the commonest species—indeed, his numbers on the whole are probably small compared with those of guillemot, puffin and fulmar-petrel. Probably only a small proportion of the kittiwake population is involved. I imagine the Saksun parade embraces the off-duty and non-breeding birds from the ten mile stretch of the north Streymoy coast beyond Vestmanna, but there are no colonies for some distance about Eiði, and I am at a loss to know where these hosts come from. Perhaps they make a round trip of thirty or forty miles from the scattered colonies of the Norðuroyar.

Saksun is certainly a magnificent place. It is at the western end of a long valley, Saksunardalur, which runs across the whole island. For the last mile the stream runs through a deep ravine into an almost circular pool, the Pollur, well-known to many British anglers, which lies in the deep shadow of towering crags, and which harbours sea-trout up to fifteen pounds in weight. Seawards, beyond the Pollur, the narrow ravine continues between precipitous walls, carrying the stream to the sea more than a mile away. For most of this distance you can walk dryshod on the black sand of the chasm's floor and I believe that when the tide is low you can follow the river to its mouth and obtain splendid views of the magnificent fowling-cliffs to north and south.

One day I cycled with some Hvalvík friends to the Saksun lake, and we left our machines on the hillside and climbed to the moor above. Soon we entered a shallow valley (one of many which supply water for the majestic cascades of the Saksun bowl and in and out of the thin mists about us arctic skuas flew by the score. They are more numerous here than I have found them in any part of the Faeroes, with the possible exception of Fjallavatn, the lovely lake on Vágar. Shortly we changed direction and entered another and shorter valley running down to the western coast. Here the arctic skuas gave place to the best colony of their larger relatives, the bonxies, now remaining in the islands, where the species at one time must have been a common bird. Only ten or a dozen pairs are left on Skúvoy, its classic home, and there are about the same number on Svínoy, and scattered pairs on Vágar and elsewhere. I estimated the breeding strength in this valley, Svínaskorá, at between sixty and eighty pairs, and even at this late date—July 25th—we found newly-hatched chicks, though other young were very nearly fledged. Our passage through Svínaskorá was unpleasant, the big brown skuas swooping at our heads as we crossed their nesting-ground, always from behind in malevolent silence so that the first intimation was a sudden " whoosh " of air as the bird curved past one's head.

For a time we sat on the clifftop, and then some of us, not content with the view we were getting from above, clambered a fair way down. We found an excellent vantage point from which we could look along the immense spread of bird-mountains reaching almost to the northern tip of Streymoy. The cliffs leaned back from the Atlantic in grassy bastions, where the earth was scored with innumerable puffin-burrows, and brown basalt walls, to which numbers of kittiwakes, guillemots and fulmars clung like white flies to an immense flypaper. Strewn along the foot of the cliffs were huge stacks and tall spires of rock, each thronged with sea-birds, each adding to the picturesqueness of the scene. The sunshine brightened the green of the grassy slopes and seemed to pour molten gold on the sea against the stacks ; it slashed the jagged cliffs with blue-black shadows, and made each bird a gleaming speck of white against the land. A typical stack beneath us had its walls dappled with kittiwakes, and guillemots clustered thickly on its flat top in a beautiful mosaic of black and white. Fulmars slid past on still wings, glancing inquiringly at these strange visitors to their domain, turned with a shudder of feathers, and slid past again. Puffins came up on busy wings with their wet orange legs shining and the small fish like silver slivers in their painted bills, and occasionally a bonxie flew over, lifting himself with effortless, almost lazy strength to the mouth of the valley.

All the time the incredible noise from the stack below rocked the air, and the updraught against the cliff carried with it the strong smell of the birds. The din was indescribable—queer, unbirdlike music—but this and the peculiar taint of the air were wholly characteristic of that throbbing life whose realm is the border-line of earth and sea.

3

When I went to Hvalvík from Eiði, intending to make it my base for excursions to Saksun and Mýrinar, I had no idea where to stay. I knew no one and had no introductions. Fortunately for me, as I stood by the roadside just outside the village, wonder-

ing what to do, a man aged about sixty passed by with a satchel
of food on his back and a *torvskeri* in his hand. I asked him if he
knew English, and he replied in the affirmative ; it turned out
that he was a blacksmith and had learnt his trade more than forty
years before in Leith. I asked him if he had any idea where I
might find a lodging for three or four days, and he promptly
put down his satchel and his turf-spade, returned with me to the
village, and took me to his home.

Quite apart from the pleasant and most friendly atmosphere
of Carl Olsen's house, my stay was memorable on account of the
food I consumed ! I do not remember ever to have fared better
in so short a time. There was heavy rain on my first morning at
Hvalvík, so I got up to date with my diary and had a lazy time.
The laziness was induced by the breakfast I devoured at about
ten o'clock—four fried eggs with an equal number of fried
herrings, fresh that morning from the Sundalagi. At midday a
tray was brought into my little room, bearing a pot of tea and a
plate of cakes which, I understood, would " carry me on " until
lunch-time. This came actually less than an hour later—more
of the lovely fresh herrings, with potatoes, and a very tasty
blanc-mange with a raspberry-flavoured sauce to follow. When
I had done justice to this I felt confident that I should be allowed
to rest in peace for a while : all I asked of life just then was a
quiet corner in which to curl up and sleep !

I was soon disillusioned. My hostess, thinking I was still
ravenously hungry, brought me a plate of warm, rolled pancakes,
with rhubarb jam exuding lusciously from their folds, and set
this on the table with the coffee-pot. My feeble protestations
were drowned by her departing cry of " Eat ! Eat ! Eat ! " The
protestation, which in Faeroese is " Eg eri mettur ! " I had learned
long before in self-defence, for it implies that the speaker is " fed
up " in the literal sense. I often wondered why I had troubled
to learn it, since few Faeroe housewives ever believed that a state
of repletion could possibly exist beneath a rapidly tightening
battledress blouse ! Petra Olsen merely laughed at me, and I
could almost hear her thinking " The poor boy doesn't know what
he's talking about ! " So I ate one of the pancakes for appearance's
sake, and then two more because the first had been so delicious ;
but I quailed at the thought of tackling a fourth, and gave in.
Sigmund Andrias Dam, a happy and handsome little fellow, came
in to show me his pet leveret soon after I had resigned ; and I
encouraged him to eat a few of the remaining pancakes, so that

his mother, when she should remove the débris of the meal, would
believe that I had a reasonably healthy appetite after all. I sat
at the table for a long time after lunch, too frightened to move.

The afternoon turned out to be beautifully warm and sunny,
and Sigmund and his grandfather·accompanied me over the hill
behind the houses to put me on the track to Mýrinar.
It is a long stiff climb from Hvalvík to this marshland area
on the high moors. To get there we must toil up the northern
slope of Sneis, here and there crossing rocky gulleys which chute
cascading rills down to the wide valley below. Along the rim
of one of these, Rosserikke, the widest and rockiest of them all,
the thin and often indiscernible pathway ascends. When we have
put some three hundred metres between ourselves and the sea
the cairns lead us round the shoulder of Sneis to Hvalvíkskarð,
the water-shed beyond which Mýrinar lies, and the pass through
which men go when journeying to Vestmanna or to Kvívík on
the western coast.
If the day is fine then we will do well to stop before we reach
the shoulder and admire Saksunardalur, for this is unquestionably
the finest valley in the Faeroes. We can see two-thirds of the way
along it, and look upon the great moors sweeping up to the
summits on its northern flank. The sun strikes deep into the
contours of the hills, creating black shadows on the rocky ground ;
and the clouds spill vast pools of shade which move quickly
over the panorama, engulfing the slopes and the valley floor,
extinguishing once-bright colours where the greens were gilded
and the sunlight gleamed on the yellows and the browns. The
hamrar loom above the valley, dark and disrupted, and above the
high moors the pale clouds seem to rest on the summits of
mountains as strange and lovely as their names—Rossafjall,
Sandfjall, Givrufjall and finally Mélin, a proudly-pointed peak
in the west. Its spaciousness, its pastel colouring in the sunlight,
and its soft warm beauty are quite unusual features in a Faeroe
landscape, but the absence of farms and tilled fields is typical.
With these, and trees in place of turbaries along the valley floor,
breaking up the twin threads of stream and roadway as they wind
along, their winding without harmony, Saksunardalur would be
a perfect dale in any of the Celtic provinces of Britain.
The highway we follow as we go on our way is more ancient
and important than the one winding through the great valley
below. It is one of Streymoy's arterial roads, and yet is no more

than a meagre track struggling to preserve a shadowy identity
in an inhospitable wilderness, its route marked at regular
intervals by old and sturdy cairns of moorland stones heaped
in prominent places on the rough hillside. These cairns are
comforting, for the path is never very sure of itself. Here, a patch
of denuded gravelly ground swallows it up, or a tiny streamlet
uses it as a ready-made bed ; there, the fast-growing mosses of a
marshy tract have annihilated it, or its course has become confused
by sheep tracks which, more often than not, have a character more
definite than its own. But always, when the main road to Kvívík
and Vestmanna disappears, one can appeal confidently to these
squat pillars of stone which march line ahead across the moor.

Below Middalfjall, just over the watershed, the meagre
pathways branch apart, and round the base of that hill to the
western slope of Loysingafjall the cairns punctuate the way to
Vestmanna ; whilst the Kvívík track turns southwards with the
telephone wires behind Sneis, and, showing a splendid contempt
for the fastness of the hills, runs in a straight and dogged line
towards its journey's end. Between the two is a wide bowl of
marshland and small pools, rough moorland and peat-hags—
Mýrinar.

I shall always remember it for the little birds living on its
assorted ponds, the red-necked phalaropes I went there specially
to seek. To any one who is without a knowledge and appreciation
of birds the name red-necked phalarope can convey nothing at
all, which, of course, is the great fault with the so-called common
" English names " of birds. They are not nearly common—that
is to say, vulgar—enough, and the English is so stilted and
grammatical that " cuckoo," " corncrake," " robin " and " skylark " stand out as gems of poetry among the rest. The British
(or Nothern) greater (or lesser) spotted (or speckled) this (or
that) is worse than the worst museum label and the height of
ornithological conceit. For much of my Faeroe birding I was
grateful for the necessity of having to rely on the Faeroese names,
which, in almost every case, are refreshingly complete in two or
three short syllables. *Likka* is a vast improvement on British
lesser blackbacked gull, and *kjógvi*, " the thief " is much neater
than arctic skua. Similarly, when one is left with the choice of
red-necked phalarope or *hálsareyði*, red-throated diver or *lómur*,
the outcome is a foregone conclusion.

Mýrinar was as interesting and promising a sight in reality

as its greatly reduced outline had suggested when I had studied the map. It was a wide basin in the midst of the hills, with slightly undulating ground full of little pools and a network of small streams, as well as two fairly large lakes lying close together on the southern side. Over them, the long and rakish outline of Egilsfjall slanted down towards the west, and beyond its shoulder was the peak of Reynsatindur, the second highest of the Vágar hills. Egilsfjall and Loysingafjall are separated by a long, steep-sided rift which sears the moor from east to west, and ultimately forms the natural haven on the coast where the pleasant, tidy town of Vestmanna lies. All this wide, wet moorland, with its intricate venation of streams born in the mountain ring, its gleaming pools and twin lakes side by side, seemed to me a perfect breeding-ground for phalaropes, and my hopes of finding these fascinating little creatures ran high.

The first pool, near Hvalvíkskarð, was covered with a forest of bogbean, and as I came down to the shore I saw that the stems were being set in troubled motion by the first *hálsareyði* of the day. He swam in and out of the forest by devious ways, obviously in a state of considerable nervousness—which, in a male phalarope, can mean only that there is at hand a nest or young whose safety he feels is imperilled. The female is one of nature's rebels, leaving the dull household routine of incubation and care of the young to her mate. Not only this, but she carries her domination to the extreme by wearing the brighter plumage, which in birds is normally, of course, the prerogative of the male. It is an inexplicable reversal of natural law in which the phalaropes are unique among northern birds, although in the dotterel the greater share of domestic duties also falls to the male bird.

Certainly this particular male had a thorough grasp of his tremendous responsibilities, and my search for the young birds, which I felt sure were very close at hand, made no headway. Sometimes his rising anxiety led me to believe that I was getting warm, for then his jerky swimming through the maze of bogbean would grow ever faster and more erratic. Finally even this was an insufficient outlet for his pent-up emotions. Something more energetic was required, so he flew up and circled the pool with wayward flight, returning in a few seconds to flop into the water and pursue his aimless swimming once again. On two or three occasions he worked himself up to the pitch of frenzy, his sharp " twik, twik," callnote becoming a louder, rapidly repeated " twerrik, twerrik " as mind and body grew more and more restive. But he need have had no qualms : I did not find his chicks, much to my disappointment ; and, becoming increasingly afraid that he would do himself some organic harm if I stayed much longer, I moved on.

I walked past other small pools, occasionally putting up phalaropes from their margins or from the moor. Lesser black-backs wheeled overhead, protesting at my presence in churlish voices : they are thinly distributed over the whole area, and twice I found well-grown young squatting quietly in some slight cavity of the uneven ground, hoping to pass unnoticed. Away behind me the plaintive mewing cries of arctic skuas floated across from the lower slopes of Middalfjall, where they chased and chivvied each other across their breeding-ground. Now and then snipe drummed on the sky, or a golden-plover called, and by the first of the larger lakes parties of oyster-catchers tried to outsing each other as they clustered about the outlets of the little streams that crossed the wide, shingly shore.

The lakes were interesting mainly for more phalaropes, and for the red-throated divers on the more southerly one. There were two pairs swimming together on the farthest side, and they always contrived to keep on the farthest side no matter how close to them I tried to get. The *lómur* is without doubt the most shy and difficult of Faeroe birds to approach, but the *hálsareyði* is a delightful and quite astonishing contrast. I sat down on the shore of the first lake to eat my bread and *skerpikjót* (without which my hosts at Hvalvík would not let me out of the house) with no less than seven of these charming creatures swimming about within as many yards of me.

Judging by their tameness, and the presence of males and females in the party, they were birds that had finished breeding, but only one of the seven was a bird of the year—creamy white with markings of grey and brown, and every whit as handsome as his elders, though so different in plumage that one might have been forgiven the thought that he belonged to a different species. They had the sides of their necks a rich, warm chestnut in the sunlight, and the mottling of black and brown and streaking of buff on back and wings was almost as intricately beautiful as in the snipe. Some waded on the margin, pecking so rapidly at the sand to pick up food that their short brown bills hardly seemed to touch the earth. The others swam close inshore, whispering to each other with a barely audible " poo-ip " or now and then a louder more definite, " twip." For a long time the little flotilla remained within a short distance of my point of vantage on the bank above, before dispersing up and down the shore.

The sun was still warm and a long way from setting, although it was after nine o'clock. The temptation to remain in this fascinating area was strong, but the thought of the fried eggs which Fru Olsen would most certainly place on the table within five minutes of my return to Hvalvík put the spirit and the flesh at one. I turned towards the pass at Hvalvíkskarð. It seemed an appalling distance, and all of it uphill, but I resolutely set out, reluctantly resigned to the thought that bird-watchers have to be human sometimes!

4

Sandur has a lovely setting. The beauty is in the district rather than in the village, which straggles in customary disorder along a low peninsula jutting out in the eastern corner of the south-west coast. The peninsula forms one arm of a narrow bay, down which one can look towards the isles of Skúvoy and Stóra Dímun, and the hazy coast of northern Suðuroy beyond. At the head of the bay is that unique physical feature, a sand-dune formation, which has given this village and this island its name. It is not the golden sand of English coasts, but a greyish-brown basalt powder washed down through centuries from the island's hills. Nevertheless, it has the same amenable disposition as English sand, possessing those properties which small children with toy spades and buckets demand of any worthy beach, and the seclusion, warmth and comfort required by bathers and those who merely sit at ease and bask in the sun. I should add that here, as in Suðuroy, the Faeroe summer is more of a reality than a myth!

I have heard Sandur called the Blackpool of the Faeroes, because it attracts so many holidaymakers from Tórshavn and other parts of the country. My wife and I spent our own holiday there in early July of 1944, and found the climate agreeably fine and warm, and the countryside even more interesting and enjoyable than the enthusiastic recommendations of others had led us to expect. One quickly sees that life here ought to be brighter than in most *bygdir* for Sandur is not encompassed by huge bleak hills, nor flanked by towering cliffs. One finds a welcome release from the claustrophobia that inhabits a number of Faeroese villages, where gloomy mountains shut out the sky and dominate the houses and the fields, restricting man's dominion to a mere fragment of the land and continually reminding him of his infinitesimal size and place. The open situation and the wide, free vistas are perhaps the district's primary virtues : nature has withdrawn her tyranny and the relaxation of mind so essential to a beneficial holiday is easy to achieve.

In this congenial atmosphere, and the sand on the beach, the resemblance to Blackpool begins and ends. Substitute Windermere for Blackpool, and I will agree that the simile is a little less inapt—for Sandur is indubitably the lakeland of the Faeroe isles. The village peninsula extends inland as a ridge of low heath separating two valleys, one large and one small. The big one in the east contains Sandsvatn, which is about a mile and a third long and varies from half to three-quarters of a mile in width ; and the small valley in the west holds the shallow Gróthúsvatn and its pretty, attendant pools. This is a comparatively narrow valley and a veritable sun-trap on a summer's day, and we spent most of our time in being lazy on the lakeside heath. If you are interested in birds such laziness brings ample reward, for this is the haunt of some of the rarest species in the country.

Sandsvatn itself is most beautiful along the eastern side, for here the valley is shut off by a sheer wall reaching upwards to the high moorland of the central hills. Under this wall, where two neighbouring streams cascade over the face of the cliff and hurry over rocky beds to the lake, there is a colourful hamlet called í Trøđum. I revisited Sandur in October on a day when a strong westerly wind was pounding against the wall and whipping the upper reach of the twin falls into great white plumes of spray which curled gracefully backwards into the hills, as though the water had found a new course in defiance of all natural laws. It is not an unusual effect in the Faeroes in stormy weather and one which never ceases to impress, but I have nowhere seen it to better advantage. These two streams are harnessed in the hills above to provide the district with its water-supply, and perhaps the falls could be used to give electric light and power, but as yet this blessing of civilisation has not found its way to Sandoy.

One blessing the island does possess, however, is the radio-telephone. Communication is established four times a day between Tórshavn and Skopun, a village on the north coast, whence messages can be passed by line to Sandur, and through it to í Trøđum or Skarvanes, or to Skálavík, Húsavík and Dalur, the settlements on the eastern coast. There is a re-transmitting station at Sandur serving the outlying islands of Skúvoy and Stóra Dímun. The Skopun station is in the nature of an emergency measure, for before the war there was a submarine cable linking this village with the Tórshavn Telephone Exchange.

Sandoy has a good system of unmetalled roads which greatly facilitates the movement of passengers, goods and mail, and the half-dozen light lorries and cars on the island are busy almost every day keeping appointments with the inter-island steamer at Skálavík on its journeys to and from Suđuroy, or with the small motor vessels which come more frequently to Skopun to collect milk and other produce for Tórshavn. There is a through road form Skopun to Skálavík via the western shore of the large lake, and branches turn to í Trøđum, Skarvanes and Húsavík. Dalur, in fact, is the only settlement accessible by hill-track alone. Skopun and Sandur both have good stone-built harbours, suitable for boats up to sixty or seventy tons ; but the latter is still under construction—work was commenced in 1936—and use of the former is much restricted by the uncertain weather in Skopunarfjørđur.

The most interesting road goes past the end of Gróthúsvatn and strikes north-west across the low, undulating moorland to the four-mile distant creek of Søltuvík. It passes the lake on a natural causeway which separates the water from the low coastal rocks—a picturesque barrier of huge sea-rounded boulders cast up by long centuries of winter storms. The road was constructed primarily so that the great quantities of seaweed cast ashore at the distant creek could be brought to Sandur and used to fertilise the fields, and secondly in order that the peat so abundant on this moorland could be the more easily carried home. One direct result of this development is the recent commencement of a trøđ farm at Søltuvík—a village, perhaps, in embryo.

Sandsvatn, unlike its sister-lake, feeds the sea by a short and shallow stream which flows swiftly behind the dune area and across the open shore. This is the thoroughfare of the sea-trout when they come to the lake from the bay in autumn to spawn. Sandsvatn is famed for its sea-trout fishing, and in pre-war days was the venue of anglers from as far away as Demark and Britain. A century and a half ago Landt praised this virtue of the lake, and said that the inhabitants themselves did not take the oppor-

Klakksvik—the harbour and Kunoy

Klakksvik—
the town

tunity it afforded of increasing their bill of fare. The outlook is
certainly different to-day, and the rod, reel and line are to be
found in a good many households. Worm is the popular bait—
the gentle art of spinning a fly does not appear to have gained
much favour among local anglers as yet. Our host, David
Davidsen, told me on my October visit that he had landed
150 sea-trout on four excursions to the lake during the previous
month, which is the best time of the year. The majority were
between 1½ and 2 lbs. in weight, and the largest—about twenty
inches long—tipped the scales at 6 lbs. The fact that we heard
of even bigger ones which, true to the best traditions of the
piscatorial art, had got away, suggests that the sport has a bright
future before it here !

Sea-fishing remains the more profitable pursuit when the
weather is favourable. East and north-east winds give the best
sea-conditions on the fishing-ground, which lies to the north-west
of Suđuroy and west of Dímun and Skúvoy, between twenty and
thirty kilometres out. The *seksmannafar* and *áttamannafar*, motor-
powered, are used, and make the journey in about 2½ hours in
good weather, though a laden boat may take five hours against a
strong head-wind on the way home. The catch is almost entirely
cod, and prior to the war the quantity fished off Sandoy was the
third largest in the Faeroes, coming next after Suđuroy and the
north islands, and amounting to nearly twenty per-cent of the
total harvest.

There is a great deal of fertile and well-tilled land in the
district and one of my pleasant memories of Sandur in the
summer is of the warm air charged with the sweet smell of white
clover—so noticeable because it is an experience rare among the
islands. So impressive was it that I found myself chiding nature for
not having provided the Faeroes with bees to benefit from it !
The scentless mayweed is also an abundant plant, especially in
the fields between Sandsvatn and the stream, and, generally
speaking, Sandur appears to have a richer flora than most other
localities. The dune, incidentally, is the only habitat in the
Faeroes of the stiff grey-green marram-grass characteristic of
such situations, and among it a good deal of barley, escaped from
the nearby fields, is growing wildly.

As a result of this unique shore-formation the people of
Sandur are fortunate in possessing one of the very few grass-grown
(and non-tidal !) football fields, for at many of the villages this
game can be played only on the beach. Football, however, is

s

less popular with the youth of Sandur than handball, at which both sexes are proficient. Other social activities are afforded by a social club, a choral society run by the parson's wife and Sunday evening dances to the strains of a piano-accordion in a tiny hall in the fields on the way down to the shore

The commonwealth of 96 *merkur* comes second only to that of Hvalbøur in north Suđuroy in point of size. Of these, 42 m. are farmed by *kongsbøndur* : there are four holdings of 6 m. each at í Trøđum, and seven others of varying sizes in Sandur itself. Much of the remaining land is " Óđals," but formerly there were also 16 m. " kongs " attached to the living of the pastor. This was sold without rights in the outfield to a number of smallholders when the government began to pay the clergy fixed salaries. There is a very large extent of *trađir* at this settlement, much of it very old, and examples of this type of holding are to be seen in the enclosed fields on the western side of Gróthúsvatn and in the big potato growing area along the western shore of the bay. The village of Skopun, incidentally, was established rather more than a hundred years ago on *trađir* bought by the settlers from the outfield of Sandur.

The chief crop in the *bøur* and *trađir* is of course meadow grass, and although most of the hay is stored in barns quite a lot of small, neat *desir* are left standing outside in the yards. Barley has been largely replaced, as elsewhere, by potatoes. There are two wooden mills standing on the twin streams at the back of í Trøđum, and these are used by the " kongs " farmers for grinding their corn. Potatoes are grown extensively and this is one of the very best places for them. The then comparatively new crop was already flourishing here in Landt's time, and Sandur was probably one of the first places in the Faeroes to adopt it. There are innumerable small potato patches all along the western shore, where the fine sandy soil is particularly suited to them. Much of the harvest is exported to Tórshavn, along with the excess milk, mutton and wool. Lettuce, cabbage, carrot and rhubarb also grow well under the mild weather conditions, and Sandur is one of the few places where strawberries can be raised.

There are about two hundred cattle in the village and fifty ponies. No man may have a cow unless he owns a certain amount of *bøur* or 10,000 square metres of *trađir*. In summer the cattle pasture is the moorland between Sandur and Søltuvík, and wet or fine the *neytakonur* make a double journey of between three and four miles, morning and evening, in order to milk the herd, carrying the skin-covered pails strapped to their backs. The ponies are used for draught purposes, and it is only natural that with such good and comparatively level roads in the district carts are in more regular use than in most villages. They are all of the same type, small and shallow box-carts with two wheels and shafts for a single horse.

In a good lambing year the *hagi* may produce twenty sheep to the *mørk* for slaughter, whilst the *kongsbøndur* at í Trøðum regularly kill some three hundred each a year. A curious fact is that the sheep on Sandoy are smaller than in other places : some say that interbreeding is the cause, and others that it is due to the poor quality of the moorland grass, for sheep sent to other islands quickly grow to a normal size. In October whole " sides " of sheep were hanging outside many of the houses, generally beneath a loft window, so that the meat would dry in the sun and wind. This treatment is common here and in Suðuroy because most of the houses do not have a special meat *hjallur*, as do those of Mykines and the north islands, the classic homes of prime *ræst kjøt* and *skerpikjøt*. A *hjallur* should always be sited alongside a fast-running stream or on a clifftop—features absent from Sandur—where there is a continual current of air, and wind-dried meat should never be prepared in a *hjallur* that is used for drying fish, turves, hay, the week's washing, or other purposes.

5

One of the reasons why I chose Sandur for this holiday was my hope and belief that this would prove to be the breeding-ground of the redshank, a bird whose status in the Faeroes appeared to be in some doubt. According to the chief authorities, the redshank " probably bred " but none seemed to be quite sure. I had sought it in the season at Toftavatn, Fjallavatn and other lakes without success, and Sandur seemed to be the only feasible haunt remaining unexplored.

On the first evening of our stay we set out to make a circuit of the larger lake, but as we passed through the road gateway near the parsonage, where the road joins the lakeside, our good intention was quickly forgotten. From away to the west, beyond the ridge of brown heathland, came a breeze faintly punctuated with the tell-tale " tewk, tewk, tewk " of the bird I had sought so long. At last, the hunt was up !

We hurried across the moor in the direction of the challenging voice, and soon arrived at the wall dividing the poor, unproductive land and the *traðir* meadows of Klettur which have been won from it, and which rise from the south-eastern corner of Gróthús-vatn. There on the wall, facing some real or imagined danger in the fields, was the redshank, in slender silhouette. When she spotted us she rose to circle above with characteristic slow and jerky flight, each flick of her white-edged wings releasing a high-pitched " tewk "—behaviour denoting that she had youngsters not very far away. We soon decided that they were somewhere in the meadowland, and therefore unattainable, for in this country where hay is more valuable than gold the desire to establish an ornithological record would have been a poor excuse for trampling down the ripening grass.

The following day we encountered another noisy, nervous bird by the lakeside, and the reward of an afternoon's sun-bathing beneath the *hamar* of the ridge was one half-grown youngster found and ringed, and the breeding of the redshank definitely proved. On the evening of July 12th, by which time I was satisfied that there were only the two families in the area, and that the *traðir* young were already on the wing, we ran to earth the remainder of the lakeside brood. I was surprised that their parent let us get so near before rising in alarm and sending her young into hiding, for the redshank is one of the wariest of wading-birds ; but we caught her napping, and saw the nearly-fledged young swimming on the edge of a pool as they searched for food. They hid under the bank, were ruthlessly marked down and ignominiously fished out with yards of slimey green weed hanging from their lanky yellow legs.

The bird I always associated with the redshank at home was the peewit—a not unnatural association, since they both like the same types of land. It was an appropriate encounter, then, which followed our meeting with the redshank on the first evening ; for, chancing to look up as we retraced our steps across the moor, I saw a flock of over thirty peewits swinging and swaying through the sky. I recalled the only other occasion on which I had seen them in the Faeroes, a grey January afternoon two and a half years before, when walking between Tórshavn and Hoydalur. A flock of fifteen had risen lazily from the streamside, passing inland with unmistakable, undisciplined flight. The lapwing has stronger personality than most birds, and leaves a greater imprint on the countryside : whenever I call to mind the Lancashire and Cheshire fields, or the fascinating Ayrelands of the Isle of Man, the picture has peewits tumbling and twirling through it. On that January day, and that evening in July, the unexpected meetings in an alien countryside brought with them waves of nostalgia which served to confirm the lapwing's subtle power to influence his scene. In that moment, with the redshank still crying " tewk " behind us, and these companions of his flying above, Gróthúsvatn appealed to me as more English than any other Faeroe scene.

I think the lapwings' breeding season must have been over by the time we went to Sandoy, for only one bird on the heath behaved as if it had domestic cares, and its performance was by no means convincing. Perhaps the young were too well-grown to need much care. We watched it closely on the afternoon when we discovered the first redshank chick, for the two adults were only fifty yards apart, but if it had any secrets it was careful not to let them out. Probably few of the lapwings breed successfully every year, for our host David Davidsen told us that a number of the villagers have a taste for the eggs. In view of the bird's undeniable value to the farmer, and its equally undeniable desire to colonise the Faeroes, the Løgting should certainly give it some measure of protection.

A few years ago Sandoy was its only regular breeding haunt, apart from sporadic excursions to other islands, and Gróthúsvatn remains its stronghold. During the war years, however, four or five pairs established themselves between Miðvágur and Sørvágsvatn, whilst others have nested on Eysturoy, and in 1944 a pair bred for the first time on Koltur, rearing four young. It has also nested in the past on both Nólsoy and Mykines, and if protection were afforded the " pool " from which these pioneers are drawn its increase and spread might be of considerable benefit to Faeroe agriculture.

The two lakes were the resort of several interesting species of duck in July, but when I returned to Sandur for a day in October I was surprised to find them almost bare of waterfowl. A majestic whooper swan, probably on passage, and a solitary red-breasted merganser were all I saw. This must be the best island for the merganser, and in addition to several pairs seen on Sandsvatn and Gróthúsvatn on the summer visit, there were others on Stóravatn and Lítluvatn between Sandur and Skarvanes, and on the two pools at the top of the Skopun pass. Mallard were surprisingly scarce, and the little teal which I had expected to find here was apparently absent. The most interesting paired ducks, possibly breeding, were pintail and common scoter. The former are truly handsome birds, and we had many excellent opportunities for admiring them as we sat or walked by the Gróthúsvatn shore. There are only two records of their having bred in the Faeroes, and none at all for the scoter, but I feel sure a resident ornithologist at Sandur (and what a pity there is none !) would soon show that these and other ducks nest regularly here.

Some of the species we saw were probably spending a lazy and comfortable summer on the lakes to save themselves the trouble of journeying to their Iceland home. There were three female scoters in addition to the paired birds, and several small parties of scaup. On the first evening we watched a party of tufted-ducks, and among them an incredibly lovely long-tailed drake in breeding dress, the chestnut of his wet plumage shining like polished bronze in the slanting sunlight. The tufted-duck was no stranger, for I had come across him several times, and already that year had watched parties of males and females on Sørvágsvatn in May. He can no longer be considered the " very rare vagrant " of the books, and my own impression is that the species is a regular and probably increasing passage-migrant, especially in the spring.

Lastly, there were the red-necked phalaropes who live on the lake edge of Gróthúsvatn and the large and lovely pool nearby. As at Fjallavatn and Mýrinar, they seemed to like this pool for its extensive growth of bogbean, a plant which must be a useful shelter for the tiny young when arctic skuas and blackbacked gulls are about. For many hours we watched this pool for a sight of chicks—again whilst sunbathing !—and eventually patience brought its reward. For a long time, one beautiful afternoon as we sat under the *hamar*, the agitated males refused to settle down, swimming lightly and with nervous manner about the bogbean stems, and complaining with low, uneasy calls which gradually increased in tempo until the birds rose and flew low over our heads, to remind us that we were not forgotten. But eventually the one farthest from us dropped his guard, and soon a tiny dot was seen bobbing about in the water like an animated cork near to where he stood preening on a stone.

At first I could hardly believe that this was a bird—so very tiny was it. The glasses were brought to bear, and proved that it was indeed a phalarope in miniature, swimming with astonishing dexterity for a mite so small among the towering stems of weed. Close by was a golden-spangled clump of late-flowering kingcups, and as I ran down to the shore and the anxious parent came to meet me, I fully expected that the tiny prodigy would go there to hide. I removed my shoes and socks and waded out, whilst the nearly demented father thrashed about in the water in a magnificent " false-bathing display," and sure enough the chick was crouching among the tangled leaves and stems of the marsh marigold. He squirmed and wriggled in my hand, shooting out his neck to an astonishing length in his efforts to be free. His dark brown down, like a young redshank's, was beautifully marked with black, and lightened to buffish-white on the underside. The curious lobed feet were amusingly large, but they were disproportionately big for an excellent purpose, as we saw on returning him to the water. He could not have been more than two or three days out of the shell, but even so early in his career there was no mistaking the nature of his future life.

At Sandur, as elsewhere, the typical inland birds—oyster-catcher, whimbrel, golden-plover, Faeroe snipe, wheatear and meadow-pipit—are well represented, and we found nests or young of all of them during our stay. But it is to the gentle, slender phalaropes, the handsome waterfowl, and the English association of noisy redshanks and homely lapwings that memory most often returns. For they are a reflection of the singular peace and charm of this lakeland of the Faeroes, a commentary on the very structure of the environment which makes their presence possible. When one assesses Sandur, one is inclined to think of its topography and the nature of its setting largely in terms of birds. For the ornithologist there is only one better place among the islands, and that is western Mykines, for while the birds of Sandur belong only to the spirit of the land, the seafowl of Mykines belong also to the life and soul of the people. And of the two, the latter provides the greater intellectual adventure.

References to Chapter Eleven

LANDT, J. (1810) ; NICLASSEN, P. (1938-39) ; SALOMONSEN, F. (1935) ; WILLIAMSON, K. (1945 b).

Chapter Twelve

OTHER ISLANDS

1. We go on a picnic to Koltur, and see how the people behave (*page* 280).
2. We revisit Koltur, and on this occasion see how the people live (*page* 287).
3. We sail between Kallsoy and Kunoy, and spend an hour ashore at Kunoyarbygd (*page* 293).
4. We go to Nólsoy to see the village and its setting, hear about the people and see something of the birds (*page* 298).

I

MY FIRST Faeroe holiday began on a Sunday afternoon in mid-July of 1942. It seemed a propitious time to start, for I had been invited to join a party which Sverri Patursson, local ornithologist and antiquary, was taking on a day visit to Koltur and Hestur islands. These are two of the Atlantic outposts of the Faeroes which I had long wanted to visit, for like many of my friends, I have a consuming passion for small islands. That is perhaps because I am a naturalist, and feel that it is good to get away to places far removed from human domination ; and an island, which lives intimately with the elemental nature of earth and sky and sea, is therefore the perfect retreat. On a small island the tiniest manifestations of nature— her flowers, insects, birds—somehow seem so much more personal in relationship to oneself.

I was at the redezvous at the appointed time, but my eager anticipation suffered a rude shock, for I was met by a perplexed Patursson who was at a loss to understand why the remaining members of the party had forgotten to come. So I had to cool my heels on the corner for a time, during which I reflected that the natural history society and its derivatives are probably the same the world over, human nature being what it is, and that it is no good a naturalist belonging to one at all if what he wants is freedom to move as he will about his pleasure of watching and recording the ways of wild life. However, I thought, its power does not lie in its passion for picnicking on the grand scale, but in its commendable indifference to the fate of the annual subscription. If it were not for this indifference, the majority of the papers that have enriched the scientific annals of the world would never have achieved permanent record in print.

A few members of the party arrived, followed by the transport, and I fell to contemplating instead the probable nature of the early part of the journey. Our carriage was a curious one, a light lorry that had seen many better days, and was now trying hard to pass muster as a *char-à-banc*. On weekdays I had seen it going about its lawful occasions, hauling almost anything from coal to household furniture ; but, this being a Sunday, it was dressed for the occasion, carrying on its back a wooden superstructure which had two rows of box-seats covered by a hard leather upholstery. It was an open-air bus that took the climate too optimistically on trust, for the passengers' part was quite open to the sky. This was a grey day with mist hiding the hills, but the weather was fortunately, if precariously, fine.

At last we were all met. An internal combustion engine was discovered and coaxed into life, and we shuddered off. We bumped out of the town along the Velbastaðvegur, which runs above the Sandá river to a bridge half-way along Havnadalur. There the road began to climb to the wet, grey mists shrouding the rocky face of Tvørfelli and the stony moorland beneath. We rumbled past the Tjaldar Tarns—as I call them (because in spring they are the centre of oyster-catcher activity for the moors around)—and came to the top of the pass.

Shortly we began a winding descent which reprieved us of the fog and drizzle and brought us above the scattered homes of Velbastaður on the western coast. We could make out the lower part of our islands' shapes as they lay half-smothered under pillows of cloud. It was a pity we could not see these splendid islands at their best, for that best is impressive and picturesque in a high degree. I know of no isle which has such beautiful form as Koltur, with the high conical peak at its northern end sweeping down to the low farmland, and continuing to a gently-rounded hill near the rocky southern point. Nor do I know any island which enjoys such friendship with the evening clouds. I have admired this sunset-isle many times from Kirkjubøreyn, and each time Koltur has been enriched by a different setting of sea and sky and sinking sun. The strongly raked back of Hestur, with cloud-wisps streaming like a mane from the upland plateau of Eggjarók, is often equally inviting, but to-day only the lower reaches of the dark hillside, and the lighter fields surrounding the single village, could be seen. It was no use regretting that to-day was not one of the better days : after a short time in the Faeroes one learns to be grateful for any weather that does not have frequent recourse to rain.

Turning off the road at a hairpin bend, where there was so little space that the bus had to reverse two or three times before its snout could be brought to bear in the required direction, we entered the spacious *bøur*. We sidled up to one of the houses and the party got down, woodenly, to stretch its cramped legs. Gradually we infiltrated through the door, and when I, the last, went inside, it seemed to me that the expedition was tottering for the second time that day. Our leader was loudly declaiming into the old-fashioned telephone set whose type is universal in the Faeroes, and is the most frightening feature of an otherwise satisfactory service. Our boat had not turned up, but eventually it was traced to Kirkjubøur farther down the coast, and was recalled.

By this time the remainder of the company was settling down to the table in the guest-room, where a light repast had been conjured forth in characteristic Faeroe style. There was plenty of cake and delicious coffee, and lively conversation which I did not understand. Then one of my companions, Jóanes av Skarði learned that I had come from the Isle of Man, and immediately showed an enthusiastic and intelligent interest in the political structure and historical background of that little country, so that I had my work cut out to prevent my wish to gratify his curiosity from interfering with the craving of a hearty appetite. It was not the first time (nor the last) that a Faeroeman displayed a lively interest in this remnant of the Viking empire in Britain's seas, whose story has so many analogies with that of the Faeroe Isles.

When we saw that the little boat had appeared in the distance, a small, bounding oval dot with a shimmering white " V " running away behind, the evacuation of the house was precipitate. We each said " Manga tøkk ! " to our hostess as we rose from the table, and received her blessing " Vælgagnist ! " in reply. This has no literal English interpretation : " Manga tøkk ! " is an expression of thanks reserved for food alone, and the traditional response is a wish that the food you have eaten will do you good.

It is one of the essential formulæ which one very quickly learns in this land where politeness is not regarded as a virtue, but as normal, everyday behaviour—where men are considered rude if they do not doff their hats to each other in the street, and where the ceremony of taking one's partner's arm and escorting her to her seat has not yet been banished by the boorish influence of the " Palais de Danse." It seemed to me, in contrast, that we bustled from this house in a hurry which an English family would have considered downright improper, but this directness of motive and tacit understanding that each has his own task before him and his own way to go is again characteristic of Faeroe life.

The way to the landing-place was a steep zigzag road down the hillside, for the most part of Velbastaður is high above the sea on a wide levelling of the coastal slope. Our arrival was nicely timed, for the boat shut off her engine as we came to the last short scramble over the rocks. She was that typical Faeroe miniature of the Viking longship of a thousand years ago : originally designed for six oarsmen, she had now dispensed with man-power, having a good inboard engine to send her scudding lightly over the waves. The waves in the fiord were playfully robust, as usual, but our little craft was as light and dainty as a phalarope, and as imperturbable.

Koltur came quickly to meet us. The green grass roofs of the older and more southerly of the two settlements escaped from the green grass of the hill behind, making a picturesque and primitive scene which charmed the eye, and contrasted in odd fashion with the well-built two-story house of the Niclassens a little way to the north. Ahead of the boat was the concrete sea-wall, with a gap of a few feet half-way along it, protecting the little landing-place. Behind the gap, fifty feet high on the cliff, was the *neyst* of old boathouses, with a winch at the head of the steep slipway to drag the craft out of harm's way of the winter seas.

As we drew close to the rocks, the oldest and the youngest of the Niclassens—grandfather and six years'-old grandson— appeared in the gap, and they took the painter whilst we jumped ashore. When we had landed and words of greeting had been exchanged, they suddenly lost all interest in us, and returned to whatever job they had been doing prior to the interruption. We were the first visitors to this lonely outpost for many days, yet the meeting was dominated by that same recognition of each other's immediate need which had marked our flight from Velbastaður. In that sane and healthy spirit we left the old man and the very young man to their destiny, and made our way up the cliff path to the fields before the farm.

We were warmly greeted and ushered in by the good lady of the house, who, I could not but notice, spoke the word " Vælkomin ! " to each of us in turn as he set foot across the threshold. I must confess that I began to feel restive, for I very much wanted to see the island and do some birding, and instead was faced with the inevitablility of another meal ! We moved about the living-room and the *glasstova* beyond, whilst out hostess bustled ominously about in the kitchen, and her husband engaged his visitors in conversation.

In the airy and comfortably furnished sitting-room, a photographic family history festooned the walls. Family ties are strong in the Faeroes, and the people are not at all embarrassed by the stern gaze of many ancestors. I looked long at a hand-coloured portrait of Harra Karl Niclassen and his charming bride, handsomely attired in the long *stakkur* of heavy silk, the traditional wedding-gown which is, alas, no longer much in favour. It is customarily of a dark red or blue colour, and is worn beneath a white embroidered shawl ; it has large embroidered cuffs, and a heavy ornamental gold or silver belt, whilst the bodice is laced with a thin chain of the same metal. I examined other photographs, and a tour of the room only served to strengthen my impression that these mural exhibitions are often as remarkable for their portrayal of the development of photographic art as for their pictorial recording of genealogy.

Again characteristic of this little nation, there was on a round table in the middle of the room a shallow dish containing a heap of loose snapshots of places and people—but mainly of people. You meet with this in almost every Faeroe house, and it is hoped that you will delve into these varied glimpses of family life with gay abandon, and so improve the shining hour. It does not matter if nobody is at hand to explain the various occasions and relationships. The Faeroese have found a philosophy in photographs, and use them with skill and insight to foster friendship and make the chance visitor feel more at home. Snapshots on the table are always a sure and certain guarantee of homeliness and good fellowship, of a real desire to enfold you to the family bosom, so to speak. The camera, one might say, writes " Welcome ! " on the doormat.

By what accident did the English overlook this magnificent virtue of the photo-album ? Their collections, which are certainly as varied and as numerous, are stowed away in cupboards or drawers, there to " rust unburnished, not to shine in use." It would be an impertinence, if not an effrontery, to pore through the pages of an Englishman's album without his express invitation or permission. It is probable that in a strange house one would be saved from boredom—as in the dentist's waiting-room or barber's shop—with out of date copies of the illustrated magazines, but no personal encroachment on family life is admissible. Why ? Perhaps the defences of the Englishman's castle would totter and crumble if he left such intimate documents as his photographs exposed to prying eyes !

Soon our busy hostess raised the cry " Verð so góður ! "— " Be so good ! "—and we shuffled into our seats at the table. " Verð so góður ! " is a borrowing from Danish, although in homes where the spoken tongue is invariably Faeroese its equivalent, " Gerð so væl ! "—" Do so well ! " as to take your place—is now often used. Coming so soon after the Velbastaður spread, the sight of the table with its white bread and farm butter, *skerpikjøt*, rhubarb jam and assortment of biscuits and cakes was a little overpowering ; but to have excused oneself on the grounds that one was not in the least hungry would rightly have been thought churlish. The offer of refreshment is a *sine qua non* of hospitality in the islands, where your caller may have had to travel long and arduous miles by land or sea. Even in modern Tórshavn this first act of grace towards the traveller survives in many homes, and I have heard the housewife press the offer of refreshment on callers from only a few hundred yards away, who had come on the most fleeting errands.

Interwoven with the fabric of Faeroe hospitality is a charming code of manners, the apparent complexity of which at first appals the timorous newcomer who is eager to conform to the good old adage " When in Rome, do as Rome does ! " But the code is easy enough to learn, and one need not undergo the rigorous education of the Faeroe child in order to master the intricacies of social behaviour. In good homes small boys and girls are taught to say as a grace on leaving the table, " Góði Jesus-pápi, tøkk fyri matin." Then they go to their father and mother in turn, offer a hand, and say the traditional word of thanks, " Manga tøkk ! " The boys bow as they do so, and the girls curtsey. Parents do not insist on this behaviour after the age of ten or eleven years, but by that time the niceties of courteous deportment have been thoroughly instilled, by precept and example, into the rising generation.

During our meal the eldest of the Niclassens came into the room, and at once wished us " Vælgagnist ! " The company murmured its thanks. Here is another of the proprieties—if you approach any person who is at meat, whether at the dinner-table or merely eating a sandwich by the side of his turbary, you should always preface your conversation with this blessing on his food. On special occasions, as when you have been invited to a birthday or other party, you do not rise from the table until your hostess herself rises and bids the company " Vælgagnist ! " In addition to replying " Manga tøkk ! " you thank your host and hostess again with a word and a handshake as you leave the room. Later, when departing from the house, the polite leave-taking is " Tøkk fyri í kvøld," or " Thank you for the evening." Your gratitude does not end there ; indeed, the responsibility of it will weigh heavily on your mind until you next meet your host and hostess, either on the street or at some future function, a day or a week or even a year or more later. Your greeting should always include the phrase " Tøkk fyri síðst," which means " Thank you for the last time."

So we ate and drank, trying to take as little as possible, but having small success because Faeroe hostesses are much too attentive to permit a mere pretence at eating. One hardly dared to empty a cup, for it would be mysteriously filled from a pot which loomed over one's shoulder almost before the cup had settled itself in the saucer again. The table was revictualled with a like alacrity ; there was an abundance of everything, at the end no less than at the beginning of the meal. I shall always remember this as the first occasion when I realised that there was something really good about *skerpikjøt*, a commodity I had been secretly trying to get the better of for some considerable time. The leg on the Niclassens' table was hard and tough, as *skerpikjøt* is when in beautifully prime condition. In those early days I had not learned the knack of carving it—a knack which one must have in order to enjoy it to the full—and did not know, until that day at Koltur, that the only way to master a *kjógv* is to assault it with vigour and determination, and dominate it completely.

So it was that when my turn came I went to the leg timidly, and after a few moments fiddling about managed to cut a sliver of the size that is given to Faeroe children just after they have cut their teeth. I was thoroughly ashamed of it, lying microscopically on my plate, and, feeling a distinct grudge against the *kjógv*, returned to the fray in something of a fighting mood. But the *skerpikjøt* had sensed my weakness and had no intention of lightly relinquishing the advantage it had gained. My next piece sprang away from the leg like a piece of steel clock-spring, whistled across the table, and came to rest with a sickening ring in Jóanes av Skarði's saucer. Everybody went on eating as though this was quite the normal way for a piece of *skerpikjøt* to behave, but if a hole had opened in the floor I would have gone through it with a superlative exultation. Greatly cowed, I was about to apply myself meekly to the leg once more when my next-door neighbour with charming diplomacy, expressed mild surprise at the shameful bluntness of my knife, and intervened to avert what might well have become a dangerous situation. I watched closely as the *kjógv* wilted beneath his gaze, and trembled in his grip as the knife flashed to its work : the piece he gave me would have pleased a giant, but I ate it and enjoyed it, for I felt that *skerpikjøt* had no secrets for me now !

2

Koltur is said to be " the colt " island, and although it has no superficial resemblance to a horse that I can call to mind, it is a logical assumption that it may have been dubbed " the colt " because it lies next to the larger island of Hestur, " the horse." There are those who hold that this is a fanciful view, and that Koltur was originally *kollur*, a term applied by Faeroese to a large " sugar-loaf " of land. Certainly the huge northern hill is the most striking natural feature of this beautiful island, but *kollur* is too prosaic and obvious to appeal to my mind. Still another theory links Koltur with *kultur*, the belly portion of the butchered sheep, for when the *kultur* is hung up in the cellar its sectional outline is supposed to resemble Koltur's outward shape. I have seen the sheep's undercut, and am not impressed. I believe in the poet who saw the white clouds streaming like a mane from Hestur's high back, and in a moment of inspiration called the island after man's faithful servant and friend—and who saw the little island rearing up in the sea alongside, and named it, happily enough, " the colt."

Meanwhile, the twenty-one inhabitants of this picturesque island pursue their vigorous, hardy lives without any thought for such academic diversions. It is enough for them that Koltur has soil to grow crops, rocks to house a myriad birds, and seas to yield their toll of fish. These kindly people—for so we found them when we landed again in late August of 1944—live at four farmsteads, two of which lie in the shelter of the low southern hill, and two farther north towards the mountain hump. Their houses are wooden buildings raised on stone cellars in the traditional Faeroese way, and they are simply but substantially furnished according to the middle-class standards of the great majority of Faeroe homes. The dwellings are surrounded and almost smothered by a miscellany of *gróthús* and *hjallar* and other offices inseparable from the farming life.

The southern settlement was one of the most charming old groups in the Faeroes until the sod roofs were stripped from the dwellings and replaced by asbestos sheets in the summer of 1944. Development and improvement are desirable and laudable virtues, but when I revisited Koltur in that year I found myself thinking how hard it is sometimes to reconcile progress with one's aesthetic tastes. However, it is none of my business. I do not have to live the hard toil of a lonely island life, wrestling for half the year's course with the frenzy of Atlantic storms. My own life, like that of most people who will have leisure to read this book, is made easy by the innumerable blessings of twentieth-century science. The light by which I read and write, and my good wife knits and sews, does not depend on my ability to shoot a seal and deprive him of his oil. For a payment my fuel is delivered at the door—not dug by the sweat of my brow from the slope of a distant hill. I did not have to site my house (and build it with the help of my friends) above a trickling stream so that I could have water ready to hand ; nor must I carry water from a spring in the field in summer when the trickle runs dry ! What a curious contrast is this business of water-supply on Koltur !—none in the cellar for weeks, perhaps, and then a sou-westerly storm flings so many wave-tops over the sixty foot cliff that the cellars, a quarter of a mile to the east, are flooded ! It has happened more than once at the Niclassens' during the winter months.

There is also the problem of the children. Yours (if you have any) doubtless go to school regularly each day for five days a week. Here they attend school, in the Niclassens' sitting-room, for six days every month, during the week when the teacher from

Hestur is staying on the isle. But do not think that the Koltur children are idle and illiterate as a result : they are shy, perhaps —which is only natural considering their isolation—but as mentally alert and knowledgeable as most town children at the same age. Koltur's case is not exceptional, for many of the outlying villages share their teachers, just as they must share the parson and doctor, and I cannot find any evidence that the youngsters suffer harm from this system. The teacher doubtless leaves his or her legacy of homework, but there are other and more important factors in the training of the young. The parents are fully alive to their own responsibilities in this respect, and a good deal of unofficial schooling goes on especially during the long and dreary winter when little work can be done out-of-doors. In the summertime education is more subtle : the children, without knowing it, seek and find mental and manual training themselves by imitating their elders in the fields, learning and acting real life in a way which is not possible to those who live in large towns. When they grow older, more orthodox facilities are available in Tórshavn, either at the High School or the Fólkaháskúli.

There is no church on Koltur, and the people conquer this deficiency as easily as they do the others. The family gathers in the sitting-room on Sunday morning for a simple service at which the head of the household reads the lesson and conducts the prayers ; or they listen to a broadcast service from some church in Copenhagen and join in the prayers and the singing of the hymns. Sometimes in the summer, when the weather is fine, one or more boats will go to Hestur or even to Kirkjubøur, and the family will attend divine service there.

The doctor comes to Koltur only when there is an urgent call for him over the radio-telephone. Normally the clergyman comes only for funerals and christenings, and you may guess that in so small a population these events are rare. We were told that the last time the burial service was read was in 1937. The little cemetery lies in a comparatively sheltered spot on the south-eastern corner of the mountain : it is roughly square, and is surrounded by a stone-built wall with a wicket gate in the middle of the lowest side. The graves are without headstones : those who have been laid to rest in this quiet spot need no monuments, no epitaphs, other than those engraved on their neighbours' hearts.

T

The men go fishing when the weather and other work permit, sometimes for cod but mostly for saithe, and the greater part of the catch is salted or dried for winter use. Of the two chief occupations, however, the farming takes precedence, for the holdings are fairly large and the soil is fertile. There are seventeen milking-cows and several heifers, and dairy produce is one of the few items of export. A number of bullocks were fattening for the market on the long grass at the south of the island, and mutton, wool and that peculiarly Faeroese commodity *skerpikjøt* are also produced in excess of the people's needs. Some barley is grown and there is an interesting *sódnhús*, rather smaller than the one at Froðbøur and different in that it boasts a wooden chimney. Most of the corn is ground in hand-querns, but there is a neat little mill, erected ten years ago by Niclas Niclassen on a small stream behind his house, in which a hand-quern has been adapted to a horizontal wheel. If there is a good flow in the streamlet, Niclas lets the water do the work ; but if there has been a spell of fine weather, he has the advantage of other millers in that he can always do the work himself ! Peat is the only fuel used on the island and it is cut at turbaries on the eastern flank of the big hill and carried by pony to the farms.

At the time of our visit almost everybody was busy making *sátubørn* or scattering grass in the fields, which are incidentally the finest *teigar* fields I have seen among the islands. The small children seemed to be just as busy as their parents (for this was not a schooling week), but were not taking the business quite so seriously. Even though their help is invaluable, Faeroe children can enjoy a hayfield just as much as their English cousins. A few of the older men were absent, being away on the cliffs drawing the young of the Manx shearwaters from their burrows. Niclas took us to the nearest of the fowling-cliffs and showed us the ropes dangling down over the edge, held to the ground by a most insecure-looking wooden peg no more than eighteen inches in length. From a clifftop burrow he took a fine fat *líri* who was an unkempt mixture of brown feathers, blue quills and fluffy greyish down, just at the right age for eating. He looked much more akin to the child's golliwog than to any existing species of bird. Our presence was his salvation, for he was spared the usual fate of *lírar* to wear an aluminium ring.

Two other occupations, one old and obsolete, the other in a new and flourishing condition, are worthy of mention. Landt records that a small amount of pottery was formerly made on

Koltur from a hard green clay which appears on the hill between the basalt strata. Our party hoped to find examples of this art, or, failing that, discover some new information concerning the manner in which the pots were made. One old man told us that the clay was mixed with the white of sea-birds' eggs to make it plastic, and was then fired in the houses and moulded by hand into small vessels used for containing milk. Beyond that our inquiries elicited only the name of the ware, *koltursdollir*, and it must be a very long time since this rustic handiwork vanished from the island scene. The other venture is a much more profitable one, for Niclas at any rate, for he has a fine reputation among the islands as a builder of small boats, and in winter travels up and down the country practising this craft. Although only in his middle thirties he already has well over a hundred first-class boats to his credit.

Koltur is rich in legend and story. It is not known when the first residents arrived on the island, but the remains of an old chapel show that it was inhabited long before the Reformation in 1536. In catholic times a priest came regularly from Kirkjubøur to minister in this building to the people's spiritual needs, and it is told that the last one to preach here met his death by drowning on the return trip. The chapel fell into disuse and later became a dungeon for those who displeased the chief farmer, who set himself up as " king " with power to pronounce judgment on his fellow men. It is said that part of the original stonework still stands in the walls of an outhouse at the southern settlement. The landing-place was here before the cement sea-wall was built below the Niclassen's farmstead several years ago, the boats coming ashore on a small sandy beach—one of the very few strands in the Faeroes—where I spent a part of this very delightful August afternoon watching some knots and turnstones resting on their migratory journey into the south.

A good yarn is told about a large stone which stood in the middle of a cattle-way or *geil* leading through the cultivated land to the heath beyond. This stone partly blocked the way, but it had come to be regarded with a superstitious awe, and one Tummas, the grandfather of the present head of the southern farms, declared that ill would most certainly befall anybody who was rash enough to move it. One day Tummas went away to Hestur, and in his absence some of the younger men levered the stone from its bed and rolled it to one side. Later in the day they too went to Hestur to get hay, and whilst there they told Tummas what they had done. They expected wrath, but the old man only shook his head sadly. He was asked to return with them, but refused to do so. They set sail for Koltur in favourable weather, and were nearing the sandy beach when the boat quite suddenly and mysteriously capsized, so that all the hay was lost and the men had to swim for their lives. Fortunately they got ashore safely, but they were so upset by the incident that they went straight away to the *geil* and restored the boulder to its rightful place.

There is an older legend with a fine romantic flavour which seems to me to be too like the classic saga-piece of Sigmund Brestisson's swim from Skúvoy to Sandvík in Suðuroy to have had an independent origin. The young man, called Magnus, lived on Koltur, the maiden on Hestur. They were deeply in love, but the girl's father was set against the match, and it was therefore impossible for the young couple to meet openly. So Magnus used to swim across Koltursund during the hours of darkness to a secret trysting-place among the rocks, crossing on the *eystfall*, which normally lasts about six hours, and returning on the *vestfall* when the tide sets north-west between the islands. These clandestine meetings went on for some time before the girl's father became suspicious. Confronted by his wrath, the unhappy maid confessed to the time and place of the next meeting with her beloved. On that night the old tyrant confined his daughter to the house, and, arming himself with an axe, he set out for the lonely spot where the pair were wont to meet. He seated himself on a rock, the axe across his knees, and waited. Soon the lapping of the water heralded the coming of the young man of Koltur : the watcher rose, grasped his axe firmly, and went down to the water's edge.

" He who is honest, and would have business at Hestur," said the old man, " Will come openly to the public landing-place, and not creep ashore by stealth at night ! " He gave Magnus a hard choice—to come ashore and take the consequences of such rashness, or return whence he had come. Weary after his swim, Magnus was in no condition to fight, so he attempted to go back across the sound. But the current, of course, was against him . . . The young man of Koltur swam out into the darkness, and was seen no more.

We ate our "unexpired portion of the rations," the Army's classic term for a tin of corned beef, on the slope to the north of the main farmstead, sitting among the blue jewels of the devil's-bit scabious which enlivened the close-cropped heath and which is called in this country *líragras* because it blooms at the time the young shearwaters are captured. The friendly Niclassens sent a can of fresh milk and a leg of *skerpikjøt* to increase our meagre fare, and although most of the party viewed the latter with some diffidence and clutched their bully the more tightly in their fists, there was no mistaking the approbation accorded the can. Before our departure we were given tea and cakes in the house, a similar repast to the one which had been our welcome to the island six hours before. We doubted, as we said good-bye, if there are more charming, forthright or hospitable people anywhere.

The wind was freshening and there were white caps, *grísarnir*, on the waves rushing tide-borne through the sound. They are said to have first appeared with a current of unprecedented violence on the night that young Magnus kept his last, fatal tryst. Koltur grew smaller and ever more beautiful (for it is best when seen from the south) as our ship sailed down the fiord, and the folk whose lives we had been privileged to glimpse and admire became the merest specks toiling against the soft yellow of the sloping fields.

3

We were very fortunate in the weather for our visit to Kunoy : a warm, sunny and wonderfully clear day enhances the beauty of any landscape, but is absolutely essential to an appreciation of the grandeur and strangeness of these north-eastern isles. Kunoy and Kallsoy, between which we sailed, are long and narrow mountain chains standing high out of the sea, touching the sky with pyramidal peaks seldom less than two thousand feet in height, and there is perhaps no part of the Faeroe coastline so impressive when examined from the sea.

A peculiarity of Kunoy, and the source of much of its picturesqueness, is the regular alternation of steep mountain-slope and *dalur* or round valley formation as you sail along its coast. The *dalur* is not a valley in the generally accepted sense, but a deep half-bowl scooped out of the mountain mass, with immense walls of rocky *hamrar*, rising tier upon tier, forming its sides. The walls descend, often in a beautifully even curve, to a small green floor irrigated by a network of streams whose upper reaches are foaming white cataracts against the grey-brown cliffs. Looking into Jarðadalur and Skriðudalur is like looking outwards from the central point of a tremendous natural amphitheatre, a magnified Roman ruin with broken-crested, time-worn walls around its rim. This same feature occurs on other islands—in Kálvadalur on Mykines, for instance—but there is no doubt that its best development is on Kunoy. When you consider that this island is just over eight miles in length, has an average width of less than two miles, and seldom falls below two thousand feet along its central ridge, you can perhaps imagine the splendid grandeur of these deeply cut dales scored in the great hillsides which descend to the low rocks of the coast.

Kallsoy has this kind of topography too, but viewing this island—which is even longer and narrower than Kunoy—one's chief impression is of the strongly raked back where pyramid succeeds pyramid along the full length of the land. Kallsoy has the most settlements, and they are all on the eastern side. We entered the fiord from Klakksvík to the south, and saw first of all the tiny lighthouse, then the green fields and houses of Syðradalur, with the largest of the villages, Húsar, a mile or more farther along the coast. Mikladalur, said to be the most beautiful by those who know these islands well, came in sight as we drew close to Kunoyarbygd. Trøllanes, the most northerly one, remains hidden behind a projecting headland until you reach the far end of the fiord.

The coastal path linking these two northern settlements of Kallsoy is reputed to be the grandest, and at the same time the most frightening pathway in the Faeroe Islands. My mother-in-law, who was the schoolteacher for these communities in her younger days, tells hair-raising stories of winter journeys from one place to the other, through snow and storm, securely roped between two of the toughest of Kallsoy men. She tells also of two women of Trøllanes who travelled this way regularly every summer morning, plucked three hundred puffins each at Mikladalur, and walked home again at the end of their day's work !

The track between Mikladalur and Húsar is longer, but much less dangerous ; and in fact the only risk is that you might forget to stop and lay down your load by a certain boulder in Ritudalur. Custom demands that you must rest there, if only for a few moments, and in former times you had also to place some small coin beneath the stone. This done, all was sure to go well with you on your errand. Periodically, I am told, an old man used to come out from Mikladalur, and take the wayfarers' offerings for the collection-box belonging to the church. A similar ritual had also to be observed on the road between Skopun and Sandur, but on Sandoy travel was cheaper, for to ensure a successful journey all you were required to do was throw yet another stone on a certain wayside cairn.

Kunoy village is to my mind one of the prettiest in the Faeroes. It stands on the brink of Lítlidalur, with a semi-circular rock wall away behind it, and a spur of the hills called Lítlujfall immediately above, separating this dale from a lesser one lying to the north. The typical old church, sombre and plain with its white walls and red roof, overlooks the landing-place from the tip of a rocky point, and the majority of the houses are grouped behind it. This is the main settlement, but there are also two small groups a few hundred yards distant on either side, Nordur í Húsi and Sudur í Bø.

We landed at a brand-new concrete landing-place which the men of Kunoyarbygd had spent all the summer in building, and had completed only a week or so before our visit in early September. It comprises a small but adequate quay wall, and behind it a steeply inclined rampart against the low cliff. In the middle of this rampart is a channel, fitted with wooden rollers, down which the boats are lowered by a capstan above. On either side of the channel is a flight of steps, so that men may walk beside and steady the boats as they slide down. This is but one of several landing-places in the islands which were constructed about that time, always by the combined labour of the men in the villages concerned, and with the financial help of the Løgting.

It being such a fine day, and late in the season, almost everybody was working in the fields, tying big swathes of grass to wire fences to dry in the sunshine, or bearing home hay that was already made. This new way of drying grass is quite general on Kunoy and Kallsoy, and on looking across to the sister isle one could see the full frames in the fields as short, dark, even streaks like crayon-marks on the pastel-green of the stubble—a peculiar effect quite unlike the distant prospect of hay-fields in other places.

Christoffer Kunoy, the chief *kongsbóndi* at the village and a very pleasant host, told us that this method of harvesting the grass was introduced in 1911, and has since spread to many other settlements. He also said the the first Faeroe rowing-boat to adopt engine-power was a Kunoy boat, about 1903—so there is ample evidence that this little village, though remote from the tide of progress, keeps its eyes open and is quick to learn. Kunoyarbygd is a 34 m. village with a population of 139 : its high outfield supports about seven hundred sheep which normally yield sixteen lambs to the *mørk* for slaughter, and there are about three dozen cattle.

This is one of the three places in the Faeroes to boast a small plantation of mixed conifer and deciduous trees. It is a very pleasant little park in a sheltered spot beyond the cultivated fields, and we strolled through it along a narrow shady path rimmed by ditches full of yellow lesser spearwort flowers. Below, the main stream, called Millá, flows out of Lítlidalur and down past the schoolhouse to the coast. The schoolmaster took us into this simple one-roomed building, where he teaches the Kunoy children for a fortnight in each month. The remaining fortnight he spends at Haraldsund on the opposite side of the island, attending to the pupils there.

One mill, a comparatively new one, remains on the little stream, and one feels that the name Millá indicates that this is a very old site. Very little barley is grown in the village now because rats, which got a footing on Kunoy during the last war, are numerous and damage the crop severely. There is a story that these destructive animals were put ashore at Haraldsund by a Klakksvík man who had a grudge against the people there! They have done irreparable harm in another direction too : formerly the young of the Manx shearwater were taken for food at a colony on the east coast near the deserted village of Skarð, but the rats have now almost extirpated these birds. The only fowling indulged in nowadays by the Kunoy men is " fleyging " for puffins at three small promontories near the north-western tip of the isle, and their usual catch in a good year is about 13,000 birds. This summer, however, the puffins got off Scot-free, for the men were too busy building their new landing-place to have any time for the birds.

The flora and avifauna of Kunoy are more characteristically alpine than on any other island, with the possible exception of Viðoy. Many interesting " alpines " have been recorded by Rasmus Rasmussen and other infrequent visitors, but the island's natural history has been little worked, and it would prove a happy hunting-ground for any energetic botanist. Christoffer

Kunoy told me that the snow-bunting breeds in the hills, but it is apparently rather rare, and another northern species, the purple sandpiper, is said to nest in some numbers. The most interesting of the Kunoy birds is undoubtedly the *rýpa*—either grouse or ptarmigan, but which of the two no one knows ! There have been several introductions of game-birds ; some Greenland ptarmigan were turned down near Tórshavn in 1890 and quickly spread to other islands, whilst six years later some Scottish red-grouse were introduced. According to Salomonsen, all these birds are supposed to have died out in the early years of the present century, since when no further attempt to establish them has been made. There is good local information from Kallsoy, however, that the *rýpa* was common there up to about 1930 : Hr. Jógvan Hansen, a farmer at Húsar, told me that he sometimes used to see as many as twenty during an afternoon's walk through Knútsdalur in the south of the isle. Although none is present on Kallsoy to-day, Christoffer Kunoy not infrequently comes across one or two birds when going among the hills on his own island, and he found a nest with eleven eggs a few years ago. It would be most interesting to know which of the two birds, the Greenland or the British, has managed to survive the rigorous climate of this northern isle, and what conditions have made its survival possible. One suspects that it is the ptarmigan—but in ornithology it does not always pay to trust too much upon one's expectations !

Skarð, a ruined village on the eastern coast, a little north of Kunoyarbygd, is a place with a tragic history. One evil day in 1913 all the active menfolk lost their lives in a mysterious accident at sea. Although the women and the old men tried nobly to carry on the farm-work for a while, the task was too much for them, and the old homesteads had to be left behind. Hr. Jóanes av Skarði, the headmaster of the Fólkaháskúli at Tórshavn and our companion on this day, still receives sheep every autumn from the land which his family had to leave in that fateful year. Skarð, like Haraldsund, was a 17 m. village, and after the departure of the inhabitants the Haraldsund folk took over the outfield under the customary arrangement of working for a third part of the produce. There are other settlements in the North Islands which were evacuated just as abruptly, though not under so great a cloud of misfortune. Strond and Skálatoftir on Borðoy are now but place-names on the older maps ; they were *traðir* villages whose inhabitants found themselves unable to wrest a livelihood from the poor soil. Blankskála on Kallsoy was deserted in 1809 because of the ever-present danger of destruction by avalanches of snow from the hills above.

Unfortunately we had no time to walk to Skarð—a pity, for the route is tempting, and the path over the island's ridge must afford grand views of the Norðuroyar on a clear, sunny day. You can see the line of the pathway as your boat comes in to Kunoyar-bygd, climbing the long hillside behind Norður í Húsi, at one point traversing an almost perpendicular cliff-face, and finally vanishing in the entrance of a tremendous cleft. This is Skarðsg-jógv, separating Middagsfjall and the great rocky pyramid of Kúðungafjall, both of which tower to a height of over 2,500 feet, and on our visit were still streaked with white where drifts of snow had lain under their summits since the spring. It must be an exciting journey—exhausting, alarming, and magnificently picturesque by turn, and perhaps a little sad when one comes through the ravine and stands within sight of the ruins on the other coast.

As we raised our eyes towards the dark gash between the mountains when our boat sailed out again into the fiord, Jóanes told us a good story about the amazing acoustics in the cleft. His grandfather, the hero of the tale, was known far and wide in the Faeroes as a man of powerful voice. One day *grind* was sighted in the sound between Skarð and Borðoy, and of course Símun av Skarði was elected to climb the hill and run through the *gjógv* to yell " Grindaboð ! " to the people of Kunoy village beneath. He did so—and the men of Lorvík, seven miles to the south on Eysturoy, put out their boats !

I have since asked several people about this story and have yet to find one who does not believe it. I am not at all surprised to find that it has become a Faeroe legend !

4

" The inhabitants of this island are distinguished by their industry, the care which they take of their sheep, and the neat manner in which they prepare their turf for fuel." Any com-munity of whom the Rev. Jørgen Landt in 1800 could write this glowing commendation, and of whom, nearly a century and a half later, many impartial Faeroe people express much the same opinion, ought to be worth a visit. So I thought in May of

1943, when the opportunity of sailing to Nólsoy, the " Needle Island," first came my way.

I found there an interesting settlement, in many respects—especially in its quiet, conservative atmosphere—reminiscent of Mykinesbygd. The village lies on a low and narrow isthmus connecting the rocky lower slopes of the stately Skúvafjall, the central hill, with the long and comparatively low northern section where is much of the cultivated land, and which nature has very nearly succeeded in making a holm.

The most striking feature of the panorama as one closes the shore, entering the small semi-circular bay at whose head the concrete landing-place awaits, is the contrast of new and ancient buildings. First to meet the eye is a long row of old wooden dwellings along the northern waterfront, between the little pier and the neat, white church which stands on the furthermost point. I looked upon this scene with interest mingled with surprise, for it is the one and only row of houses I have come across in the islands, where almost every home, from the finest to the most lowly, is detached. In common with most of the older Faeroe houses the row presents a dark and dreary aspect with its tar-coated, weather-beaten walls, but the dreariness is saved to some extent from ugliness by the refreshing green of the long grass on the roofs, and by the sharp contrast with the new houses of pleasant shades of yellow, white and brown which stand on the rising land behind.

One enters the village street, after landing, beneath a picturesque archway made from the jaw-bones of a sperm-whale which some of the villagers found drifting several miles east of the island fifty years ago. Five rowing-boats were required as tugs to bring this unusual prize ashore. Beyond the arch, one finds a curious juxtaposition of the old and the new—the village water-pump, the only source of supply during summer droughts, and the painted petrol-pump which provides a world-famous fuel for the little boats.

Many of the older houses have a single central chimney of wooden boards or imported hand-made bricks, some of them enclosed in a bush of straw thatch, possibly as a safeguard against the winter frosts. On raised ground just to the south of the isthmus is one of the finest and most primitive groups of *hjallar* I have seen among the islands (page 300), well-sited to get the fullest benefit from the salt winds. They huddle together, forming a cosy group, with rough walls of water-worn basalt stones obviously derived from the litter on the shore below. Their roofs are of the usual grassy sods, and they have slatted fronts and doorways fitted with the ingenious wooden locks peculiar to the Faeroes. That these locks, which work on the same principle as the modern Yale-lock, are not yet things of the past was amply proved by one brand-new example with a key-hole in the form of a narrow-armed cross, thus +, suggesting that its only concession to modernity lay in the use of a metal instead of wooden key. Each key and its corresponding lever are cut to a different pattern, and when inserted and turned in its own lock the key lifts two wooden pegs, *hvølpar*, which release the lever, so that it can be moved freely to and fro. When the key is taken out the pegs fall into position again, holding the lever fast. A story is told that an American, inspired by the mechanism of the *hvølpalás*, applied the principle to a metal lock

HJALLAR on NÓLSOY.

and patented it ; and when a Dutchman began to produce an identical lock a few years later he took the man to court on a charge of stealing his patent. The Dutchman produced a Faeroe *hvølpalás*—and the American lost his case.

Down below the *hjallar* is the curious eastern " shore " : I give it that name, although it stands some thirty feet above the level of the sea, for it is everywhere strewn with rounded basalt rocks flung on to the land by the force of the waves. During easterly gales, the seas crash and sweep over the low cliff and drench the greater part of the village with froth and spray. One has the impression that this precarious isthmus is gradually wearing away, and the time may not be far hence when much of the village will have to be re-sited in a safer place. There is a fine natural archway against the shore where the encroaching sea, within the present century, has eaten through the soft sandstone conglomerate sandwiched between two more resistant layers of basalt. The same geological feature also occurs between Tórshavn and Argir, nearly five miles due west of Nólsoyarbygd, although there it is without the caves and archway which make the Nólsoy *eiði* so picturesque.

At points along the cliff-edged coast which curves away to north and south of the isthmus the sea has bored numerous caves, which the seals use as nurseries for their calves. Landt mentions a cave with a hidden entrance, on the western side, which " proceeds almost through the whole island ; it is entirely dark, and in some places can be passed with difficulty ; but people have penetrated so far into it, that they could hear distinctly the roaring of the waves at the other side of the island." Nólsoy is an isle of caverns and arches, and the most picturesque is perhaps that at the extreme south of the western coast—the " eye " from which the " Needle Island " was fancifully named.

The inhabitants, if tradition is to be believed, form a heterogenous assembly. The first settlers are reputed to have been Celtic monks who came here about the time that Kirkjubøur was settled, but whether or not there is any historical foundation for this belief I do not know. Some people claim descent from the daughter of James II of Scotland, Princess Margaret, who, having fallen in love with a commoner, married him in defiance of her father's will, and eloped. The couple sailed to the Faeroes, and settled on Nólsoy in the belief that they had found an asylum sufficiently remote from the monarch's wrath. But the king discovered their retreat, and would have had them slain had not his heart melted at the sight of his little grandson so that instead all was forgiven.

The ruined walls of what is said to have been their " castle " are to be seen in the coastal fields a few minutes' walk from the village ; but whether they are so ancient as tradition would have them is a moot point. They should certainly be excavated, however, for if they produce nothing more, they will at least provide Faeroe historians with an excellent ground-plan of an old farmstead—perhaps the oldest for which there is any record in the islands.

Although Nólsoy is only just across the fiord from Tórshavn, a matter of half-an-hour's sailing, the villagers speak quite a distinct dialect from the townsfolk. In this, however, they are not alone, and there are other villages at no great distance on

Streymoy and Eysturoy where idiom and pronunciation are again different. Kollafjørður, which is only a few miles to the north of Tórshavn, is famous as a home of picturesque figures of speech, and many of the words and phrases used are not to be found elsewhere in the Faeroes. In former times the dialects were many and various, and much more in evidence than now : indeed, Hans A. Djurhuus tells me that he knew a man, years ago, who claimed that he was able to tell which one of the hundred or so villages a stranger belonged to as soon as the fellow opened his mouth !—a commentary on the immense difficulties with which the pioneers of written Faeroese had to contend at the end of the last century, when Dr. Jacobsen and V. U. Hammershaimb put in a tremendous amount of time and labour in organising the rules of grammer and syntax, and for the first time established a standard written language. One of the present literary leaders, Rasmus Rasmussen, points out that it is precisely this absence of a written Faeroese which enabled so many dialects to develop. In Iceland, where the famous sagas of the twelfth century and after have always been regarded as the basis of the national tongue, such dialects—despite the greater isolation of the settlements—are quite unknown.

Nólsoy is indubitably Tórshavn's most valuable asset from a scenic point of view, for without this shapely island shutting off the eastern horizon, the panorama about the town would be dull indeed. During my four years in Tórshavn there were countless occasions when one could look across the fiord and see some rich, new beauty in the isle, or in the great cloud-masses beyond. Sunrise on a winter's morn, with high, bloodshot cumulus or feathery fronds of cirrus heaped above the low isthmus ; moonrise on a winter's night, a scarlet lantern poised above the village, and the island's snow-gleaming satin form clearer than during the light of day . . . these were occasions when the wonder of Nólsoy was beyond description, and so full of the loveliness of colour and cloud-shapes that even now the mind thrills to the memory. But of all occasions, perhaps the most memorable were those long, light summer evenings when, by some trick of slanting light as the sun slipped at last behind Kirkjubøreyn, the whole length of the island's rocky face changed in a trice from the drab grey-brown of the basalt to a delicate rosy pink. This marvellous phenomenon was invariably short-lived : the roseate suffusion grew deeper, and then, in a few minutes, vanished as suddenly as it had come. Whilst it lasted this incredible transformation was perhaps the most exquisite vision that it is possible to experience in these islands—more wonderful even than the swaying green and blue and scarlet curtain-folds of the most brilliant displays of northern lights.

Like Mykines, Nólsoy is a wonderful island for birds. The little bay at the approach to the *bygd* is full of the brown eiderducks and their handsome black and white mates, so astonishingly tame that they appear to be almost domesticated. In the summer it is also the haunt of busy sea-swallows, constantly bickering as they hover and plunge, with consummate grace, to seek their food in a silvery splash. These terns nest in tight groups on the rocky flats below the rising hill, glittering against the greensward in almost the same dizzying multitudes as the host I found in Kálvadalur. Though Nólsoy has not so vast a population of sea-birds as Mykines, it has many interests for the ornithologist, and indeed is well worth a visit by any traveller to the capital who would see, close at hand, something of the immense wealth of the fowler's preserves.

This character of the island is best seen by taking a trip in a small boat along the eastern coast. In the middle of the southern reach there is a long, wide shelf below the precipitous fall of Skúvafjall, where lie massive mounds of great boulders which have tumbled from the weather-beaten *hamrar* above. This talus, which the fowlers call *urð*, is a metropolis of puffins, and the haunt of Manx shearwaters and stormy petrels, who come only in the dusk. The puffins fly between the dappled sea and the pulverized land as thickly, it seems to me, as about the puffinries of Dalið and Lambi on Mykines. On the wide ledges of long, rich grass which interrupt the precipitous wall of Skúvafjall one is astonished to see grazing sheep, and wonders how on earth they could have reached such dizzy places. The boatmen will tell you that the animals are let down by rope from above in the spring, and that when the villagers wish to take the wool, or segregate lambs for slaughter, they too go down from the hilltop in the same manner to do their work.

In the cliffs of the eastern coast, below the *urð* and to the north of it, lives the finest colony of rock-doves in the Faeroes ; and those butterfly sea-birds, the tysties or black guillemots, are much more numerous than I have seen them elsewhere. There are innumerable eiders on the water, and many shags, and if you are fortunate you will see one or more of the seals who live in the island's caves. The only usual sea-birds that are not much in evidence are the kittiwakes and guillemots, for the cliffs are not of the kind which suit them best. There is a small colony of the little gulls, however, at the south-western extremity of the isle, near the needle's eye, and on the low shore at Borðan a few hundred yards to the east there is another colony of arctic terns.

Everywhere on the cliffs and in the east-side *hamrar* the fulmars have staked their claims. I would not care to guess how many hundred thousand birds resort to this island to-day, and I defy any one to make even an approximate assessment of their strength. Yet this was one of the last of the islands to be colonised, the birds reaching it only when they had completed a circuit of the western and northern coasts of the Faeroes, little more than fifty years ago. The vast and amazing range-expansion of this species in the Faeroes and Britain within recent years remains one of the unexplained mysteries of nature.

I could write much more about the Nólsoy birds, but throughout this book I have tried to deal with the bird-life only in so far as it affects the character of the countryside and the life and work of the people. It is difficult to write about Nólsoy, however, without mentioning that here lives the best of Faeroe ornithologists, Niels Fr. Petersen, better known there as Niels á Botni. He is a farmer, and Faeroe *bøndir* are always busy men ; yet he finds time to indulge this study with important results for our knowledge of the bird-life of these Atlantic Isles. No less remarkable is his extensive knowledge of Faeroe life and customs in former times, and this book owes to him—and no less to many other good Faeroe folk—most of whatever virtues it may be found to possess.

References to Chapter Twelve

FISHER, J. and WATERTSON, G. (1941) ; LANDT, J. (1810) ; SALOMONSEN, F. (1935) ; WILLIAMSON, K. (1945 b).

Nólsoy—
the village
and quay

Inter-island communications   (*Top*) The old " Smiril "

(*Bottom*) A modern helicopter

Chapter Thirteen

THE FAEROES TODAY

by

Einar Kallsberg

I

R EADERS of the preceding chapters will probably have drawn the conclusion that the Faeroese must be a society of much charm and excitement, spared of penetration by the materialism of the twentieth century. A visitor to the Faeroes today will quickly realise this is a dynamic community endeavouring to adjust itself to the requirements of modern time. He might need the intuition of a detective to discover anyone cutting peats, and he will look in vain for the faint beams of indoor paraffin lamps lighting the intimate village streets. Electricity is now available in every single village. The charm and excitement, nevertheless, are plentiful everywhere.

Tremendous progress has been achieved in the Faeroes since the end of the Second World War, and in particular over the past 10–15 years. This is true not only of production and investment, but of social conditions, education and cultural activities as well. In addition, relations between the Faeroes and Denmark underwent a profound change in 1948 when the Faeroes were granted the status of a self-governing community within the Kingdom of Denmark (*heimastýri*). The economic and social structure differs widely from the pattern of a score of years ago, though fishing and fish-processing still saturate the economy, which consequently is extremely sensitive to catches and market conditions for fish products.

An attempt is made in the following pages to describe the main features of the political, economic and social affairs in the islands, devoting most attention to present-day conditions.

U

2

During the Second World War the Faeroes and Denmark were occupied by opposing sides. Complete separation from Denmark for five years compelled the Faeroe Islanders to fend for themselves. Their success in supplying fish to the British market at high war-time prices fostered among Faeroese a belief in themselves as a self-sufficient community. Politically this was reflected in strong electoral support for the People's Party (*folkaflokkurin*), who wanted self-government.

When the war ended, normal relations with Denmark were resumed. However, both the Danish Government and the majority of the political parties in the Faeroes were disinclined to reintroduce the pre-war county status as a lasting arrangement. (When Denmark ceded Norway to Sweden under the Peace of Kiel in 1814 the Faeroes remained with Denmark, along with Iceland and Greenland. Since 1816 the Faeroe Islands had been a Danish county.)

In the Faeroes as in most other countries elections were held shortly after the end of the war. Four political parties took part. The People's Party claimed self-government, though an exact definition of this concept was not stated. The Unionist Party (*sambandsflokkurin*) favoured the closest possible ties with Denmark. The Social-Democratic Party (*javnadarflokkurin*) and the Old Self-government Party (later re-named the Self-government Party) wanted a form of autonomy with the Løgting as the legislative assembly and full recognition of the Faeroese language and flag.

Besides their different positions with regard to the relationship with Denmark, the political parties, as elsewhere, have differing views on economic and social issues. Using the traditional distinction between right and left, the People's and Unionist Parties are broadly-speaking right wing, while the Social Democratic Party is labour or left wing and the Self-government Party is social-liberal.

Prolonged negotiations between representatives from the Faeroes and the Danish Government led to a proposal from the latter granting self-government on a very limited scale, but this proved unsatisfactory to any of the Faeroese parties. A referendum was held on September 14th, 1946; at which 31·9 per cent of the electorate voted in favour of the proposal, while 32·8 per cent voted for the only alternative put by the Danish Government, namely complete separation from Denmark.

The People's Party hailed the result as a vote for independence, and supported by one Social Democrat gained a majority for this view in the Løgting (12 out of 23 representatives). The Danish Government then declared the referendum indecisive and the King dissolved the Løgting. Subsequently new elections were held.

The result this time was a majority in the Løgting against separation but also against the Danish Government's proposal. Afterwards fresh negotiations between representatives of the Løgting and the Danish Government were begun, resulting in the Self-government Act (*heimastýrislogin*) of March 27th, 1948. This law granted the Faeroe Islands the status of "a self-governing community within the Kingdom of Denmark".

3

Under the Self-government Act the Løgting has legislative power in all affairs subject to self-government. The administrative responsibility for these affairs lies with the Local Government (*Landsstýri*) which is appointed by the Løgting on the basis of the parliamentary representation of the respective political parties. Traditionally the Landsstýri has been made up of three or four members headed by a Prime Minister (*Logmadur*). The number of seats in the Løgting can vary between 20 and 30.

The Self-government Act specifies a number of various fields which immediately after the enactment of the law, or later upon the request of either the Landsstýri or the Danish Government, should be transferred as special Faeroese affairs. The takeover of some affairs, i.e. the police and the national church, is subject to prior negotiations between the Local and Danish Governments. Those affairs not explicitly enumerated in the Act, such as defence, foreign relations, foreign exchange regulations and the judicial system are joint affairs; they are handled as matters of common concern by the Danish Government and do not involve expense to the Landsstýri.

On the other side the Landsstýri defrays all expenses in connection with those affairs which are fully transferred. Almost all these were effected when the Act came into force on April 1st, 1948, very few having been made subsequently. In the first place the specifically Faeroese fields are local government and municipal matters, economic affairs including taxation, culture, commerce, industry and transportation. The Faeroese are not subject to any Danish taxes but pay income tax and indirect taxes such as import duties to the Landsstýri. In addition, approximately fifty municipalities also collect income tax. There is no property tax.

Although they were not the subject of negotiations before transference to the Landsstýri, substantial parts of the social and health services and educational matters (e.g. primary schools) are handled by the Danish and Local Governments in co-operation. The expenditure involved in running these " mixed affairs " is defrayed by both governments, frequently on an approximately fifty-fifty basis. The legal and executive powers in these cases are in principle the concern of both.

Down to 1948 when the Faeroes were a Danish county the chief administrative officer was the county sheriff (*Amtmaður*). The Self-government Act replaced this appointment by a Resident High Commissioner (*Rikisumbodsmaður*) who is the principal representative of the Crown in the Løgting (without having the right to participate in its resolutions) and to the Landsstýri and is head of the Danish executive branch in the Faeroes.

The Self-government Act provides that Faeroese is recognised as the principal language. Danish may be used in all public affairs, and must be thoroughly taught in the schools. The Faeroes were also granted the right to their own flag. This is the same flag which at the beginning of the Second World War was recognised by the United Kingdom and her Allies and was introduced as the sixth of the crossed flags of the Nordic countries.

Also, outside the framework of the Self-government Act, other provisions have been enacted underlining the special position of the Faeroes. An example is that in 1949 the Islands got their own currency notes, but not coins. The notes in circulation in the Faeroes are convertible into Danish kroner at parity price.

It should be noted that the Constitution of the Kingdom of Denmark provides for two representatives from the Faeroes to the Danish Parliament, which is a single chamber parliament with a total of 179 seats. As far as possible the public election in the Faeroes of these two representatives coincides with elections in Denmark.

4

The Self-government Act has been in force unchanged for 22 years. This is a remarkable achievement considering the presence during this period of six political parties all with different views regarding the relationship with Denmark. Except for the years 1962–6 the Landsstýri has been backed by a majority in the Løgting of parties accepting the Self-government Act as the basis regulating the association between the two countries. During the years 1962–6 the Local Government was composed of a coalition of the four parties which regard the Act as unsatisfactory. The Republican Party (*tjodveldisflokkurin*) wants complete separation from Denmark; this is a labour party, supported mainly by fishermen, established in May 1948 by many of those who voted for separation in 1946. The People's Party wants progressively increased self-government towards an association acknowledging the Crown and Danish conduct of foreign affairs. This view is shared by the Progressive Party (*framburdsflokkurin*) founded in 1954 mainly by discontented members of the People's Party. The Self-government Party, while accepting the Act, requests that it should be modified and modernised. In spite of the declared intention of these four coalition parties to initiate an evolution towards greater independence for the Faeroes the Self-government Act has remained unaltered.

The last public election was held in November 1966. In January 1967 a coalition of the Social Democratic Party, the Unionist Party and the Self-Government Party, representing a majority (14) of the 26 seats in the Løgting, formed the Landsstýri. The next election should be held not later than November 1970.

It is noteworthy that no action to modify or otherwise alter the Self-government Act has materialised in official requests to the Danish Government, or vice versa. From this it may be inferred that the political scene in the Faeroes as to relations with Denmark has been stabilised. The importance of such stability is difficult to evaluate but undoubtedly it has had strong bearing on the readiness of the Danish Government to support in many ways the efforts of the Faeroese to improve their living standards.

5

More than one-third of the population earns its living directly from the fishing industry, which accounts for approximately one-third of the gross national product. More than 90 per cent of the total export consists of fish and fishery products. At the end of the Second World War the Faeroese economy was flourishing, due to the remunerative export of fish to the United Kingdom; the remaining years of the 1940's continued to be profitable, as the former markets for wet salted cod and " klipfisk " again became accessible.

Under these circumstances many Faeroese felt an urgent need to expand and re-equip the fishing fleet, and this led to a wave of hectic investment in fishing vessels. Unfortunately, what seemed advisable in the short run proved to be a serious setback a few years later. Many obsolete trawlers were bought from the United Kingdom (and even Iceland), frequently requiring heavy expenses before becoming operational. Thus the experience of the late nineteenth century and the first decade of the present century was repeated, for during that period British owners converted their fleet to modern vessels and the Faeroese bought the obsolete smacks. There were of course exceptions, and a few new modern trawlers were ordered. In addition, modern small vessels of seine-net type were bought in Denmark, partly assisted by a separate loan-financing scheme initiated by the Danish Government.

This expansion of the fishing fleet implied a substantial increase in the catch capacity, but on the whole the Faeroese vessels were obsolete, a major part of them being composed of 40–60 year old smacks. Due to a faster increase in costs than in prices the rate of return diminished and in the early 1950's the industry was faced with a serious crisis. Many shipowners went bankrupt and the crisis was felt throughout the community. The first half of the 1950's can be considered years of economic standstill, and a period of deliberations on ways and means of how to restore confidence in the future. Negotiations between the Faeroese and Danish authorities led to the setting up in 1955 of the Mortgage Institution of the Faeroes. This has played a tremendous role in the subsequent programme of converting the fishing fleet into modern vessels.

In addition, shipowners can obtain loans from the Danish Fishery Mortgage Bank. Further, the Løgting introduced an assistance scheme by rendering grant-loans to buyers of fishing vessels. These three sources of finance leave it to the investor himself to supply 10 per cent of the estimated cost of the vessel. Most of the shipowners are joint stock companies and frequently the fishermen themselves are shareholders. In some cases also local units (kommūnir) are shareholders in a vessel.

Unquestionably the conversion of the Faeroese fishing fleet from the post-war pattern of small wooden long-line vessels, smacks, schooners and steam-trawlers to its modern composition of wooden long-line vessels, large steel ships for the long-line and herring fishery, and big diesel-powered trawlers, could not have been accomplished so swiftly and extensively without the aid of these various loan facilities.

In 1953—the middle of the economic standstill period—the fleet consisted of 200 vessels with a total of 25,000 gross registered tons. In 1968 the comparable figures were 160 and 33,000 respectively, thus indicating an increase in the average size of vessels by approximately 60 per cent. Since the outmoded ships have been replaced by new ones, the average age of the fishing fleet has decreased substantially. Among the newest additions to the fleet are three large factory trawlers. Although long-line fishing has replaced the hand-line to a large extent this method is still practised, but new technical devices have reduced the input of manpower. Long-line and trawl are the main methods at the present day. Since the middle of the 1950's drifters have accounted for substantial catches of herrings, but today steel vessels equipped with power blocks permitting an impressively efficient use of nets account for most of the herring catches.

6

Disregarding the trawlers, the Faeroese fishing traditionally has been limited to the summer season. The transformation of the fleet into large modern units has permitted all-the-year-round fishing, the various grounds being frequented according to their respective seasons.   Wet salted cod from Greenland waters has usually formed the major share of the total catch, which in 1968 was 170,000 tons fresh weight.   Mainly engaged in this are the trawlers and steel-built long-line ships, with crews of approximately 50 and 25 men respectively, away on fishing trips lasting from two to four months.   Haddock has ranked second to cod in the ground-fish group, and is sought mainly in waters close to the Faeroes.   The herring fishery in the Norwegian Sea has expanded markedly in late years and accounted for about 40 per cent of all catches in 1968.   An interesting feature in recent years has been the growth of fishing in home waters, providing the basis for an expanding production of frozen fish fillets in the Faeroes.   In their efforts to broaden the variety of species some vessels are now catching salmon in Greenland waters, while others have fished for porbeagle sharks off the east coast of North America.

After Iceland decided to extend her fishing limits to 12 nautical miles in 1958, a provisional agreement was reached between Denmark and the United Kingdom fixing the Faeroese limits at 12 nautical miles, but granting those nations which up to then had customarily fished inside these limits (in particular the U.K.) the right to continue to do so up to six miles from land.   When the United Kingdom officially recognised the new Icelandic 12-miles-limit the Anglo-Danish provisional agreement was terminated by the Danish Government at the request of the Faeroese.   From March 12th, 1964 the fishing limit in the Faeroe Islands was fixed as 12 nautical miles from straight baselines, without any traditional rights for foreign nations.   As a retaliation against this expansion of the fishing territory the U.K. enforced limitations upon the import of Faeroese iced fish.   As a result the export of iced fish from the Faeroes has decreased substantially and it is now of very limited importance to the industry.   Eventually the British action led to increased landings at Faeroe ports of iced fish catches from the long-line vessels, thus supplying the home filleting industry with much needed raw material.

The greater part of the codfish catches are still processed on board as wet salted fish, primarily for export to Italy, Spain and Portugal.   The production of " klipfisk " (pp. 88-9) was of great importance during the 1950's but has dwindled to insubstantial amounts. This is mainly due to hard competition from Spain and Portugal both of whom were large importers until a few years ago. Spain especially has expanded her own production of salted cod to such an extent that she herself has become a large net exporter of "klipfisk," primarily to Brazil. With labour costs only a fraction of those in the Faeroes it is profitable for the Spanish and Portuguese to import wet salted cod and process it as "klipfisk." Since this is a much more highly processed commodity than wet salted cod, the decline in its export has of course been unfavourable to the Faeroese economy. The change in marketing conditions for the traditional Faeroese export commodities has stimulated the search for new products, and underlines the necessity for a more varied production.

In this respect important results have already been achieved. Modern plants for producing frozen fish fillets have been built and the output is increasing, the main customers being the United States and Great Britain. New factories for the reduction of herrings to herring meal and herring oil have been constructed, receiving their raw material from the power-block equipped seine-netters. In addition salted herrings in barrels have become an export commodity of some importance.

It appears justified in the light of events of the last two decades to conclude that the Faeroese fishing industry is a dynamic enterprise reacting vigorously to developments in the market and to competition from other countries. It should not be inferred however that the Faeroese fishing fleet is lacking problems to fight. World market prices for fish products have not moved upwards at the same rate as the costs of production. But these are terms of reference with which the Faeroese fishing industry is experienced. The vulnerability of the economy to conditions in the fishery is obvious and no effort will be spared to solve the present difficulties, which after all are similar to those which the industry is encountering in other North Atlantic countries.

The agricultural production is very limited. The main produce is lamb, mutton, potatoes and milk, but the quantities are insufficient for home consumption. Approximately 40,000 sheep and lambs are slaughtered annually. There are about 3,000 cattle in the Islands. The hunting of pilot whales (see Chapter 4) still plays a role although the importance of whale meat as food is less than formerly.

8

Modernisation and expansion have not been confined to the fishery industry. In other sectors of the economy similar developments are apparent. Many new small scale factories have come into operation, mainly producing equipment such as nets, trawls and fishing-lines, etc., while modernisation of the shipyards has made possible the construction of steel fishing vessels and small cargo ships.

The level of investment in the private sector has increased, although at a fluctuating rate corresponding to variations in the purchases of fishing vessels. Meanwhile the public investments have expanded vigorously and steadily, especially in the last decade. The Landsstýri in co-operation with the local units (kommūnir) have improved and enlarged the harbour facilities in many villages. The Local Government has initiated an ambitious road construction programme which is not yet complete, so that most of the isolated villages have now been connected with larger and more centrally-situated settlements. For topographical reasons road construction in the Faeroe Islands is difficult and very expensive, and it is even necessary to lead roads through tunnels in some places, as for example the 1,550 m. stretch between Trongisvágur and Hvalbøur (Suđuroy).

Regular air services have been established in the last few years, and there are flights several times a week to and from Denmark, Norway and Iceland, and, in summer time, Scotland (Glasgow). The air services with Denmark have succeeded at the expense of the traditional seaway connection with Copenhagen; the Faeroese-owned M.V. Tjaldur was withdrawn from this route in 1968, but there is still connection by Danish passenger vessel sailing between Denmark and Iceland, as well as by small cargo/passenger vessels. Communications by sea between the Islands have shown considerable improvement and almost all the ferry-boats, publicly and privately operated, are new and modern. The Faeroese have had their own broadcasting service since 1957.

The first hydro-electric power station was erected in the 1920's, but in the course of the last 16 years the intercommunal electric power company SEV has brought electricity to every single village. Due to almost exhausted resources of water-power (almost unbelievable in view of the climate!) any future expansion is likely to have to rely on diesel-powered units.

The high level of investment, both private and public, notably since the late 1950's, has required financial resources far in excess of the aggregate savings in the Faeroes. There are two commercial and three savings banks. In general the lending capacity of the commercial banks can meet the demand for current operations of trade and industry. The savings banks are mainly engaged in financing house-building and lending to the local units (*kommūnir*). Considerable inflow of capital from abroad has been necessary and most of this capital has come from Denmark. With regard to investments in fishing vessels the resources of the Mortgage Institution of the Faeroes originate mainly from bond issues on the Danish capital market. The Danish Fishery Mortgage Bank may give loans to Faeroese buyers of fishing vessels. Most of the new factories and frozen fish-fillets plants have received loans from the Regional Development Board in Denmark. In short Faeroese industry has access to Danish Government financing facilities on equal terms with Danish industry.

The investment expenditure of the Landsstýri has also exceeded the amounts available through annual budget appropriations. In consequence it has made substantial borrowings in the Danish capital market. In 1963 the Danish Government established a revolving investment fund for the Faeroes, which may given loans on concessional terms to public and semi-public investment projects. Up to the present, road construction and electricity projects have been the major beneficiaries.

Access to the Danish capital market, however, does not by itself result in investments. The initiative remains largely with Faeroese business. Beyond any doubt the Landsstýri, through grants and guarantees, has greatly stimulated Faeroese companies to invest in modern vessels and plant. The Faeroese investor has reacted favourably.

9

Social security and health and hospital services are joint affairs, but under the Self-government Act they could at any time be transferred to the Landsstýri as specific Faeroese affairs. Thus the costs of running the social and health services are divided on the whole on a fifty-fifty basis, both current expenses and investments, between the Landsstýri and the Danish Government. Because of this, development in these fields in the Faeroe Islands has been closely linked with their development in Denmark. Generally speaking, the Danish system has been introduced in the Faeroes but frequently with a certain time lag, and usually adjusted to the special conditions of the Islands. Thus the Faeroes have benefited from the substantial recent expansion and improvement in Danish social legislation. The new regional hospital at Tórshavn is an impressive tower building; it is linked by a tunnel with a new (the first) mental hospital, due to be completed in the middle of the 1970's. Responsibility for the care of mental defectives, epileptics and other heavily handicapped persons lies with the Danish government, which defrays all costs. Until the new mental hospital is in operation Faeroese sufferers from these handicaps will be treated in hospitals and similar institutions in Denmark.

Education in the Faeroes is at a similar standard as in Denmark and by and large follows the pattern of the Danish educational system. The basis of this is the primary school with compulsory education for all children between the ages of 7 and 14, with an option to continue general education at a " comprehensive " level to the age of 16. For those who wish to continue academic studies to university entrance there is a three-years' course at a resident college in Tórshavn. Educational facilities in the Faeroes have improved much during the past decade, and a few years ago an institute of higher learning (fróðskaparsetri) concentrating mainly upon research and teaching in Faeroese language and literature was opened. It is still necessary for anyone who wants a university degree to go abroad, however.

10

The conversion of the Faeroese fishing fleet into larger units which now operate throughout the year has naturally changed the character of the fisherman-crofter's existence. The deep-sea fishing is no longer confined to the early spring through to the autumn seasons as was formerly the case, and in consequence few fishermen are now able to supplement their livelihood from the produce of the cultivated fields.

During the 1950's when the fishery became outmoded while the other maritime nations such as Norway, Britain and Iceland extended and modernised their fleets, hire on foreign vessels offered better pay and more comfortable accommodation on board in comparison with Faeroe ships. A considerable number of Faeroemen—in some years approximately 1,000 persons— were employed at this time chiefly on Norwegian and Icelandic vessels. The renewal of the home fleet has reversed this trend, though some Faeroemen still prefer to sail in foreign ships.

Fishing has always been beset by two fundamental uncertainties—weather and catches. Even with good market conditions these incalculable factors may result in a poor income for fishermen and shipowners. To relieve this disadvantage a wage equalisation scheme was established in 1957. The scheme guarantees a minimum income to the fisherman, which presently amounts to about 1800 kroner (say £100) a month. The finance for this scheme came originally from the revenues of an export duty but it is now wholly covered by annual appropriations from the budget of the Landsstýri. In addition, the Løgting grants direct subsidies to maintain the price of fresh and wet salted fish for the benefit of the fishermen. The shipowners on the other hand receive no price-subsidy.

In spite of the minimum wage scheme and the substantial subsidies, owners have been faced with growing difficulties in respect of hiring crews. An important adverse factor is the strong demand for labour from the various public works schemes in recent years, pushing up hourly wage-rates. In modern times even those who have had long experience of earning their living at sea have shown a preference for employment on land. Thus the Faeroese fishery is faced with a serious manpower problem. If the level of investment within the public sector proves to be transitory many of these former fishermen will have to return to the ships in the absence of alternative employment. From a long-term point of view a better remedy would be to enable the fishing fleet to offer better remuneration than work ashore. To accomplish this a continuous investment in new ships with higher productivity, and more comfort and conveniences for the crew, is

required. It is essential that the Faeroese fleet should keep up
with the standards of other North Atlantic countries, otherwise
the seafarer will find it more attractive and profitable to seek
employment either on land or on board alien ships.

II

The preceding pages will have revealed that in the after-war
years the Faeroese have been a progressive community. The
public authorities have supported a flourishing private initiative
to improve and expand production, and as a result there has been
a substantial increase in the standard of living.

Since the second war the population of the Faeroe Islands has
increased by approximately 9,000 individuals to a present figure
of 38,200. This equals an average annual rate of growth of
1·3 per cent, somewhat above the comparable figure for Denmark.
The population growth has fluctuated remarkably, however, and
mainly due to substantial emigration the rate was particularly
low during the setback in the 1950's. This experience is probably
not particular to the Faeroes. What is perhaps peculiar to the
situation in the islands is the increasing trend of emigration in
the course of the 1960's, despite a rapidly expanding economy
and favourable conditions of employment. This has naturally
caused concern to the Local Government and other authorities.

The anxiety is aggravated, moreover, by an imbalance in the
composition of the emigrants, since females in the age-range
17–25 account for a substantial part of the total. Indeed, female
emigrants have been in the majority throughout the post-war
period. There is in consequence a deficiency of females in the
population at the present day—greater than in any other of the
North Atlantic countries except Ireland and Iceland. Five years
ago this deficit was running at about 20 per cent for the age
group from 20–35 years, to which one looks for the largest number
of weddings and births. If not soon reversed this trend could be
perilous to the future stability of the population. The relatively
high fertility rate—currently about twice the Danish rate—is
likely to decrease, contributing to a much reduced growth rate.

A reply to the question of why there is a net emigration is not
easily given. Many factors contribute. Being citizens of the

Kingdom of Denmark no impediments whatever arise in taking up residence there except for the distance. As far as the younger generation is concerned the motive for moving to Denmark is in most cases the demand for some type of education which cannot yet be obtained in the Faeroes. Faeroese who graduate from university have no longer a good chance of returning to the Islands, should they want to do so, as was the case in the immediate post-war years. Although there is an excellent nautical school at Tórshavn the " brain-drain " is such that no fewer than 10–15 per cent of the officers in the Danish merchant marine are Faeroese.

With young girls the demand for higher education is less likely to be in the forefront of the problem, although there are indications that many of them begin their stay in Denmark as students in folk high schools and domestic science colleges. A considerable number, however, are attracted by the better pay in practical work in Denmark and the more varied way of life compared with the monotonous daily round in a Faeroese village.

Whatever the reason for their departure, very few of these Faeroese emigrants actually consider themselves as exiles, for the desire to return to the homeland is persistent. Even if the net emigration during a period of prosperity seems surprising, it has to be borne in mind that this is an experience shared by small and isolated communities the world over, and the drain would certainly have been greater in the absence of growing prosperity. Parallel with this trend, a concentration of the population in the larger communities, and the port of Tórshavn in particular, has been evident. During the last 20 years Tórshavn has grown from 17·6 per cent to 26·6 per cent of the total population of the Islands, and presently has some 10,000 inhabitants. The other main settlement areas are Klakksvík (Norðuroyar) and Skálafjørður (Eysturoy), the comparable figures being from 9·7 to 11·6 per cent, and from 3·5 to 4·0 per cent respectively.

To a certain extent the concentration of the population in larger places may reflect the same motives as the emigration. The educational facilities are better and more diverse, and there are improved possibilities of employment. The heavy demand for labour in Tórshavn during the past decade is a main reason for its rapid growth. The development of the fishing as an all-year-round rather than seasonal task has tempted many

families to move from the outer villages to the neighbourhood of
the home-port of the vessels.   The construction of new roads may
help to reduce this tendency.   The net result, nevertheless, is of
small remote villages becoming gradually depopulated and left
with a dangerously high proportion of old age pensioners.

12

The post-war years on the whole, and particularly the last
ten years, have been years of progress.   The capacity of the
fishing-fleet and industry ashore to produce has been expanded.
Road and sea communications and port facilities have been
improved.   A better basis for future growth in trade and industry
has been established.   All this could not have been achieved,
however, without a substantial import of capital, and consistently
the Faeroese balance of payments has been in deficit on current
account.

For most other countries a deficit of this kind could not
continue for too many years because it might prove difficult to
secure the foreign finance.   The deficit on current account during
recent years has amounted to as much as 10–15 per cent of the
Faeroese gross national product, and the major part of it has been
covered by grants from Denmark.   In addition the main part of
foreign loans to the Faeroes have been obtained through the
Danish Government and the capital market in Denmark.   In
the fiscal year ending March 31st, 1968, the expenses of the
Danish Government in the Faeroe Islands amounted to approximately 65 million kroner, the comparable figure for the Local
Government being 83 million kroner.   This implies that out of a
total expenditure of 148 million kroner the Danish Government
defrayed some 40 per cent.   This clearly indicates the extent as
well as the need for close co-operation between the Faeroese and
Danish authorities.   Until now this co-operation, achieved
within the framework of the Self-government Act, has been
fruitful in developing a higher standard of living among the
Islands.

The growth of the Faeroese economy has definitely led to a
better foundation for further expansion in the future through a
more widely diversified production and decreased sensitivity to

" S.E.V."—the Faeroe electricity undertaking

Fisher girl

shifts in market conditions. The economy and the prosperity of the islanders is still and for the forseeable future fundamentally linked with the fishery. The initiative and concerted actions of private business and Local Government, strongly encouraged by Denmark, justify the belief that in years to come the Faeroes will continue to be a vigorous and flourishing community.

APPENDIX "A"

Faeroe Mammals

FAEROE MAMMALS, like some Faeroe birds, present an interesting case of differentiation from the typical form of their species, such as often happens among small mammals and resident birds living on remote islands. In their struggle for survival they have had to adapt themselves to unusual and sometimes harsh conditions imposed by climate, environment and food-supply, and their specialisation has brought about distinct, if slight, morphological changes. Such changes may take many hundreds, or even thousands of years to effect in many cases, but—incredible though it seems—they may also become apparent almost within the living memory of man.

The first hares were introduced into Streymoy from south Norway in 1854 or 1855, but Magnus Degerbøl, after the critical examination of many specimens, considers that the present population constitutes a good "forma geographica" quite distinct from the parent stock. Whereas the Norwegian hares assume a completely white pelage in the winter months, this change has not been noted in the Faeroe hares since the end of the last century. Their coats change from the deep reddish-brown of summer to a greyish-blue which harmonises wonderfully with the colour of the rocks, gravel-beds and scree on which they live ; in this, and certain structural characters, they more nearly match the Scottish blue-hare than their Norwegian ancestors. It is rather remarkable that this protective change, probably induced by the winter mildness and humidity (and therefore, the relative scarcity of snow), should have come so quickly to a creature so obviously not in need of it : for in the absence of foxes and the great scarcity of large birds of prey the Faeroe hare has no other enemy than man.

House-mice can hardly have been in the Faeroes much longer than a thousand years, yet there are two very distinct insular races (and may soon be a third !) in addition to the typical house-mouse of Europe. The first of these was described in 1904 by William Eagle Clarke from specimens captured on Nólsoy ; the second described and named by Magnus Degerbøl, is confined to Mykines, whilst Evans and Vevers have shown that the mouse population of Fugloy may be in process of divergence from the Nólsoy type. The Nólsoy mice are larger and have more robust feet and tails than the common house-mouse (examples of which exist so near as Tórshavn), and in addition to these differences the Mykines mice are more brightly coloured and exhibit a marked difference in the structure of the skull. Like the wren, indeed, the Mykines mouse is much more akin to its opposite number on St. Kilda than to the mainland form.

The greater size and robustness of these mammals is due to their more exacting environment, for here "house-mouse" is almost a misnomer, the majority of the little creatures inhabiting the great "bird-mountains" or *fuglabjørg*. Even so, their emancipation from human kind is not quite complete, and on Mykines I heard amusing stories of fowlers so intent upon their "fleyging" that they forgot to keep an eye on their lunch-packets lying beside them—with the result that the mice benefitted and not they ! Incidentally (though no scientist, of course, will take this seriously), *skerpikjøt* is probably a contributary cause of their excellent physique, for they are said also to be frequent despoilers of the *hjallur* ! The Mykines folk are convinced that their mice hibernate in the winter time, and indeed it is not improbable that some such change in habit (or, more likely, survival of an ancestral habit) has occurred along with the morphological changes which make the Mykines mouse what it is.

Brown rats, fortunately, have failed to reach many of the small islands : one hopes they will be long kept at bay, for the damage they would inflict on the native fauna might eventually have very serious consequences to the bird-fowling. A great many rats must be wild-living too, and I have seen them from time to time in the great gullery south of Kirkjubøreyn, some 4-5 miles from Tórshavn. Probably the offal of the gull's meals, as well as eggs and young birds, keeps them alive, and they may be responsible for the disappearance of the puffin in comparatively recent years from this part of the coast. That their's is a dangerous life is also apparent, for I have found their remains lying besides the gulls' nests.

Landt wrote that the islands where there were no rats were free from mice also, though this cannot have been true of Nólsoy, Fugloy and Mykines, and he further adds, " it has been supposed that the soil of these islands has something in it which these animals cannot endure. Earth, therefore, has been brought from the northern islands, to some of the houses at Thorshavn infested with rats and mice, and although the experiment succeeded in some cases, it failed in others." Norman F. Ellison tells of a similar belief in " enchanted soil " related to him by the late Duncan John Robertson, founder of the bird-sanctuary at Eynhallow, Orkney, who "remembered clearly as a boy that a load of Eynhallow soil was brought to the mainland and placed under the foundations of any house being built, in order to ' keep away all vermin.' " Eynhallow was a ' holy ' island : can it be that the belief was carried to the Faeroes from Orkney, undergoing a change of interpretation (for it seems to have been regarded as a cure rather than preventative) in the process ?

Landt spoke of the black or ship's rat as being known in the Faeroes, but Degerbøl, having no specimen, wisely excluded it from his list. Much of my work during the war was done on the quay, and occasionally I had fleeting glimpses of " black " rats about the transit sheds. Without a corpse, however, one could never be sure of the species. Probably the black rat does occur as a ship-borne vagrant, and if local legend is reliable it is something rather more than that ! The " black rats " of the trawler *Nýggjaberg* are said to have been seen coming ashore before she set sail for Iceland in March, 1942—to vanish with all hands a few days later.

The scientific nomenclature of the mammals mentioned in this book, based on Degerbøl's list, is as follows :—

ORDER RODENTIA

Epimys (Rattus) norvegicus (Erxleben). Brown rat, *rotta*. (Viđoy, Borđoy, Kunoy, Eysturoy, Streymoy, Vágar, Hestur and Suđuroy.)

Epimys (Rattus) rattus Linnaeus. Black rat, *svørt rotta*. (Tórshavn?)

Mus musculus musculus Linnaeus. House-mouse, *mús*. (Tórshavn only, so far as is known.)

Mus musculus faeroensis Clarke. Faeroe house-mouse, *mús*. (Type-locality Nólsoy ; probably also Streymoy and Eysturoy ? Fugloy, Sandoy, Hestur, Suđuroy ?)

Mus musculus mykinessiensis Degerbøl. Mykines house-mouse, *mús*. (Confined to the type-locality, Mykines.)

Mus musculus muralis Barrett-Hamilton, the St. Kilda house-mouse, is also mentioned.

Lepus timidus seclusus Degerbøl.   Faeroe hare, *hara*.   (Suđuroy, Sandoy, Vágar, Streymoy, Eysturoy, Nólsoy and the Norđuroyar except Svínoy.)
Lepus timidus timidus Linnaeus, the Norway alpine hare, and *Lepus t. scoticus* Hilzheimer, the Scottish blue hare, are also mentioned.

ORDER CHIROPTERA

Vespertilio murinus Linnaeus.   Parti-coloured bat.   Henry Feilden's MS. Diary records that in December 1870 or January 1871 the occupants of a house at Húsavík, Sandoy, were alarmed by scratching noises behind the wooden panelling. Their cat solved the mystery by catching a bat which was sent to Copenhagen and identified as *Vespertilio discolor* (= *V. murinus*). This vagrant from the Continent has also occurred on Whalsay, Shetland, in late March 1927 (J. Ritchie, *Scottish Nat.*, 1927).

ORDER CARNIVORA

Phoca vitulina Linnaeus.   Common or Harbour Seal, *steinkópur*.
Halichoerus grypus (O. Fabricius).   Grey or Atlantic Seal, *láturkópur*.

ORDER CETACEA

Balaenoptera musculus (Linnaeus).   Blue whale, *roydur*.
Balaenoptera borealis Lesson.   Sei whale, *seidhvalur*.
Balaenoptera physalus (Linnaeus).   Fin whale, *nebbafiskur*.
Megaptera nodosa (Bonnaterre).   Humpback, *kúlubøka*.
Physeter catodon Linnaeus.   Sperm whale, *avgustur*.
Lagenorhynchus albirostris (Grey).   White-beaked Dolphin, *springari*.
Lagenorhynchus acutus (Grey).   White-sided Dolphin, *springari*.
Globicephala melaena (Traill).   Caũing whale or Blackfish, *grindahvalur*.
Hyperoodon ampullatus (Forster).   Bottlenose whale, *døglingur*.

APPENDIX "B"

Faeroe Birds

THERE HAVE BEEN a number of lists of Faeroese birds, and a history of ornithological research among the islands was included by Dr. Finn Salomonsen in the definitive taxonomic review "Aves" which appeared as part of *The Zoology of the Faroes* in 1935. In compiling this excellent and very comprehensive work he searched through a scattered and extensive literature and critically examined the many Faeroese specimens kept at the Universitetets Zoologiske Museum, Copenhagen. His survey will for long remain the firm foundation on which subsequent workers will build. Since that time newer lists have been drawn up by myself in the first edition of *The Atlantic Islands* in 1948, and by Anders Holm Joensen in his beautifully illustrated *Fuglene pa Faerøerne* published in Copenhagen in 1966.

A number of reasons have induced me to embody an annotated systematic list of Faeroese birds in this book. Several previous writers on the Faeroese life and scene, notably Svabo and Landt, did the same, so the course is not without precedent. Such a list will serve to give a brief indication of the status, and also the all-important scientific names, of the many birds whose importance in the Faeroese economy and folk culture is described in the foregoing chapters. An ever-growing number of visitors—not least the expeditions of young people—are interested in the bird-life of the islands, and will find an up-to-date list a useful guide to what is already known, and also to those aspects (in particular the breeding of waterfowl and small song-birds) which urgently require further exploration.

The sequence of orders and families follows Charles Vaurie's *Birds of the Palearctic Fauna* (London, 1959 and 1965), but the nomenclature of species and subspecies differs in some instances where my own experience and preference depart from his. The common English name of the species is followed by the Danish name, and then by the Faeroese name where one exists. The scientific designation immediately afterwards is that of the sub-species or geographical race most usual in the Faeroes, any less

326

important subspecies which occurs there being mentioned later in the brief summary of status as at present known from notes and papers published down to the spring of 1969. Most of such work has appeared in the journal of the Danish Ornithological Society, *Dansk Ornithologisk Forenings Tidsskrift* (abbreviated to D.O.F.T.), and a selected list of the more important contributions since 1947 is given at the end.

The present list contains 224 species of which 53 breed regularly, with the possible exceptions of Cormorant and Snow Bunting, whose present status is obscure. Only one of these, the Purple Sandpiper, does not nest in the British Isles. A further 20 species breed irregularly or have done so in the past; of these, the Great Auk is extinct, while Grey Lag Goose, Whooper Swan and White-tailed Eagle ceased to be regular breeders long ago. Deliberate introductions have resulted in two gains, Greenland Ptarmigan and Mute Swan; and the growth of the plantations and gardens at Tórshavn has quite recently attracted Blackbird and Robin as regular nesters, while one or two warblers and perhaps other species nest there from time to time. The list of breeding birds is small by comparison with other countries, due partly to the Faeroes' isolation, and also to the very narrow limits of variation in the environment—a fact which will be obvious to readers of this book.

Of the above regular and occasional breeders at least 56 also occur on migration, while a further 56 use the islands only in transit, making 112 passage migrants and winter visitors. The next largest category comprises the vagrants, birds with up to ten or a dozen appearances scattered over two centuries; these number 95, with the possibility that three (Canada Goose, Snow Goose and Red-headed Bunting) could have escaped from captivity. Four species have crossed the North Atlantic from America. Some obvious "escapes," unsuccessfully introduced birds, or records for which there is perhaps insufficient evidence, have been placed in square brackets.

As happens in island habitats the world over, certain of the resident birds have evolved as well-marked geographical races or subspecies, through long centuries of isolation and adaptation to special conditions of food, climate and environment generally. These are the Eider Duck, Tystie, Common Guillemot (less well defined than the others), Raven, Starling and Wren. The

" Faeroe Snipe " is really a northern form, found also in Iceland, Shetland, and St. Kilda; and the " Faeroe Rock Pipit " also breeds in Shetland and St. Kilda. The Faeroe Islands are a meeting-place for northern and southern subspecies; thus, it may be said that Snipe, Golden Plover, Guillemot and Wheatear have northern affinities, while Dunlin, Ringed Plover, Lesser Black-backed Gull, Puffin and others are southern forms. This state of affairs has resulted in a mixed population in the case of a few species, some Wheatears and Golden Plovers, for instance, showing intermediate characteristics.

ORDER GAVIIFORMES

Family GAVIIDAE

RED-THROATED DIVER; rødstrubet lom; lómur. *Gavia stellata stellata* (Pontoppidan). Formerly common, now scarce, breeding summer visitor. Passage migrant and winter visitor.

BLACK-THROATED DIVER; sortstrubet lom. *Gavia arctica arctica* (Linnaeus). Once, before 1860.

GREAT NORTHERN DIVER; islom; havgás. *Gavia immer* (Brünnich). Common winter visitor. Scarce non-breeding summer visitor, but may have bred in colder climatic periods, since Svabo (1783) says " it is seen with young ones that cannot fly."

ORDER PODICIPIDIFORMES

Family PODICIPEDIDAE

DABCHICK OR LITTLE GREBE; lille lappedykker. *Tachybaptus ruficollis ruficollis* (Pallas). Vagrant, Nólsoy and Tórshavn, both in November.

SLAVONIAN OR HORNED GREBE; Nordisk lappedykker; gjøðr. *Podiceps auritus auritus* (Linnaeus). Scarce breeding summer visitor, Eysturoy (since 1935) and Vágar (since 1942). Passage migrant and winter visitor.

RED-NECKED GREBE; gråstrubet lappedykker. *Podiceps griseigena griseigena* (Boddaert). Once, Norðuroyar, winter 1918.

ORDER PROCELLARIIFORMES

Family DIOMEDEIDAE

BLACK-BROWED ALBATROSS; sortbrynet albatros; súlukongur. *Diomedea melanophrys* Temminck. Vagrant: one summered with the Gannets on Mykineshólmur for 34 years until May 1894; one was taken on a fishing-bank 40 miles southwest of the Faeroes in May 1900.

Family PROCELLARIIDAE

FULMAR; mallemuk; havhestur. *Fulmarus glacialis glacialis* (Linnaeus). Abundant resident, all islands, first bred *c.* 1816. Winter visitor. Dark morph birds from high-arctic colonies occur in winter (Salomonsen, 1935), a few remaining into the summer.

MANX SHEARWATER; almindelig skråpe; skrápur. *Puffinus puffinus puffinus* (Brünnich). Breeding summer visitor with colonies on most islands.

[LITTLE SHEARWATER. *Puffinus assimilis* subsp. Recorded (as *Puffinus obscurus*) by Andersen (1898), but extremely doubtful.]

GREAT SHEARWATER; storskråpe; havskrápur. *Puffinus gravis* (O'Reilly). Regular summer and autumn visitor from the South Atlantic.

SOOTY SHEARWATER; sodfarvet skråpe; svartur havskrápur. *Puffinus griseus* (Gmelin). Summer and autumn visitor from the southern hemisphere.

MEDITERRANEAN SHEARWATER; Kuhls skråpe. *Calonectris diomedea diomedea* (Scopoli). Once, 1877 (Salomonsen, 1935, 1942).

Family HYDROBATIDAE

STORMY PETREL; lille stormsvale; drunnhvíti. *Hydrobates pelagicus* (Linnaeus). Breeding summer visitor, colonies on most islands. Passage migrant.

LEACH'S OR FORK-TAILED PETREL; stor stormsvale; havtiril. *Oceanodroma leucorrhoa leucorrhoa* (Vieillot). Breeding colony on Mykineshólmur; observed at Trøllhøvdi, but nesting not proved.

ORDER PELECANIFORMES

Family SULIDAE

GANNET; sule; súla. *Sula bassana bassana* (Linnaeus). Breeding colony on Mykineshólmur and adjacent stacks (*c.* 1615 pairs in 1937; *c.* 1950 pairs in 1957; *c.* 1080 pairs in 1966). Passage migrant.

Family PHALACROCORACIDAE

CORMORANT; storskarve; hiplingur. *Phalacrocorax carbo carbo* (Linnaeus). Formerly a common breeder, latterly scarce with small colonies on Sandoy and Viðoy; present status obscure.

SHAG; topskarv; skarvur. *Phalacrocorax aristotelis aristotelis* (Linnaeus). Common resident, breeding all islands.

ORDER CICONIIFORMES

Family ARDEIDAE

BITTERN; rørdrum; *Botaurus stellaris stellaris* (Linnaeus). Vagrant, 2, Tórshavn (May 1887) and Borðoy (January 1951).

AMERICAN BITTERN; Amerikansk rørdrum. *Botaurus lentiginosus* (Montagu). Vagrant, 2, Sandoy (1930) and Viðoy (November 1952).

LITTLE BITTERN; dvaerghejre. *Ixobrychus minutus minutus* (Linnaeus). Vagrant, 4, Streymoy, Suðuroy and Norðuroyar.

NIGHT HERON; nathejre. *Nycticorax nycticorax nycticorax* (Linnaeus). Once, Streymoy (July 1870).

[SQUACCO HERON. *Ardeola ralloides* (Scopoli). Said to have been taken in the Faeroes, but there are no details.]

GREY HERON; fiskahejre; hegri. *Ardea cinerea cinerea* Linnaeus. Fairly regular visitor, all seasons, mostly immature birds.

PURPLE HERON; purpurhejre. *Ardea purpurea purpurea* Linnaeus. Once, Suðuroy (June 1946).

Family THRESKIORNITHIDAE

SPOONBILL; skestork. *Platalea leucorodia leucorodia* Linnaeus. Vagrant, 2, one before 1655 and another on Sandoy (November 1896).

GLOSSY IBIS; sort ibis; svartur spogvi. *Plegadis falcinellus* (Linnaeus). Vagrant, only 2 specimens, but a number have been seen.

ORDER ANSERIFORMES

Family ANATIDAE

CANADA GOOSE; kanadagås. *Branta canadensis canadensis* (Linnaeus). Once, Streymoy (November 1866). Possibly an escape from captivity.

BARNACLE GOOSE; bramgås; bramgás. *Branta leucopsis* (Bechstein). Irregular passage migrant and winter visitor, occasionally seen in summer.

BRENT GOOSE; knortegås; helsugás. The Pale-breasted *Branta bernicla hrota* (Müller) is a fairly regular and sometimes common passage migrant; the Dark-breasted *Branta bernicla bernicla* (Linnaeus) has been taken twice on Nólsoy.

SNOW GOOSE; snegås. *Anser hyperboreus* subsp. One lived for some time with tame geese near Tórshavn in 1914; it may have been an escape.

GREY LAG GOOSE; gragås; gragás. *Anser anser anser* (Linnaeus). Formerly a common breeder (until *c.* 1840) but now scarce and very irregular (Sandoy 1939 and 1942, S. Streymoy 1943). Common passage migrant.

WHITE-FRONTED GOOSE; blisgås; korngás. *Anser albifrons* subsp. Irregular passage migrant; no specimens are preserved so the subspecies is in doubt.

PINK-FOOTED GOOSE; kortnaebbet gås; svalbardsgás. *Anser brachyrhynchus* Baillon. Probably a regular passage migrant, but there are few certain records.

MUTE SWAN; knopsvane; knubbsvannur. *Cygnus olor* (Gmelin). Introduced resident at Tórshavn (*c.* 1940) and Vágur, Suðuroy.

WHOOPER SWAN; sangsvane; sangsvanur. *Cygnus cygnus* (Linnaeus). Formerly bred, until seventeenth century. Passage migrant and winter visitor, a few remaining in summer in recent years.

[BLACK SWAN. *Cygnus atratus* (Latham). One lived for a few years on Sørvágsvatn, Vágar, *c.* 1937. Doubtless it had escaped from captivity.]

SHELDUCK; gravand; tjaldursont. *Tadorna tadorna* (Linnaeus). Vagrant, 7, including 3 in January.

[RUDDY SHELDUCK. *Casarca ferruginea* (Pallas). Said by Witherby *et al.* (1941) to be " casual " in the Faeroes, but there is no formal record.]

MALLARD; gråand; villdunna. *Anas platyrhynchos platyrhynchos* Linnaeus. Breeds on the larger islands, some staying the winter. Passage migrant and winter visitor.

TEAL; krikand; krikkont. *Anas crecca crecca* Linnaeus. Scarce breeder. Regular passage migrant.

GADWALL; knarand. *Anas strepera strepera* Linnaeus. Twice on Sandoy, a pair in May 1953 and a ♀ in July 1955.

WIGEON; pibeand; pípont. *Anas penelope* Linnaeus. Has bred on Vágar (1948, 1950); Streymoy (?1872, 1949), and probably Sandoy. Pairs are frequently seen in summer. Regular passage migrant and winter visitor.

PINTAIL; spidsand; stikkont. *Anas acuta acuta* Linnaeus. Has bred on Eysturoy (1871) and Nólsoy (1926). Pairs are frequently seen in summer. Regular passage migrant and winter visitor.

GARGANEY; atlingand. *Anas querquedula* Linnaeus. Vagrant, 2 old records.

[SHOVELER; skeand; sp).nont. *Spatula clypeata* Linnaeus. Vagrant; has appeared a few times on Nólsoy, according to Niels á Botni.]

POCHARD; taffeland. *Aythya ferina* (Linnaeus). Vagrant, 2.

[FERRUGINOUS DUCK; hvidøjet and. *Aythya nyroca* (Güldenstadt). Once, a bird received by Niels á Botni for skinning: no data available.]

TUFTED DUCK; troldand; trøllont. *Aythya fuligula* (Linnaeus). Has bred on Suðuroy (1966) and Eysturoy (1967). Pairs are frequently seen in summer. Common passage migrant since *c.* 1940, previously apparently scarce.

SCAUP; bjergand; gråbøka. *Aythya marila marila* (Linnaeus). Has bred on Eysturoy (1894). Regular passage migrant, a few remaining in summer.

[MANDARIN; mandarinsand. *Aix galericulata* (Linnaeus). Adult ♂ ♂ on Nólsoy (1904) and Streymoy (1907), also a pair from Sandoy now in Tórshavn Museum, had doubtless escaped from captivity.]

EIDER; ederfugl; aeða ♂, aeðublikur ♀. The endemic *Somateria mollissima faeroeensis* Brehm is a common resident at all the settlements. The arctic race *Somateria mollissima borealis* Brehm is said to occur at sea off Nólsoy in winter.

KING EIDER; kongeederfugl; aeðukongur. *Somateria spectabilis* (Linnaeus). Vagrant, 12 or more, including 6 in summer.

COMMON SCOTER; sortand; kolont. *Melanitta nigra nigra* (Linnaeus). Has bred on Sandoy, where pairs are frequent in summer. Regular passage migrant, mostly in spring.

VELVET SCOTER; flojlsand. *Melanitta fusca fusca* (Linnaeus). Vagrant, 3 or more.

SURF SCOTER; brilleand. *Melanitta perspicillata* (Linnaeus). Vagrant from America, Streymoy (November 1847) and Vágar (September 1896), and possibly Suðuroy *c.* 1860.

[HARLEQUIN. *Histrionicus histrionicus* (Linnaeus). Has been included in most lists but without satisfactory evidence (Williamson, 1947).]

LONG-TAILED DUCK; havlit; ogvella. *Clangula hyemalis* (Linnaeus). Regular winter visitor and passage migrant, often common; occasionally seen in summer.

GOLDENEYE; hvinant; suðont. *Bucephala clangula clangula* (Linnaeus). Vagrant, though formerly an irregular visitor on passage and in winter.

BARROW'S GOLDENEYE; Islandsk hvinand. *Bucephala islandica* (Gmelin). Vagrant, 3, Eysturoy (May 1944) and Nólsoy (April 1949, January 1945).

RED-BREASTED MERGANSER; toppet skallesluger; toppont. *Mergus serrator* Linnaeus. Breeds on the larger islands, apparently increasing. Regular passage migrant.

GOOSANDER; stor skallesluger; tannont. *Mergus merganser merganser* Linnaeus. Vagrant, 4, February–March and a pair on Eysturoy in June.

ORDER FALCONIFORMES

Family PANDIONIDAE

OSPREY; fiskeørn; fiskaørn. *Pandion haliaëtus haliaëtus* (Linnaeus). Vagrant, 4, May–June and November.

Family ACCIPITRIDAE

HONEY BUZZARD; hvepsevåge. *Pernis apivorus* (Linnaeus). Vagrant, 2, Nólsoy (June 1884) and Streymoy (May 1949).

WHITE-TAILED OR SEA-EAGLE; havørn; ørn. *Haliaëtus albicilla albicilla* (Linnaeus). Scarce breeder until mid-eighteenth century, winter vagrant since, last recorded in 1902.

SPARROWHAWK; spurvehøg. *Accipiter nisus nisus* (Linnaeus). Vagrant, 2, *c.* 1874 and Nólsoy (May 1918).

[COMMON BUZZARD. *Buteo buteo* (Linnaeus). One is said to have been shot on Nólsoy late in the last century, but there are no details.]

ROUGH-LEGGED BUZZARD; laddenbenet musvåge. *Buteo lagopus lagopus* (Pontoppidan). Once, Nólsoy (October 1931).

HEN HARRIER; blå kaerhøg. *Circus cyaneus cyaneus* (Linnaeus). Vagrant, 3, Nólsoy (October and January).

MARSH HARRIER; rørhøg. *Circus aeruginosus aeruginosus* (Linnaeus). Vagrant, 3, Streymoy and Eysturoy (September–October) and Nólsoy.

Family FALCONIDAE

GYRFALCON; jagtfalk; falkur. Both the Iceland *Falco rusticolus islandus* Brünnich and the Greenland *Falco rusticolus candicans* Gmelin are uncommon passage migrants and winter visitors.

PEREGRINE; vandrefalk; ferðafalkur. *Falco peregrinus peregrinus* Tunstall. Vagrant, 6 or more, Suðuroy, Mykines and Nólsoy.

MERLIN; dvaergfalk; smiril. *Falco columbarius subaesalon* Brehm. Uncommon breeder on the larger islands. Passage migrant, especially in autumn.

KESTREL; tarnfalk; grýtismiril. *Falco tinnunculus tinnunculus* Linnaeus. Irregular visitor, especially in autumn.

ORDER GALLIFORMES

Family TETRAONIDAE

PTARMIGAN; fjeldrype; rypa. Of several introductions only that of Greenland birds *Lagopus mutus rupestris* (Gmelin) at Tórshavn in 1890 proved successful, birds having been seen in recent years in the Norðuroyar (Williamson, 1945, 1954; Petersen, 1949). Vagrant on Mykines (1903).

[RED GROUSE. Scottish birds *Lagopus lagopus scoticus* (Latham) introduced in 1896 were unsuccessful.]

[BLACKCOCK ♂ AND GREYHEN ♀. Remains of a ♀ identified at the British Museum (Natural History) as *Lyrurus tetrix tetrix* (Linnaeus) were found on Nólsoy in January 1942. It seems unlikely to have reached the Faeroes unaided.]

Family PHASIANIDAE

[PHEASANT. *Phasianus colchicus* Linnaeus. Post-war attempts to establish it in the Tórshavn area were unsuccessful.]

QUAIL; vagtel; vaktil. *Coturnix coturnix coturnix* (Linnaeus). Formerly a scarce and irregular breeding summer visitor to Suðuroy, Sandoy, Nólsoy and Streymoy, but not recorded in this century.

ORDER GRUIFORMES

Family GRUIDAE

COMMON CRANE; trane. *Grus grus grus* (Linnaeus). Vagrant, 3, Norðuroyar (1857, May 1872) and Suðuroy (June 1922).

Family RALLIDAE

WATER RAIL; vandrikse; jarðakona. The Icelandic *Rallus aquaticus hibernans* Salomonsen is a regular passage migrant and winter visitor. The Continental race *Rallus aquaticus aquaticus* Linnaeus has been collected on Nólsoy (a pair, October 28th, 1946), and one or the other form has nested there.

BAILLON'S CRAKE; dvaergrørvagtel. *Porzana pusilla intermedia* Hermann. Vagrant, 2, Streymoy (September and November).

SPOTTED CRAKE; plettet rørvagtel. *Porzana porzana* (Linnaeus). Vagrant, 2, Mykines (September–October, 1953).

CORNCRAKE OR LANDRAIL; engsnarre; akurskrift. *Crex crex* (Linnaeus). Formerly a scarce breeding summer visitor to the southern islands, but only a few summer occurrences (mostly on Mykines) in this century.

MOORHEN; rørhøne. *Gallinula chloropus chloropus* (Linnaeus). Irregular winter visitor in recent years (Petersen, 1949), formerly a vagrant.

COOT; blishøne; sjóhøna. *Fulica atra atra* Linnaeus. Irregular winter visitor.

ORDER CHARADRIIFORMES

Family HAEMATOPODIDAE
OYSTERCATCHER; strandskade; tjaldur. *Haematopus ostralegus ostralegus* Linnaeus. Abundant summer visitor, breeding on all islands. Passage migrant.

Family RECURVIROSTRIDAE
AVOCET; klyde. *Recurvirostra avosetta avosetta* Linnaeus. Once, Sandoy (May 1882).

Family CHARADRIIDAE
RINGED PLOVER; stor praestekrave; svarthálsa. *Charadrius hiaticula hiaticula* Linnaeus. Rather uncommon summer visitor, breeding on most islands, occasionally several pairs together. Passage migrant.

KILLDEER PLOVER; kildire. *Charadrius vociferus vociferus* Linnaeus. Vagrant from America, Nólsoy (winter 1939–40).

DOTTEREL; pomeransfugl. *Charadrius morinellus* Linnaeus. Once, a flock on Mykines (June 3rd, 1902).

GOLDEN PLOVER; hjejle; lógv. *Charadrius apricarius altifrons* Brehm. Abundant summer visitor, breeding on all islands; also a passage migrant, a few wintering. Some are intermediate between this and the typical race *Charadrius apricarius apricarius* Linnaeus (Williamson, 1948) and migrants corresponding to this southern form have been seen on Sandoy in May.

GREY PLOVER; strandhjejle; fjorðulógv. *Charadrius squatarola* Linnaeus. Vagrant, Nólsoy (November 1929, and a small party, late October 1938).

LAPWING; vibe; vípa. *Vanellus vanellus* (Linnaeus). Scarce but regular breeder in recent years on Sandoy; has also nested on Suðuroy, Vágar, Mykines, Koltur, Nólsoy and S. Streymoy (1875, 1953). Passage migrant and winter visitor.

TURNSTONE; stenvender; tjaldursgraelingur. *Arenaria interpres interpres* (Linnaeus). Abundant passage migrant and (in recent years) winter visitor, small numbers staying in summer but not breeding.

Family SCOLOPACIDAE

LITTLE STINT; dvaergryle. *Calidris minuta* (Leisler). Vagrant, Nólsoy (1918 and 1937), both September.

PURPLE SANDPIPER; sortgrå ryle; grágraelingur. *Calidris maritima maritima* (Brünnich). Scarce breeder, formerly rather common, but in recent years found only on Skúvoy, Sandoy, Mykines, Vágar and N. Streymoy. Passage migrant and winter visitor.

DUNLIN; almindelig ryle; fjallmurra. *Calidris alpina schinzii* (Brehm). Scarce breeding summer visitor and passage migrant. The northern *Calidris alpina alpina* (Linnaeus) has been recorded on passage but there are no specimens.

KNOT; Islandsk ryle; islandsgraelingur. *Calidris canutus canutus* (Linnaeus). Passage migrant and winter visitor, a few staying in summer.

SANDERLING; sandløber; sandgraelingur. *Calidris alba* (Pallas). Scarce but regular passage migrant, a few staying occasionally in summer.

RUFF ♂ AND REEVE ♀ ; brushane; brushøna. *Philomachus pugnax* (Linnaeus). Regular autumn passage migrant in recent years, formerly rare.

WOOD SANDPIPER; tinksmed. *Tringa glareola* Linnaeus. Vagrant, 4, Nólsoy, Mykines and Streymoy (August–September).

COMMON SANDPIPER; mudderklire. *Tringa hypoleucos* Linnaeus. Vagrant, 2, Suđuroy (May 1946) and Sandoy (July 1967).

REDSHANK; rødben; stelkur. *Tringa totanus robusta* (Schiøler). Scarce breeding summer visitor in recent years, mainly on Sandoy, perhaps also Suđuroy, Vágar, Mykines, Eysturoy and N. Streymoy. Passage migrant and winter visitor.

GREENSHANK; hvidklire. *Tringa nebularia* (Gunnerus). Vagrant, Nólsoy, according to Niels á Botni.

BLACK-TAILED GODWIT; stor kobbersneppe; reyđspógvi. *Limosa limosa islandica* Brehm. Scarce and irregular breeding summer visitor, S. Streymoy (1856, ?1872), Vágar (1914–18) and Sandoy (1951–52), perhaps also Suđuroy (1946). Irregular passage migrant.

BAR-TAILED GODWIT; lille kobbersneppe. *Limosa lapponica lapponica* (Linnaeus). Scarce and irregular passage migrant.

CURLEW: stor regnspove; tangspógvi. *Numenius arquata arquata* (Linnaeus). Regular summer visitor, but no indication

Y

of breeding. Common passage migrant and winter visitor.

WHIMBREL; lille regnspove; spógvi. *Numenius phaeopus phaeopus* (Linnaeus). Abundant breeding summer visitor, all islands. Passage migrant.

WOODCOCK; skovesneppe; skogsnípa. *Scolopax rusticola* Linnaeus. Scarce but regular passage migrant, occasionally found in winter.

SNIPE; dobbeltbekassin; mýrisnípa. *Capella gallinago faeroensis* (Brehm). Abundant breeding summer visitor, all islands. Passage migrant to and from Iceland, some wintering. The typical race *Capella gallinago gallinago* (Linnaeus) is said to have occurred in autumn.

JACK SNIPE; enkeltbekkasin. *Lymnocryptes minimus* (Brünnich). Scarce and irregular winter visitor.

Family PHALAROPODIDAE

GREY PHALAROPE; Thorshane; sildhøna. *Phalaropus fulicarius* (Linnaeus). Scarce passage migrant, mainly Mykines and Nólsoy, September–November.

RED-NECKED PHALAROPE; Odinshane; hálsareyði. *Phalaropus lobatus* (Linnaeus). Scarce breeding summer visitor to Sandoy, Vágar, N. Streymoy and Eysturoy; has bred on Nólsoy. Passage migrant.

Family STERCORARIIDAE

BONXIE OR GREAT SKUA; storkjove; skúgvur. *Catharacta skua skua* (Brünnich). Breeding colonies on N. Streymoy (*c.* 230 pairs), Svínoy (*c.* 200 pairs), Skúvoy (*c.* 45 pairs), and scattered small groups on Sandoy, Borðoy and Viðoy. Commoner in nineteenth century than now. Passage migrant.

POMARINE SKUA; mellemkjove; jói. *Stercorarius pomarinus* (Temminck). Regular and rather common passage migrant.

ARCTIC OR RICHARDSON'S SKUA; almindelig kjove; kjógvi. *Stercorarius parasiticus* (Linnaeus). Common breeding summer visitor, all islands. Passage migrant.

LONG-TAILED OR BUFFON'S SKUA; lille kjove; snaeldukjógvi. *Stercorarius longicaudus longicaudus* Vieillot. Irregular passage migrant.

Family LARIDAE

LITTLE GULL; dvaergmåge. *Larus minutus* Pallas. Vagrant, 7, mostly in winter.

BLACK-HEADED GULL; haettemåge; fransaterna. *Larus ridibundus ridibundus* Linnaeus. Small but rather unstable breeding colonies on a few islands; has increased in this century. Passage migrant and winter visitor.

LESSER BLACK-BACKED GULL; sildemåge; likka. *Larus fuscus graellsii* (A. E. Brehm). Abundant breeding summer visitor, colonies on all islands. Passage migrant.

HERRING GULL; sølvmåge; mási. *Larus argentatus argentatus* Pontoppidan. Common resident, passage migrant and winter visitor. One of the yellow-legged forms *Larus argentatus omissus* Pleske, was reported from Nólsoy in May 1939.

ICELAND GULL; hvidvinget måge; islandsmási. *Larus glaucoides glaucoides* Meyer. Scarce but regular winter visitor from Greenland.

GLAUCOUS GULL; gråmåge; valmási. *Larus hyperboreus hyperboreus* Gunnerus. Common passage migrant and winter visitor.

GREAT BLACK-BACKED GULL; svartbag; bakur. *Larus marinus* Linnaeus. Common resident, small colonies on most islands. Passage migrant and winter visitor.

MEW GULL OR COMMON GULL; stormåge; gneggjus or skáta. *Larus canus canus* Linnaeus. Breeding summer visitor, small colonies on most islands; has increased in this century. Passage migrant.

SABINE'S GULL; Sabinemåge. *Larus sabini* Sabine. Vagrant, 5.

KITTIWAKE; ride; rita. *Rissa tridactyla* (Linnaeus). Large breeding colonies on all islands. Passage migrant; uncommon in winter.

ROSS'S GULL; rosenmåge. *Rhodostethia rosea* (MacGillivray). Vagrant, 4, Suðuroy (February 1863) and Nólsoy (autumn 1922, summer 1927 and December 1942).

IVORY GULL; ismåge. *Pagophila eburnea* (Phipps). Scarce and irregular winter visitor. A considerable number appeared in spring 1895.

BLACK TERN; sortterne. *Chlidonias niger niger* (Linnaeus). Vagrant, 3, Nólsoy and Tórshavn (June and September).

WHITE-WINGED BLACK TERN; hvidvinget terne. *Chlidonias leucopterus* (Temminck). Once, Nólsoy (May 1943).

CASPIAN TERN; rovterne. *Hydroprogne tschegrava* (Lepechin).
Vagrant, 2, Vágar (May 1887) and Nólsoy (April 1949).
ARCTIC TERN; havterne; terna. *Sterna paradisaea* Pontoppidan.
Breeding summer visitor, colonies on all islands. Passage
migrant.
LITTLE TERN; dvaergterne. *Sterna albifrons albifrons* Pallas. Once,
Kallsoy (June 1941).

Family ALCIDAE

LITTLE AUK; søkonge; fulkubbi. *Plotus alle alle* (Linnaeus).
Common passage migrant and winter visitor.
RAZORBILL; alk; alka. *Alca torda islandica* Brehm. Abundant,
breeding on all islands.
GAREFOWL OR GREAT AUK; gejrfugl; gorfuglur. *Pinguinus impennis*
(Linnæus). (Extinct.) Formerly an irregular visitor, ap-
parently scarce: may have bred.
GUILLEMOT; lomvi; lomvigi. *Uria aalge spiloptera* Salomonsen.
Abundant on all islands, with immense colonies on many.
BRUNNICH'S GUILLEMOT; kortnaebbet lomvi. *Uria lomvia lomvia*
(Linnaeus). Probably a regular winter visitor; there are
several records from Nólsoy.
TYSTIE OR BLACK GUILLEMOT; tejst; teisti. *Cepphus grylle faeroensis*
Brehm. Resident, breeding colonies on all islands.
PUFFIN; lunde; lundi. *Fratercula arctica grabae* (Brehm). Abundant
on all islands, with immense breeding colonies on many.
Northern Puffins *Fratercula arctica arctica* (Linnaeus) are
regular and probably common winter visitors, some staying
in summer.

ORDER COLUMBIFORMES

Family PTEROCLIDAE

PALLAS'S SAND GROUSE; steppehøn. *Syrrhaptes paradoxus* (Pallas).
Several occurred in summer 1863 (Streymoy) and in spring
1888 (most islands) during invasions of this asiatic species
into Europe.

Family COLUMBIDAE

ROCK DOVE; klipperdue; bládúgva. *Columba livia livia* Gmelin.
Fairly common resident on most islands. There is a scarce

mutant variety with spotted wing-coverts (á Botni and Williamson, 1949).

WOODPIGEON OR RINGDOVE; ringdue; manansdúgva. *Columba palumbus palumbus* Linnaeus. Frequently seen in summer in the plantations, but not yet proved to breed. Passage migrant and winter visitor.

TURTLE DOVE; turteldue; turtildúgva. *Streptopelia turtur turtur* (Linnaeus). Scarce but regular autumn passage migrant, occasionally seen in summer.

ORDER CUCULIFORMES

Family CUCULIDAE

CUCKOO; gøg; geykur. *Cuculus canorus canorus* Linnaeus. Vagrant, 10 or more, mostly in summer.

ORDER STRIGIFORMES

Family STRIGIDAE

SNOWY OWL; sneugle; snjóugla. *Nyctea scandiaca* (Linnaeus). Scarce and infrequent winter visitor, occasionally staying through the summer.

LONG-EARED OWL; skovhornugle; hornugla. *Asio otus otus* (Linnaeus). Vagrant, 7 or more.

SHORT-EARED OWL; mosehornugle; kattugla. *Asio flammeus flammeus* (Pontoppidan). Infrequent passage migrant.

[TAWNY OWL. *Strix aluco* Linnaeus. Has been included in some lists but the record is due to a confusion of dates and locality with *Asio otus* in Feilden (1882).]

SCOPS OWL; dvaerghornugle. *Otus scops scops* (Linnaeus). Once, Nólsoy (May 1954).

ORDER CAPRIMULGIFORMES

Family CAPRIMULGIDAE

NIGHTHAWK; nathøg. *Chordeiles minor minor* (Forster). This American species has occurred once, according to Joensen (1966).

NIGHTJAR; natravn. *Caprimulgus europaeus europaeus* Linnaeus. Vagrant, 9 or more, mostly May–July.

ORDER APODIFORMES

Family APODIDAE
SWIFT; mursejler; feigdarsvala. *Apus apus apus* (Linnaeus).
Scarce passage migrant and non-breeding summer visitor.

ORDER CORACIIFORMES

Family UPUPIDAE
HOOPOE; haerfugl. *Upupa epops epops* Linnaeus. Vagrant, 3,
Eysturoy (October 1885), Vágar (late summer 1888) and
Mykines (April 1901).

Family CORACIIDAE
ROLLER; ellekrage. *Coracias garrulus garrulus* Linnaeus. Vagrant,
4, June and July.

ORDER PICIFORMES

Family PICIDAE
WRYNECK; vendehals; snuđurkríki. *Jynx torquilla torquilla* Lin-
naeus. Rare and irregular passage migrant, May and
September–October.
GREAT SPOTTED WOODPECKER; stor flagspaette; stóra flekkuspetta.
Dendrocopos major major (Linnaeus). Scarce and irregular
autumn visitor in " eruption " years.

ORDER PASSERIFORMES

Family HIRUNDINIDAE
SAND MARTIN; digesvale. *Riparia riparia riparia* (Linnaeus).
Vagrant, 6, May and August.
SWALLOW; landesvale; svala. *Hirundo rustica rustica* Linnaeus.
Scarce and irregular breeding summer visitor, sometimes
nesting in cliffs. Passage migrant.
HOUSE MARTIN; bysvale. *Delichon urbica urbica* (Linnaeus). Scarce
passage migrant, mainly in spring. Reported nesting at
Skúvoy (1956) and at Mykines (1966).

Family ALAUDIDAE
SKYLARK; sanglaerke; lerkur. *Alauda arvensis* Linnaeus. Scarce

and irregular summer visitor, breeding occasionally on the southern and central islands. Common passage migrant.

WOODLARK; hedelaerke. *Lullula arborea arborea* (Linnaeus). Once, Nólsoy (October 1950).

Family MOTACILLIDAE

MEADOW PIPIT; engpiber; títlingur. *Anthus pratensis theresae* Meinertzhagen. Common breeding summer visitor, all islands, though numbers fluctuate. Abundant passage migrant to and from Iceland, a few remaining in winter.

[RED-THROATED PIPIT. *Anthus cervinus* (Pallas). Mentioned by Hartert (1910) but no specimen is known.]

ROCK PIPIT; skaerpiber; grátítlingur. *Anthus spinoletta kleinschmidti* Hartert. Common resident, breeding on all islands.

BLUE-HEADED WAGTAIL; gul vipstjert. *Motacilla flava flava* Linnaeus. Scarce and irregular passage migrant, mainly in spring. The northern Grey-headed Wagtail *Motacilla flava thunbergi* Billberg has occurred on Vágar and Mykines (May 1900).

YELLOW WAGTAIL; gul vipstjert. *Motacilla lutea flavissima* (Blyth). Vagrant, 2, Vágar (August 1872) and Mykines (May 1903).

GREY WAGTAIL; bjergvipstjert. *Motacilla cinerea cinerea* Tunstall. Once, Mykines (October 1898).

WHITE WAGTAIL; hvid vipstjert; erla kongsdottir. *Motacilla alba alba* Linnaeus. Scarce breeding summer visitor to most islands. Common passage migrant to and from Iceland. The British Pied Wagtail *Motacilla alba yarrellii* Gould has occurred on Mykines (April 1904) and Nólsoy (spring 1926 and October 1950).

Family LANIIDAE

RED-BACKED SHRIKE; rødrygget tornskade. *Lanius collurio collurio* Linnaeus. Once, Koltur (September 1919).

GREAT GREY SHRIKE; stor tornskade. *Lanius excubitor excubitor* Linnaeus. Vagrant, 6, October to March, mainly on Nólsoy.

Family ORIOLIDAE

GOLDEN ORIOLE; pirol. *Oriolus oriolus oriolus* (Linnaeus). Once, Streymoy (May 1893).

Family STURNIDAE

ROSY STARLING; rosenstaer. *Sturnus roseus* (Linnaeus). Vagrant, 7, June–October.

STARLING; staer; stari. *Sturnus vulgaris faeroensis* Feilden. Abundant resident, breeding at all settlements and often in cliffs. The Continental *Sturnus vulgaris vulgaris* Linnaeus is probably a regular passage migrant though few have been identified.

Family CORVIDAE

JACKDAW; allike; rókur. The Scandinavian *Corvus monedula monedula* Linnaeus appears to be an irregular visitor, mainly to Nólsoy. The British *Corvus monedula spermologus* Vieillot appears irregularly in winter and spring on Mykines, Vágar and W. Streymoy.

ROOK; råge; hjaltakráka. *Corvus frugilegus frugilegus* Linnaeus. Regular winter visitor in varying numbers.

HOODED CROW; gråkråge; kráka. *Corvus corone cornix* Linnaeus. Common resident, breeding on all islands.

RAVEN; ravn; ravnur. *Corvus corax varius* Brünnich. Resident, breeding sparsely on all islands. The name *varius* was given to a piebald variety, once fairly common, but extinct since about 1870 (Salomonsen, 1935).

Family BOMBYCILLIDAE

WAXWING; silkehale. *Bombycilla garrulus garrulus* (Linnaeus). Occasional winter visitor in " eruption " years.

Family CINCLIDAE

DIPPER; vandstaer. *Cinclus cinclus cinclus* (Linnaeus). Twice, Tórshavn (*c.* 1800 and *c.* 1869).

Family TROGLODYTIDAE

WREN; gaerdesmutte; musabródir. *Troglodytes troglodytes borealis* Fischer. Common resident, breeding at all settlements and on cliffs.

Family PRUNELLIDAE

DUNNOCK OR HEDGE-SPARROW; jernspurv. *Prunella modularis modularis* (Linnaeus). Vagrant, 4, Mykines (November, January and April) and Nólsoy (May).

Family SYLVIIDAE

SEDGE WARBLER; sivsanger. *Acrocephalus schoenobaenus* (Linnaeus). Once, Nólsoy (May 1920).

REED WARBLER; rørsanger. *Acrocephalus scirpaceus scirpaceus* (Hermann). Once, Nólsoy (September 1953).

GREAT REED WARBLER; drosselrørsanger. *Acrocephalus arundinaceus arundinaceus.* Once, Nólsoy (September 1945).

BARRED WARBLER; høgesanger. *Sylvia nisoria* (Bechstein). Scarce and irregular late summer passage migrant, young birds.

GARDEN WARBLER; havesanger. *Sylvia borin* (Boddaert). Has bred, Tórshavn (1948). Scarce but fairly regular passage migrant.

BLACKCAP; munk. *Sylvia atricapilla atricapilla* (Linnaeus). Regular passage migrant; observed at mid-summer and mid-winter.

WHITETHROAT; tornsanger. *Sylvia communis communis* Latham. Scarce but fairly regular passage migrant.

LESSER WHITETHROAT; gaerdesanger. *Sylvia curruca curruca* (Linnaeus). Has bred, Tórshavn (1964). Scarce but fairly regular passage migrant.

WILLOW WARBLER; løvsanger. *Phylloscopus trochilus acredula* (Linnaeus). Regular and fairly common passage migrant.

CHIFFCHAFF; gransanger. *Phylloscopus collybita abietinus* (Nilsson). Regular and fairly common passage migrant. The southern *Phylloscopus collybita collybita* (Vieillot) has been taken once on Nólsoy (October 1912) as has also the Siberian form *Phylloscopus collybita tristis* Blyth (November 1921).

WOOD WARBLER; skovsanger. *Phylloscopus sibilatrix* (Bechstein). Vagrant, 6, Mykines, Nólsoy and Suðuroy, mid-August to mid-October.

[ARCTIC WARBLER; *Phylloscopus borealis* (Blasius). A pair reported on Nólsoy (September 1949).]

YELLOW-BROWED WARBLER; hvidbrynet løvsanger. *Phylloscopus inornatus inornatus* (Blyth). Once, Nólsoy (September 1949).

GOLDCREST; fuglekonge; kongafuglur. *Regulus regulus regulus* (Linnaeus). Regular and sometimes common passage migrant; one mid-summer record.

FIRECREST; rødtopper fuglekonge. *Regulus ignicapillus ignicapillus* (Temminck). Once, Tórshavn (c. 1895).

Family MUSCICAPIDAE

PIED FLYCATCHER; broget fluesnapper. *Ficedula hypoleuca hypoleuca* (Pallas). Scarce and irregular passage migrant, May and September.

RED-BREASTED FLYCATCHER; lille fluesnapper. *Ficedula parva parva* (Bechstein). Once, Nólsoy (September 1947).

SPOTTED FLYCATCHER; grå fluesnapper. *Muscicapa striata striata* (Pallas). Vagrant, 4, Nólsoy (April–May) and Suđuroy (August).

[BROWN FLYCATCHER. *Muscicapa latirostris* Raffles. Reported seen on Nólsoy (September 1949).]

Family TURDIDAE

WHINCHAT; bynkefugl. *Saxicola rubetra rubetra* (Linnaeus). Vagrant, 4, Tórshavn (December 1852) and Nólsoy (May).

STONECHAT; sortstrubet bynkefugl. Four specimens, from Tórshavn and Mykines, are in worn spring plumage and the race is therefore indeterminate, but Salomonsen (1935) considers they are most likely to be *Saxicola torquata hibernans* (Hartert) "overshooting" from the British Isles. The Siberian *Saxicola torquata maura* (Pallas) has been taken once on Nólsoy (September 1946).

WHEATEAR; stenpikker; steinstólpa. *Oenanthe oenanthe schiøleri* Salomonsen. Abundant breeding summer visitor, all islands. The big Greenland race *Oenanthe oenanthe leucorrhoa* (Gmelin) is a common passage migrant.

BLACK REDSTART; sort rødstjert. *Phoenicurus ochruros gibraltariensis* (S. G. Gmelin). Vagrant, 6, Mykines (including small flock, November 12th–January 12th, 1902–03) and Nólsoy (including one, December–April 1946–47).

COMMON REDSTART; rødstjert. *Phoenicurus phoenicurus phoenicurus* (Linnaeus). Scarce and irregular passage migrant, May and September.

ROBIN; rødhals; reyđbristingur or bringureyđi. *Erithacus rubecula rubecula* (Linnaeus). Bred successfully at Tórshavn 1960, 1964 and 1966. Regular passage migrant and scarce winter visitor. The British race *Erithacus rubecula melophilus* Hartert has occurred once on Mykines (January 1900).

RED-SPOTTED BLUETHROAT; blåhals. *Luscinia svecica svecica* (Linnaeus). Twice in May, Nólsoy (1898, 1953).

DUSKY THRUSH; brundrossel. *Turdus naumanni eunomus* Temminck. Once, Nólsoy (December 1947).

FIELDFARE; sjagger; fjalltraestur. *Turdus pilaris* Linnaeus. Common passage migrant and winter visitor. A statement by Witherby *et al.* (1941) that it has bred has no foundation.

SONG THRUSH; sangdrossel. *Turdus philomelos philomelos* Brehm. Scarce and irregular winter and spring visitor. The British race *Turdus philomelos clarkei* Hartert has been taken thrice on Mykines (February 1901 and 1909; spring 1903).

REDWING; vindrossel; óðinshani. The Icelandic *Turdus iliacus coburni* Sharpe breeds regularly in small numbers at Tórshavn (since 1928, though a nest was recorded in 1869), and has probably bred elsewhere (e.g. Sørvágur, Kunoy). It is a common passage migrant and some stay the winter. The Scandinavian *Turdus iliacus iliacus* Linnaeus is probably a regular passage migrant though so far recognised only on Nólsoy.

RING OUSEL; ringdrossel. *Turdus torquatus torquatus* Linnaeus. Vagrant, 6, Mykines and Nólsoy, including 3 in winter.

BLACKBIRD; solsort; kvørkveggja. *Turdus merula merula* Linnaeus. Bred at Tórshavn in 1947 and has done so regularly during the past decade; bred on Kunoy, 1948–49. Common passage migrant and winter visitor.

WHITE'S OR GOLDEN MOUNTAIN THRUSH; gulddrossel. *Zoothera dauma aurea* (Holandre). Once, Nólsoy (November 1938).

Family PLOCEIDAE

HOUSE SPARROW; gråspurv; gráspurvur. *Passer domesticus domesticus* (Linnaeus). Has bred on Suðuroy since 1935–36, at Tórshavn since 1946, and has since settled at a number of villages. Previously a vagrant on Nólsoy (May 1900).

TREE SPARROW; skovspurv. *Passer montanus montanus* (Linnaeus). Small breeding colony at Sunnbøur, Suðuroy, in 1966. Formerly bred on Skúvoy (from 1866) and Sandoy (from 1872), vagrants reaching Tórshavn (bred 1888), Mykines (1901) and Kunoy (1906). This colonisation died out *c.* 1910. Since then it has occurred on Mykines (5 in summer 1934) and near Tórshavn (2 in July 1966).

Family FRINGILLIDAE.

CHAFFINCH; bogefinke; bókfinka. *Fringilla coelebs coelebs* Linnaeus. Regular passage migrant and winter visitor.

BRAMBLING; kvaekerfinke. *Fringilla montifringilla* Linnaeus. Bred at Tórshavn in 1967. Irregular passage migrant and winter visitor.

[SERIN. *Serinus canarius* (Linnaeus). Recorded by H. C. Müller (January 1858) but the record is considered doubtful (Salomonsen, 1935).]

HAWFINCH; karnebider. *Coccothraustes coccothraustes coccothraustes* (Linnaeus). Twice, Streymoy (July 1927 and November 1947).

GREENFINCH; grønirisk. *Chloris chloris chloris* (Linnaeus). Scarce and irregular winter visitor, September to April.

SISKIN; grønsisken. *Carduelis spinus* (Linnaeus). Once, Tórshavn (May 1953).

LINNET; tornirisk. *Acanthis cannabina cannabina* (Linnaeus). Once, Mykines (April 1904).

TWITE; bjergirisk. *Acanthis flavirostris flavirostris* (Linnaeus). A small colony was resident on Nólsoy from 1938–50 (Williamson, 1945, 1948). There are vagrant records from Mykines (winter 1903 and August 1962).

REDPOLL; gråsisken; reyðkollur. Has perhaps bred, pairs having been seen at Tórshavn (July 1960) and Sørvágur (August 1962). The Mealy Redpoll *Acanthis flammea flammea* (Linnaeus) is an irregular, occasionally common, winter visitor in "eruption" years. There is probably regular passage of the Greenland low-arctic form *Acanthis flammea rostrata* (Coues)—up to 12 were present on Nólsoy in April 1949—and the Greenland high-arctic form *Acanthis flammea hornemanni* (Holböll) has been taken on Kallsoy (April 1945).

COMMON CROSSBILL; lille korsnaeb; krossnev. *Loxia curvirostra curvirostra* Linnaeus. Sporadic late summer immigrant in "eruption" years.

WHITE-WINGED OR TWO-BARRED CROSSBILL; hvidvinget korsnaeb. *Loxia leucoptera bifasciata* (Brehm). Vagrant, 4, Suðuroy, Tórshavn and Mykines.

SCARLET GROSBEAK; karmindompap. *Carpodacus erythrinus erythrinus* (Pallas). Once, Nólsoy (September 1953).

BULLFINCH; dompapa. *Pyrrhula pyrrhula pyrrhula* (Linnaeus). Vagrant, 2, Mykines and Nólsoy, both in November.

Family EMBERIZIDAE

CORN BUNTING; bomlaerke. *Emberiza calandra calandra* Linnaeus. Once, Suðuroy (March 1897).

YELLOWHAMMER; gulspurv. *Emberiza citrinella citrinella* Linnaeus. Scarce and irregular winter and spring visitor, once 4 in summer.

RED-HEADED BUNTING; brunhovedet vaerling. *Emberiza bruniceps* Brandt. Twice, Vágar (July 1963) and Mykines (July 1967), possibly escapes.

ORTOLAN; hortulan. *Emberiza hortulana* Linnaeus. Vagrant, 4, Nólsoy (May and November).

REED BUNTING; rørspurv. *Emberiza schoeniclus schoeniclus* (Linnaeus). Vagrant, 6, Nólsoy, Mykines and Tórshavn, mostly April–May.

LAPLAND BUNTING; laplandsvaerling. *Calcarius lapponicus* subsp. Vagrant, 2, Mykines and Eysturoy.

SNOW BUNTING; snespurv; snjófuglur. *Plectrophenax nivalis nivalis* (Linnaeus). Formerly a not uncommon breeder, in the Norðuroyar especially, but its present status is obscure. Abundant passage migrant and winter visitor, occasionally seen in summer.

REFERENCES

ANDERSEN, C., *Faerøerne i Farver* (photographs by Leo Hansen), Copenhagen, 1958.

ANDERSEN, K., Meddelelser om Faerøernes fugl (from notes contributed by P. F. Petersen, Nólsoy, and S. Niclassen, Mykines), *Naturhist. Foren. Vidensk. Meddelelser i Kjøbénhavn,* 1899–1904.

BAERENTSEN, C. F., *Forslag og Betaenkningur opgivne af dens Faerøske Landbokkommission,* Copenhagen, 1911.

BAYES, J. C., DAWSON, M. J., JOENSEN, A. H. and POTTS, G. R., " The distribution and numbers of the Great Skua breeding in the Faeroes in 1961, " *D.O.F.T.,* 58: 36–41, 1964.

BAYES, J. C., DAWSON, M. J. and POTTS, G. R., " The food and feeding habits of the Great Skua in the Faeroes," *Bird Study,* 11: 272–279, 1964.

BONNEVIE, E. and MITENS, E., *Faerøsk Lovsamling 1599–1923,* Tórshavn, 1932.

BRØGGER, A. W., *Løgtingssøga Føroya,* Bd. 1, 36–45, Tórshavn, 1937.

BUCKLEY, T. A. and HARVIE-BROWN,.J. A., *A Vertebrate Fauna of the Orkney Islands,* Edinburgh, 1891.

CLARKE, W. E., " On some forms of *Mus musculus* Linn., with description of a new sub-species from the Faeroe Islands," *Proc. Roy. Physical Soc. Edinburgh,* 25, 1904.

CURWEN, E. C., " The problem of early water-mills," *Antiquity,* 19: 130–146, 1944.

DANJALSSON á RYGGI, M., *Midvinga Søga,* Tórshavn, 1940.

" List of Faeroese animal names," Part LXVI of *Zoology of the Faroes,* 3, pt. ii, Copenhagen, 1940.

DAHL, L., " Firvaldar i Føroyum " (Lepidoptera from the Faeroes), *Fródskaparrit,* 3: 128–154, 1954.

DARE, P. J., " Notes on birds seen in the Faeroe Islands in May and June 1965," *D.O.F.T.,* 60: 88–91, 1966.

DEBES, L., *Faeroae et Faeroa Reserata,* Copenhagen, 1673 (New ed., Tórshavn, 1903).

DEGERBØL, M., " Mammalia," Part LXV of *Zoology of the Faroes,* 3, pt. ii, 1–132, Copenhagen, 1940.

EDMONSTON, E., *Sketches and Tales of the Shetland Islands*, Edinburgh, 1856.

ELKJAER-HANSEN, N. and HERMANSEN, C., *The Faroe Islands* (Royal Danish Ministry of Foreign Affairs), Copenhagen, 1959.

ELLISON, N. F., "Eynhallow," *North-west. Nat.*, 19: 124, 1944.

EVANS, E. E., *Irish Heritage*, Dundalk, 1944.

EVANS, F. C. and VEVERS, H. G., "Notes on the biology of the Faeroe Mouse (*Mus musculus faeroensis*)," *J. Anim. Ecol.*, 7, 1938.

FEILBERG, C., Paper in *Botany of the Faeroes based upon Danish Investigations*, 3. London, 1908.

FEILDEN, H. W., "The birds of the Faeroe Islands," *Zoologist*, 2nd ser., 7: 3210, 3245, 3277, 1872.

"Ornithological notes from the Faeroe Islands," *Zoologist*, 3rd ser., 2: 153–155, 1878.

"On the reported occurrence of a Gare-fowl in the Faeroe Islands," *Zoologist*, 3rd ser., 2: 199–201, 1878.

"Introduction of the Ptarmigan into the Faeroe Islands," *Zoologist*, 3rd ser., 16: 413–414, 1892.

FERDINAND, L., "Studier af fuglelivet på Faerøerne" (Studies of the bird-life in the Faeroes), *D.O.F.T.*, 41: 1–37, 1947.

FISHER, J., *The Fulmar*, London, 1952.

FISHER, J. and VEVERS, H. G., "The breeding distribution, history and population of the North Atlantic Gannet," *J. Anim. Ecol.*, 12: 173–213; 13: 49–62, 1943.

FISHER, J. and WATERSTON, G., "The breeding distribution, history and population of the Fulmar in the British Isles," *J. Anim. Ecol.*, 10: 204–272, 1941.

GIBBS, R. G. and MAWBY, P. J., "Ornithological observations in the Faeroes, 1966," *D.O.F.T.*, 62: 137–140, 1968.

GORRIE, D., "Summers and winters in the Orkneys," in GUNN, J., *The Orkney Book*, Edinburgh, 1909.

GOUDIE, G., "On the horizontal water-mills of Shetland," *Proc. Soc. Antiquaries Scotland*, 20: 257–297, Edinburgh, 1886.

GREG, E. H., *A Narrative of the Cruise of the Yacht Maria among the Faeroe Islands in 1854*, London, 1855.

GUNN, J., *Orkney, the Magnetic North*, Edinburgh, 1932.

HAMMERSHAIMB, V. U., *Faerøsk Anthologi*, Copenhagen, 1891.

HARTERT, E., *Die Vogel der palaarktischen Fauna*, Berlin, 1910.

HARVIE-BROWN, J. A. and POPHAM, H. L., " Albatross at the Faeroe Isles," *Zoologist*, 3rd ser., 18: 337–338; 4th ser., 4: 324, 1894.

JACOBSEN, M. A. and MATRAS, C., *Foroysk-Donsk Ordabók*, Tórshavn, 1927–28.

JAKOBSEN, J., *Faerøsk Folkesagn og Aevintyr*, Copenhagen, 1898–1901.

JOENSEN, A. H., "Ynglefugle på Skúvoy, Faerøerne, deres udbredelse og antal " (The breeding birds of Skúvoy, their distribution and numbers), *D.O.F.T.*, 57: 1–18, 1963.
Fuglene pa Faerøerne, Copenhagen, 1966.

JONES, G. I., " Faeroe ships and boats," *Fanfaroe*, 4, Tórshavn, 1943.

JONSSON, S. and LINNMAN, N., *Faröarna—fåglar och fångster*, Stockholm, 1959.

KILERICH, A., " Geography, hydrography and climate of the Faeroes," Part I of *Zoology of the Faroes*, 1, pt. i, 1–51, Copenhagen, 1928.

LANDT, J., *A Description of the Feroe Islands*, London, 1810 (original ed. Copenhagen, 1800).

LEACH, E. P., Reports on " Recoveries of marked birds " in *Brit. Birds*, London, 1937–44.

MACGREGOR, A. A., *The Haunted Isles; or, Life in the Hebrides*, London, 1933.

MEGAW, B. R. S., " The harvest of the turbary," *J. Manx Mus.*, 4: 95–101, 1939.
" The fiery cross, and the Manx ' crosh vusta '," *J. Manx Mus.*, 5: 35–37, 1941.

MILLAIS, J. G., *The Mammals of Great Britain and Ireland*, 2 vols., London, 1906.

MÜLLER, H. C., " Faerøernes fuglefauna med bemaerkninger om fuglefangsten," *Naturhist. Foren. Vidensk. Meddelelser i Kjøbenhavn*, 1862 (separately published, Copenhagen, 1863).
" Whale-fishing in the Faeroe Isles " (reprint of a paper in English, source not stated), n.d.

MUNCH, P. A., *Chronicle of Man and the Sudreys*, Christiana, 1860 (republished by Manx Soc., 1874, Douglas).

NICLASEN, B. (Ed.), *The Fifth Viking Congress, Tórshavn, July 1965* (contains papers on Faeroese subjects), Tórshavn, 1968.

NICLASSEN, P., " Faeroe fisheries," *Dan. Foreign Office J.*, no. 196, 50–55, Copenhagen, 1937.

Føroya Addressubók, Tórshavn, 1938–39.

NØRLUND, N. E., *Faerøernes Kortlaegning*, Geodetisk Instituts Publicationer, 6, Copenhagen, 1944.

NØRREVANG, A., " Nogle ornithologiske iagttagelser fra Faerøerne " (Some ornithological observations from the Faeroes), *D.O.F.T.*, 44: 192–199, 1950.

" Skråpe og skråpefangst på Faeroerne " (Manx Shearwater fowling in the Faeroes), *D.O.F.T.*, 45: 96–101, 1951.

" S. F. Niclassens ornithologiske optegnelser fra Faerøerne," *D.O.F.T.*, 48: 150–155, 1954.

" Forandringer i den faerøske fugleverden i relation til klimaaendringen i der nordatlantiske område " (Changes in the Faeroese avifauna in relation to climatic change in the North Atlantic), *D.O.F.T.*, 49: 206–229, 1955.

" On the breeding biology of the Guillemot," *D.O.F.T.*, 52: 48–74, 1958.

" Søfuglenes udvaelgelse af ynglebiotop på Mykines, Faerøerne " (Habitat selection of seabirds on Mykines), *D.O.F.T.*, 54: 9–35, 1960.

OSTENFELD, C. H., " The land vegetation of the Faeroes," *Botany of the Faeroes based upon Danish Investigations*, 3, London, 1908.

PATON, C. I., " The calendar customs of the Isle of Man," *Folklore*, 51 and 52, 1940–41.

PATURSSON, S., *Fuglameingi er landsvirði*, Tórshavn, 1948.

PEDERSEN, A., *Fågelberg i Atlanten* (Mykines), Uppsala, 1954.

PETERSEN, E., " Nogle ornithologiske notitser fra Faerøerne," *D.O.F.T.*, 44: 121–126, 1950.

PETERSEN, I. and ASKANAR, T., " Tva veckors exkarsioner på Färöarna sommaran 1955 " (Two weeks' bird studies in the Faeroes in summer 1955), *Vår Fågelvärld*, 15: 182–187, 1956.

PETERSEN á BOTNI, N. F. and WILLIAMSON, K., " Polymorphism and breeding of the Rock Dove in the Faeroe Islands," *Ibis*, 91: 17–23, 1949.

PETERSEN, S., " En samling sjaeldne fugle fra Faeróerne " (Collection of rare birds from the Faeroes), *D.O.F.T.*, 43: 87–90, 1949.

" Gråspurven på Faerøerne," *D.O.F.T.*, 43: 166–167, 1949.

354   REFERENCES

POTTS, G. R., " Observations on birds in the Faeroes, 1960,"
D.O.F.T., 55: 152–160, 1961.

PRESS, M., *The Saga of the Faeroe Islanders*, London, 1934.

RASMUSSEN, R., " Lundasina: eitt merkiligt tilbrigdi av grassa-
slagnum *Festuca rubra*," *Vardin*, 8, Tórshavn, 1928.

SALOMONSEN, F., " Den Faerøiske ornithologis historie indtil aar
1800," *D.O.F.T.*, 28: 79–114; 29: 67–100, 1934–35.

" Aves," Part LXIV of *Zoology of the Faroes*, 3, pt. ii, 1–268,
1935 (also Supplement, pp. 6, 1942).

" The distribution of birds and the recent climatic change in
the North Atlantic area," *D.O.F.T.*, 43: 87–90, 1948.

" The food production in the sea and annual cycle of Faeroese
marine birds," *Oikos*, 6: 92–100, 1955.

" Systematisk oversigt over Nordens fugle," *Nordens Fugle i
Farver*, 7, Copenhagen, 1963.

SAYCE, R. U., Paper in *Folkliv*, 2, 3, 1939.

" Some recent trends in Swedish folk studies," *Folklore*, 54:
378–389, 1943.

av SKARDI, J., " Føroyski leypurin " (The Faeroese " leypur "),
Fródskaparrit, 4: 32–60; 5: 108–152, 1955–56.

SVABO, J. C., " Føroyaferðin, 1781–82" (extracts from original
MS. in Royal Library, Copenhagen, ed. by Mads Jacobsen,
Tórshavn, 1924).

TUDOR, J. R., *The Orkneys and Shetlands, their Past and Present State*,
London, 1883.

VEVERS, H. G. and EVANS, F. C., " A census of breeding Gannets
on Myggenaes Holm, Faeroes," *J. Anim. Ecol.*, 7: 298–302,
1938.

WALKER, F. and DAVIDSON, C. F., " A contribution to the
geology of the Faeroes," *Trans. Roy. Soc. Edinburgh*, 58, pt. iii,
869–897, 1935–36.

WARMING, E., Paper in *Botany of the Faeroes based upon Danish
Investigations*, London, 1908.

WEIHE, A., *Tjodminni*, Tórshavn, 1938.

WILLIAMSON, K., " The ' Puffins ' of the Calf Isle," *J. Manx
Mus.*, 4: 178–180, 203–205, 1940.

" Turf-cutting in the Faeroe Islands," *North-west. Nat.*, 17:
332–335, 1942.

" The economic importance of sea-fowl in the Faeroe Islands,"
Ibis, 87: 249–269, 1945.

" Some new and scarce breeding species in the Faeroe Islands,"
   Ibis, 87: 550–558, 1945.

" The economic and ethnological importance of the Caaing
   Whale in the Faeroe Islands," *North-west Nat.*, 20: 118–136,
   1945.

" The horizontal water-mills of the Faeroe Islands," *Antiquity*,
   20: 83–91, 1946.

" Birds in Faeroe folk-lore," *North-west Nat.*, 21: 7–19, 155–166,
   1946.

" Field-notes on the breeding biology of the Whimbrel,"
   North-west Nat., 22: 167–184, 1947.

" Field-notes on the nidification and distraction display of the
   Golden Plover," *Ibis*, 90: 90–98, 1948.

" Nesting of the Faeroe Snipe," *Brit. Birds*, 42: 394–395, 1949.

" The distraction behaviour of the Arctic Skua," *Ibis*, 91:
   307–313, 1949.

" Notes on the Caaing Whale," *Scott. Nat.*, 61: 68–72,
   1949.

" The distraction behaviour of the Faeroe Snipe," *Ibis*, 92:
   66–74; 93: 306, 1950.

" Regional variation in the distraction displays of the Oyster-
   catcher," *Ibis*, 94: 85–96, 1952.

" Beretning om nogle faerøske ynglefugle " (Report on some
   Faeroese breeding birds), *D.O.F.T.*, 48: 139–149, 1954.

" Spring migration (1953) in the Faeroe Islands," *D.O.F.T.*,
   48: 221–234, 1954.

WILLIAMSON, K. and BOYD, J. M., *A Mosaic of Islands*, Edinburgh,
   1963.

WILLIAMSON, K., and PETERSEN á BOTNI, N. F., " Recent occurrences of rare vagrants and passage migrants in the Faeroe
   Islands," *Ibis*, 87: 25–32, 1945.

" Notes on the occurrences and habits of some passage-migrants
   and rare vagrants in the Faeroe Islands," *Ibis*, 89: 105–117,
   1947.

" Notes on the ornithology of the Faeroe Islands, 1945–47,"
   D.O.F.T., 42: 202–215, 1948.

" Fugletraek pa Faerøerne i 1949 med notater fra Fair Isle til
   sammenligning " (Bird migration in the Faeroes in 1949,
   with comparative notes from Fair Isle), *D.O.F.T.*, 45:
   121–138, 1951.

WITHERBY, H. F., JOURDAIN, F. C. R., TICEHURST, N. F. and TUCKER, B. W., *The Handbook of British Birds*, 5 vols., London, 1938.

WOLFF, N. L., " Lepidoptera," Part XXXIX of *Zoology of the Faroes*, 2, pt. i, Copenhagen, 1937.

GLOSSARY OF FAEROESE WORDS USED IN THE BOOK

áarpisur : Fledgling Puffins which travel downstream to the sea from inland nesting-burrows.
adam og eva : The Spotted Orchis.
akurknívur : Reaping-hook.
akurskrift : The Corncrake.
álka : The Razorbill.
Annar Jóladagur : St. Stephen's Day, December 26th.
árarskeyti : That part of the oar which works against the *tollur.*
áttamannafar : Boat for 8 oarsmen.
áttingur : Eighth part of the village commonwealth (Mykines)

ballingar : " Lapped " swathes of grass laid to dry in the hayfield.
barkastokkur : Celebration on launching a new boat.
Bartolsmessa : First day of autumn, August 24th (St. Bartholomew).
bátsgildi : Party given by the owner of a boat for the crew.
beltisgyrði : " Belt " or " skirt " of slain Puffins carried by the fowler round his waist.
belti : " Belt " of rope securing a hayrick.
bendil (bendlar) : Rope twisted from hay.
bendlasneis : Small wooden instrument used in making hay-rope.
bládúgva : The Rock Dove.
blóðmørur, blóðpannukøka, blóðpylsa : " Black pudding " or pancake made from sheep's blood, tallow, etc.
bógvur : Shoulder of dried mutton or *skerpikjøt.*
bóndi : Farmer.
boráskeyti : Wooden " cushion " on the gunwale on which the oar moves.
botnur : Head of a fiord.
bramgás : The Barnacle Goose.
breiða (at breiða) : Turning grass with the rake in haymaking.
brenna krakk : Custom of burning the three-legged stool after turning down a suitor.
brennivín : " Aquavit " or brandy.
brúshøna : The Black-tailed Godwit.
brúðarvísa : Wedding ballad, accompanying the *dansuringur.*

357

bundi : Bundle of corn-sheaves.
bygd : Village.
byrða : A man's load of hay.
byrðarleypur : Wooden box used for carrying turves or potatoes.
bøkkar : Blocks of soil cut with the *haki* in tilling ground.
børkuvísa : Rhizomes of Tormentil.
bøur : Cultivated " infield " surrounding the village.

dagligstova : Best room or sitting-room in modern houses.
dalur : Valley.
dansuringur : Faeroese ring-dance.
dartari : Stick trailing on the upper millstone and shaking the corn out of the " shoe " in the horizontal mill.
desir : Hayrick.
desasneið : " Harvest-home " celebration following completion of the *des.*
draga lundar, dráttrar lundar : Puffins caught by drawing them from their burrows.
drunnhvíti : The Storm and Leach's Petrels.
drýlur : Bread baked from barley-flour.
dumbur : Chaff.
dylla : Wooden yoke, from which pails are suspended, carried by *neytakonur.*
døglingur : The Bottlenose Whale.
døgurði : Midday meal.

einmánaður : Third month of the old Faeroe calendar.
einnáttarsodnur : Corn of the first night's drying in the *sodnhús.*
eiði : Isthmus.
eldkast : A skin-disease.
erla kongsdóttir : The White Wagtail.
eyrgraelingur : The Sanderling.
eystan : East.
eystfall : Tide setting SE. in the fiords.

falkur : Falcon.
feigdarsvala : The Swift (" death swallow," a bird of ill-omen as it is in many countries).
feitilendi : " Fat land " covered with a rich growth of grass, as on the fowling-cliffs (see *lundasina).*
felagsogn : Owned by the community ; for division according to the worth of the holding.

fellingi : Outer track of lower millstone.

finningarfiskur : The biggest whale of a *grind,* presented to the finding-boat.

fiska gratin : Dish prepared from fish.

fiskaørn : The Osprey.

fjall (á fjall) : To go into the hills to work among the sheep.

fjallmurra : The Dunlin.

fjallstavur : Staff carried when going among the hills.

fjarðalás, fjarðaringur, fjarðaskot : Toys made from goose-feathers.

fjós : Byre.

Fjøruti Riddarar : ;" The Forty Knights," March 9th.

fláborð : One of the 6 strakes of a boat.

Flaggdagur : see *Markusarmessa.*

flaghaldi : Narrow plank at the eaves, supporting a sod thatch.

flagtak : Roof of grassy sods.

flagvelta or *fleygastong :* A type of cultivation.

flesjar : Low inshore rocks.

fleyg, fleygistong or *fleygastong :* The net, and the long handle to which it is affixed, used in bird-catching.

Fólkaflokkur : Political party with strong nationalist " home-rule " policy.

fótur : Lower part of haft of a spade ; " shoe " feeding corn to the quern in a horizontal mill.

fransaterna : The Black-headed Gull.

frikkadellir : Fish-cakes.

frýggjarastavur : Courting staff.

frælsi : Grazing right.

fuglabjørg : Bird-fowling cliffs.

Fuglakvæði : Mediaeval bird-ballad.

fulkobbi : Dovekie or Little Auk.

fygling : Catching Guillemots in the *fleyg* on the cliff-face.

fýramannafar : Boat for 4 oarsmen.

Fyrstifleygidagur : The first day for " fleyging " Puffins with the fowling-net (*fleyg*), July 2nd.

Føstu inn Gangur : First Monday in Lent.

garðarærsgildi : Celebration held in the Autumn.

gás (gæs) : Goose (geese).

geil : Cattle-way through the " infield."

gil : Small glen.

gjógv : Cleft or gorge in the hills or on the coast.

gjóðr : The Slavonian Grebe.

glasstova : Best room (sitting-room) in an old farmhouse.
gneggjus : The Common Gull.
Gomlu trettandi : The Thirteenth Day (old style calendar).
gorfuglur : The Garefowl or Great Auk.
grábøka : The Scaup-duck.
grágás : Grey-lag (and other species of " grey ") Goose.
grágrælingur : The Knot.
grannastevna : Annual meeting of landowners.
gráspurv : The House and Tree Sparrows.
grásúla : Gannet in juvenile plumage.
grátítlingur : The Rock and Meadow Pipits.
gravarferð : Burial.
grev : Iron blade of a spade.
grind : School of Caaing-whales ; meat of Caaing-whale.
grindaboð : Message that a *grind* has been located.
grindadistrikt : Political division for administrative purposes in
    connection with the distribution of whale-meat.
grindadráp : Slaugher of a school of Caaing-whales.
grindaformaður : Whaling-captain.
grindaglaða : Beacon lighted to transmit *grindaboð.*
grindahvalur : The Caaing-whale.
grindalokkur : Crane-fly or " daddy-long-legs."
grindapláss : Beach selected for the slaughter of a *grind.*
grindarakstur : Driving a school of Caaing-whales.
grindareiðskapur : Whaling implements and accessories.
grísarnir : " White horses " on the waves.
gróthús : Stone outhouse for storing turves, etc.
grótleypur : Special *leypur* for carrying building stones.
grotti : Hole in the centre of the nether-stone of a quern.
grúgva : Open hearth.
grunningshøvd : Cods' heads served as food.
grýla : A " fikt " in the form of a sheep with two legs, which
    lives in the hills (a " bogey-man ") ; also the children who
    dress up at *Føstu inn Gangur.*
grækarismessa : St. Gregory's feast-day, March 12th (*Tjaldurs-
    dagur*).
grønlandslundi : Large northern Puffin, *Fratercula a. arctica*
    (Linn.).
gyllin : A unit of land or produce valuation.
gø : Second month of the old Faeroese calendar.

hagi : Uncultivated " outfield " of valley, hill, cliffs, etc.

haki : Spade.

hálsareyði : The Red-necked Phalarope.

Halvarðsøka : Half-year's festival, May 15th.

hamar (hamrar) : Exposed edges of the lava-flows, forming rocky walls in the hill or cliff sides.

Handilsskúli : Commercial school.

hara : Hare.

Harra : Mr.

havgás : The Great Northern Diver.

havhestur : The Fulmar.

havskrápur : The Great Shearwater.

hegri : The Heron.

heimabeiti : " Home-field " about the houses.

heimahvonn or *hvonn :* Cultivated form of *Archangelica officinalis.*

heimapartur : Unit of whale-meat for general distribution.

hellufuglar : Sea-birds " fleyged " when flying at the foot of the cliffs.

helsingagás : The Brent Goose.

heystfiski : Autumn fishing-season.

hjallur : Small outhouse for drying meat and fish, etc.

hjaltakráka : The Rook (" Shetland crow ").

hólgasáta : Stack of *hólgar* or bundles of barley-straws.

hólgi (hólgar) : Bundle of barley-straws.

hornaklingra : Hoop made of rams' horns.

hoyggja : Haymaking.

hoyggjhús : Barn.

hoyríva : Hay-rake.

hoyrúgva : Loose cock of partly-made hay.

huldufólk : " Grey people " who live among the hills.

hundaland : Toadstools (*Agaricaceae*).

húskallur : " House-karl " or male servant.

hvalvákn : Whale-weapon or lance.

hvast : " Haf-name " for knife.

hvølpalás : Wooden lock.

høvuðkambur : The Ruff; a " bossy " person.

jarðarhvalur : " Ground-whale " paid to the landowners at a *grindapláss.*

jarðarkona : The Water-rail.

jarðarsipa : A lichen, *Peltigera canina* Linn., used medicinally.

Jóansøka : Festival of St. Joan, June 24th.

Jólaaftan : Christmas Eve.

Jóladagur : Christmas Day.

jólaseyður : A sheep fattened for the Christmas festivity.

jólatræ : Christmas-tree.

jólatrøll : Items of sewing, knitting, etc. unfinished by Christmas Eve.

kalvafiskur : The Halibut.

kast : White stone attached to a line, used for driving whales.

kattakongur : Winner of the barrel-breaking competition on the first Monday in Lent.

kattugla : The Long-eared and Short-eared Owls.

kenning : System of sheep-marking and ownership in Suðuroy.

keppur : A kind of sausage.

ketta : Cat (a kitten is *kettlingur*).

kjalarborð : Strake of a boat next to the keel.

kjallari : Basement of the house.

kjógv : Leg of mutton or lamb.

kjógvi : The Arctic Skua.

kjøtpylsa : Sausage made from minced meat and fish.

klárur : Instrument for pounding corn-field on completion of sowing.

klasseksdrongur : " Luggage-boy " applied to the Puffin.

kleppar : Implements for gaffing halibut and other large fish.

klibbari : Wooden crook-saddle from which *rossaleypar* are slung.

klíggjagrót : Stones, fastened to ropes, used in holding down a *sáta* or hayrick.

klinkubygdur : Clincher-built (boats).

klipfiskur : Cod-fish split and dried in the sun.

klipping : Slaughter of the ewes in autumn.

klokka : Clock ; time of day.

klóta : Kind of driftwood used in boat-building.

klúkur : Small mound of grass in the hayfield.

knettir : Dish made from fish and tallow.

knívur : Knife.

kola : Lamp burning seal or whale-oil.

kollur : " Sugar-loaf " hill.

kolont : The Scoter-duck.

komuna : Village council.

kongafuglur : The Goldcrest.

kongsbóndi : Farmer leasing crown land.

kópakona : The " Seal-wife " heroine of a folk-story.

kópur : Seal.

korkabreyð : Red dye produced from *Lecanora tartarea.*
kornfari : Inner track of lower millstone.
kornríva : Broad rake with double row of tines used in cornfield.
kornskurátíð : Corn harvest.
koyggja : Small cubicle, containing a bed, in the old farm-kitchen.
kráka : The Hooded Crow.
krákumáni : A short time.
krákuting : An assembly of crows ; also an assembly of gossips or politicians.
krakkur : Three-legged stool.
krikkont : The Teal.
krógv : A " clamp " of turves walled on two sides.
króna : A unit of money, value about one shilling.
Krossmessa : May 3rd.
krossmessuposi : Bag containing varied articles, such as the one in which servants carried their belongings in old days.
kúgv : Cow (a calf is *kálvur*).
kvarnkallur : Driving-shaft of a horizontal mill.
kvastur : Goose-wing brush.
kverkveggja : The Blackbird.
kvøldseta : Evening meeting in the *roykstova* for story-telling, singing ballads, etc.
kvørn : Quern.
kyllingar : Hand-cocks made in the hayfield.
Kyndilsmessa : Candlemas.
kyrnumjólksuppa : Soup made from fresh and sour milk mixed.

landnyrðingur : NE. point ; NE. wind.
landsynningur : SE. point ; SE. wind.
lerkur : Lark.
letivelta : Type of cultivation corresponding to " lazy-beds."
Leypársmessa : February 24th.
leypur : Wooden box carried on the back and supported by a head-band.
líggi : Scythe.
líkka : The Lesser Black-backed Gull.
Líradagur : August 24th, the day for taking young Shearwaters.
líri : Young Manx Shearwater.
lívflýggj : One of the 6 strakes of a boat.
Ljósamessa : Candlemas (" Festival of the Light ").
lógv : The Golden Plover.

lómur : The Red-throated Diver.

lomvigi : The Guillemot.

lundakrókur : Instrument used in drawing Puffins from their burrows.

lundaland : Area inhabited by colony of Puffins.

lundanavari : Special trowel for excavating nest-burrows for Puffins.

lundapísa : Young Puffin.

lundasina : Luxuriant growth of *Festuca* grasses in the bird-fowling cliffs.

lundi : The Puffin.

lutur : A mound of turves on the moor.

lúður : Bench in mill on which the quern is mounted.

lyftustong : Lever for raising or lowering upper millstone.

lættitræ : Handle of *lyftustong*.

lættikorn : Chaff which remains after winnowing corn.

Løgting : Parliament.

Mariumessa : March 25th.

Markusarmessa : Festival of St. Mark, April 25th. National Flag-day.

mási : Herring-gull (also *fiskimási*).

matarhvalur : Whale-meat set aside for free distribution at the *grindapláss*.

mellingi : Middle track of lower millstone.

metingarmenn : Officials who measure up and assess the value of whales.

Mikkjalsmessa : Festival of St. Michael, September 29th.

mylda (at mylda) : Treatment of cornfield after sowing.

millumáli : Afternoon tea.

mið : Fishing-ground

morgunmatur : Breakfast.

mortítlingur : The Wren.

munni : Partition wall in the *sodnhús*, containing *munnhella* or hearth.

mús : Mouse.

músabróðir : The Wren (" brother to the mouse ").

mylnuspæl : Horizontal wheel of a water-mill.

mýrisnípa : The Snipe.

møna : Apex of roof.

mørk (merkur) : Basic unit of land and property valuation.

mørur : Heart, liver and lungs of the sheep.

náti : Young Fulmar.
nátturði : Supper.
nes : Headland.
nevtollur : Tax formerly payable in beaks of Ravens and other predacious birds.
neyst : Boathouse.
neytakona : Milk-maid.
norðan : North.
nulvingar : Small bundles of grass in the hayfield.
nykur : A " fikt " in the shape of a horse, inhabiting lakes.
nœvur : Birch-bark used in roof construction.

ógvella : The Long-tailed Duck.
Olavsøka : Summer festival of St. Olaf, the great national holiday, July 28th-29th.
omanfleyg : Catching *hellufuglar* from a boat at the foot of the cliffs.
ompil : Nestling Gannet.
oyðisúla : immature, brown-and-white Gannet.
oyri : Unit of money, one hundredth part of a *króna*.
óðalsbóndi : Freeholder.
óðinshani : The Redwing, Fieldfare and Song-thrush.

Pálsmessa : Festival of St. Paul, January 25th.
partahvalur : Amount of whalemeat available for general distribution following a *grindadráp*.
pinnagrev : Part of the iron blade of a turf-spade.
pisa : Young sea-bird ; also a " dram."
prestakragi : White ruff-like collar worn by Lutheran clergyman.
prestaleypur : Special *leypur* used by the parson for carrying his books and vestments.
prestur : Parson.
próstur : Dean.
Pætursmessa : Festival of St. Peter ; first day of Spring, February 22nd.

ravnabøli : An untidy house (like a Raven's nest).
ravnur : The Raven.
Realskúlin : The High School.
reinavelta : Traditional type of cultivation in the old *bøur*.
remmuborð : One of the 6 strakes of a boat.
rennustokkur : Wooden trough leading water to mill-wheel.
reyðbreystingur : The Robin.

reyðskalli : The Redpoll.
rímin : Strake of a boat next to the gunwale.
ringdúgva : The Wood-pigeon.
ripa (at ripa) : Removing ears of barley from the straws, done with the aid of an iron comb or *ripari.*
rista (at rista) : Shaking out swathes of grass in haymaking.
rita : The Kittiwake.
rómastampur : Curds and whey.
rók (røkur) : Bird-catching place on the cliffs.
rókur : The Jackdaw.
rossaleypar : Large *leypar* carried by pony, fixed in position by equipment known as *rossatýggj.*
rotta : Rat.
rotuskógvar : Skin shoes.
roykstova : Combined kitchen and living-quarters in old farm-house.
rullupylsa : Dish made from the meat on a sheep's ribs.
rýpa : Ptarmigan or Grouse.
rystari : See *dartari.*
ræstur fiskur : Wind-dried fish.
ræst kjøt : Mutton after a few months of drying in the *hjallur ;* the basis of *ræst súpan,* a soup.

Sambandsflokkur : Political party supporting union with Denmark.
sáta : Tramp-cock made in the hayfield.
sátubørn : Hand-cocks made in the hayfield.
seiður : The Saithe or Coal-fish.
seksáringur : Boat for 12 oarsmen.
seksmannafar : Boat for 6 oarsmen.
septembersjúka : Illness contracted from *nátar,* young Fulmars.
setralundar : Puffins which sit about ashore on fine days.
seyðarhøvd : Sheep's heads.
seyðamaður : Shepherd.
seyður : A Sheep.
siggj : Tallowed hemp or wool for caulking seams of boats.
sigli : " Sile " in upper stone of quern.
sildafiski : Herring-fishery.
sildberi : Puffin carrying fish in its bill.
sildhøna : The Grey and Red-necked Phalaropes.
sjógrælingur : The Purple Sandpiper.
sjóhøna : The Coot.
skarvabøli : An untidy house (see *ravnabøli*).

skarvur : The Shag.

skaðahvalur : Whalemeat sold by auction to defray damages to boats.

skeinkjari : Man who goes among the wedding-guests offering them drink.

skerpikjøt : Mutton after several months drying in the wind—more advanced than *ræst kjøt.*

skinn : A unit of land and produce valuation.

skipstroyggja : Fisherman's jersey.

skrápur : The Manx Shearwater.

skúgvur : The Great Skua or Bonxie.

skurð : Slaughter of the rams in autumn.

sláa (at sláa) : Mowing (with a scythe).

slagborð : One of the 6 strakes of a boat.

slúsa : Sluice-gate.

smyril : The Merlin ; name of inter-island passenger steamer is s.s. *Smiril.*

snàra (at snara) : Method of trapping Guillemots, etc., at sea.

snjófuglur : The Snow-bunting.

snjóugla : The Snowy or Arctic Owl.

snúðurkriki : The Wryneck.

snældukjógvi : The Buffon's or Long-tailed Skua.

snøristól : Rope-making machine.

sóbil : Miller's goose-wing brush.

sodnhús : Kiln for drying barley (*sodnker, sodnspølir, sodnur* are various parts of it).

sókn : Parish.

sóknarongul : Iron hook used in whale-hunting.

spenniskógvar : Black shoes with silver buckles worn with the national dress.

sperra : Rafter.

sperðil : " Parson's nose " of the sheep, filled with tallow.

spik : Blubber of the Caaing-whale.

spísustova : Dining-room.

spógvi : The Whimbrel.

springari : A Dolphin.

spæla (at spæla) : Play.

stakkur : Long silk gown, often used as wedding-dress.

stari : The Starling.

stavnhetta : High double-peaked hat worn with national dress.

steinamosi : A moss, *Parmelia saxatilis* Linn., which gives a brown dye.

steinstólpa : The Wheatear.
stelkur : The Redshank.
stikkont : The Pintail.
stiltari : See *dartari*.
stýri : Steering-oar or rudder.
súla : The Gannet (adult) ; also a wooden holder for the fishing line.
súlukongur : The Black-browed Albatross.
summarfiski : June-July fishing season.
Summarmáladagur : First day of summer, April 14th.
sunnan : South.
súsonnuvísa : A ballad.
súðbygdur : Clincher-built (boats).
svala : The Swallow.
svanur : The Whooper and Mute Swans.
svartaspilla : A blackish blight which attacks potatoes.
svartbakur : The Greater Black-backed Gull.
svarthálsa : The Ringed Plover.
svíni : " Shoe " feeding corn to the quern of a mill (*Kvívík*).
Syftunsøka : St. Swithin's.
syftunsøkugras : Meadow Cat's-tail grass.
sýslumaður : Chief district officer.

tangspógvi : The Curlew.
tannhali : " Haf-name " of the Manx Shearwater.
tarakøstar : Seaweed middens.
teigur : Field in the old *bøur*.
teisti : The Tystie or Black Guillemot.
terna : The Arctic Tern.
ternusnertur : Cold, stormy weather at Halvarðsøka, May 15th.
teymaspjaldur : Implement for making fishing lines.
tíggjumannafar : Boat for 10 oars.
ting : A court or meeting for law-giving purposes.
tingakrossur : Sign sent among the people to summon meetings.
tjaldur : The Oyster-catcher.
tjaldursgraelingur : The Turnstone.
tjaldursont : The Shelduck.
Tollaksmessa : " Little Christmas Eve," December 23rd.
tollar : Flat wooden pegs in the gunwale of a boat, serving as rowlocks.
toppont : The Red-breasted Merganser.
torri : First month in the old Faeroe calendar.

torrafiski : February fishing season.
torskur : The Codfish.
torv : Block of peat or turf, cut with a special spade, *torvskeri*.
treskja (*treskjur*) : Bat used in threshing.
tríbekkur : Boat with two pairs of oars, also called *tristur*.
tróðr : Ties joining rafters.
trøð (*traðir*) : Newly-cultivated " intake " from the *hagi*.
trøll : Gnome.
trøllont : The Tufted Duck.
turkageykn : Barley given in payment to the woman attending the drying-kiln.
tvørvelta : A method of cultivation.
tøðleypur : The *leypur* for carrying manure.

urð : Rock debris at the foot of the cliffs.
útnyrðingur : NW. point ; NW. wind.
urtagarður : Small enclosure reclaimed from the moorland.
útróðrarskrín : Rectangular box for carrying fishing tackle and food.
útskift : Redistribution of holdings in the *bøur*.
útsynningur : SW. point ; SW. wind.

vaktarhald : Men appointed to watch over, and assist in the distribution of, whale-meat.
válgari : First 3 ribs of a sheep's carcase.
valmási : The Glaucous and Iceland Gulls.
várfiski : Spring fishing season.
vatiskolli : The Wren.
venda (*at venda*) : Turning *klúkar* in the hayfield.
vesa : " Haf-name " for smoke.
vestan : West.
vestfall : Tide setting NW. in the fiords.
vevlingur : Cord tied round the sleeve when digging for Puffins.
vevur : loom.
villdunna : The Mallard or Wild-duck.
vindskeið : Transverse planks on the roof holding the sod thatch in place.
vípa : The Lapwing or Peewit.

æða, *æðublikur* : The Eider duck and drake.
æðukongur : The King Eider.
økt : Eighth part of a day (1½ hours).
ørn : The Sea-eagle.

SUBJECT INDEX

(Page numbers in italics refer to line drawings reproduced in the text)

Abrahamsen, A., 127, 133, 145-6, 153-4, 168, 175, 182; J., 132
Acknowledgments, 7, 8, 304
Advent, 230
Agarics, 47
Airfield on Vágar, 187
Air Services, 314
Albatross, Black-browed, 135, 329, 352
Allodial ownership of land, 48-51, 53
Alpine plants, 42, 296
Althing, Icelandic, 245-6
Andersen, C., 350; K., 167, 329, 350
Angelica, 47, 129, 239
Angling, 262-3, 272-3
Auk, Great, 158, 327, 340, 351; Little, 340
Avocet, 336

Ball, R. D., 7
Ballad, Bird-, 40, 84, 164; Wedding-, 171
Banks, Mrs., 237
Baptists, 32
Barley crop, 45-6, 57, 68, 76, 223, 274, 296; drying kiln, 206-14, 207, 216, 224, 290; harvesting, 206-14; milling, see Watermills
Barns, 201-2, 201, 216, 274
Basalt rocks, 18, 190
Bat, Parti-coloured, 325.
Bayes, J. C. et al., 350
Beacons, 102
Beds, 27, 35, 148, 242

Bees, 273
Birds, Persecution of, 66, 123; Ringing of, 42, 132-3, 138-42, 153, 166, 173, 276; Systematic list of, 326-49
Bitterns, 330
Blackbird, 327, 347
Blackcap, 345
Bluethroat, Red-spotted, 346
Boat-building, 71-4, 291; -houses, 126, 216, 283; -ownership, 76; -parties, 72, 84; -races, 243-4
Boats, 70-4, 71-2, 114-5, 119, 283, 296, 352; equipment of, 77-8, 79, 82, 83, 104, 104-5; register of, 108-9; use of old, 64, 254
Bogbean, 47, 258, 268, 278
Bonnevie, E. and Mitens, E., 119, 350
Botany, 351, 353
Botni, Niels á, 68, 84, 147, 153-4, 161, 183, 228, 238, 254, 304, 332, 341. See Williamson, K.
Boyd, J. M. See Williamson, K.
Braddan, Saint, 20
Brambling, 348
Bread, Barley-, 148, 220, 228-9
Brestisson, Sigmund, 21, 52-3, 240-1, 245-6, 292
British occupation, 6, 24, 39, 60, 187
Broadcasting, 314
Brøgger, A. W., 20, 43, 350
Buckley, T. E. and Harvie-Brown, J. A., 119, 350

Bull, Regulations concerning, 194
Bullfinch, 348
Bullocks, 131, 176-7, 290
Buntings, 327, 349; Snow-, 38, 297, 327, 349
Burdens, Carrying, 58-60, 152-3, 173, 202, 354
Burials, 254-5
Buttercups, 46, 129
Butterflies. See Lepidoptera
Buttermilk, 239
Butterwort, 41
Buzzards, 334
Bærentsen, C. F., 69, 350

Campion, Moss, 41; Red, 129
Candlemas, 236
Carrots, 34, 45, 274
Carts, 59, 275
Cat, 84, 246-7
Catholics, Roman, 32, 53
Cattle, 28, 45, 51, 189, 256, 290, 296, 313; fodder, 45, 75, 203, 209, 211; milking, 172-3, 274-5; regulations concerning, 193-5, 274
Caves on Nolsoy, 301
Celebrations connected with farming, 196, 202-3; fishing, 82, 84; fowling, 130, 162-3; whaling, 101, 106. See Festivals
Cellar, 28
Chaffinch, 348
Character, Faeroese, 5-6, 23, 35, 78-80, 115, 127, 166-7, 204, 231, 261, 282-6, 298
Chess, 32
Chickweed, 45, 130
Chiffchaff, 345
Children's games, 246-50, 250;

pets, 161, 173-4, 265; training, 285-6, 288-9
Christenings, 251-2
Christian IV of Denmark, 22
Christianity, introduction of, 21, 52, 241, 245
Christmas, 84, 126, 155; fare, 82, 232; festivities, 230-3, 248
Churches, 205, 216, 261, 307
Clarke, W. E., 322, 324, 350
Climate, 19, 322, 353-4
Clothing, 27, 230. See Dress
Clover, 46-7, 273
Coal, 18, 60, 190-1, 193
Cod-fishing, 76, 80, 88, 273, 290, 312; -liver, 80. See Klipfisk
Compass points, 84-6
Convent, 32-3
Coot, 335
Cormorant, 148, 162, 327, 330
Corn. See Barley
Councils, Village, 51, 109, 311, 314
Courtship customs, 253-4; stories, 137, 292-3
Cow, 28, 84, 204. See Cattle
Crakes, 335
Crane, 335
Craneflies, 114, 228, 256
Cranesbill, 46-7
Cross, Fiery, 102-3, 352
Crossbills, 348
Crosswort, 47
Crow, Hooded, 41, 66-7, 128, 174, 176, 236, 344
Cuckoo, 341
Cultivation, 22, 44-6, 49, 54-8, 55, 194. See Barley, Grass, Hay, Potatoes
Cultural Foundation of the Faeroese Løgting, 8

AA*

Curlew, 173, 337
Currency, 308
Curwen, E. C., 221-2, 229, 350
Customs, 248-55, 282-6; Calendar, 84, 230-3, 353; Fowling, 130, 149-53, 163

Dahl, J., 32; L., 350
Dance, Ring-, 101, 106, 170-1, 231, 244, 255
Danjalsson, Mikkjal á Ryggi, 67, 69, 227, 350
Dansk-Færøsk Kulturfond, 8
Dansk Ornithologisk Forening, 327
Dare, P. J., 350
Davidsen, D., 273, 277
Davidson, C. F. See Walker, F.
Dawson, M. J., 350
Day, Working, 64, 87
Debes, L., 66, 69, 222, 229, 350
Degerbøl, M., 94, 119, 322, 324, 350
Dew, 238
Dialects, 301-2
Dicuil, 20
Dipper, 344
Diver, Red-throated, 68, 255, 258-9, 267, 269, 328, others; 328
Djurhuus, H. A., 228, 232, 302
Dog, 43, 46; -days, 239
Dolphins, 93, 325
Dotterel, 268, 336
Doves, Rock, 68, 303, 340-1, 353
Dress, National, 114, 243; Wedding, 169
Driftwood, 72, 136
Drying-sheds, 29, 126, 275, 299, 300

Duck, Long-tailed, 278, 333; Scaup, 258, 278, 332; Tufted, 258, 278, 332; others, 332-3. See Eider, Mallard, Merganser, Pintail, Scoter, Teal, Wigeon
Dunes, Sand-, 270, 273
Dunlin, 328, 337
Dunnock, 344
Dyes from plants, 46-7

Eagle, White-tailed, 66, 122-3, 327, 334
Edmonston, Eliza, 103, 116-9, 351
Education, 24, 33, 308, 316, 319. See Schools
Eggs, Easter, 129; Seabirds', 139, 146, 148, 152, 161; Superstitions concerning, 84, 236, 238
Eider, Faeroe, 41, 84, 259, 303, 327, 333; King, 84, 333
Eiderdown, 148, 162
Electricity, 305, 314-5
Elkjær-Hansen, N. and Hermanson, C., 351
Ellison, N. F., 324, 351
Emigration to Denmark, 24, 318-9
Employment, 317, 319
Evans, E. E., 50, 64, 69, 201, 205, 351; F. C. and Vevers, H. G., 323, 351
Eyebright, 46

Faeroe Saga, 20-1, 52-3, 240-1, 292, 354
Fairies, 248-9
Falcons, 334
Farmers, 48-51
Feathers, 148

Feilberg, C., 46, 69, 351
Feilden, H. W., 69, 158, 167, 325, 351
Ferdinand, L., 351
Festivals, Candlemas, 236-7; Christmas, 230-3; Easter, 129; Flag-day, 240; Gannet-welcoming, 130; Harvest-home, 202-3; Joansøka, 237, 239-40; Lent, 246-8; miscellaneous, 40, 68, 76, 233, 237-40; New Year, 232-3; Olavsøka, 240-6; Shearwater hunt, 162-3, 238
Fieldfare, 347
Fields, 54-6. See Cultivation
Finance and investment, 311, 315, 320
Finsen, Niels, 31
Fjords, 18, 35, 37, 45, 260
Firecrest, 345
Fisher, J., 351; and Vevers, H. G., 164, 167, 351; and Waterston, G., 147, 167, 304, 351
Fishing banks, 78; fleet, 87, 89-90, 310-1; industry, 19, 24, 44, 87-90, 305, 310-3, 317-8; limits, 312; lines, 77, 79; methods, 74-5, 77-8, 88, 311; perils, 78, 89, 114-5, 129, 297; seasons, 76, 312; superstitions, 83-4, 249
Flag, Faeroe, 240, 308
Flies, 42, 82, 114, 128, 130, 256
Flycatchers, 346
Fodder, 45, 197, 203, 209, 211
Food, 6, 239, 265, 286; Christmas, 232-3; Wind-dried, 29, 45, 75, 166, 229; from birds, 68, 143-8; from fish, 75, 80-3; from sheep, 29-30, 286-7;

from whales, 94, 96, 113; from wild plants, 47, 129, 239. See Bread, Meals
Football, 32-3, 245-6, 273
Footwear, 27, 47, 243
Forget-me-not, 33, 129
Fowling, 19, 28, 44, 51, 77, 96, 130, 133, 143-67; cliffs, 19, 130, 143-4, 160, 176, 263-4; customs, 130, 151, 155, 162-3, 166; implements, 149-52, 150, 155, 157, 163, 290; rights, 157, 163, 178-80; social aspects of, 130, 144-5, 162-3, 166-7
Fowls, Domestic, 27-8
Fraser, C. I., 7
Frederick II of Denmark, 22
Frode, Legend of, 189-91
Fulmar, 125, 130, 133, 144, 159-60, 174, 176, 263-4, 304, 329, 351; fowling, 147, 159, 180

Gannet, 126, 131-2, 135, 137, 148, 185, 329, 330, 351, 354; folklore, 130, 137; fowling, 132-3, 144, 147, 164-7, 178-9; ringing, 132-3, 166
Gardens, 34, 47
Geese, Domestic, 195, 220; Grey-lag, 124, 137, 327, 331; others, 327, 331
Geil, Poul í, 226
Geology, 18-19, 190, 260, 300-1
German occupation of Denmark, 6, 24, 79, 240
Gibbs, R. G. and Mawby, P. J., 351
Godwits, 337
Goldcrest, 345
Goldeneyes, 333

Gorrie, D., 117, 119, 351
Goudie, G., 220-1, 229, 351
Grass, 45, 57, 130, 237, 274, 276; Marram, 273. See Hay
Grebes, 328; Slavonian, 248, 328
Greenshank, 337
Greenfinch, 348
Greg, E. H., 351
Grosbeak, Scarlet, 348
Grouse, Red and Black, 334-5
Guillemots, 340; Faeroe, 138-9, 144, 146, 148, 154, 156-9, 233-4, 304, 327, 340, 353. See Tystie
Gulls, 68, 161, 176, 183, 339; Black-headed and Common, 257-8; Glaucous, 36, 161; Great Blackbacked, 66, 161, 174, 257; Herring, 125, 161, 257, 325; Lesser Blackbacked 41, 126, 173, 257, 267-9, 323, 328, 339
Gunn, J., 117, 119, 351
Gaesa of Kirkjubøur, 124
Gøtu, Trondur í, 21, 32, 52, 241

Haakon, Hertug, 22
Haarfager, King Harald, 20
Haddock fishing, 76, 81, 312
Haf names, 84
Halibut fishing, 76, 82, 83, 88
Hammer, Emil and Olaus, 208, 213
Hammershaimb, V. U., 32, 167, 302, 351
Handball, 245, 274
Hansen, Dr. S., 156; Hans Pauli, 171-2, 182-3; Jógvan, 297; Leo, 8, 350
Harbours, 272, 314

Hares, 38, 42, 148, 265, 322, 325
Harriers, 334
Harrows, 208
Hartert, E., 351
Harvest-home, 202-4
Harvie-Brown, J. A. and Popham, H. L., 142, 352. See Buckley, T. E.
Hawfinch, 348
Hawkbit, 129
Hay and haymaking, 45-6, 51, 54, 77, 160, 162, 197-205, 239, 274, 290, 295
Heinason, M., 22
Hemp-nettle, 45
Herbs, 46-8, 237-8
Herons, 84, 330
Herring fishery, 312-3
History of the Faeroes, 18-24
Honeysuckle, 47
Hoopoe, 243
Horse, River, 249
Hospitality, 6, 31, 242, 265, 282, 284-6, 293
Hospitals, 32, 254, 315-6
Houses, 25, 26-8, 167, 284, 288, 299, 301

Ibis, Glossy, 331
Ibsen, M., 93
Ice Age, 19
Iris, Yellow, 33
Isholm, E., 226

Jacobsen, M. A. and Matras, C., 7, 114, 119, 212, 229, 352; Mads, 354; N., 228, 254
Jackdaws, 344
Jakobsen, Dr. J., 32, 233, 255, 302, 352
James II of Scotland, 301

Jensen, D. J., 208; O. J., 76
Joansøka, 84, 237, 239-40
Joensen, A. H., 8, 326, 350, 352
Jones, G. I., 352
Jonsson, S. and Linnman, N., 352

Kamban, Grim, 20
Kallsberg, E., 8, 305-21
Kelly, F. C., 116
Kestrel, 334
Kilerich, A., 43, 352
Kingcup, 256, 279
Kitchen, Farmhouse, 25, 27, 230
Kittiwake, 125-6, 133, 144-5, 159, 171, 173, 185, 264, 304, 339; bathing, 64, 121, 133, 140, 161, 173, 262-3; colonies, 127, 129, 130-1, 138-40; folklore, 138, 161, 174; fowling, 77, 148, 161, 180; migration, 138-42
Klipfisk, 87, 88-9, 310, 312-3
Knife superstitions, 84, 234
Knitting, 43, 230-1, 255
Knot, 291, 337
Kunoy, C., 295, 297

Land, Ownership of, 48-54, 274, 297; taxation, 54; tenure, 44, 48-51, 197; valuation, 52-4. See Cultivation, Fields
Landing-places, 109, 126, 174-5, 283, 291, 295, 299
Landsstýri, 307-10
Landt, Rev. J., 22-3, 46-8, 57-9, 67, 69, 78, 84, 94, 148, 157-8, 161, 167, 178, 188, 206-9, 212-3, 223, 229, 237, 255, 259, 272, 274, 279, 290, 298-9, 301, 304, 323, 326, 352

Language, Faeroe, 23-4, 32, 302, 308, 316; Icelandic, 302; Norn, 32
Lapwing, 40, 276-7, 279, 336
Laws concerning fowling, 156-8 160, 179-80; geese, 195; inheritance of land, 48, 51; persecution of harmful birds, 66, 128; whale-killing, 104, 106-12
Lazy-beds, 57
Leach, Miss E. P., 142, 352
Legends concerning eiderdown, 162; fairies, 248-9; Frode, 189-91; ghosts, 234; Koltur, 291-3; Mykines, 135-7; Nolsoy, 301; 'seal-wife,' 234-5; stones, 248, 294-5
Lent, 246-8
Lepidoptera, 42, 350, 356
Library, 32
Lichens, 46
Lighthouses, 58, 130, 294
Lighting appliances, 47, 136, 184, 213, 226, 232-3, 238, 288
Lights, Northern, 303
Linklater, E., 7, 13-16
Linnet, 348
Liver, Cod-, 80; -fluke, 195; Sheep-, 195; Saithe-, 229; Whale-, 99-100
Locks, Wooden, 64, 300
Loom, 27, 28
Luther, Martin, 32, 80
Lutheran Church, 32
Løgting, 21, 52, 67, 104, 108, 110, 156-7, 188, 244-6, 277, 295, 307-10

MacGregor, A. A., 117, 119, 352

Mail deliveries, 5, 38, 121, 126, 188, 260-1

Mallard, 277, 233

Mammals, Faeroese, 322-5, 350

Manners, 282-3, 285-6

Manure, 56-8, 114, 118, 135, 178, 254, 272

Maps, early, 112; of Mykines, *134*

Margaret, Princess of Scotland, 301

Marigold, Marsh, 256, 279

Marriage superstitions, 169-70, 236-7

Martins, 342

Matras, C. See Jacobsen, M. A.

May Day, 236, 238

Mayweed, 213

Mawby, P. J. See Gibbs, R. G.

Meadowsweet, 47

Meals, 30-1, 81; folklore concerning, 84, 229

Medical services, 32, 254, 289, 315-6

Megaw, B. R. S., 69, 119, 352

Merganser, Red-breasted, 64, 277, 333

Merlin, 68, 334

Michelsen, P., 92

Milk-maids, 172-3, 274; -puddings, 239

Mill. See Watermill

Millais, J. G., 95, 116-9, 352

Mitens, E. See Bonnevie, E.

Monopoly, Danish Crown trade, 23, 73, 87

Monument to Mykines fishermen, 129; to Niels Finsen, 31

Moorhen, 335

Mosses, 40, 42, 46-7, 130, 133, 260

Mouse, House, 322-4, 350-1

Müller, H. C., 112, 115, 119, 348, 352

Munch, P. A., 20, 43, 352

Museums, 32, 135, 309

Mutton, 313; special dishes, 29-30, 239; wind-dried, 29-31, 166, 238, 247, 275, 286-7, 290, 293

Mykines, Joensen, 254

Names, Christian, 251; " Faeroe," 20; Faeroese and Danish bird-, 148, 267, 328-49; Faeroese mammal-, 324-5, 350; haf, 84; mill,-228; street-, 31-2, 226

Navy, Royal, 23, 35

New Year, 232-3

Niclassen, B., 352; P., 43, 69, 94, 204, 279, 353; S. F., 350, 353

Niclassens of Koltur, 283-8, 290

Nielsen, J., 132, 147, 154, 168, 184

Nighthawk, 341

Nightjar, 341

Nørlund, N. E., 119, 353

Nørrevang, A., 353

Occupation by British Forces, 6, 24, 39, 60, 87; of Denmark by German Forces, 6, 24, 79, 240

Olav I and II of Norway, 240-1

Olavsøka, 193, 198, 240-6

Olsens of Kvalvik, 265-6, 270

Omen-seeking rites, 236-7

Orchid, Heath Spotted, 46

Oriole, Golden, 343

Ornithology, British Trust for, 132

Orthography, 7
Osprey, 333
Ostenfeld, C. H., 69, 353
Ousel, Ring, 347
Owls, 341
Oystercatcher, 34, 39-43, 128, 173, 176, 256-7, 269, 279, 281, 336, 355

Pállson, Páll, 39
Parson, 56, 58, 84, 110, 115, 118; visiting islands, 168-9, 252-3, 289
Paton, C. I., 236-7, 248, 255, 353
Patronymics, 251
Patursson, Sverri, 68, 148, 280, 353
Peat. See Turf
Peace of Kiel, 306
Penal settlement, 191
Pennywort, Marsh, 195
Petersen, E., 353; I. and Askanar, T., 353; Niels, F., see Botni, Niels á; P. F., 350; S., 334-5, 353
Petrel, Leach's, 180-5, 329; Stormy, 166, 180-5, 303, 329
Pets, 161, 173-4, 265
Phalarope, Grey, 84, 338; Red-necked, 267-70, 278-9, 338
Pheasant, 335
Photographs, Family, 284-5
Pintail, 257-8, 272, 332
Pipit, Meadow, 34, 41, 43, 68, 257, 279, 343; Red-throated, 343; Rock, 41, 58, 328, 343
Pirates, 72, 102
Plantations, 33, 43, 260, 296, 327
Plough, 51, 56
Plover, Golden, 34, 39, 42, 269,

279, 328, 355; other species, 328, 336
Police Force, 23, 226, 307
Politics, 23, 40, 306-10
Pondweed, 195
Ponies, 59, 152, 176, 245, 275
Poor, Provision for, 51, 110
Popham, H. L. See Harvie-Brown, J. A.
Population growth, 19, 106, 111, 318-20
Potatoes, 34, 45-6, 56-7, 68, 223, 274, 313
Pottery, 290-1
Potts, G. R., 350, 354
Press, M., 21, 43, 69, 255, 354
Privateers, 72, 102
Psittacosis in Fulmars, 160
Ptarmigan, 297, 327, 334, 351
Puffin, 84, 125, 133, 143, 153-5, 159, 164, 175-6, 238, 263-4, 303, 323, 328, 340; colonies, 127-31, 133, 151-3; fowling, 145, 149-56, 178-9, 183, 296; folklore, 151, 153-6

Quail, 335
Quern, 219-20; Hand, 221-3, 290

Radio-telephone, 130, 271-2
Rails, 335
Rainfall, 19
Rams on Mykines, 130
Rankin, Dr. M. N. and D. H., 142
Rasmussen, Dr. 160; Rasmus, 40, 225, 252, 296, 302, 354
Rats, 164, 296, 323-4
Rattle, Yellow, 129
Raven, 64-6, 128, 174, 176, 327, 344

Razorbill, 146, 148, 154-9, 340
Redpolls, 348
Redshank, 257, 275-7, 279, 337
Redstarts, 346
Redwing, 347
Reformation and land-tenure, 53
Rein, Hansina, 40, 248, 251; Niels, 58, 72, 82, 229
Religion, 32
Resident High Commissioner, 118, 308
Rhubarb, 34, 146, 274, 285
Ribwort, 237
Rigsdag, 23, 308-9
Ritchie, J., 325
Ring Ousel, 347
Roads, 51-2, 60, 109, 272, 314, 320
Robertson, D. J., 307, 324
Robin, 327, 346; Ragged, 46
Roller, 342
Roman Catholicism, 32
Roof construction, 64, 216-7
Rook, 66-7, 344
Root-crops, 34, 45, 274
Rope, Hay-, 77-8, 77, 200-2
Round-valleys, 260, 293-4
Royal Danish Ministry of Foreign Affairs, 8
Ruff and Reeve, 337
Rush-lights, 37

Saga, Faeroe, 21, 52, 240-1, 292, 354; Icelandic, 20
Saithe, 81, 229; fishing, 74-6, 290
Salomonsen, F., 167, 180, 188, 258, 279, 297, 304, 326, 329, 344, 254
Salvation Army, 32
Sanatorium, 33

Sanderling, 337
Sandpipers, Purple, 297, 327, 337; others, 337
Sand-dunes, 270, 273; -grouse, 340
Saxifrage, 42
Sayce, R. U., 200, 205, 255, 354
Scabious, Devil's-bit, 47, 293
Schools, 33, 51-2, 289, 296, 308, 316, 319
Scoters, 278, 333
Scott, Sir Walter, 221
Scouting movement, 32, 244
Scythes, 58, 198, 208
Seals, 84, 234-5, 288, 303, 325
Seaweed, 57-8, 84, 178, 238, 272
Sedge, Cotton, 47, 173
Self-Government Act, 307-10, 320
Serin, 348
Servants, 76, 230, 238-9
Shag, 148, 162, 174, 180, 303, 330
Shearwater, Manx, 84, 144, 181, 185, 296, 303, 329, 353; folklore, 84, 163, 239; fowling, 148, 162-3, 290; others, 329
Sheep, 19-20, 22, 42, 45, 51, 65-6, 84, 122, 174, 188, 195-8, 239, 275, 298, 303, 313; ownership of, 178-9, 192-3; slaughter of, 29, 178-9, 232, 238; wild, 191
Ship-building, 70-4, 87, 314
Shipwreck, 254
Shipwrights, 73-4
Shrikes, 343
Sileage, 197-8
Silverweed, 47
Siskin, 348

Sivertson, Sofus, 132-3, 139, 166, 175, 181-2

Skardi, Jóanes av, 247, 253, 282, 297-8, 354; Símun av, 298

Skins, Tanning, 47

Skua, Arctic, 41, 125, 155, 173, 262-3, 267, 278, 338, 355; Great, 161-2, 263-4, 338, 350; others, 338

Skylark, 342

Skaelingi, Hanus á, 228

Snowfalls, 19, 239, 298

Snipe, Faeroe, 34, 39, 42, 68, 256, 269, 279, 328, 338, 355; others, 338

Social organisations, 32, 244, 274; security, 315-6

Sorrel, 46-7, 129

Soups, 30

Spades, 56, 61-2, *61*

Sparrows, 347, 353

Sparrowhawk, 334

Spearwort, Lesser, 296

Spoonbill, 330

Sports festivals, 240, 243-5; ground, 33; organisations, 32, 244

Springs, 237, 288

Starling, Faeroe, 41, 68, 128, 176, 327, 344; others, 68, 344

Stint, Little, 337

Stonechat, 346

Stool, Three-legged, 253-4

Strawberries, 274

Sturlassen, Snorre, 21, 67

Summarmáladagur, 155, 193, 238-9

Sunday observance, 67, 83, 118, 204, 229, 251, 289

Superstitions concerning eggs, 84, 236, 238; farming, 65-9,

292; fishing, 83-4, 249; house building, 307; knives, 84, 234; marriage, 169-70, 236-7; seaweed, 84, 238; whaling, 114-5, 135

Svabo, J. C., 32, 158, 167, 222, 229, 326, 328, 354

Swallow, 141, 342

Swans, 255, 277, 327, 331

Swift, 342

Swithun's Day, 237, 239

Sýslumaður, 61, 107-8, 192

Tanning, 47

Tax on harmful birds, 66, 123; land, 54; whales, 104, 110

Taxes, 308

Teal, 278, 332

Telephone service, 102, 260, 271-2, 282

Tenure of land, 44, 48-51, 197; of mill, 228

Tern, Arctic, 68, 121, 125, 128, 131, 140-1, 148, 174, 185, 259, 262, 340; others, 339-40

Theatre, 32

Thor, 32

Thrushes, 347

Tides, 86, 293

Time of day, 85-7

Tithes, 110, 148

Tormentil, 47

Tórur and Oli legend, 136

Tourist accommodation, 31, 188

Toys, 250, *250*

Trade, Danish Crown monopoly, 23, 73, 246; in early times, 21, 67; with Britain, 24, 31, 89, 312; with Denmark, 31, 148; with Mediterranean countries, 88, 312-13

Transport and travel, 58-60, 64, 152, 175, 185-8, 259-60, 272, 281-2, 308, 314

Trondur í Gøtu, 21, 32, 52, 241

Trout, Sea-, 262-3, 272-3

Tudor, J. R., 116-9, 354

Turf and turf-cutting, 19, 51, 58, 60-5, 69, 76, 173, 178, 193, 227-8, 288, 290, 298

Turnstone, 43, 291, 336

Twite, 348

Tynwald, Manx, 245-6

Tystie, 125, 131, 303, 327, 340

Vaurie, C., 326

Vevers, H. G. and Evans, F. C., 167, 354. See Fisher, J.

Vikings, 19-20, 37, 71, 74, 85, 102, 189, 191, 221-2, 282-3

Villages, Deserted, 296-7; Sites of, 37, 45

Wagtail, White, 41, 43, 67, 343; others, 343

Wahl, Mogens, 8

Walker, F. and Davidson, C. F., 43, 205, 330

Warblers, 327, 345

War losses to fishing fleet, 89

Warming, E., 69, 354

Watch-houses, 22

Watermills, Horizontal, 214-5, 217-28, 218, 224, 274, 294, 296

Waterston, G. See Fisher, J.

Waxwing, 344

Weather lore, 67-8, 115, 151-2, 154, 239

Wedding, 168-72; stories, 252

Weihe, A., 94, 122, 142, 163, 167, 205, 230, 238-9, 247, 255, 354

Whale, Bottlenose, 93, 136, 325; Caaing or Pilot, 94-119, 220, 313, 325; meat, 58, 81, 91, 94, 107-13, 117; offal, 57, 114, 118; oil, 94, 112-3; other species, 91-2, 325

Whaling, 5, 28, 44, 93-119, 298, 313; Commercial, 91-3; districts, 111-2; folklore, 114-5; implements, 98-9, 103-5, 104, 105, 114, 118

Wheatear, 34, 41, 43, 114, 173, 238, 256, 279, 328, 346

Whimbrel, 34, 41-3, 64, 170, 256, 279, 338, 355

Whinchat, 346

Whitethroats, 345

Wigeon, 258, 332.

Williamson, K., 43, 69, 119, 167, 188, 229, 279, 304, 334, 336, 341, 348, 353, 354-5; and Petersen á Botni, N. F., 355

Winds, 85

Witherby, H. F. et al, 356

Wolff, N. L., 356

Woodcock, 338

Woodlark, 343

Woodpecker, Great Spotted, 342

Woodpigeon, 341

Wool, 21, 178-9, 195-6

Wormius, Olaus, 158

Wren, Faeroe, 41, 68, 129, 306, 310, 316, 323, 327, 344; St Kilda, 323

Wryneck, 342

Yellowhammer, 349

INDEX TO PLACE NAMES

(Page numbers in italics refer to line drawings reproduced in the text.
Page numbers in bold refer to photographs—pages facing.)

Aberdeen, 79, 89
Antrim, Co., 18, 142
Argir, 46, 51, 77, 102, 301
Árnafjall (Mykines), 175 ;
   (Vágar), 123, 175

Bear Island, 88
Blankskála, 298
Bólið, 134-5, 165-6
Borgardalur, 134, 136, 175,
   178-9
Borðoy, 17, 112, 157, 297-8
Brandansvík, 20
Britain, 87-90, 95, 103, 192,
   201, 221, 266, 272, 310
Bøur (Streymoy), 51 ; (Vágar),
   201, 215 ; mill, 223-4, 224

Copenhagen, 24, 79, 289, 309

Dalið (Mykines), 127-30, 179,
   181-5, 303
Dalur, 272
Denmark, 6, 21, 59, 114, 148,
   231, 272 ; Faeroese in, 24 ;
   influence in Faeroes, 23, 246,
   249 ; relations with Faeroes,
   23-4, 33, 88, 225 ; return of
   Faeroese from, 79-80
Dímunar, 39, 52, 93, 156, 175,
   273. See also Stóra and Lítla
   Dímun
Dúgvugarður (Saksun), 25, 215

Egilsfjall, 268
Eiði, 22, 111, 259, 261-3 ;
   church, 261 ; mill, 223 ;
   turf-cutting, 63
Eiðisvatn, 249, 262

Eynhallow (Orkney), 324
Eysturoy, 17, 35-7, 86, 111-2,
   225, 261, 277 ; roads, 60, 63

Fámjin, 60, 112, 190, 208, 213
Fjallavatn, 41, 263, 275, 278
Flatidrangur, 126, 133, 164-5,
   179
Froðiarbotnur, 192
Froðiarnípa, 189, 191
Froðbøur, 45, 60, 189-95 ; hay-
   making, 198-200, 203-4 ;
   land, 50, 52, 177, 192-5 ;
   mills, 214, 217-20, 223
Fuglafjørður, 17, 20, 60, 237
Fugloy, 17, 111, 158, 242, 246,
   252-3, 323-4
Fútaklettur, 60, 177, 186-7
Gásadalur, 45, 123, 136, 175
Gáshólmur, 18, 122, 123
Germany, 88
Gjógv, 111
Glivursnes, 89, 248
Glyvrar, 37, 257
Góðidrangur, 134, 142
Greece, trade with, 88
Greenland, 18, 37, 70, 81, 88,
   95, 141, 154, 161, 297
Grimsby, 87
Gróthúsvatn, 271-2, 274, 276-9
Gøtuvík, 60, 73, 241

Haldorsvík, 261
Hamar (Froðbøur), 45, 190-5,
   208, 211, 213-5
Haraldsund, 296-7
Harris (Hebrides), 117
Havnadalur, 226, 281
Hebrides, 18, 21, 61, 102 ;

mills, 220-1 ; whale-hunts, 116-9

Heimay (Westmann Is.), 164

Hestur, 18, 38, 102, 108-9, 111-2, 146, 175, 205, 223, 280, 282, 287, 289, 291-2 ; church, 205 ; turf-cutting, 65

Hólmgjóv, 130, 134, 136-7 ; bridge, 130, 166

Hósvík, 260

Hoydalur, 33-5, 276

Hoyvík, 51, 54, 96

Hull, 87

Húsar, 223, 294, 297

Húsareyn, 34, 38

Húsavík, 112, 272, 325

Hvalbøur, 45, 52-3, 93, 112-3, 192, 274, 314; coal, 190; fowling, 156

Hvalvík, 90, 259, 260, 262, 264-6

Hvítanes, 51

Iceland, 17-8, 20, 24, 37, 70, 79, 81, 88-9, 92, 154, 157-8, 161, 173, 198, 238, 245, 249, 253, 261, 278, 302, 310

Ireland, 18, 50, 57, 62, 64, 70, 142, 189, 200, 202, 254 ; mills, 221

Italy, trade with, 88

Kaldbak, 53, 249, 260

Kaldbaksfjørður, 90, 260

Kallsoy, 17, 47, 67, 111, 200, 223, 234, 253, 293-5, 297

Kálvadalur, 135, 174-5, 178-9, 294

Kirkjubøreyn, 38, 281, 302, gullery, 41, 323

Kirkjubøur, 20, 32, 46, 102, 148, 160, 178, 282, 289, 291, 301 ; farm, 45, 48

51, 53, 75-6, 124, 162, 196, 198

Klakksvík, 17, 19, 22, 33, 60, 73, 240, 243, 252, 272, 273, 294, 296, 319; whale-hunting, 111-3

Knúkur (Mykines), 172-5

Kollafjørður, 53, 90, 186-8, 208, 260, 302

Kollur, 287 ; (Eiði), 22, 261-2

Koltur, 18, 38, 45, 53-4, 65, 92; 109, 111-2, 164, 208, 215, 277; fowling, 145, 148, 155, 159, 163, 290; visits to, 280-93

Kongshavn, 37, 83, 257

Krákustein, 66

Kunoy, 17, 67, 112, 145, 272 haymaking, 200, 295; mills, 223, 227, 296 ; visit to, 293-8

Kvívík, 53, 56, 60, 177, 186-8, 254, 267 ; mills, 220, 227-8

Lambi (Mykines), 129-30, 137 179, 181, 185, 303

Lewis (Hebrides), 164

Leynar, 102, 111, 187, 228

Leynarvatn, 188

Lítla Dímun, 18, 53-4, 112, 123, 191; fowling, 156; sheep, 191

Loysingafjall, 267-8

Man, Isle of, 20, 61-2, 66, 70, 102, 163, 195, 215, 232, 245, 248-9, 254, 277, 282 ; mills, 221 ; Calf of, 163

Middalfjall, 267, 269

Mikladalur, 234-5, 294-5

Miðvágur, 53, 60, 65, 102, 112-3, 141, 186, 277 ; whale-hunt, 110, 112-3

Mjavøtn, 188

Mjóvanes, 73, 86

Múli, 111

Mykines, 18, 46, 52, 54, 57, 111-2, **112**, **129**, **161**, 164, 168-85, 188, 190, 193, 198, 200, 252, 277, 279, 299, 303, 323, 353; fowling, 144-5, 148, 151-2, 159, 161-2, 164-7; journey to, 120-7; legends, 135-7; map, *134*; puffinries, 127-31, 151-2; turf-cutting, 64, *69*
Mykineshólmur, 18, 92, 131-5, 176, 178, 180-5, 254, 329, 330
Mýlla, 223
Mýrinar, 266-70, 278

Nes (Eysturoy), 37, 53, 60
Newfoundland, Kittiwake recoveries, 140-2
Niðri á Bø, 190, 211 ; farm-buildings, 214-6; mill, **208**, 217-20, *218*, 223, 225, 227
Nólsoy, 17, 33, 39, 68, 73, 83, 102, 108-9, 111-2, 145, 147, 153-4, 159, 238, 248, 255, 277, 322-4; mills, 223, 228; turf-cutting, 65, 238-9, 298 ; visit to, 298-304
Nólsoyarbygd, 46, 57, 77, **208**, 299, **304**
Norway, 19, 20-1, 24, 38, 52, 85, 95, 102, 140, 154, 198, 217, 241, 253-4, 305 ; mills, 220-3
Norð í Sund, 111, 113
Norðradalur, 38-9, 54, 160
Norðragøta, 52, 111, 215, 237
Norðskála, 86, 260
Norðuroyar, 17, 19, 111, 191, 240, 263
Núgvan, 39, 160

Orkney Islands, 21, 50, 65, 70, 102, 307, 310 ; mills, 221 ; whale-hunting, 116-9
Oyri, 260

Píkarsdrangur, 126, 144, 164-6
Pollur (Saksun), 263
Portugal, trade with, 88

Risin and Kellingin, 261
Rituvik, 108, 111
Rógvukollur, 129-30, 134, 136, 138, 179, 181-5

St. Kilda, 323, 328
Saksun, 42, 90, 111, 160, 262-4
Saksunardalur, 263, 266
Saltangará, 37, 63, 257 ; mills, 225
Sandagerði (Tórshavn), 54, 226
Sandavágur, 51, 54, 60, 65, 102, 187 ; mills, 215, 227-8
Sandoy, 18-9, 39, 112, 123, 141, 147, 175, 191, 234 ; visit to, 270-9
Sandsvatn, 271-3, 275, 277-9
Sandur, 250, 270-9, 295 ; fields, 46, *49*, 50, 57, 59, 273 ; fowling, 157-8, 161
Sandvík, 21, 292
Scotland, 18, 50, 65, 89, 102, 221, 229, 232, 246, 297
Selatrað, 260
Shetland Islands, 17, 21-2, 32, 50, 62, 70, 73, 102, 234 ; mills, 220-3, 227 ; whale-hunts, 116-9
Skálafjørður, 35-7, 63, 73, 83, 225, 257, 319; roads, 60
Skálatoftir, 297
Skálavík, 112, 226, 234, 272
Skansin Fort, 22, 66, 226
Skarvanes (Froðbøur), 189 ; (Sandoy), 272, 277
Skarð, 296-7

Skarðsgjógv, 298
Skipanes, 37, 60
Skopun, 271-2, 274, 277, 295
Skúvafjall (Nolsoy), 299, 303
Skúvoy, 18, 21, 42, 45, 52-3, 112, 123, 158, 161, 164, 175, 191, 241, 252, 263, 270, 272-3, 292, 352; fowling, 146, 156, 159
Skælingsfall, 90, 160, 187, 260
Skælingur, 53-4
Slættanes, 51
Slættaratindur, 64, 261
Spain, trade with, 88
Spitzbergen, 88
Stiklestad, Battle of, 241, 245
Stiðjafjall, 39, 90, 160
Stóra Dímun, 18, 45-6, 112, 164, 191, 270, 272 ; farm, 48, 53, 196 ; fowling, 146, 158-9 ; penal settlement, 191
Stremnes, 259-60
Strendur, 193
Streymoy, 17, 86, 111-2, 159, 175, 177, 260-1, 264 ; roads, 60, 187-8
Strond, 297
Sula Sgeir (Hebrides), gannetry, 164
Sulnasker (Westmann Is.), gannetry, 164
Sund, 51, 53, 73, 196
Sundalagi, 63, 83, 86, 259-62, 265
Sunnbøur, 60, 148, 191, 208, 253
Suðiravatn, 63, 65, 261-2
Suðuroy, 18-9, 39, 45-6, 73, 93, 112-3, 123, 175, 177, 190-1, 220, 270, 273, 275 ; barley-growing, 206 ; fowling, 147, 157, 160 ; roads, 60 ; sheep-ownership, 192-3

Svínaskorá, 263-4
Svínoy, 17, 263
Sweden, 21, 24, 221-2
Syðradalur (Kallsoy), 294 ; (Streymoy), 38-9, 198
Sølmundarfjørður, 37, 73
Søltuvík, 58, 272
Sørvágsvatn, 65, 124, 187, 277-8
Sørvágur, 60, 113, 120, 135, 175, 177, 186

Tangafjørdur, 51, 73, 102
Thurso, 117
Tindhólmur, 18, 112-3, 122-3, 177
Tinganes, 226 ; Fort, 22
Tjørnuvík, 261
Toftavatn, 63, 225, 249, 256-9, 275
Toftir, 37, 60, 63, 256
Tórshavn, 5, 17, 20, 22, 24-6, 31-5, 46, 51, 60, 64, 65, 66, 73, 80, 94, 102, 123-4, 147, 157, 177, 186, 188, 190, 230-1, 248, 253, 257, 259, 261, 270-2, 274, 285, 289, 297, 301-2, 306-7, 316, 319, 323; communal saithe-netting, 74-5; haymaking, 198, 200, 202; mills, 220, 223, 225-7; Ólavsøka celebrations, 240-5; ting, 241, 244-6; whale hunt, 96-101, 105, 109-11, 113
Trongisvágur, 112, 115, 190, 193, 314
Troðum, í, 271-2, 274-5
Trøllanes, 294
Trøllhøvdi, 18, 38, 164 ; fowling, 148, 162, 329
Tungulifjall, 38
Tvørfelli, 281

Tvøroyri, 18, 20, 32, 60, 157, 193, 214-5, 240, 243 ; church, 216

Vágar, 18, 39, 57, 92, 111-3, 121, 123, 175, 177, 240, 253, 263 ; airfield, 187 ; roads, 60, 186-7
Vágur, 18, 20, 93, 112, 213, 216, 240
Varmakeldueiđi, 237
Velbastađur, 45, 53, 102, 178, 257, 281-4

Vestmanna, 17, 20, 50, 60, 200, 243, 263, 267-8 ; fowling, 157; whale-hunts, 107, 112-3
Vestmannasund, 102, 186-7
Víkar, 51
Víđ Air whaling-station, 91
Viđareiđi, 45, 252; fowling, 145
Viđoy, 17 ; fowling, 145, 157

Westmann Islands, 161, 164, 310

Øradvík, 60, 193